THE COLD WAR FROM THE MARGINS

THE COLD WAR FROM THE MARGINS

A Small Socialist State on the Global Cultural Scene

Theodora K. Dragostinova

CORNELL UNIVERSITY PRESS

Ithaca and London

First published 2021 by Cornell University Press

Library of Congress Cataloging-in-Publication Data

Names: Dragostinova, Theodora, 1972– author.
Title: The Cold War from the margins : a small socialist
    state on the global cultural scene / Theodora K.
    Dragostinova.
Description: Ithaca [New York] : Cornell University Press,
    2021. | Includes bibliographical references and index.
Identifiers: LCCN 2020034764 (print) | LCCN 2020034765
    (ebook) | ISBN 9781501755552 (paperback) |
    ISBN 9781501755569 (epub) | ISBN 9781501755576 (pdf)
Subjects: LCSH: Cultural diplomacy—Bulgaria—History—
    20th century. | Cold War—Social aspects. | Politics and
    culture—Bulgaria—History—20th century. | Bulgaria—
    Cultural policy—20th century.
Classification: LCC DR92 .D73 2021 (print) |
    LCC DR92 (ebook) | DDC 949.903/1—dc23
LC record available at https://lccn.loc.gov/2020034764
LC ebook record available at https://lccn.loc.gov/2020034765

To my parents

Contents

Illustrations

PREFACE

I grew up as a child of developed socialism in Bulgaria. I remember well the endless barrage of propaganda during the late 1970s: the newly envisioned laws of beauty would transform young Bulgarians into multifaceted personalities. As the state promoted this vision of the important place of each individual in society, during gym one day the teacher lined up the girls by height. The two tallest girls, including myself, were pulled out and told we wouldn't be going to summer camp on the Black Sea where the other pupils spent a month training for a mass sports event, the Spartakiada, held in autumn 1979. I later sat in the stadium bleachers while my classmates performed complex figures constantly in flux, viewing a lavish spectacle that sought to convey the care of the developed socialist state for its citizens.

Those were days full of hectic, state-sponsored activities, both at school and in our free time. In 1979 and 1981, the International Assemblies for Peace brought children from across the world to Sofia. I did not represent my country in the chalk art, music, or dance competitions, but every pupil in Bulgaria was mobilized to visit cultural sites, participate in mass events, and marvel at the new monument, The Bells, featuring examples from seventy-nine countries on the outskirts of Sofia. The exhilaration of being a part of a grand vision for the world was palpable. In 1981, my grandmother, Baba Keti, took me to see a film that had become a sensation: *Han Asparuh* (which premiered as *The Glory of the Khan* in English) told the story of the founder of the Bulgarian state. An epic saga, it had taken years to film the mass scenes of migration, combat, and settlement of the Proto-Bulgarians beyond the Danube River. The Bulgarian authorities had nominated the film for an Oscar, and as an elementary student I imagined that the entire world had seen it. I also remember visiting the newly built People's Palace of Culture (NDK) in downtown Sofia. The 1300 Years Bulgaria Monument nearby caught my attention because it told the story of the country's historical achievements in a modernist visual imagery distinct from the canons of socialist art. I recall sitting in the last rows of Hall One of NDK, listening to speeches delivered

on the occasion of either the Twelfth Congress of the Bulgarian Communist Party (BKP) or the 1300th anniversary celebrations and thinking what
a glorious moment this was to witness. I wandered the monumental building, up and down the escalators, soaking in the frescoes, murals, wood carvings, giant chandeliers, and luxurious leather furniture that could only be
the doings of a state, I assumed, that was an important global actor. I also
remember vividly the sudden death of Liudmila Zhivkova, the daughter of
the communist leader Todov Zhivkov and a key figure behind these events.
The announcement, which came during summer 1981, felt like collective
shock to the developed socialist nation pursuing new global paths.

I went on to high school in the mid-1980s. I passed the exams for a special school, the National Gymnasium for Ancient Languages and Cultures
(NGDEK), which had first opened in 1977 to put Zhivkova's vision of multifaceted personalities into practice. As I began my studies at what was called
the classical high school, I heard rumors that many of my classmates belonged
to the political and cultural nomenklatura. This was a period of tremendous
intellectual growth for the child of average members of the technical and
medical intelligentsia; my dad was an engineer and my mom a pediatrician,
and they had never become BKP members. Sporadically, they discussed if
they should join the party because our family needed larger living quarters.
Beginning in 1977, my parents spent two years working in Nigeria with the
hope that hard currency would allow them to purchase the desired home.
But by the mid-1980s, they were still at the bottom of the waiting list, as they
were neither BKP members nor working class. My parents decided that our
family would at least enjoy consumer goods from the hard currency store,
Korekom: a sewing machine, a stand mixer, a cookie press, and a new Lada
that facilitated regular ski and Black Sea vacations as well as a tour of Hungary, Czechoslovakia, and the German Democratic Republic (GDR) in 1987.

Back at the classical high school, we continued to balance universal knowledge about the ancient world with the requirements of developed socialism.
We studied Caesar in Latin and Plato in Greek, the debaucheries of gods and
humans in Greek and Roman mythology, the New Testament in Old Church
Slavonic, and Dostoyevsky in the original. At the same time we discussed
the Marxist-Leninist principles of ethics and Gorbachev's perestroika ideas.
During eighth-grade physical education class the girls rehearsed gymnastics
moves for the Celebration of Beauty, which was held at the Home of the
Party (the BKP headquarters) where we danced the cancan in scanty costumes that exposed our changing bodies to the scrutiny of parents, teachers, and our male classmates sitting in the audience. During our tenth-grade
trip to Greece to witness the miracles of antiquity, we toured the Acropolis,

FIGURE 1. The author at a celebration of the Bulgarian children's mass organization, Chavdarche, likely in 1982

FIGURE 2. The author's family in Nigeria, 1979

Delphi, and Olympia, but during our free time we went shopping for dis-
counted clothing. Up until 1989, uniform rules were strictly enforced while
the teachers ignored the *pushkom* (smoking committee) across the street or
the miniskirts and jeans some students wore under their uniforms. As a special school, we were spared the obligatory summer harvest-picking brigades
because we went to archaeological excavations instead, but we still attended
military camps where we fired Kalashnikovs and slept in enormous, unsani-
tary barracks with dreadful bathroom facilities.

Then on 10 November 1989, walking home after school with my friends,
I learned that Todor Zhivkov had stepped down. Several days later, on
18 November, the first oppositional demonstration took place in central
Sofia; our school was nearby, and some classmates went to the rally. In subsequent weeks our teachers ignored attendance when we skipped class because
many of us joined the demonstrations to experience the exhilaration of
change. We were shaken when a classmate, the son of a Politburo member,
was beaten up. Yet, late 1989 was a hopeful, optimistic time full of political
discussions in lieu of chemistry labs and marches in front of the parliament
or the mausoleum instead of Latin homework. I was in my junior year.
By senior year in 1990, the transition was in full speed: stores were empty,
a rationing system was in place, and prom was on the horizon. Procuring a
decent dress proved a challenge. My mom offered the only viable solution:
a glittery fabric from Nigeria she had saved. With a sewing pattern from

FIGURE 3.   The author and other students from the classical high school at archaeological excavations at Nicopolis ad Istrum, summer 1989

the German *Burda* magazine in hand, we took the cold bus across town to a high-rise on the outskirts of Sofia where a kind, middle-aged seamstress, looking to make extra cash, made what I considered a mediocre dress. My mom saved the situation again by borrowing a corduroy trench coat from a family friend, so I could cover up the dress. When my classmates started showing up for prom, it transpired that some families had done extremely well under the transition—they sported flashy foreign-bought outfits that screamed Western consumerism and capitalist prosperity.

At the end of senior year, many of my classmates enrolled in universities in the West. Some hugely talented people earned full scholarships to Ivy League schools in the United States. But others had undisclosed acquaintances abroad that miraculously allowed them to pursue education in places out of reach to the average Bulgarian. An unspoken tension between the haves and have-nots was emerging in our previously equal circle of friends. Going West was what everyone desired in 1991. I had been accepted to several U.S. universities, earning partial scholarships, but my family was in no way capable of paying the expenses for an education abroad, so I enrolled at Sofia University to study history. The following year, I won an educational exchange scholarship to continue my studies in Greece. In the fall of

1992, my tortuous international path began on a bus headed to Athens where I was supposed to figure out how to enroll in a Greek language class and find a room in the dorms. With the transition to capitalist prosperity stalling, in 1995 my father took his second African job, working for the United Nations Industrial Development Organization (UNIDO) in Tanzania. At the end of a taxing, lonely year, my family finally purchased a new apartment. But then came 1997, the hardest year of the Bulgarian transition, which featured bank runs and the devaluation of wages and savings. When a U.S. university gave me a full scholarship to pursue a PhD in 1998, the choice was clear.

In the years of extended postsocialist transition, the Eastern Europeans of my generation kept their eyes on the West. In the 1990s and 2000s, preoccupied with our return to Europe, we wished to discover the world beyond the Iron Curtain. In the process of asserting our European identities, however, we often forgot other experiences. In my case, my family's two-year stay in Nigeria between 1977 and 1979 had triggered my curiosity throughout my childhood. As a teenager, I wrote down my memories of Nigeria in a "memoir" reflecting on my first time traveling by airplane; my majority Black school; my new friendships with kids from England, Syria, and India; and my encounters with unfamiliar animals, flowers, weather, and food. In 1995, I visited my father in Tanzania. One memory stands out from this trip, in addition to our tours of Zanzibar and Victoria Falls in Zimbabwe. Traveling to a game reserve, our car broke down in a small village. When the local people asked where we were from, our reply triggered unexpected enthusiasm. The villagers congratulated us for Bulgaria's victory against Germany in the quarterfinals of the World Cup in 1994 and thanked us for building a bicycle factory in Tanzania during the Cold War. Eastern Europe had nurtured other contacts in the world, which we forgot in the rush to join Europe. Considering all these historical forces that have shaped my life—the reality of late socialism, the pursuit of East-West contact, and the desire to know the world—I hope to make sense of the long 1970s, the time of my childhood but also the time of uneasy, shifting, difficult to define global transformations, much like the anxious transformations of today.

I owe gratitude to many people and institutions for their support as this project evolved. I am indebted to numerous Bulgarian archivists and librarians at the Central State Archives, the National Library, and the Archives of the Ministry of Foreign Affairs who facilitated my research while working under often challenging conditions. I thank these institutions for their permission to publish materials from their collections. In the United States, I thank Angela Cannon at the Library of Congress and Sarah Patton at the Hoover Institution Library and Archives. Working at the Open Society Archives in Budapest, Hungary, was a tremendous pleasure. In the United Kingdom, I am grateful to Milan Grba at the British Library and the staff of The National Archives in London. At Ohio State, Pasha Johnson and David Lincove have always been helpful answering my questions and directing my searches. I thank John Fine, Victor Friedman, Charles Gribble, Gail Kligman, John Lampe, and Predrag Matejic for sharing memories from their work in the late socialist Balkans.

I am grateful to the College of Arts and Sciences, the Mershon Center for International Security Studies, the Center for Slavic and Eastern European Studies, the Global Arts + Humanities Discovery Theme, and the Department of History at Ohio State University for their financial support of my research, writing, and manuscript preparation. A TOME (Toward an Open Monograph Ecosystem) Grant from the Ohio State Libraries made possible the publication of my book as an open access digital monograph.

I have presented early drafts of this work at the University of Illinois at Chicago, the American University of Bulgaria, the Red House for Culture and Debate in Sofia, the Institute of Culture and Memory Studies of the Slovenian Academy of Sciences and Arts, Indiana University, Vanderbilt University, and the University of Wisconsin–Madison. I am grateful for the hospitality of Ulf Brunnbauer at the Institute for East and Southeast European Studies in Regensburg, Germany, where I polished parts of the book. I completed the final manuscript while in residence at the Center for Advanced Studies in Sofia, where Rumen Avramov and Diana Mishkova provided excellent support and good company.

Numerous colleagues provided insightful feedback on my work, including Rachel Applebaum, Dimitar Bechev, Maria Bucur, Malgorzata Fidelis, Kristen Ghodsee, Irina Gigova, Emily Greble, and Małgorzata Mazurek. Maria Todorova remains a source of wisdom, inspiration, support, and critical intervention. At Ohio State, I am grateful to Robin Judd, Tina Sessa, Mytheli Sreenivas, and Ying Zhang for their wonderful friendship and constant encouragement over the years of our writing group; Elizabeth Bond joined us during my last year of intense revisions. Alice Conklin, Philip Gleissner, Yana Hashamova, David Hoffmann, Stephanie Smith, and Sarah Van Beurden provided excellent comments on select chapters. The best writing buddy, Robin Judd, and the best walking buddy, Jennifer Siegel, have helped me think through this book and other things that matter.

Parts of this book first appeared as "The East in the West: Bulgarian Culture in the United States of America during the Global 1970s," *Journal of Contemporary History* 53, no. 1 (2018): 212–239, and "The 'Natural Ally' of the

'Developing World': Bulgarian Culture in India and Mexico," *Slavic Review* 77, no. 3 (2018): 661–684. I reprint this material with permission.

At Cornell University Press, Roger Haydon gave me his strong support throughout the process and provided razor-sharp commentary on early drafts of this book. I thank Marlyn Miller for her excellent copy editing and Karen Hwa for expertly supervising the editing and production process.

I completed this book as the country came to a standstill during the global pandemic in 2020, which has given me a keen perspective on what is essential in life. I am endlessly grateful for my family, who helped me stay focused, connected, and lucid. My parents, Violeta Nikolova and Koytcho Dragostinov, and my brother, Kiril Dragostinov, who reside in Bulgaria, kept my perspective on the world in check. My life remains a life between two motherlands, my birthplace and my adopted country. In the United States, my husband, Bud Barnes, and my two boys, Alex and Daniel, provide a daily reminder of the joys and challenges of human closeness. I wouldn't have it any other way.

By telling this story, I express my gratitude to my parents, who gave me a meaningful, happy childhood during turbulent times.

Abbreviations

ASEEES	American Association for the Advancement of Slavic Studies
BAN	Bâlgarska akademiia na naukite (Bulgarian Academy of Sciences)
BANU	Bulgarian Agrarian National Union
BKP	Bâlgarska komunisticheska partiia (Bulgarian Communist Party)
BTA	Bâlgarska telegrafna agentsiia (Bulgarian Telegraph Agency)
COMECON	Council for Mutual Economic Assistance
CPI	Communist Party of India
CSCE	Conference on Security and Cooperation in Europe
DAAD	Deutscher Akademischer Austauschdienst (German Academic Exchange Service)
EEC	European Economic Community
FCO	Foreign and Commonwealth Office
FESTAC 77	Second World Black and African Festival of Arts and Culture
FRG	Federal Republic of Germany
GDR	German Democratic Republic
KGB	Komitet Gosudarstvennoi Bezopasnosti (Committee for State Security)
KIK	Komitet za izkustvo i kultura (Committee for Arts and Culture)
KK	Komitet za kultura (Committee for Culture)
MAK	Museum für angewandte Kunst (Museum of Applied Arts)
MPO	Macedonian Patriotic Organization
MVnR	Ministerstvo na vânshnite raboti (Ministry of Foreign Affairs)
NARA	National Archives and Records Administration
NATO	North Atlantic Treaty Organization
NDK	Naroden dvorets na kulturata (People's Palace of Culture)
NGDEK	Natsionalna gimnaziia za drevni ezitsi i kulturi (National Gymnasium for Ancient Languages and Cultures)
NIEO	New International Economic Order

NITsAA   Nauchno-izsledovatelski tsentâr za Afrika i Aziiia (Scientific-Research Center on Africa and Asia)

NKK   Natsionalna koordinatsionna komisiia 1300 godini Bâlgariia (National Coordinating Committee 1300 Years Bulgaria)

NRB   Narodna Republika Bâlgariia (People's Republic of Bulgaria)

NWFZ   Nuclear-weapons-free zone

OSA   Open Society Archives, Budapest, Hungary

PASOK   Panellinio sosialistiko kinima (Panhellenic Socialist Movement)

PCR   Partidul Comunist Român (Romanian Communist Party)

PRI   Partido Revolucionario Institucional (Institutional Revolutionary Party)

RFE   Radio Free Europe

SELA   Sistema Económiko Latinoamericano (Latin American Economic System)

SKJ   Savez komunista Jugoslavije (The League of Yugoslav Communists)

SRM   Socialist Republic of Macedonia

TNA   The National Archives, Kew, United Kingdom

TsDA   Tsentralen dârzhaven arhiv (Central State Archives), Sofia, Bulgaria

UNAM   Universidad Nacional Autónoma de México (National Autonomous University of Mexico)

UNESCO   United Nations Educational, Scientific, and Cultural Organization

USIA   United States Information Agency

USICA   United States International Communications Agency

VOA   Voice of America

NOTE ON TERMINOLOGY

My sources often conflate the terms "commu-
nist" and "socialist" to describe different aspects of the political order in Bulgaria in the 1970s. I generally refer to the political system and the time period as
"socialist"; often, I speak about "developed socialism" and "real socialism,"
two terms used at the time. I tend to use the phrases "communist regime"
and "communist elites," because the vast majority of those in positions of
power were Communist Party members. When I need to differentiate the
political system in Eastern Europe from democratic socialist practices elsewhere, I speak about "state socialism." I use "late socialism" to refer to the
post-1968 period.

I often use the phraseology of the 1970s to describe policies and their
outcomes; I usually put those phrases in quotation marks on first use and
provide the Bulgarian original. The use of this vocabulary is meant to capture the rhetorical reality of the times and does not reflect my views of the
political system or its aspirations.

I am using a modified version of the Library of Congress transliteration
system for Bulgarian; namely, I use "â" instead of "û," which is closer to the
common Bulgarian rendition of the hard sign.

Introduction

Bulgaria on the Global Cultural Scene of the 1970s

A flurry of international events marked public life in late socialist Bulgaria: the visits of out-of-the-ordinary, often flamboyant foreign dignitaries, such as Angela Davis from the United States, Muammar al-Gaddafi from Libya, Mengistu Haile Mariam from Ethiopia, or Svetoslav Roerich from India; the appearance of recognizable Western cultural icons like Tina Turner, Ray Charles, Erskine Caldwell, or Henry Moore; the exhibition of masterworks by Leonardo da Vinci at the Alexander Nevski Cathedral or the showing of Rubens, van Gogh, Monet, and Rembrandt from the Armand Hammer Collection at the National Gallery of Art; the appearance of world-class performers and artists at the Varna International Ballet Competition, the Golden Orpheus Pop Music Festival, the Red Poppy Political Song Festival, or the Gabrovo International Festival of Humor and Satire. In this maelstrom of activity, one event stood out: the International Assembly of Children, which was held under the auspices of the United Nations and brought hundreds of children from throughout the world to Bulgaria in 1979. The elites in the entourage of long-time communist leader Todor Zhivkov believed that such vibrant public activities and stimulating cultural events would enrich daily life by exposing Bulgarians to the shared legacy of the world's civilizational treasury. The world now came to Bulgaria, a small socialist state that proudly embraced its role in advancing a new global cultural flourishing.

1

While the country welcomed the world, Bulgarians also traversed the globe, sending economic, scientific, technical, educational, and cultural experts throughout Europe, North and South America, Africa, Asia, and the Middle East. These Bulgarian representatives advertised the successes of their country as they helped launch industrial plants and agricultural enterprises, provided medical and dental care, constructed homes and public buildings, launched campaigns to fight illiteracy, and taught technical and scientific skills to emerging postcolonial elites. But they also opened museum and art exhibits, presided over book discussions and film screenings, received musical and performance prizes, and spoke about the importance of preserving one's historical heritage and making culture accessible to the people. The Bulgarian stories about bringing culture to the masses were attractive—as was their focus on the mysterious Thracians and tenacious Slavs that challenged the dominant tropes of Western civilization. International observers realized that the "Bulgarians today clearly want the world to know that they are . . . ancient people with pride in their history."[1] Bulgarian officials were especially proud that a small state could accomplish such an extensive cultural program, claiming that "while Bulgaria ranks in size among the smaller European nations . . . in the field of culture there are neither big nor small nations, and the dynamism of modern Bulgaria is firmly rooted in a cultural heritage spanning thirteen centuries."[2] By the official record, between 1977 and 1981 small Bulgaria, with a population of 8.7 million in 1975, organized 38,854 cultural events across the world, highlighting the far-reaching global aspirations of the communist elites in charge of the country.[3]

This ambitious cultural program was linked to the lavish celebrations of a national anniversary in 1981—thirteen hundred years since the establishment of the medieval Bulgarian state in 681. Using the occasion of the jubilee, state and party officials embarked on an extravagant, wide-ranging project to showcase Bulgarian culture abroad and thus boost the prestige of their country and establish its presence on the global scene. Using the celebration of the 1300th anniversary—or 1300 Years Bulgaria, as it was often called—to promote the international image of the small socialist state was a smart choice. The motto of the jubilee was brief and catchy: Bulgaria was both "ancient and modern," or as the glossy pamphlets emphasized, "A modern nation salutes its past."[4] The goal was to inform the public of the rich historical contributions of "one of the oldest states in Europe" and to advertise the contemporary achievements of modern Bulgaria and "real socialism" in the context of the Cold War competition with the capitalist

West. The January 1981 issue of *Bulgaria Today*, a magazine produced by the state agency Sofia Press for foreign audiences, summed up the logic of the celebration for global consumption:

In this new year Bulgaria strides forward into her 13th centenary with a proudly raised torch whose purified light illumines the path traversed and the path ahead. Spiritual greatness and [a] heavy yoke have been known to the people who found their homeland on both sides of the Balkan Range. But the 36 years of socialist renewal and transformation have been enough to heal the bitter wounds and to promote to unprecedented heights the virtues which this people suffered during many centuries. . . . Such is now Bulgaria, ancient and new, striving to reach the peak of her 13th centenary.[5]

Bringing together past, present, and future, the jubilee celebrated past glories and emphasized the inevitable march toward communism of a people that had always been in the vanguard of history. Conveniently, the year 1981 also marked the ninetieth anniversary of the establishment of the Bulgarian Communist Party (BKP), so the two central ideas of the celebrations merged seamlessly.

The 1300-year jubilee—whose celebration consumed vast amounts of labor and money from 1976 to 1982—had both domestic and international dimensions. In Bulgaria, the communist regime sponsored excavations and historical studies; built new monuments and museums; funded film productions, television series, and radio programs; engaged in a prolific publishing enterprise; and organized concerts, conferences, and mass celebrations. The commemorative program aimed to involve every single person, from school children to university students to work collectives to pensioners. Abroad, the events included exhibitions of ancient treasures and medieval icons, performances by folk and classical music ensembles, and the organization of art exhibits, film weeks, and book readings, whose ultimate goal was to secure favorable media coverage in the foreign press, radio, and television and advance the country's reputation as an active global player. Meetings between representatives of socialist Bulgaria and "progressive elements" in the host societies occurred regularly, as did more spontaneous encounters between performers and audiences. The aspiration was to expose sympathetic global publics not only to the richness of Bulgarian culture, but also to the achievements of Bulgarian tourism, sports, industry, agriculture, education, and social policies—or the state socialist way of life in general. Bulgarian elites expected that these events would reinvigorate developed socialist

FIGURE 4.   1300 Years Bulgaria poster. Source: Angelina Todorova, ed., *1981–681: 1300 godini ot sâzdavaneto na bâlgarskata dârzhava; Plakati* (Sofia: Septemvri, 1981), held in the National Library, Sofia.

society at home and promote the prestige and agenda of the country abroad; throughout this period, domestic and global agendas went hand in hand, creating a vibrant state-run cultural program that stands out in late socialist Eastern Europe.

While at first suspicious of "communist propaganda" or wary of the "marked revival of Bulgarian nationalism," international observers came to see these cultural events as the clever public relations campaign of a small state that wished to advance its international standing, redefine its reputation, and gain support for its policy agenda. According to Reuters, in 1976 the "high-powered campaign to put Bulgaria on the international cultural scene was already showing results."[6] In the opinion of the *Guardian*, the Bulgarian exhibitions of ancient treasures and medieval icons made the gold of Troy and Mycenae look "like something out of a Christmas cracker" and introduced the world to new historical traditions that deserved to be marveled at as much as those that were better known.[7] American media similarly found this emphasis on newly discovered lavish civilizations appealing: "Western museums cannot get enough of it," wrote the *Washington Post*.[8] According to the *Observer*, these events were "a brilliant success as an exercise of international public relations by putting this small, obscure Balkan country on the western world's cultural map."[9] In the end, in the words of the *Economist* from 1981, the 1300-year jubilee showed the "more liberal face" of the regime and its willingness to give "greater cultural freedom" to the population, normalizing the country in the eyes of the West.[10]

The Bulgarian events also found resonance in the developing world. The *National Herald* of New Delhi declared: "Small nations know a lot about big nations, but the big nations know very little or almost nothing about the small nations." The newspaper admired the "exceptional success" of Bulgarian culture in India and appreciated the fact that the Bulgarian cultural events showcased "an ancient civilization outside the traditional Greco-Roman world."[11] In 1981, Prime Minister Indira Gandhi proclaimed, "friendship between counties can spring and grow in numerous ways." Emphasizing the "common endeavor" of Bulgaria and India, she declared that "[cultural] kinship develops other exchanges in trade and in ideas."[12] Culture, in other words, was just the first step.

The Bulgarian investment in culture seemed to be paying off by the early 1980s as a shift in international public opinion vis-à-vis the country was underway. Throughout the 1970s, Paris, Vienna, London, Munich, New York, Tokyo, New Delhi, and Mexico City all hosted Bulgarian events that were widely and sympathetically reported in the international press. During a meeting of Western European public figures who were helping to organize celebrations dedicated to the 1300th anniversary in their respective countries, one speaker concluded, "all of us, who represent different nations in Europe, need to seek out the roots of our historical development and common spiritual past." Small Bulgaria was now helping the old continent embrace its common past: by using the language of European civilization and adhering to universal historical values, the Bulgarians presented a cultural program that was an "honor for the entire European continent."[13] Not least, to the apparent satisfaction of Bulgaria's new partners in the West, these cultural events "irked the Russians." By highlighting its role in the evolution of Slavic civilization—as the first Slavic nation to convert to Christianity and create a literature in the Cyrillic alphabet—Bulgaria now charted a path that was "independent of, and predated, the Russian connection."[14] Culture allowed the Bulgarian leaders to project a degree of independence and change opinions of their role in the Soviet bloc. In Radio Free Europe's eloquent characterization, Bulgaria's new cultural prominence "offset western views of the country as a Balkan backwater or Soviet satrapy."[15]

Why were the Bulgarians heavily investing in international culture during this time? Not surprisingly, this type of nation branding served the domestic and international policy agendas of Bulgaria's authoritarian regime. At home, the extensive state-sponsored attention given to culture sought to energize society and bolster the authority of the communist elites in charge of the country by creating new visions of national unity and historical pride. Abroad, the events pursued prestige-making goals by seeking to revise the image of the Zhivkov regime as the most loyal ally of the Soviet Union while emphasizing Bulgaria's national uniqueness and contributions to humanity. But soft power aspirations also contributed to hard power goals, as cultural outreach facilitated a series of new political, economic, and cultural partnerships across the globe. Bulgaria now had dynamic, multifaceted relations with Greece, Austria, West Germany, France, India, Mexico, and Japan, among others. While one might criticize the motivations of the communist elites who orchestrated these events, there is no doubt that cultural diplomacy provided a good strategy for the small socialist state to redefine its global standing in concrete ways. Bulgaria now became an active international player pursuing ambitious agendas.

This book centers the historical experience of a small state to emphasize the importance of actors on the margins in our understanding of how the global order works. The majority of states are "smaller powers" that constantly seek to maneuver their roles in world affairs.[16] We have numerous frameworks that allow us to appreciate the power of the weak, the agency of the periphery, or the advantages of backwardness in how political and social dynamics unfold. I focus my analysis on the "advantages of smallness" to claim that in the Cold War, formulating a country's objectives from the position of geopolitical marginality could provide that state with unexpected opportunities. Given that the superpowers viewed culture as secondary to political, economic, or military objectives, cultural diplomacy emerged as a good strategy for smaller states to articulate and project their global visions. This view of the Cold War from the periphery takes seriously "the story of people who weren't at the center of things" in order to reframe "the dominant . . . narrative from the inside."[17] Being situated on the margins allows small places unique openings to find their place and voice in the world.

Why Culture Matters

We now understand the importance of studying culture during the Cold War alongside political and diplomatic crises, economic shake-ups, social transformations, and protest movements. Détente, nonalignment, the Sino-Soviet rift, and the Helsinki Accords were all important aspects of the Cold War, but so were the publications of Alexander Solzhenitsyn's *Gulag Archipelago* and Václav Havel's "The Power of the Powerless," the defections of the Czech film director Miloš Forman and the Soviet conductor Mstislav Rostropovich, the appeal of rock and roll and other aspects of Western mass culture in the Soviet bloc, the controversies surrounding the Moscow and Los Angeles Olympics in 1980 and 1984, as well as the World Youth Festivals, Congresses for Peace, and American and Soviet National Exhibitions held during the Cold War. Throughout Eastern Europe, a wide range of transborder contacts across a porous Iron Curtain occurred with regularity after 1956. Trade agreements, travel and tourism, mass culture, and a range of consumer practices from shopping to fashion to cooking all reflected the constrained but determined contacts between East and West. Cultural diplomacy remained an important tool for the superpowers as they engaged in international projects, but soft power strategies were even more important for small states as it allowed them to advance their hard power agendas in alternative ways. Building upon the findings of two bodies of scholarship that do not always converse—international histories of the global Cold War and cultural histories of transnational contact across the Iron Curtain—I explore the importance of culture for the political agenda of a small state that navigated the complex dynamics of the late Cold War.

In the last two decades, we have expanded our view of the Cold War as a global phenomenon. Instead of focusing on diplomacy, we now examine postwar developments from the viewpoint of decolonization, the Third World, internationalism, economic globalization, human rights, environmentalism, technology, or ideology.[18] Here, I study the Cold War through the prism of international cultural contact. I use the insights of what has been called cultural internationalism or cultural transnationalism, two notions that allow us to think about state-driven international cultural projects and transnational cultural contacts outside of the state framework in tandem.[19] Because ideology was so important in the Cold War, and culture was often perceived as a strategy to showcase the superiority of each side's way of life, cultural contact across borders provides a unique perspective in comprehending how conflicting worldviews clashed, conversed, and accommodated each other in a global context. By studying culture during the Cold War, we better understand the ideological rationale of the conflict between the superpowers, their allies, and those on the sidelines.[20]

This focus on ideology allows me to analyze culture as a discursive system or "the sets of signifying practices through which people know and understand the world."[21] This approach—based on Antonio Gramsci's ideas of cultural hegemony—is appealing to me as a cultural historian because it puts the production, dissemination, and control of cultural representations at the center of analysis. The cultural "struggle for hearts and minds" during the Cold War—as manifested in the creative production of artists, musicians, writers, and filmmakers—becomes a manifestation of competing understandings of modernity. In this analysis, culture acquires the broad meaning of "struggles to control the meaning of words and ideas."[22] In the Bulgarian case, culture functioned as an expression of the state socialist way of life, merging cultural and ideological messages to serve a regime that wished to boost its reputation, agenda, and legitimacy domestically and internationally.

Throughout this analysis, I focus on what we might call official culture to chart the decisions made by the leaders of a small state as they sought to insert themselves into the global scene. I engage with practices that can be variably described as cultural diplomacy, soft power, nation branding, public relations, or image projection to analyze the events that Bulgarian elites orchestrated to advance their political visions domestically and globally.[23] This choice is largely determined by my sources, which mostly come from state or other institutional archives and predominantly reflect the views of those in power. "Representative" exhibitions of Thracian gold, medieval icons, monastery treasures, and contemporary art as well as "prestigious" appearances by the best Bulgarian performers, artists, writers, filmmakers, and scholars were the core elements of these cultural programs. While the role of bottom-up reactions to state policies, local variations in the implementation of these decisions, and countercultural practices articulated outside of the state framework are all fascinating topics of analysis, I leave these perspectives in the hands of those whose source base and theoretical grounding allow them to tackle these themes.[24]

Socialist, internationalist, national(ist), local, global, and transnational forces all shaped how culture functioned in socialist-era Bulgaria. The exhibitions, concerts, book readings, and cultural meetings described here were orchestrated at the highest levels of the Bulgarian state and cultural bureaucracy to project the ideological superiority of the state socialist system vis-à-vis the West and to express solidarity with the Third World according to the rules of socialist internationalism. These cultural campaigns also pursued a national, or one might say nationalist, objective: to demonstrate the prominence of Bulgaria as a representative of one of Europe's and the world's leading civilizations. Often, cultural programs reflected the personal choices of Bulgarian "power elites," as they were called in the West, and most notably, the worldview of first lady (or first daughter) Liudmila Zhivkova, who promoted her close associates so that they could translate her idiosyncratic visions into cultural policy. Bulgarian officials used eclectic languages to convey these ideas: the emphasis on folk traditions and ancient artifacts from the past went hand in hand with modernist artistic visions of the present. These international programs followed foreign cultural templates and technologies, taking advantage of the expansion of global interconnectivity in the post-1945 period. In this sense, they were also evidence of the acceleration of contemporary cultural globalization in the 1970s. Finally, these cultural contacts were, by their nature, transnational, so as Bulgarian representatives crossed borders to present their cultural products, the inevitable cross-pollination of different cultural experiences occurred. Thus, in addition to the meticulous plans for state-sponsored cultural exchange, there were also global trends, local conditions, diverse audiences, and idiosyncratic practices that shaped this global Bulgarian affair. Every so often, unlikely cultural accommodations led to unexpected outcomes. The warm welcome of Bulgarian culture in Greece, usually a fierce national competitor; the uneasy encounters between Bulgarian officials, Orthodox priests, and anticommunist émigrés in the West; the enthusiastic reading of Bulgarian poetry by Indian students at Delhi University; and the presence of Bulgarian representatives at the Second World African Festival of Arts and Cultures in Nigeria are just a few examples of these surprising cultural entanglements.

How did culture become a key Bulgarian export during late socialism? The "cultural front" always held an important place in socialist Bulgaria (similar to the rest of the Soviet allies). In the 1970s, in the spirit of socialist internationalism, which sought to create a unified cultural scene across the Soviet sphere of influence, Bulgaria continued to have an active cultural

FIGURE 5. Opening of the exhibition *Contemporary Bulgarian Print Makers* in Lagos, April 1980. Source: MvNR, op. 36, a.e. 4648, l. 41.

presence in the Soviet Union and the rest of the socialist states. Bulgarian cultural events of the 1970s often followed templates of socialist solidarity established in the late 1940s; Red Army parades, World War II memorials, and Bolshevik Revolution celebrations remained a permanent staple of the Cold War cultural landscape. All socialist countries had cultural-informational centers in other socialist capitals that coordinated activities while cultural attachés from throughout the bloc met regularly to discuss common strategies of cultural exchange.

But over the course of time, and especially after 1956, as the Eastern European countries opened to foreign influences, cultural events became more varied. International youth festivals; meetings of writers, artists, and musicians; and popular culture events brought East and West together with some regularity in the 1960s. These transnational contacts often facilitated grassroots initiatives outside of direct state control, leading to brisk interactions between East and West during the remainder of the Cold War. Bulgaria was a latecomer to these trends when compared to the rest of Eastern Europe; after a cautious opening to foreign influences in the 1960s, however, the country embraced international cultural outreach during the 1970s.[25] Sometimes, international gestures had an explicit ideological rationale, such as the visit of U.S. antiwar activist Angela Davis in 1972 during the last stages of the Vietnam War. When Tina Turner and

Ray Charles appeared on Bulgarian television, this served as criticism of U.S. racial policies. Other times, however, the focus was on the universal appeal of culture. At the international pop music festival Golden Orpheus, Western Europeans performed regularly—including the Italian pop stars Al Bano and Romina Power, many Bulgarians' favorites. The Varna International Ballet Competition (which began in 1964) crowned its first Western prizewinners in the 1970s: Patrick Dupond and Élisabeth Platel, both from the Paris Opera Ballet. Over time, the country's cultural outreach also became more global. In 1979 Bulgaria hosted the International Assembly of Children, which brought 1,361 children from across the world for ten-day cultural celebrations in the name of world peace. International writers' meetings, congresses of Bulgarian studies scholars, children's assemblies, and joint sessions with UNESCO (the United Nations Educational, Scientific and Cultural Organization) became an inextricable part of the experience of late socialism.

As a result of expanding cultural cooperation, there was an increase in Bulgarian events organized in the West. Bulgaria had long-standing cultural contacts with Austria and France, two countries where many members of the Bulgarian national intelligentsia had received their education in the late nineteenth and early twentieth centuries. Bulgarian musicians, artists, and

FIGURE 6. Children visiting The Bells monument on the outskirts of Sofia in 1981, built on the occasion of the International Children's Assembly in 1979. Source: P. Kolev, published with permission.

academics continued to work with French and Austrian colleagues throughout the Cold War. Gradually, culture also helped reestablish contacts with the Federal Republic of Germany (FRG), and a series of cultural programs paved the way for the full restoration of Bulgarian-West German diplomatic relations in 1973. Bulgarian officials also reached out to Great Britain, the United States, and Canada, where cultural relations were often created from scratch. To facilitate those contacts, Bulgarian diplomats approached émigré communities, even if those contacts were risky from ideological perspective. Throughout the 1970s the Bulgarian elites persevered in their attempts to establish a high-profile cultural program in the West, allocating money, cultural products, and personnel in extravagant ways. Nurturing East-West contacts, albeit carefully and selectively, had become a state priority as communist elites promoted Bulgaria's European pedigree.

Scholars have advanced the idea that Cold War cultural exchange served as a precursor to and manifestation of cultural globalization in the post-1945 period. Together with the flow of people, capital, technology, and ideas, the acceleration of global interconnectivity was also evident in the faster circulation of cultural and media images, or what Arjun Appadurai has called "mediascapes."[26] While this process of global integration began in modest ways in the late 1940s, by the 1970s the global condition was becoming universally palpable, also influencing societies that were typically thought of as being isolated behind the Iron Curtain. But the Bulgarian encounter with global cultural flows also highlights the limits of the concept of cultural globalization, because what some describe as the Bulgarian "cultural opening" generated highly controlled and uneven contacts that in my interpretation primarily reflected the desire of communist power elites to seek new global directions.[27] While these international entanglements may have also created new grassroots opportunities, in late socialist Bulgaria the elites were the real agents of the faster transmission of ideas, people, finances, or technologies. Contacts remained meticulously planned and vigilantly controlled, as state and party elites as well as the police services carefully filtered which individuals and what types of culture would cross the East-West divide.

In addition to expanding communications with the West, the Bulgarians made more distant cultural contacts in the Third World. In the midst of Cold War tensions, Iraq, Syria, Egypt, Libya, Tunisia, and Algeria all had friendly relations with Bulgaria. Bulgarians were actively involved in "brotherly" Cuba from the 1960s on. After decolonization and the establishment of friendly socialist regimes in Ethiopia, Mozambique, Angola, and Tanzania,

FIGURE 7.   Tina Turner giving an interview on Bulgarian television, 1981. Source: P. Kolev, published with permission.

the Bulgarians also reached out to subequatorial Africa. From the late 1960s, the leaders of many newly independent Third World states visited Bulgaria in their search for allies. In addition to the customary public parades of comrades from the East and the new carefully curated partnerships with the West, now foreign leaders from developing states regularly visited the country. Students from Africa, Asia, and Latin America made their first appearance in Bulgarian universities in the 1960s; newly built dormitories housed those international students while the Institute for Foreign Students taught them Bulgarian language skills and Marxist orthodoxy. Relations with Vietnam had grown closer during and after the Vietnam war, but Bulgarian representatives now also actively sought contacts with two other Asian nations, India and Japan. In the 1970s, relations between Bulgaria and India intensified as a personal friendship developed between Liudmila Zhivkova and Indira Gandhi. Bulgaria had prior contacts with select countries in Latin America, notably Argentina, where a large Bulgarian community resided, but it now looked to expand its presence in that region, too. In 1974, Bulgaria and Mexico established diplomatic relations, followed by an unusually quick expansion of cultural cooperation. The Bulgarians also began to venture into non-socialist African states, such as Nigeria, where they constructed the National Theatre in Lagos. While we still do not know enough about the logic, execution, and especially reception of this outreach in the Third World, I conclude that unlike the highly controlled opening to the West, contact with the developing world allowed a larger, more diverse group of state socialist citizens to pursue international contacts across multiple geographies and chart new global visions of East-South cooperation. Bulgaria embraced the world while the world also began to discover Bulgaria.

The global agenda of small Bulgaria illustrates the importance of socialist globalization during the 1970s. This notion allows us to contest narratives that understand globalization as a process of westernization only and to recover the existence of competing models of global interconnectivity during the Cold War.[28] Despite well-entrenched ideas of Eastern European captivity behind the Iron Curtain, the socialist states of Eastern Europe engaged in extensive political, economic, and cultural projects outside of Europe. Often, the Eastern European states showed solidarity with the developing world at the direct expense of the superpowers (including the Soviet Union), promoting alternative notions of regional cooperation and global integration.[29] So far, this encounter between Eastern Europe and the world has been studied predominantly from political, economic, and military viewpoints, but our understanding of the global dynamics continues to evolve. Łukasz Stanek shows how Eastern European architects advanced a socialist vision of urban development in Africa and the Middle East, promoting the unique modernization agenda of "socialist worldmaking" by negotiating socialist and global practices.[30] In the case of Bulgaria, Kristen Ghodsee documents the critical role of the official women's organization that worked with African feminists during the International Decade for Women (1976–1985) to challenge the role of U.S. feminists in the United Nations, successfully undercutting their appeal in the global women's movement.[31] By reconstructing Bulgaria's cultural contacts with a range of actors, I enhance these debates by demonstrating the ability of a small state to influence the cultural imagination of the 1970s outside of the East-West and North-South lines of communication. As I show on multiple levels, these interactions led to the emergence of new global visions and alternative mental geographies along an East-South axis, which actively shaped the world from the margins. Many of these partnerships outlasted the Cold War; despite the firm orientation of Bulgaria toward the West after 1989, we are now beginning to appreciate the role of foreign students and workers in the country; the impact of Japanese economic investment during and after socialism; the influence of Indian, Mexican, and African art in

Bulgarian cultural life; and the continued Bulgarian involvement in large infrastructure projects in North Africa and the Middle East.

The Global 1970s

To understand the logic of the Bulgarian cultural extravaganza, we need to grasp the logic of the 1970s, or "the first truly global decade," when transnational linkages expanded rapidly and people experienced "the shock of the global" in multifaceted ways.[32] Historians have only recently started to analyze the 1970s as a period of major, disorienting, and consequential reorganization of the world order. A "decade of ill repute," "depressing and forgettable," the 1970s was a time of political crises, economic adjustments, and social upheaval.[33] On the one hand, the global economic shakeup after 1973 created an overwhelming sense of instability, yet on the other, the acceleration of political reconciliation between East and West during détente encouraged hope for a more secure future. The 1970s was the decade of various crises but also new opportunities for the superpowers and their partners, as evident in Vietnam and Watergate, Ostpolitik and Helsinki, the Eastern European dissidents and the Polish trade union Solidarity, or the U.S. hostages in Iran and the Soviet invasion of Afghanistan. This was the decade when actors outside of the superpower orbit—such as Deng Xiaoping, Fidel Castro, or Josip Broz Tito—became global icons by offering their visions for a different future. In the 1970s, as a precursor to the anxious globalism of today, the world experienced the convergence of peacetime extremes: this was the time of oil shortages, energy rationing, rising unemployment, and an upsurge in anti-immigrant moods, but also the era of human rights, the international women's movement, environmental and antinuclear activism, and Third World solidarity. A global perspective on Bulgarian cultural efforts that teases out the intersections of these extremes is necessary to explain their meaning and relevance.

To grasp the essence of the 1970s, one has to consider how much the decade differed from the defiant 1960s, best known for the mass culture that challenged established social norms and the global protest movements that shook the political order. For Tony Judt, the 1970s was "the most dispiriting decade of the twentieth century"—in Western Europe, pessimism prevailed "because of the contrast with what had gone before," while in Eastern Europe people inhabited "a stifling space in which enthusiasm was replaced by acceptance."[34] For Matthew Connelly, the world saw a "loss of faith in institutions and the very idea of progress" while "no one appeared capable of restoring order."[35] Yet, the experiences of state socialism allow us to introduce nuance into these gloomy analyses that reflect the Western vantage point. As Paulina Bren demonstrates, both the Czechoslovak regime and its citizens actively sought normalization after 1968; while the state embraced "the politics of the (a)political" to empty city squares from potentially unruly crowds, ordinary people pursued quiet lives focused on social comforts, family life, and the development of one's best self, or "self-realization."[36] In the Soviet context, too, Alexei Yurchak documents how the citizens of late socialism saw the political system as both "bleak and full of promise." Up until the end of the "eternal [Soviet] state," people felt "affinity for many of the meanings, possibilities, values, or promises of socialism."[37] Importantly, in the 1970s the smaller states of Eastern Europe actively used East-West contacts "as levers for a cautious but determined reconfiguration of hierarchies in the socialist bloc."[38] This more palpable agency in international matters in turn reinvigorated society at home. The 1970s is also the classic period of Third World solidarity. During this time, the Global South took the lead in discussions for a New International Economic Order (NIEO), the United Nations actively represented the agendas of developing states, human rights debates were at the center of public consciousness, and actors outside of the Western world successfully built coalitions. Notably, the United Nations declared the 1970s as the Second Development Decade, the Decade to Combat Racism and Racial Discrimination, and the Decade for Women, providing the global periphery with tools to articulate a common cause that required common action.[39] If for the West the 1970s was the period of major political, economic, and social shake-ups, in other parts of the world the manifestations of crisis were less acute and many nations were able to imagine a better future.

My analysis of the 1970s from the margins of Europe—with its focus on contradictions, uneasy accommodations, and unlikely encounters—captures well the character of those years. In my interpretation, the 1970s was the time of tortuous attempts to balance the contradictory agendas of the First, Second, and Third Worlds. In the 1970s, the Three Worlds model of the 1950s that divided the world into the West, the East, and "the rest" underwent reconfiguration. As seen through Bulgarian eyes, the First World of the developed capitalist states—the West—no longer constituted a bloc as it was torn by the multiple priorities of its various actors in Europe, North America, East Asia, and Australia. The Third World of the developing states became more prominent and created new global opportunities that deserved attention. The Second World of recently developed states—the Soviet Union and its partners in Eastern Europe—played an important intermediary role between the West and the Third World, yet increasingly the socialist states did not act as a predictable bloc either. In this context, the 1970s was as much a decade of lost certainty and anxious search for stability as it was the time for promising global partnerships and new paths forward. For Bulgaria, these were the years of normalized state socialism when "everything seemed forever," but also the years when many Bulgarians became active players in the world. My analysis highlights the variety of experiences in the Soviet bloc during late socialism and challenges interpretations of the 1970s as the prelude to the collapse of the Eastern European regimes. Overall, this view from the margins captures the contradictory spirit of the 1970s better than the view from the center, which privileges the experiences of select actors (usually big states) at the expense of more "peripheral" players whose reality might be more representative of the wider global mood. In this book, I present an argument about the 1970s in Bulgaria that might be valid elsewhere, yet I argue that there was no single, coherent 1970s—the fractured world we know today was in the making.

The story of Bulgaria's cultural flirtations with the world reveals the ability of a small state to chart an active international agenda during the 1970s when small states dominated discussions of the new global order. The cultural extravaganza examined here was specific to the country and its political system, state socialism, which allowed vast, state-directed investment in culture during times of precarity. However, its dynamics also captured well the spirit of the 1970s as a decade. First, Bulgarian cultural outreach was the direct result of increased East-West contacts during the classic period of détente and lessening of Cold War tensions in the 1970s. Second, the Bulgarian attempts at a global presence reflected the new dynamics after decolonization when the Global South disturbed the equilibrium between West and East. Finally, these cultural programs reflected the spirit of the 1970s as the time when societies started internalizing the contradictory experiences of increasing global contacts. These three factors—the dynamics of East-West reconciliation during détente, the competition between the First and Second Worlds in the Third World, and the expanding forces of global interconnectivity—shaped Bulgaria's cultural efforts.

I offer a "pericentric" perspective—an approach that puts the periphery in the center—on these three manifestations of the 1970s to trace the evolution of historical processes that from the perspective of the margins were both liberating and intimidating.[40] In line with Jeremi Suri's analysis of détente as a conservative reaction of political elites in search of stability after 1968, I conclude that the political reconciliation between East and West in the 1970s fundamentally benefited Bulgarian elites who sought new sources of legitimacy for a political system that needed reinvention.[41] The supposedly reenvisioned "developed socialism" of the 1970s was the flip side of détente: in the same way the opening to the West was partial and highly controlled, reforms at home were selective and decisively top-down. At the same time, like other Eastern European states, in the 1970s Bulgaria actively pursued the development of new partnerships in the Third World, which provided yet another set of possibilities for reinvention. While political, military, and economic priorities drove these developments, they opened up broader prospects—Bulgarian architects, engineers, and physicians now exported urban plans, computing technologies, and medical training to the Third World. These new East-South contacts attracted global attention. British diplomats diligently followed and caustically commented on Bulgaria's "jungle offensive" in Africa, showing that the actions of the small state were touching a nerve. The Soviet Union was not happy with the unorthodoxy of its formerly predictable ally either, and Zhivkov often had to defend his country's new foreign policy before Soviet leader Leonid Brezhnev. Finally, in Bulgaria as well as globally, societies in the 1970s were grappling with the conflicting forces of an increasingly interconnected world that they did not fully understand but whose dynamics they wished to reconcile and benefit from. The growth in cross-border contacts became unavoidable during this time. Bulgarian officials tried to articulate the nature of this shift by speaking about "radical changes, linked to the scientific-technical revolution, which drives the gigantic and perpetual acceleration in the scientific and cultural potential of humanity."[42] Every so often, they used the words "extremes" (*poliusi*) and "contradictions" (*protivorechiia*) to describe their experiences. While unnamed at the time, the struggle between conflicting trends in the global condition of the 1970s foreshadowed the anxiety-ridden globalism of today.

What is the time span of the 1970s? For the purposes of my analysis, which takes into consideration both European and global dynamics, the aftermath of 1968 marked the inception of a new global experience: while still recovering from the challenges of political unrest in 1968, after the economic recession began in 1973 elites justified conservative reaction through political and economic exigencies that tried to control bottom-up imaginings of the world order. This search for political and social consensus lasted through the early 1980s when renewed Cold War following the Soviet invasion of Afghanistan reset the tone of political debates yet again. In my analysis, the 1970s refers to the period between 1968 and 1982, a time characterized by cynicism about the prospect for radical political change, silent private efforts to resolve the contradictions of the times, and tortuous paths forward that were both daunting and hopeful. This definition is specifically meant to allow room for the agency of the people who lived through the 1970s, and not simply condemn them to doom and gloom. This periodization further makes sense for Bulgaria because the late 1960s and early 1980s bookmark the cultural extravaganza that I discuss. Importantly, the 1970s was not a time of acute economic crisis or political instability in Bulgaria, showing that from the margins, the global order had a different flavor indeed. Yet, far-reaching reforms associated with the building of developed socialism and an active foreign policy agenda forced Bulgarian society to grapple with change. In this context, culture provided an important channel through which various actors articulated and negotiated their conflicting expectations of the domestic, regional, and global order.

I explore Bulgaria's programs at home and abroad to uncover the messy logic and unlikely outcomes of Cold War cultural contact in the Balkans, the West, and the Third World. Chapter 1 describes the Bulgarian domestic political and cultural scene to bring nuance to stereotypes about "the Soviet master satellite," emphasize the contradictions of developed socialism, and explain the dynamic interrelationship between national and international considerations in the conception of Bulgaria's cultural agenda. As the regime built monuments and museums, sponsored exhibitions, concerts, and film showings, or organized international meetings and mass events, the prominence of cultural projects, lavishly executed at home and abroad, contributed to the legitimization of real socialism. But the concurrent reassertion of nationalism complicated Bulgaria's cultural agenda among its neighbors in the Balkans (Romania, Yugoslavia, Greece, and Turkey), the topic of chapter 2. Analyzing the interplay between Cold War geopolitical considerations and an older history of national competition in the region, I demonstrate how the pursuit of regional cooperation undercut superpower agendas. In a regional framework, the outcomes of cultural diplomacy reveal their first surprising twist in the fact that capitalist Greece became the most reliable Balkan ally of socialist Bulgaria.

Chapter 3 engages the role of cultural diplomacy and transborder contact across the Iron Curtain to explain the logic of Bulgarian cultural engagements with Western Europe and the United States. By toning down the ideological language and embracing universal values, Bulgarian officials successfully highlighted the historical role of "one of the oldest states of Europe." Teasing out the tensions between culture, ideology, and propaganda, I tackle the different perceptions of cultural exchange by Bulgarian elites and their Western partners in the context of détente, which brought East and West together in even more systematic ways. To add one more layer to the meaning of Cold

War cultural contact, chapter 4 relates émigré reactions to Bulgarian cultural campaigns in the United States and West Germany. As Bulgarian officials encountered both "loyal" second-generation immigrants and "hostile" anticommunist exiles, unlikely contacts developed between Bulgarians of different backgrounds who frequented the same cultural sites to project their rival notions of national pride, freedom, and mobility. Because the regime actively tried to cultivate a Bulgarian diaspora, compromise emerged along national lines, demonstrating the irresistible appeal of nationalism as a legitimization tool for communist elites.

Expanding the analysis of the cultural Cold War to the developing world, chapter 5 explores Bulgarian contacts with India and Mexico in the wider context of the Second World in the Third. Here, culture was not simply a by-product of economic and political priorities, but functioned as an important tool of foreign policy. Bulgarian elites emphasized their country's role as a grand world civilization and paired their stories of courageous Thracian kings and intrepid Slavic scholars with Indian and Mexican narratives of Mughal princes, Hindu sages, Aztec warriors, and Mayan priests. Thus, new global imaginaries on civilizational grounds developed along an East-South line. Chapter 6 continues the analysis of Bulgaria's global entanglements by exploring its presence in Nigeria. Unlike India and Mexico, economic factors determined the logic of small Bulgaria's outreach to the most populous African state. Bulgarian representatives' persistent use of cultural rhetoric reflected state socialism's unique notions of development, which closely integrated economic and cultural ideas, while it also served the claims-making goals of projecting Bulgaria's own image as a developed state. As is obvious throughout the book, cultural contact served both domestic and international agendas.

Finally, the epilogue addresses the resonance of these Cold War cultural dynamics in contemporary Bulgaria. The exploration of select public debates on monuments, museums, and cultural campaigns reveals the continued interplay between cultural, ideological, national, and international factors that shape cultural discussions. Marking an uneasy continuity with the socialist period, the prominence of cultural nationalism in Bulgaria today points to one of the specters of communism still alive in eastern Europe.

In the long 1970s, gleaming golden vessels, striking icons, awe-inspiring classical musicians, and the stunning "cosmic voices" of Bulgarian folk performers (included in the 1977 golden record of the Voyager space probe) made the public image of Bulgaria. No doubt, the official cultural events that cultivated this image served the purposes of a regime that lacked transparency, directed state funds as it wished, showed little inclination for self-criticism, and did not prioritize the wishes of its own citizens. Yet, these cultural programs also promoted original humanist ideas, spurred popular excitement, and led to new global contacts and partnerships. Through culture, the Bulgarian state managed to reinvigorate its society domestically, increase its reputation internationally, and advance select policy agendas in tangible ways. This book calls attention to the role of activities that straddle the murky line between culture, public relations, and propaganda for the perpetuation of the late socialist regimes. In the pages that follow, I explore how culture worked and what it meant in each site of encounter. As I do that, I ask that we take seriously the perspective of those on the margins.

Chapter 1

The Contradictions of Developed Socialism

In his address to the Bulgarian people delivered on 20 October 1981, the general secretary of the Bulgarian Communist Party (BKP) and chairman of the State Council of the People's Republic of Bulgaria (NRB), Todor Zhivkov, reminded his listeners: "We are on the threshold of a major national celebration—the 1300th anniversary of the Bulgarian state, one of the oldest states of Europe, which emerged on the ground . . . of the ancient civilizations in our lands, covered a long distance in its development, and has now reached the highest peak in contemporary progress—the triumph of the socialist social order." The speech skillfully outlined an appealing national narrative, charting in significant detail the history of the Bulgarian people, "situated in one of the most neuralgic [sic] regions of the planet . . . at a crossroads between East and West, North and South." The rhetoric then moved to ideological ground, emphasizing that "the victory of the socialist revolution . . . marked the greatest ever radical breakthrough in our 13-century-long history" because it "unfettered the powerful forces of the nation, provided an irresistible impetus to our country's all-round progress, and marked the beginning of the implementation of the goals and tasks of centuries-long struggles and aspirations." Zhivkov finally proposed visions for Bulgaria's future development under developed socialism (razvit sotsializâm), linking the historical jubilee to domestic reforms and international initiatives already underway.[1]

While the Bulgarian communist leader's self-congratulatory view is hardly surprising, international observers confirmed the invigorating power of the 1300-year jubilee, which made evident, both domestically and internationally, the Bulgarian people's "pride in their cultural and historical heritage . . . and in current achievements in having raised the standard of living."[2] British reports from Sofia on the eve of the anniversary described, rather surprisingly, "a stable country with a growing sense of national identity, ruled by a self-confident and competent regime. Its people are better fed and better clothed than they used to be and have more opportunities for self-expression."[3] Following the 1300-year celebrations, another report concluded: "Bulgaria's reputation as the Soviet Union's closest and most willing client state has become such a cliché that the search for evidence to the contrary is irresistible. The staging of the 1300th anniversary was . . . a clear demonstration of national pride well removed from the professions of solidarity towards the Soviet Union to which we have become accustomed."[4]

Integrating Bulgarian and foreign perspectives, this chapter provides background information on the internal situation in Bulgaria during the long 1970s and engages long-lasting stereotypes associated with the country throughout the Cold War, while explaining the role of culture and the celebration of the 1300-year jubilee during late socialism. Both in historical scholarship and in contemporaneous Western diplomatic and media sources, Bulgaria is frequently presented as a ruthless dictatorship completely subservient to the Soviet Union. The country is usually described as the Soviet Union's most loyal ally, implying a strong degree of political dependence. Bulgaria also attracts attention because of its lack of a dissident movement during a time of heightened dissent in Eastern Europe, which is explained either through the regime's brutal repression or the ingrained passivity of the population. These assumptions, even though often based on insufficient information or a simplistic reading of the facts, made the country seem unworthy of attention. Here, I take a closer look at the situation in Bulgaria to complicate both opinions. What if the "eternal Bulgarian-Soviet friendship" served the country well? Or the lack of dissent meant popular acceptance of the regime's policies? This chapter adds much-needed nuance to the history of late socialism in Eastern Europe by analyzing the role of official culture in sustaining state socialist regimes. I demonstrate that Bulgarian cultural policies of the 1970s served the purpose of domestic legitimization as they reinvigorated Bulgarian "patriotism," rejuvenated the social contract between the regime and its citizens, and undercut dissent by recruiting potential critics into the cultural projects sponsored by the state.

Western observers typically defaulted to clichés in their descriptions of Bulgaria. In the standard view, because the country was dependent on Soviet economic assistance for raw materials, training, and markets, it "ha[d] surrendered much of its sovereignty" to the Soviet Union, both militarily and in foreign policy.[5] British diplomatic reports from the early 1970s spoke about its "docility" and concluded that the situation in Bulgaria served to illustrate "what Moscow would do, if it could, with the other members [of the Soviet bloc]." Because Bulgarian loyalty to the Soviet Union remained "unquestioned," one reason to study Bulgaria was to "provide insight into the Soviet system."[6] Sofia's reputation as "Moscow's loyal flag-bearer" persisted into the 1970s.[7] Western dispatches consistently spoke about "obedient Bulgaria" and "the master satellite."[8]

Throughout the 1970s, as they learned more about the country—including from its cultural programs—diplomats began refining their assumptions. Bulgarian leader Zhivkov was sensitive to accusations of Bulgarian loyalty to the Soviet Union and its satellite role because it made "his country that much less interesting to the west."[9] Thus, the regime sought to proactively correct this view. In 1979, Zhivkov joked that "the Soviet Union was really a Bulgarian colony" since Bulgaria received its raw materials from Russia and sold its finished ones there, in "the classic colonial relationship."[10] That year, the British ambassador in Sofia observed: "If they can find a way to satisfy Moscow by form and themselves by substance, [the Bulgarians] will choose it. If they can get their own way by shouting 'Eternal Friendship' a bit louder they will do so."[11] By the late 1970s, the Soviet proxy stereotype had been subjected to fine-tuning: now, diplomats saw the internal situation in Bulgaria as "not bad" while they detected "no specific obstacles to normalization, such as the human rights problems in Czechoslovakia."[12] In 1981, the Economist called Bulgaria "Un-Polish."[13] One might argue that, in the midst of turmoil elsewhere in Eastern Europe, "un-Polish" and "not bad" meant good.

At the same time, Western media covering Bulgaria usually described a climate of merciless domestic repression that allegedly eradicated all opposition. In 1975, Radio Free Europe (RFE) concluded: "apparently the intercession-intimidation mechanism is extremely intricate and always effective. The regime's elaborate bureaucratic apparatus seems to have perfected it to the point where almost nothing can be done to counteract it."[14] But this rigid view did not withstand scrutiny. British diplomats, while describing "widespread, underlying political apathy" and "lack of enthusiasm in communism, particularly amongst young people and intelligentsia," pointed out that in Bulgaria, "there was no obvious discontent."[15] The "youth problem" manifested itself in work-shyness, antipathy to public service, and craving for all things Western. Yet, while young Bulgarians wanted more consumer goods, travel, cultural choices, and a better standard of living, what they did not want was political change.[16]

Unable to offer a satisfactory explanation for the fact that discontent had not become dissent, Western diplomats spoke of Zhivkov's "benevolent dictatorship," a phrase that captures well the contradictions of late socialism.[17] Official policies benefited ordinary people: in 1981, the year of the 1300th anniversary, the economy "performed well . . . and real incomes increased," the availability of consumer goods "continued to improve," the political system was "stable," and there was "no audible discontent," while in foreign affairs the country saw the "ceaseless coming and going of delegations from overseas."[18] Thus, observers remained skeptical of the potential for radical change: "it is tempting to believe that the apathy and the social malaise . . . will lead to significant changes in the political order. This would be wishful thinking."[19]

Cultural policies provide a window into the "benevolent dictatorship" of Todor Zhivkov, as they allow us to engage the shifting political and social order of the 1970s and explain the normalization of late socialism.[20] In the 1970s, but especially after Zhivkov's daughter, Liudmila Zhivkova, took charge of culture in 1975, new ideas of aesthetic education and beauty replaced the worn-out Marxist vocabulary of domestic cultural programs. Concurrently, Bulgarian elites launched a massive campaign of cultural diplomacy to create a new image for the country. The national and international aspects of these cultural policies were closely intertwined: on the global scene as well as at home, Bulgaria was showcasing not only its communist credentials, but also its national uniqueness and broader contributions to humanity. The 1300th anniversary celebrations, in particular, had "two beneficial side-effects . . . first in helping to publicise Bulgaria and its achievements abroad, and second in encouraging a sense of national pride and self-confidence [at home]."[21] In my analysis, I show that official culture, vacillating between creative expression, national campaign, public relations plan, and propaganda, fulfilled both international prestige-making aspirations and domestic morale-building goals.

Before I examine Bulgaria's ambitious international cultural policies, it is important to outline the domestic conditions that made this new course possible. For Bulgaria, the period of late socialism was characterized by relative economic security and reform, the political solidification of the regime, an active foreign policy agenda, and attempted projects of social rejuvenation. The country also saw the revival and active promotion of "patriotism," which was at the core of cultural events embracing historical topics. In this context, the "cultural front" acquired new prominence as it actively served ideological, national, and morale-building functions, and culture became a visible priority of state policy, both financially and administratively. These processes were accompanied by the entry of a new generation into the state and party apparatuses; many members of this third generation of communist elites made their careers in the cultural sphere. Further, the new cultural policies undermined the formation of a dissident movement, as they coopted and disarmed potential detractors of the regime. An accommodation emerged between the regime and its citizens, leading to the acceptance of developed socialism by many Bulgarian citizens.

Building Developed Socialism: Bulgaria in the Long 1970s

Bulgaria's reputation as a loyal Soviet ally is connected to the origins of the communist regime. In 1946, Georgi Dimitrov, the longtime Comintern leader and close associate of Joseph Stalin, returned to Bulgaria, assumed BKP leadership, and became the prime minister, helping consolidate communist control (he passed away in 1949 and was replaced by Vasil Kolarov and then Vâlko Chervenkov). Following Stalin's death in 1953, a mid-level apparatchik, Todor Zhivkov, astutely used Soviet power struggles to undermine the Stalinist Chervenkov. Zhivkov became a secretary of the BKP in 1954, but following the Twentieth Congress of the Communist Party of the Soviet Union in February 1956 (which famously featured Nikita Khrushchev's secret speech), he orchestrated Chervenkov's removal during the April Plenum of the BKP (in the spirit of eliminating the Stalinist cult of personality). From that point on, Zhivkov pursued a two-pronged strategy for maintaining power: first, he ingratiated himself with the Soviet leader (by providing support during the Hungarian Revolution of 1956 and suggesting even closer relations and an eventual "merging" between Bulgaria and the Soviet Union in 1962) and second, he proactively removed internal challengers and promoted loyal followers (with the creation of the Committee of Active Fighters against Fascism and Capitalism in 1959 and the appointment of trusted cadres to the Politburo in 1962). When Leonid Brezhnev came to power in 1964, Zhivkov followed the same policies of reaping political and economic benefits from a close relationship with the new Soviet leader: with the slowdown of the economy in the early 1960s, Soviet financial support was critical. In 1968, Bulgaria sent troops during the Warsaw Pact invasion of Czechoslovakia and later unconditionally supported the Brezhnev

doctrine. At the same time, Zhivkov continued his skillful political maneu-
vering at home, implementing additional purges of internal opponents in
1968 and 1972 in the wake of the Prague Spring and shoring up the security
services to better detect political opposition and monitor social discontent.
Yet, Zhivkov treated his opponents with moderation. He did not imprison
or strip them of privileges but offered them retirement or appointed them
to honorary positions, successfully undercutting the development of intra-
party opposition and preventing broader social repercussions.[22]

From the mid-1960s on, the regime also started to pay closer attention to
the everyday needs of the population, using social policies to expand its base
and create a broader consensus. Political scientist Ivaïlo Znepolski describes
Bulgaria during this period as a "consensual dictatorship," a concept that
aligns with contemporary characterizations of Zhivkov's rule as a "benevolent dictatorship."[23] The period of the long 1970s was in many ways the
"golden age" of the Zhivkov regime, which saw the perfection of his "benevolent," "consensual" authoritarian rule. While periodically the general secretary had to address economic, foreign policy, political, and social challenges,
he did this confidently and calmly, assuring both the political elites and the
"masses" that developed socialism was a success.

What were the main developments in Bulgaria during the long 1970s?
The global economic crisis of 1973 caused ripple effects in Bulgarian society,
because Western countries ceased importing Bulgarian goods, which constituted its main source of hard currency. The regime continued to receive oil
supplies from the Soviet Union with prices much below their international
market value. However, the negative export balance pushed Bulgaria's ruling elites toward borrowing from Western banks, quickly inflating its foreign
debt. As it had in the 1960s, in 1979 Bulgaria received Soviet financial assistance to cover its debt obligations, and by the early 1980s the debt problem
was under control. The close relationship with the Soviet Union benefitted
the Bulgarian regime economically during this precarious period of global
economic turmoil, and compared to the other Eastern European countries,
the Bulgarian government did not perceive its economic problems as acute
during this time (that would change in the 1980s). Consistent with the initia-
tion of economic reforms elsewhere in Eastern Europe, in 1979 the Bulgarian
leadership began to discuss a new economic mechanism that included decen-
tralization, limited private property in agriculture and the service sector, and
some price corrections to align with international markets. Once the positive
effects of the Soviet debt financing became clear, however, elites lost interest
in applying the new economic mechanism and in effect the phrase became
an empty propaganda slogan that was extensively discussed in the press and

workplace, but never given real substance. Still, as Martin Ivanov argues, the public debates on the new economic mechanism throughout 1979 and 1980 created social expectations that the regime would introduce reforms when necessary and led to an "atmosphere of greater tolerance to reforms" in general.[24]

The 1970s also saw the continued political consolidation of Zhivkov's regime. The Tenth Congress of the BKP in spring 1971 officially proclaimed that the NRB had entered the period of "developed socialist society" (*razvito sotsialistichesko obshtestvo*), or "real socialism" (*realen sotsializâm*). Zhivkov pushed for a revised constitution to reflect the new times. In May 1971, the Zhivkov constitution enshrined his leading role by creating a new state council under his leadership while the functions of the prime minister became mostly representative. Zhivkov also secured the appointment of trusted new cadres in key political posts. Zhivkov's cult was further built through the anniversary celebrations of his birthdays in 1971, 1976, and 1981, accompanied by the rewriting of the history of anti-fascist resistance in Bulgaria to glorify the current leader. Other aspects of his growing power were the formation of his "hunting crew," which functioned as an informal headquarters for coordinating important state decisions; the appointment of family members, such as his daughter and son-in-law, to important state posts; and the further removal of political opponents.[25]

In terms of foreign policy, Bulgaria followed the main tenets of Soviet foreign policy with a degree of overzealousness that has caused much discussion in the literature, but is best explained through the longer history of Bulgarian Russophilism. Zhivkov diligently cultivated Bulgaria's reputation as a reliable Soviet partner: in the 1970s, he dutifully attended the ritual summer Yalta meetings of Warsaw Pact members with Brezhnev and loyally supported Soviet policies, notably vis-à-vis the West and China.[26] Zhivkov's so-called "sixteenth republic" proposition, which was a suggestion to implement the merging (*slivane*) of Bulgaria and the Soviet Union first made to Khrushchev in 1963, is a hotly debated question. In 1973, Zhivkov pitched the same idea to Brezhnev, the new Soviet leader. It is still debated whether Zhivkov wanted to literally merge Bulgaria with the Soviet Union, or rather wished to benefit economically from the Soviet "big brother" by pledging unyielding support during times of political challenges elsewhere in the Soviet bloc—the explanation advanced in his memoirs. As seen previously, the Soviet Union did treat Bulgaria preferentially in terms of economic aid and crude oil supplies: in the 1970s, Bulgaria received the second largest amount of Soviet financial assistance after the GDR. The "special relationship" between Bulgaria and the Soviet Union was steadily reinforced during this time, including through the 1978 centennial celebrations of Bulgaria's liberation by the Russian army during the Russo-Turkish War of 1877–1878, at the end of which modern Bulgaria was created.[27]

However, this special relationship became more complicated when Bulgarian leaders began to reinvigorate nationalism. Following the internationalist stage of the BKP after 1944, the rehabilitation of national ideas began in the late 1950s, with the eventual embrace of both socialist internationalism and what the regime called "patriotism" in the mid- to late 1960s. As envisioned by Zhivkov, the goal of the "patriotic turn" was to instill national pride in the history and traditions of the Bulgarian people while also proclaiming commitment to socialist solidarity. The 1960s and 1970s thus saw a significant shift in official master narratives along national lines. In the late 1960s, the regime started promoting "grandiose . . . spectacles" on national themes, such as the celebrations of 24th May as the Day of the Slavic Alphabet and Bulgarian Culture, focused on the allegedly Bulgarian scholars Cyril and Methodius who compiled the first Slavic alphabet in the ninth century.[28] "Patriotic education" programs at school ensured that the new generation of socialist Bulgarians would be exposed to literary and historical narratives focused on national topics, while film sagas and monuments filled the country with the images of khans, tsars, patriarchs, national awakeners, and revolutionaries. Cultural nationalism was thus well enshrined in Bulgarian society by the 1970s. Yet, there was a darker aspect of this embrace of nationalism, which relied on the notion of a unitary socialist nation and did not leave much room for minorities in the NRB: notably, the 1971 constitution did not include provisions on minority autonomy or protection. In the mid-1970s there were name-changing campaigns against the Pomaks and the Roma to bring them into the national fold (the regime treaded carefully vis-à-vis the Turks until 1984 when a new assimilation campaign began).[29] The revival of nationalism doubtless served the purpose of internal political consolidation—in RFE's assessment, the resurrected nationalist sentiment "provided the Zhivkov regime with an element of legitimacy" and "served as a safety valve."[30] Yet, the patriotic turn also created international complications, particularly with Bulgaria's neighbors. It also put the Soviet Union on alert in relation to its most loyal ally: as Bulgarian politicians and historians reembraced the national rhetoric, the Soviets cautiously watched to see whether "aspects of Bulgarian nationalism . . . could be divisive in the future."[31]

In addition to this clear patriotic turn, the 1970s were also a period of social reconfiguration, when a new generation that had known nothing but socialism entered the public arena. Znepolski dates to the mid-1960s the formation of a "social consensus" within Bulgaria, which he attributes to the generous social policies that the regime used as a strategy for "buying political loyalty" and "corrupting the masses." In his interpretation, which follows a totalitarian model, ordinary people were willing to accept the measures of the regime in return for modest yet stable improvements in their daily lives.[32] In contrast, Ulf Brunnbauer offers a revisionist analysis that aptly reconciles the "totalizing aspirations" of the state and the appeal of a "socialist way of life" among the masses.[33] During late socialism, "society grew ever more complex, which made it more difficult to police the behavior of individuals."[34] While the state attempted to create a top-down "socialist everyday culture" (*bit*), it did so through "flexible strategies." Brunnbauer convincingly shows that many Bulgarians accepted the ideology of real socialism promoted by the state, and the socialist system in Bulgaria enjoyed a "relatively high level of legitimacy" until the early 1980s.[35] In the end, the 1970s were not simply a period of resignation and apathy, as Western observers saw it, but also of normalization and acceptance of developed socialism as ideology and practice.

The accommodation between state and society, however, did not mean that the regime considered the situation in Bulgaria perfect; striving to build a better socialist system remained a preoccupation to the end. In a famous speech from 1966, Zhivkov spoke about the "two truths" (*dvete pravdi*) in the process of building socialism: "Our socialist reality contains ever more traits of a developed socialist society. But at the same time, we meet not a few negative phenomena. . . . There exist two realities in our life . . . [that] struggle against each other."[36] The contradiction of proclaiming the victory of developed socialism while continuously trying to improve it was at the heart of late socialism. What was different in the 1970s as compared to the 1960s was the creation of a "normalized society"—a society in which "the expectation for a stable system" and a "firm institutional hierarchy" coexisted with the "expression of intentions for change" and "social compromise."[37] This more consensual aspect of late socialism—and the accommodation between the regime and society—provided the backdrop for far-reaching cultural changes during the 1970s.

What's New on the Cultural Front?

Throughout the socialist period, the cultural front (*kulturen front*) maintained its important role in promoting the ideological goals of the regime. The relationship between culture, ideology, and propaganda was at the core of the state socialist understandings of official culture, and intellectuals played an important role in the Bulgarian power structures after 1944.[38] Zhivkov, who came to power in 1956, liked to be seen as invested in culture and socialized with intellectuals to demonstrate his commitment to cultural liberalization in the post-Stalinist period. The period of the thaw in the 1950s, however, ended with limited results: cultural producers remained dependent on the benevolence of political functionaries and carefully straddled the needs of the party and the people, on the one hand, and their own intellectual aspirations, on the other.[39]

The Bulgarian cultural scene was often subjected to top-down reforms whose goal was to articulate its exact functions in socialist society. In the 1960s, according to Evgeniia Kalinova, those reforms came in fits and starts, reflecting the primacy of political imperatives over cultural priorities. In 1963, the Committee for Arts and Culture (KIK) was separated from the Ministry of Education and Culture and given an independent role; this change promoted the role of experts in the administration of culture. In 1965, to purge Stalinist remnants after a coup attempt against him, Zhivkov launched policies of "socialist democratization," which relaxed ideological expectations of cultural production, softened criticism of Western influences, and allowed freer cultural expression. Yet, the state continued to carefully monitor the cultural sphere. The First Congress of Culture, held in 1967, promoted "social participation" in culture, but ultimately served to better align the cultural front with state priorities. With the help of loyal cultural bureaucrats (the newly elevated experts), the state controlled intellectuals in subtler yet more effective ways, without the appearance of direct orders from above. That same year, the Committee for State Security formed its Sixth Division, which focused on rooting out "ideological sabotage" in culture and the arts. In July 1968, in the midst of the Prague Spring, Bulgaria hosted the Ninth World Festival of Youth and Students, under the vigilant eye of the Sixth Division.[40] Following the Warsaw Pact invasion in August, Bulgarian intellectuals remained conspicuously silent. Soon afterward, the state used the occasion to remove inconvenient personalities from the cultural scene (such as artist Dechko Uzunov). In the late 1960s, Bulgarian cultural producers became overwhelmingly disillusioned with the prospect of cultural liberalization and silent resignation dominated cultural circles; as a sign of the new mood, the writer Georgi Markov, an active participant in Zhivkov's "socialist democratization" in the 1960s, decided to remain in Italy during a trip abroad in 1969.[41]

The far-reaching cultural reforms of the 1970s thus followed an earlier template, yet by contrast to the tense 1960s, relative tranquility characterized the late socialist cultural sphere when political functionaries and cultural producers reached a mutually beneficial accommodation. Concurrently, official culture acquired more pronounced international aspects, which provided new opportunities for advancement. In substance and in form, cultural policies became an unquestionable and visible state priority.

Emulating Brezhnev's strategy of recruiting intellectuals through encouragement and rewards, Zhivkov initiated dialogue with cultural producers and expanded state investment in culture. The new constitution of 1971 defined the role of culture as being "in service of the people" and its main goal as "develop[ing] the communist spirit." Throughout the 1970s, state investment in culture grew: according to Kalinova, from 2.4 percent of GDP in the 1960s to 3.4 percent in the 1970s.[42] A number of state and party institutions provided expertise in cultural matters. While the apparatchiks at the Central Committee of the BKP's Art, Culture, and Propaganda Department continued to vet the overall direction of cultural policy, the experts at the KIK implemented specific policies with the help of the creative unions, educational institutions, and other cultural establishments. The Ministry of Foreign Affairs (MVnR) assisted in international events, while State Security's Sixth Division kept an eye on individual cultural and artistic figures. These institutions were often in competition, but their extensive involvement in cultural matters signified the new attention to culture during real socialism.

At the same time, new ideas, phraseology, and technologies entered the cultural scene. The early 1970s saw efforts to revise the state's rigidly ideological use of culture, replacing orthodox Marxist-Leninist analysis and slogan-like propaganda with subtler interpretations of the role of culture in developed socialist society. According to cultural studies scholar Ivan Elenkov, "directing culture [wa]s no longer conceived as the organization of politico-educational propaganda-ideological campaigns, but as the management of differentiated social processes" that included the entire society, and not only the working class. To attract all social groups, the regime not only "updated the ideological narrative" but also "broadened the scope of official taste." People were engaged in cultural activities according to their age, employment, inclinations, or lifestyle and in various contexts, such as work, free time, everyday activities (bit), and family life. In 1972, KIK published a "Program for the Aesthetic Education of the Workers and Youth," which outlined the essence of "socialist mass culture" as an "active, transformational social practice"—completely different from "bourgeois mass culture and elitism"—whose goal was to create "new cultural habits among the masses."[43]

Reimagining the role of culture under real socialism also meant that there was a pronounced increase in patriotic themes entering the cultural sphere. As in Romania, eloquently described by Katherine Verdery, cultural producers became key figures in the promotion of cultural nationalism, which exalted the long-standing accomplishments of the Bulgarian nation.[44] Writers wrote historical fiction based on national themes while historians published popular historical accounts aimed at lay audiences. Archaeologists oversaw the reconstruction of the sites of the medieval Bulgarian kingdoms' capital cities. Artists and sculptors decorated public spaces and venues in patriotic imagery featuring medieval and National Revival figures. The rediscovery of the ancient past became another aspect of this shift, evident through the founding in 1972 of the Institute of Thracology to study the ancient Thracian tribes in Bulgarian territory, while the Thracians acquired the status of ancestors. The number of historical series shown of television was a particularly visible part of this campaign, which continued into the 1980s. Cultural producers were now at the forefront of the patriotic turn.[45]

This is not to say that communist ideology disappeared from cultural production. In December 1973, the Eastern European leaders of the respective ideological organizations convened in Moscow to discuss the role of ideology in the context of détente. They concluded that due to the expanding contacts between East and West, only an "ideological offensive" and "multifaceted propaganda of the success of the socialist states" could counter Western propaganda, which now focused on the lower standard of living in socialist states. As a response, in February 1974, Alexander Lilov, the secretary of the Central Committee of the BKP in charge of ideology, convened a plenum dedicated to the "ideological front" in which culture was discussed as an important aspect of ideological work. Yet, this "ideological offensive" went hand in hand with new approaches to culture in the conditions of real socialism, including pragmatism, departure from black-and-white propaganda, and the adoption of scientific vocabulary, in addition to accumulating empirical knowledge about Western reality and selectively disseminating the critical work of certain "progressive" Western intellectuals at home.[46]

In line with the new functions assigned to culture, in April 1974 the Central Committee of the BKP spelled out its goals: the reorganization of the cultural front would lead to "the satisfaction of the cultural needs and aesthetic interests of the people, [and their] turn to communist ideas." The state centralized cultural policy further: the KIK was put charge of the new vision and acquired administrative oversight over all cultural institutions. In July 1975, Zhivkov's daughter, Liudmila Zhivkova, assumed the leadership of the KIK—which in 1977 was renamed the Committee for Culture (KK) and became a ministry (Zhivkova thus became a member of the State Council).[47] Under her leadership, culture experienced far-reaching reorganization that reflected both the new spirit of the times and Zhivkova's own idiosyncratic visions.

Several projects dominated the work of the KK under Zhivkova. Discussion of what became known as "aesthetic education" had begun before Zhivkova's time, but in December 1975 the KK accepted the "All People's Program for Aesthetic Education," which framed the agenda of cultural institutions for the rest of the 1970s. In the end, the concept of aesthetic education—which emphasized the need "to awaken the creative abilities of each person," starting with children and continuing for life—became associated with Zhivkova.[48] In her conception—which she conveyed in long-winded speeches in front of her closest associates—aesthetic education was based on the "concept of beauty," which she saw as a "universal category than constitutes the basis of everything." The goal was "to teach people how to feel, think, act, and live according to the laws of beauty" so that citizens would become "harmonically developed personalities" able to balance rational and emotional elements. Instead of the worn-out Marxist-Leninist vocabulary, in the context of developed socialist society cultural functionaries offered a vision of "a new personality, reborn through beauty." By enshrining this vocabulary of beauty, in Elenkov's analysis, the regime "replaced the old proletarian enthusiasm with a new creative euphoria."[49]

As the content of culture became updated, so did its technologies. Zhivkova and her associates promoted the use of new cultural tools such as film, television, radio, photography, publishing, music, sports, and tourism to make culture more accessible and guarantee its wide social resonance. Another innovation was the creation of "national cultural complexes"—cultural projects of long duration, whose goal was to include the entire population and guarantee the effectiveness of the cultural message. The cultural experts of the KK developed new cultural forms—"new cultural phenomena"—such as television theater, television film series, radio dramas, television novels, and "synthetic concert-spectacles" that combined theater, film, photo collages, and musicals.[50] This vocabulary of cultural innovation was ubiquitous in the 1970s; often, these new technologies were implemented as a result of the study of "foreign experiences," with the goal of bringing Bulgaria in line with global cultural trends. But based on their socialist conception, the role of these new cultural mechanisms was to bring together the agendas of the "spiritual elites" who conceptualized these projects and the "mass audience" who consumed them. The ultimate objective was to cultivate new "active consumers of culture"—the new citizen of developed socialism, which was expected to be fully by 1990.[51]

Within the flurry of cultural activity during the late 1970s, two programs stand out. In March 1978, the Central Committee of the BKP affirmed "The Long-Term Complex Program for the Elevation of the Role of Art and Culture," which outlined the priorities for the next decade. This document described two cultural initiatives to be carried out under Zhivkova: first, "The Program for the Harmonious Development of Individuals and Society" focused on the cultivation of "multifaceted personalities" (*vsestranno razviti lichnosti*) and, second, the celebration of the 1300th anniversary of the establishment of the Bulgarian state in 681, which was envisioned as the focal point of all cultural efforts.[52] Until Zhivkova's death in 1981, educational and cultural institutions concentrated on implementing these two ideas. Both programs pursued domestic and international agendas, highlighting the intimate connection between local and global aspirations at the core of official cultural policy.

Zhivkova's interest in multifaceted personalities led to the launching of "complex programs" (*kompleksni programi*) dedicated to famous individuals seen as having had an indelible impact on the development of human civilization. Experts designed "complex events" (*kompleksni meropriiatiia*) that encompassed the entire year but also had a clear "culmination" (*kulminatsiia*). This model would become the signature of Bulgarian cultural outreach under Zhivkova. The program began with a celebration of the Russian artist, humanist, and peace activist Nicholas Roerich in 1978; his choice allowed Bulgaria to mollify Soviet suspicions of unorthodoxy and national self-promotion while still promoting its universalist cultural agenda.[53] The second program in 1979–1980 focused on Leonardo da Vinci; the goal here was to emphasize the "common traits between the Renaissance and Eastern Orthodox civilization," making the world aware of the unique contributions of the lesser-known civilizations in the East.[54] Next, the program celebrated Vladimir Ilyich Lenin in 1980 (the 110th anniversary of his birth) and Saint Cyril (Cyril the Philosopher to Bulgarians), the father of the Cyrillic alphabet, in 1981 (to coincide with the 1300th anniversary). These were safe choices, both ideologically and nationally, because they affirmed everlasting commitment to communism while emphasizing Bulgaria's unique contributions to Slavic civilization. By studying the impact of such extraordinary people, Zhivkova expected that these programs would reveal "the creative essence of human development" and highlight the interconnectivity between world cultures. Domestically, by learning from example, the citizens of developed socialist society would nurture a new attitude toward art and culture and become harmonious personalities. To promote these new ideas internationally, Bulgaria initiated contacts with the United Nations, UNESCO, and a range of other international organizations, governments, and independent cultural actors. Zhivkova believed that by ambitiously bringing their creative energies together, a small state would contribute to the development of a new attitude to culture in the contemporary world.[55] Both in terms of the ideas promoted and the range of activities planned, this global, humanistic approach to culture constituted a breakthrough for the relatively isolated Bulgarian society.

Next, cultural efforts focused on the celebration of all celebrations, the 1300-year jubilee, the second core element of Zhivkova's ambitions to reenvision the role of culture.[56] Anniversary celebrations were not a new phenomenon in Bulgaria: officials regularly participated in various commemorative events, both domestically and internationally. But for Zhivkova, the 1300th anniversary was no ordinary anniversary—it was the "focus," "crossroads," and "culmination" of rethinking the historical processes within the country and its contributions throughout the world.[57] Because of the critical importance of this "big event" (*goliamoto sâbitie*) in the cultural policies analyzed in this book, I engage its conceptualization in the next section of this chapter.

The reorganization of Bulgarian culture in the 1970s involved an explicit expansion of its international agenda. This trend was consistent with the pursuit of cross-border contacts by state socialist societies after 1956, but the depth and breadth of Bulgaria's reach invites us to consider the role of state socialist societies in advancing cultural globalization as it accelerated in the 1970s. In 1974, one of the "representative" (*predstavitelni*) Bulgarian exhibitions, *Thracian Treasures*, premiered in Paris, followed by an avalanche of appearances throughout Europe, North and South America, and Asia to showcase the ancient heritage of contemporary Bulgaria. With the success of the treasures concept, officials put together other high-profile exhibitions, including *1000 Years of Bulgarian Icons* (focused on the role of Orthodoxy in Bulgarian history), *Medieval Bulgarian Civilization*, *Treasures of the Rila Monastery*, and *Ethnographic Treasures of Bulgaria*, among others. The first project of the multifaceted personalities program also included an international agenda. It focused on Roerich—a Russian poet and artist who had emigrated to the West, lived in Central Asia and China, and eventually set-tled in India. In June 1978, a photo exhibit of Roerich's artwork opened in Accra, Ghana, followed by Prague, Berlin, Washington, Delhi, Damascus, Madrid, Helsinki, and Vienna; the goal was to showcase Bulgaria's role in facilitating contacts between states at the crossroads of cultures. However, these exhibitions received mixed reviews, especially in Europe, where the showing of photo reproductions did not impress.[58] This experience reaf-firmed the focus on high-profile "representative exhibitions," which became the cornerstone of international cultural policies specifically designed with global audiences in mind.

By the mid-1970s, international cultural outreach had become a core aspect of state policy. Within MVnR, the Department for International Cultural Affairs and Foreign Press coordinated events carried out by the Bulgarian embassies and monitored foreign media coverage. In 1975 the ministry created a Department of Cultural Heritage whose goal was to acquire artistic works from abroad—both Bulgarian and foreign—to enrich the holdings of Bulgarian museums and art galleries. State Security also started to recruit agents for historical espionage in foreign archives, librar-ies, and museums.[59] Another signature project of Zhivkova's was the Gallery for International Art, which opened in Sofia in 1985, several years after her death in 1981, to house the foreign masterpieces that were pur-chased by Bulgarian experts or gifted to the Bulgarian people on the occa-sion of its 1300th anniversary.[60]

Bulgaria also hosted international cultural events and famous interna-tional figures, who were carefully chosen not only to have a desired ideologi-cal impact, but also to enrich the cultural scene. In September 1972, African American activist Angela Davis visited Bulgaria to "a welcome of red carna-tions and friendly smiles."[61] In February 1973, at the last stages of U.S. involve-ment in Vietnam, Bulgaria gave a warm welcome to writer Erskine Caldwell who visited Sofia as a part of his antiwar campaign.[62] In June 1977, Bulgaria organized an International Writers' Meeting that brought 144 writers from thirty-two countries to Sofia to discuss the world after Helsinki. Despite anxi-eties over dissidents and the threat of boycotts, with the meticulous planning of the Union of Bulgarian Writers this event continued regularly throughout the 1980s.[63] In 1978, an International Conference of Bulgarian Studies was held at the Black Sea resort Druzhba (friendship), with a follow-up meet-ing in Sofia in 1980. In 1981, this event morphed into an even more ambi-tious project, the First World Congress of Bulgarian Studies, which brought together scholars from fifty-one countries to discuss the worldwide advance-ment of knowledge about Bulgaria. The World Parliament, convened by the

World Peace Council in 1980, was another high-profile event that brought foreign dignitaries to the capital.[64]

One of the most innovative and memorable international events was the Banner of Peace International Children's Assembly that Bulgaria hosted in 1979 for the United Nations' International Year of the Child. In August, 1,321 children from seventy-seven countries joined 1,100 Bulgarian pupils for a two-week visit that included artistic, musical, and performance events, from chalk art competitions in parks and squares to joint choir performances in public venues and sightseeing excursions to historical sites. The motto of the event—Unity, Creativity, Beauty—reflected Zhivkova's thinking and the new cultural phraseology in Bulgaria. At the opening of the Banner of Peace Monument on the outskirts of Sofia—which displayed bells from seventy-nine nations brought together in "peace and harmony"—Zhivkova spoke about "the unity, peace, and beauty uniting humanity" and appealed to UNESCO to recognize this "unique memorial" as a heritage site. The organization of this event reflected a core idea of the domestic focus on aesthetic education—the development of harmonious personalities began at a young age. However, Zhivkova had larger aspirations—she saw the assembly as an opportunity to cultivate a "world spiritual brotherhood" (svetovno duhovno bratstvo) with a global impact.[65] It is not coincidental that Zhivkova decided to hold the Second International Children's Assembly, with more than 2,500 participants, in the 1300th anniversary year of 1981.

These were far-reaching changes in Bulgarian cultural policies, both domestically and internationally, and they caused great excitement among the cultural bureaucracy and had wider resonance in Bulgarian society. The state invested in new ideas and projects that created a dynamic official cultural life during the 1970s. For the first time, Bulgarian citizens saw Ray Charles and Tina Turner on television and viewed da Vinci's paintings in downtown Sofia while their cultural products toured famous museums or secured international prizes and Oscar nominations. In this context, some among Zhivkova's entourage spoke about a new, second golden age of Bulgarian culture, following on the first golden age of King Simeon the Great (893–927), the most glorified of the medieval Bulgarian rulers.[66] It is important to emphasize that this state-directed cultural investment was not a selfless promotion of culture, but clearly pursued the goals of the regime. The new cultural practices were not optional; they became compulsory, all-encompassing "events" (meropriiatiia) in the life of each Bulgarian. Despite the relaxation of class and party vocabulary, the coordinated omnipresence of these events created, in the words of Elenkov, "a new official, ideologically

FIGURE 8. Participants in the International Children's Assembly, 1979. Source: P. Kolev, published with permission.

unified culture" that could only be the product of a state-managed system of cultural production that imposed its vision on its citizens without transparency or feedback.[67] As Irina Gigova demonstrates in her examination of Bulgarian writers, cultural practitioners felt that they were constantly under demand to produce for various state-sponsored events, participating in an "endless series of mandatory and carefully scripted official gatherings, conferences, and award ceremonies that kept authors mindlessly busy." If Zhivkova's policies were seen as the second golden age by some, for others they constituted the essence of "the bore of the 1970s," highlighting the con-tradictory experiences of developed socialism.[68]

The Big Jubilee: 1300 Years Bulgaria

Because the 1300th anniversary of the establishment of the Bulgarian state (also referred to as 1300 Years Bulgaria, Thirteen Centuries Bulgaria, or sim-ply 1300) became the focal point of all domestic and international cultural endeavors, in this section I analyze the core logic, organizational models, and institutional arrangements of the "big jubilee." The anniversary was envi-sioned as "the system 1300"—it had to encompass everything and every-one, and a series of secondary events led up to it—the centennial of modern Bulgaria on 3 March 1978, the thirty-fifth anniversary of the socialist revo-lution on 9 September 1979, and Lenin's 110th birthday on 22 April 1980. The celebration of 1300 Years Bulgaria in 1981 constituted the culmination of them all.[69] This "big event"—another favorite bureaucratic designation—was planned as a "chain of connected cultural events" involving a range of celebratory activities in the country and abroad, coordinated in consultation with all state institutions, from the Politburo to the neighborhood citizens' associations.[70]

The jubilee clearly pursued patriotic objectives by promoting visions of the historical unity and national glory of the Bulgarian people. In this sense, the "big event" constituted the culmination of the embrace of cultural nationalism in the long 1970s as well. The celebration of the 1300th anni-versary of the establishment of the Bulgarian state centered on a founda-tional event in Bulgarian history: in 681, the Bulgars (or Proto-Bulgarians) of Khan Asparuh crossed the Danube River and, having defeated the Byzantine troops, signed a treaty with Emperor Constantine IV who agreed to pay tribute. Khan Asparuh entered into an alliance with Slavic tribes and began the process of settlement in Byzantine Moesia in a first step toward the estab-lishment of what would eventually become the Bulgarian state. Taking this date as the starting point, the jubilee highlighted Bulgaria as one of the oldest states in Europe. However, this was a celebration of the most notable Bul-garian historical accomplishments more generally. Due to their association with the Thracians, modern Bulgarians had an ancient history that predated the Greeks and Romans.[71] By welcoming the disciples of Cyril and Metho-dius, who had created a new alphabet for the Slavic languages, the medieval Bulgarian kingdom contributed to the development of Slavic culture and became the beacon of Slavic civilization during the golden age of culture in the late ninth and early tenth centuries. Courage, vision, and progressive thinking, the argument went, were evident throughout the history of the Bulgarian people, who fought multiple invaders over the centuries (Byzantine, Ottoman, and fascist alike) but preserved their fighting spirit and rich cultural traditions. In sum, Bulgaria was a deserving match to the better-known Greek and Roman influences that were assumed to be the basis of "European civilization." Also, the Bulgarians built their unique Slavic and Eastern Orthodox civilization even before the arrival of the various "barbarian" tribes that would become the basis of the contemporary Western European states, including the Franks, Anglo-Saxons, and the Germanic tribes of the Holy Roman Empire. The goals of the 1300-year jubilee, which traced the long, glorious history of the Bulgarian people, were twofold: to chart the historical consolidation of the Bulgarian nation over the centuries and to place this process in the context of other European and world civilizations. The architects of the jubilee not only tried to construct an inspiring patriotic narrative of national uniqueness, but also sought to inscribe the history of the Bulgarian nation in the context of universal human values and shared civilizational characteristics. Bulgarian officials thus consciously avoided crude national(ist) characterizations and adhered to more refined, universal, and even cosmopolitan messages.

In addition to these national aspirations, the celebration of the 1300th anniversary had clear ideological objectives. As conceptualized by Zhivkova and her collaborators, the end goal of the 1300 Years Bulgaria program was the collective recognition of the most important figures in Bulgarian history in order to connect the past to communist mythology. By emphasizing the "unity of past-present-future," the ultimate culmination of Bulgaria's centuries-long history would be the construction of communist society in the foreseeable future. Conveniently, 1981 was the year of the 1300-years jubilee and the ninetieth anniversary of the birth of the BKP (as counted from the establishment of Dimitar Blagoev's Bulgarian Social Democratic Party in August 1891), so as the Bulgarian people were preparing for the 1300th anniversary, they were also celebrating the longevity of the BKP. The function of the jubilee, then, was "to merge the history of Bulgaria with the history of the Bulgarian Communist Party."[72] Ultimately, the 1300 Years Bulgaria events, seamlessly blending historical and ideological narratives, would skillfully serve the purpose of public relations, as they would increase small Bulgaria's reputation throughout the world while also advancing its political and economic agenda. Morale-building and prestige-making agendas conveniently came together.

The preparations for the 1300 Years Bulgaria anniversary started in June 1976 when the Central Committee of the BKP approved the celebration of

FIGURE 9.   The People's Palace of Culture (NDK) in 1981 when it first opened to host the Twelfth Congress of the BKP and the 1300 Years Bulgaria celebrations. Source: P. Kolev, published with permission.

the "big event" and established a commission that circulated a number of "idea plans" (*ideĭni planove*) for the jubilee. In 1978 the National Coordinating Committee 1300 Years Bulgaria (NKK), under the leadership of Liudmila Zhivkova, took charge of organizing the domestic and international programs associated with the anniversary. In November 1978, the NKK accepted the National Program for the Development and Coordination of Activities Related to 1300 Years. Planning for the big event sped up in 1980: in April, the KK and NKK signed off on the calendar of anniversary activities and in October they affirmed the program of important events for 1981. Many of the celebrations were conceived as "complex events" that combined diverse genres and audiences to create a lasting "multiplication effect."[73] Overall, the NKK coordinated over 3,500 meetings of various institutions and created a planning template for celebratory events. Bulgarian officials designed what can be likened to target plans for jubilee events; these "jubilee plans" were written by each state institution, sent to the NKK for approval, and required a final "general report" detailing the rationale and execution of the plan. The total cultural mobilization of the nation was underway.

To promote the narrative of national unity, the domestic celebration of 1300 Years was conceived as an "all-people's celebration" (*vsenarodno târzhestvo*) encompassing the entire nation.[74] At the end of 1980, Zhivkov launched the commemorations with a speech titled "Long Live Our Ancient and Always Young Motherland!" Mass events—meetings, congresses, openings of new monuments, youth marches, sporting events—were planned for the Thirteen Days of Bulgaria, each one organized around a distinct theme that reflected the "essence" of the "Bulgarian spirit."[75] The culmination was the official celebration of the 1300-year jubilee on 20 October 1981 in the newly built People's Palace of Culture in Sofia (NDK)—a brand-new convention center first used for the Twelfth Congress of the BKP in April. Other monumental structures built for the jubilee included the Founders of the Bulgarian State complex in Shumen, the monument of Khan Asparuh in Tolbuhin (today Dobrich), and the 1300 Years Bulgaria Monument across from the NDK in Sofia.

In Bulgaria in 1981, there were more than 3,000 exhibitions dedicated to the "big event," featuring over 800,000 artifacts. One of the most conspicuous accomplishments was the opening of the National Museum Palace in the former building of the Jurists' Council, which housed the *1300 Years Bulgaria* exhibition showing the best archaeological and historical artifacts. (Although this caused some controversy because it emptied regional museums). There were over one hundred photographic exhibits around the country, hundreds of theatrical performances, over 550 musical events, dozens of historical film productions (including the epic production *Khan Asparuh*), more than two hundred books dedicated to the 1300-year jubilee, and dozens of scientific symposia. Some 50,000 Bulgarians participated in the national television trivia competition "Bulgaria, Ancient and Young," attracting an audience of 750,000. The country was inundated with medals, pins, buttons, coins, posters, calendars, and stamps featuring the 1300th anniversary theme, which proudly disseminated the message of the national glory of small Bulgaria.[76]

Yet from the beginning, 1300 Years Bulgaria was also envisioned as a global affair. In preparation for their international plans, Bulgarian officials meticulously studied "foreign experiences" beyond the anniversary celebrations typical for the Soviet bloc. One survey of anniversary celebrations for the period 1979–1994 in fifty-seven countries compiled examples from "brotherly socialist states, Balkan, Arab, developed capitalist, and some developing countries." The countries listed under "a" included Australia, Austria, Albania, Algiers, Angola, Argentina, and Afghanistan.[77] In the end, cultural functionaries chose the anniversaries of Poland, Iran, and the United

FIGURE 10.   The 1300 Years Bulgaria Monument in the NDK park, 1981. Source: P. Kolev, published with permission.

States as the three models that most fit their needs, while also singling out two counter-models of practices to avoid, those of Belgium and Romania. Surprising cultural partnerships and unlikely exchanges of ideas framed the conception of the "big event."

Bulgarian experts studied in detail the Polish millennium of 1966, which celebrated the Christianization of Poland in 966. An appealing element of the Polish celebrations was the blending of historical and contemporary themes: the anniversary emphasized the progress of Polish socialist society throughout the centuries, but showcased the twentieth anniversary of

FIGURE 11.   The Rozhen Folk Fair held under the auspices of the 1300th anniversary, featuring a giant banner honoring the jubilee. Source: *Slaviani*, no. 2 (1982).

the establishment of the People's Republic of Poland in 1966 as the peak of the millennium celebration.[78] Experts paid close attention to the role of the "reactionary and fanatic" Catholic clergy, which had tried to "divide the population into religious and non-religious" through the organization of alternative, church-led millennial events; they tried to anticipate similar difficulties in Bulgaria due to the similarly prominent role of the Orthodox Church in Bulgarian history.[79] Finally, the mass participation of a large number of émigrés in the millennial celebrations had highlighted the "moral and political unity of [Polish] society," an appealing example for the Slavic Committee, the official Bulgarian organization for Bulgarians abroad, which similarly tried to rally the Bulgarian diaspora.[80]

While Poland was an understandable model for the Bulgarian jubilee, some of the other choices appear more eclectic. This was especially the case with the 2500th anniversary of the establishment of the Persian Empire celebrated in Iran in 1971, a lavish affair that included the opening of beautifully reconstructed historical sites, such as Persepolis, the capital of Cyrus the Great (which may have inspired the extensive reconstruction of the medieval Bulgarian capital Veliko Târnovo). The appeal of the Iranian anniversary, however, was in its international features, namely the promotion of tourism, the involvement of UNESCO, and the establishment of "national celebratory committees" to coordinate jubilee celebrations in some fifty-two countries.[81] The Bulgarians similarly pursued the recruitment of high-profile foreign public figures to spearhead Bulgarian cultural events abroad. Yet, surprisingly, Bulgarian functionaries also studied the U.S. experience in the bicentennial celebrations of the American Revolution in 1976, despite the compulsory castigation of "the failures of American propaganda" and the "important problems of contemporary American society."[82] Appealing elements of the U.S. program included the active state involvement in a long-term, complex celebratory program and the constitution of a Bicentennial National Committee; the mass participation of Americans in celebrations at the local level; the use of souvenirs, badges, banners, and other paraphernalia; and the extensive media coverage.[83] The study of these foreign anniversaries produced some curious transfers of knowledge across ideological lines. Notably, considering the "ideological overload and overdose" of the U.S. events, Bulgarian experts recommended the removal of propaganda language from events associated with their own 1300-year jubilee.[84]

This obsession with not going overboard was most obvious in the study of celebrations that Bulgarian officials believed had gone astray. The 150th anniversary of the formation of the Belgian republic occurred in 1980, but the official motto of that jubilee, "Belgium, in the Heart of Europe," was problematic because its idea of Europe consisted of "the Europe of NATO, of the [Western] European common civilization (including the USA and Canada) . . . as an antithesis of socialist Europe."[85] Rejecting the limited resonance of the Belgian celebrations—which were confined to Western Europe—the Bulgarians instead wished to engage with all European states, East and West. The 2050th anniversary of the unification of the Dacian tribes by Burebista in a centralized state, seen as the basis of contemporary Romania, also occurred in 1980. Bulgarian officials openly mocked this "fake anniversary" that "contradicts historical truth" because of Romanian "nationalism and historical revisionism." By contrast, the Bulgarians planned to use measured national language and adhere to professional historical analysis.[86]

In the end, the Bulgarian experts designed an international celebratory structure that selectively combined elements from the Polish, Iranian, and U.S. celebrations, while heeding the mistakes of Belgium and Romania. First, ideological or nationalist "overload"—like in the United States, Belgium, and Romania—was to be avoided. Instead, even if promoting a vision of national history, the 1300-year celebrations tried to embrace universal civilizational ideas and rigid historical standards. Second, international involvement became a core element of the commemorative program, whether reaching out to the diaspora, as the Poles did, or involving UNESCO and foreign dignitaries, as the Iranians did. Third, like the U.S. experience, the Bulgarian celebrations were long-term, broad-spectrum complex events that would utilize all available resources but would have a clean culmination to emphasize the core message. Fourth, based on the Iranian model, special national jubilee committees would recruit well-meaning foreign public figures to enhance the international dimensions of the events. Finally, following the Polish example, these would be mass events involving the total mobilization of the state apparatus, the population at large, and foreign participants.

With these plans in hand, in the period between 1977 and 1981, Bulgarian officials organized more than 38,000 cultural events abroad. Bulgarian

FIGURE 12.   Logo for the 1300th anniversary featured in official Bulgarian publications for foreign audiences, such as the magazines *Bulgaria Today* and *Slaviani*.

embassies throughout the world were charged with conceiving "jubilee plans," which they sent for approval to the NKK in Sofia and followed up with regular quarterly reports. As 1981 approached, priorities shifted to the organization of high-profile "complex events" to attract political and media attention. Diplomats also sought to establish national celebration committees composed of local public figures that would facilitate those events; committees were established in sixty-two countries in all.[87] Each embassy was expected to have a "culmination" marking the jubilee while they were also tasked with securing the attendance of heads of state or parliamentary representatives at the "all-people's celebration" in Sofia in October 1981.[88]

By official estimates, some 25 million visitors attended the various events abroad.[89] The demand to deliver cultural events put stress on the bureaucracy of a small state working in conditions of total cultural mobilization. In one sense, the organization of the 1300-year jubilee abroad could be understood as a series of target plans executed in conditions of fierce competition within a cultural field characterized by acute product shortages. These "cultural shortages"—to paraphrase Janos Kornai's interpretation of socialist societies as "economies of shortage"—were particularly intense during the peak of the jubilee in 1981.[90] With the high demand for cultural products, the 1300th anniversary celebrations became an aspect of the power struggles between institutions and political personas, because in the context of cultural shortages all state officials vied for the best of Bulgarian culture. Altogether, these efforts consumed a vast amount of time, energy, and resources for over five years and produced an elaborate international cultural program without precedent in Bulgaria and possibly the rest of Eastern Europe.

The People: Bulgaria's Power Elites

The elevated role of culture in Bulgaria in the 1970s went hand in hand with the promotion of a new generation of intellectuals and officials—often intellectuals in the role of officials—who were in charge of the new processes. The emergence of "new younger blood" in Bulgaria was not limited to the cultural sphere; the new generation of communist elites also entered the economic sector, foreign policy, and trade.[91] Western reports on Bulgaria remained obsessed with its "power elite," which—in the analysis of RFE—acted as a "steering mechanism" in a "closed society."[92] British diplomats, for example, compiled biographical compendiums of Bulgaria's "leading personalities" that summed up their official roles but also added vivid personal details.[93] What is striking in these bios is the sizeable presence of functionaries who launched their careers in the cultural front. Zhivkov first promoted a number of new faces among the intellectuals in the course of the state reorganization after the 1971 constitution. He saw those cadres as "new blood" with professional training and modern thinking, but also as people directly indebted to him for their careers. Some of these intellectuals became a part of his inner circle by joining Zhivkov's hunting crew, an ever-changing group of party leaders, state officials, intellectuals, and public figures whom Zhivkov patronized and who, in turn, often benefited from their proximity to him. At the same time, Liudmila Zhivkova promoted her own protégés whom she recruited to transform her ideas into policies, giving rise to what became known as Liudmila's circle. Some of "Liudmila's people" also joined Zhivkov's hunting crew. Evgeniia Kalinova speaks about a symbiosis between intellectual and political circles in the 1970s when the state generously provided loyal intellectuals with material benefits and opportunities for recognition and new informal power groups with enormous influence arose.[94] It is thus imperative to present the most prominent members of the power elites relevant to this story, who also promoted Bulgaria's reimagined position as a global player.

Todor Zhivkov, a secretary of the Central Committee of the BKP since 1954, firmly enshrined his power with the 1971 constitution. According to a British assessment, Zhivkov was "energetic and practical rather than intellectual. He has a quick mind, a bluff manner, a sociable temperament, an earthy sense of humour and a habit of laughing uproariously at his own jokes. But he . . . may deliberately play the jolly peasant role of popular consumption."[95] This psychological portrait of Zhivkov is important because many of the internal dynamics in the country were attributed to his personal style of governance. In 1977, after the removal of yet another political adversary, Boris Velchev, a longtime secretary of the Central Committee of the BKP, Zhivkov initiated a series of new appointments in the Politburo (including his daughter's promotion in 1979). In Alexander Vezenkov's analysis, after the 1977 restructuring of power, the Politburo was firmly under Zhivkov's control and consisted of a group of "veterans without any functions," "long-term collaborators of Zhivkov's," and younger technocrats who owed their rapid promotions to him.[96] With this new wave of appointments, the third generation of communist elites—following the first that came to power in 1944 and the second installed by Zhivkov after his takeover in 1954—was emerging as a powerful force; some, such as Zhivkova, were related to the old guard, but others rose from the ranks or despite their family's bourgeois origins. Many involved in the new cultural activities were part of this third generation.

The most visible member of the third generation was Liudmila Zhivkova, whose meteoric career caused much fascination, both domestically and internationally. She became highly visible in 1971 (at age twenty-nine) when she became acting first lady following her mother's death, a status augmented by her appointments as the chairperson of the KK in 1975 and a member of Politburo in 1979, positions she held until her death in July 1981 (at age thirty-nine). There is some discussion in the Bulgarian literature about whether she executed policies of "enlightened absolutism" that benefited the public or used her family background to advance personal agendas in the worst manifestation of the dynasticism and nepotism of communist elites. Her depictions in Bulgaria at the time remained dogmatic and, after her death in 1981, hagiographic.[97] But details of her biography did not follow the conventional expectations of communist elites: in one example, she did her PhD in Oxford, not in Moscow. Further, her idiosyncrasies—her practice of yoga, meditation, and theosophy; her unconventional clothing and diet; and her rumored close relation with a famous Bulgarian clairvoyant, Baba Vanga—have produced prolific scholarly and popular writing.[98]

FIGURE 13. Todor Zhivkov during an exhibition in the company of Svetlin Rusev, chairman of the Union of Bulgarian Artists. Undated. Zhivkov liked to be seen as a cultural benefactor. Source: P. Kolev, published with permission.

Even though it was taboo to talk about these peculiarities of Zhivkova's in Bulgaria in the 1970s, they were under discussion in the West. A British study of 1980 described her thus:

> [She is] well-travelled. . . . [and] small of stature, neat and expensively dressed. She is intellectual, committed, and ambitious; and holds strong (although not necessarily coherent) views of art, culture, and ideology. She is prone to regale visitors with long lectures on topics like "the public-state system of cultural management" or "aesthetic education." . . . In private she is apt to speculate on quasi-religious subjects. . . . She is interested in yoga and transcendentalism. Her latest enthusiasm is for humanism. . . . She is a formidable person in her own right and her future career is not necessarily dependent on her father's remaining in power.[99]

It is worth engaging Western coverage of Zhivkova because the foreign press was fascinated by her appearances and associated the organization of Bulgarian events abroad with her. Much of her appeal was in the perception of freshness she was supposedly bringing to Bulgarian power circles. "Having a dictator for a father was a good start to a political career," claimed the press, but observers also admired the fact that Zhivkova was "intelligent" and had an "independent mind." She was a "good Marxist-Leninist," insisted that intellectuals in Bulgaria were "monolithically united around the Party," and knew how to counter criticism of her father's regime. In 1976, when the newly minted "culture boss" was asked if she would consider becoming the head of state one day, she jokingly answered, "why not, we have no sexual discrimination."[100] Other "power kids" in the communist world also spent time in the West, and the nomenklatura everywhere had access to special stores, cars, homes, and travel, creating "red dynasties" that functioned as "family affairs." Bulgaria, too, enjoyed "a high degree of family management" because Zhivkova's goal was "to place her country's culture at the service of the regime headed by her father."[101] But when comparisons were made between Bulgaria and Romania, for example, Zhivkova earned high marks from Western observers; if Elena Ceausescu (the wife of the Romanian leader Nicolae Ceausescu who held various senior party and state positions) destroyed people, Liudmila Zhivkova promoted them.

In the end, even RFE—despite its universally negative attitude to communist elites—described her as a "politician, scholar, and widely travelled diplomat" who had gathered an "inner circle of talented young officials."[102] By 1980, "the energetic daughter of the durable [Bulgarian] president" who "combine[d] oriental mysticism, European philosophy and Marxist doctrine" had become "the most influential woman" in the communist bloc. The Western media celebrated her for promoting technocrats while observers eagerly watched her pet project, 1300 Years Bulgaria, which was "unlikely to please the Soviet Union which is traditionally suspicious of nationalist feelings that could loosen ties to Moscow."[103] In the end, she was seen as a positive phenomenon among the Eastern European power elites because she was assumed to be introducing fresh ideas that undermined the domination of ideology in the cultural sector.

There were a number of other "fresh faces" from the third generation who shaped the Bulgarian policies of the 1970s. In one British assessment, the new Bulgarian power elites shared certain common features: "They have been advanced rapidly and deliberately, and one day soon they may really rule the country. They will be more open to ideas. They would die in the last ditch in defense of what they conceive to be 'real socialism' but their concept of it will be very different from that of their predecessors."[104] First among them were three recently appointed members of the Politburo, who represented the ideological, foreign policy, and economic sectors.[105] Alexander Lilov, initially the head of the Arts and Culture Department of the Central Committee of the BKP, was made responsible for ideology in 1974, demonstrating the important role of both culture and ideology (and their close link) in the Bulgarian state apparatus. Because of the speed of his promotion and his young age, the British saw him as "effectively No. 2" after Zhivkov. Petar Mladenov, a minister of Foreign Affairs since 1971 and Politburo member since 1977, had been educated in Moscow after his father, a member of the resistance, was killed during World War II. "Confident and effective" and "generally serious, but with a fairly relaxed manner," he was well-received abroad because of his erudition and foreign-language skills. As obvious from his long-standing position as a foreign minister, he "enjoy[ed] good personal relations with Todor Zhivkov," who trusted him to represent his agenda abroad. Finally, Ognian Doïnov, one of the youngest Politburo members since 1977, became an increasingly influential voice in economic policy. Knowledgeable in the areas of industry, transportation, and science, including the sphere of electronics, he initiated a number of ambitious international projects of economic and technical cooperation.

As far as the cultural sphere was concerned, there was a precarious balance between the old guard and the "new blood" that Zhivkov constantly had to manage. While his daughter promoted her protégés, he tried to appease the secret services who viewed the newcomers with suspicion. In 1977, the philosopher Liubomir Pavlov—seen as an ally of Zhivkova's—became the head of the Department for Arts and Culture of the Central Committee of the BKP, which set the main cultural priorities and vetted proposals from cultural and creative institutions. But some old cadres remained influential, including Academician Pantaleĭ Zarev, a literary scholar, deputy chairman of the Bulgarian Academy of Sciences (BAN), and member of the State Council, who was seen as a "highly orthodox spokesman for the regime on literary matters, a hard-liner, sharply critical of western literature and its influences." In contrast, the poet and playwright Georgi Dzhagarov, recently elevated from the cultural circles by Zhivkov, was viewed as "outwardly anxious to promote better relations with the West" (despite his "contempt for foreign pop music"). A former president and secretary of the Union of Bulgarian Writers, Dzhagarov had served as the vice president of the State Council, effectively right under Zhivkov, since 1971. Dzhagarov, Zarev, and another writer, Emilian Stanev (who shied away from politics but published prolifically), were core members of Zhivkov's hunting crew, as was the sociology professor Stoian Mihailov, who joined the Central Committee of the BKP in the early 1970s and became the head of its Agitation and Propaganda Department in 1973.[106]

In the meantime, a number of Zhivkova's protégés—who formed "Liudmila's circle"—assumed important positions. Three of these stand out in particular. Alexander Fol was the son of an interwar intellectual, and his bourgeois origins had caused problems during his university studies. A specialist in ancient archaeology—"more an academic than ideologue or politician"—he was behind the establishment of the Institute for Thracology affiliated with BAN in 1972 and initiated many international cultural initiatives showcasing Bulgarian culture. He began his career in the state apparatus as Zhivkova's deputy in the KK in 1975, and in 1979 he was appointed as the minister of education. British diplomats described him as "a friendly, rather burly man, with an informal manner," who "makes good impressions on Western academics" and "continues to hanker after the academic life." Liubomir Levchev, "a poet of some distinction," also became a deputy chairman of the KK in 1975, which underlines how these functionaries relied on Zhivkova for promotion. "A leading figure in the younger generation of Bulgarian poets," he had become a member of the Central Committee of the BKP in 1972 and chairman of the Union of Bulgarian Writers in 1979 and continued to shape the larger agenda of cultural policy through his close relationship with Zhivkov's family, both father and daughter. Similarly, the artist Svetlin Rusev, a "close associate" of Zhivkova's and a "people's artist," became the chairman of the Union of Bulgarian Artists in 1973 and a member of the Central Committee of the BKP in 1976. In the assessment of the British he was "of saturnine appearance, . . . [and] a prolific artist whose painting does not offend the canons of socialist realism." His paintings and frescoes, executed in a uniquely recognizable style, were featured generously at home and abroad throughout the 1970s and 1980s. As a sign of their growing influence, in the late 1970s Levchev and Rusev joined the hunting crew, which now became a desirable destination for cultural figures.[107] Mihail Gruev describes "Liudmila's circle" as "guild elites"—educated in the West and possessing a different value system, they were frustrated by the static thinking of the second generation in charge, so they used their influence in the cultural bureaucracy and their international contacts as a channel for upward mobility and professional realization.[108]

The term power elites seems suitable to describe those shaping policies in the 1970s due to their closeness to or cooperation with Zhivkov's family. It is true that the new policies sometimes also benefited the lower echelons of society. Similarly to elsewhere in Eastern Europe, professionals and experts in Bulgaria played an important role in redefining the relationship between state and society during real socialism and successfully carved out a degree of autonomy; for example, Kristen Ghodsee has shown the active agenda of the official women's organization in guiding social policy during the exact same time.[109] Yet, the power dynamic described here remained top-down, capturing the less optimistic side of détente, eloquently described by Jeremi Suri, who insists that détente represented the conservative choice of political elites, in both East and West, who wished to impose a stable status quo through selective appearances of change in the aftermath of 1968.[110] In the 1970s, the "new blood" among Bulgarian officials, including those from the cultural sphere, successfully entered political circles and consolidated their own power. They did not push for far-reaching reforms of the existing system, but helped perpetuate it.

Where Are the Dissidents?

The dynamics of official Bulgarian culture and its changing and high-profile entanglement with the power structures of the 1970s is connected to another contentious question, namely why, during the classic period of dissidence elsewhere in Eastern Europe, dissidents were scarce in the Bulgarian intellectual landscape. Episodic manifestations of nonconformity—for example, the refusal of five Bulgarian writers to sign a 1970 telegram to the Nobel Committee protesting Alexander Solzhenitsyn's prize (engineered by Dzhagarov)—were often overblown by Western media, which fixated on highlighting protest in Eastern Europe.[111] When Bulgarian officials and cultural producers planned their international events, the question of dissidence was constantly on their mind because they expected that they would need to confront the issue of dissent (or lack thereof) in Bulgaria. The Bulgarian situation highlights the slippage between nonconformity, opposition, and dissent when thinking about the engagement between intellectuals and the late socialist regimes. While there may not have been a dissident movement that explicitly and systematically defied the regime, pushing back against the establishment through nonconformity (avoidance or refusal to comply) and opposition (criticism of and going against the official position) was certainly present.

In the mid-1970s, the cultural scene in Bulgaria seemed to have fallen in with the official line. In Kalinova's opinion, many intellectuals, despite the lack of official institutions of state-enforced censure, practiced a form of self-censure in order to be able to produce and be acknowledged publicly. Yet, various behaviors were certainly manifest; as the state generously invested in culture, intellectuals had a range of ways to respond to institutional demands. While Levchev embraced conformity and joined the Central Committee of the BKP, a fellow poet, Konstantin Pavlov, chose dissent and faced intellectual exclusion and physical deprivation that earned him the nickname "the Uncompromising" (*neprimirimiiat*). The writer Georgi Markov was initially tempted by the rewards made available to him, only to become one of the staunchest critics of the Zhivkov regime after defection to the West: as an RFE and BBC correspondent, his blistering critiques of the Bulgarian power structure and society in the 1970s turned him into the main target of State Security.[112] Markov was an exception, and he also worked from overseas; few intellectuals openly defied the regime from within. Interestingly, cultural producers now regularly traveled abroad, including to the West, but very few chose to emigrate (defectors included the sculptor Liubomir Dalchev and the writer Atanas Slavov).

This is not to say that all intellectuals were reluctant to criticize the regime: as Natalia Hristova has shown, criticism of select policies and the public "poking" of those in power had existed since 1956.[113] In 1975, a work by Blaga Dimitrova and Iordan Vassilev, a biography of the famous poetess Elisaveta Bagriana, criticized the political complicity of intellectuals and described some positive aspects of interwar society, choices unpalatable for cultural arbiters. But while Vassilev was fired from his position as the editor of a premier literary magazine and transferred to a less public academic position, Dimitrova remained an active public figure and continued publishing, showing that the regime carefully chose how to retaliate.[114] Others, such as the poet Radoĭ Ralin and writer and screenwriter Hristo Ganev, often expressed "heretical" views on "ethical" issues and had earned the reputation of being "thorns" in the side of the state since the 1950s.[115] In fact, by the 1970s, the Bulgarian state apparatuses had accepted the fact that "total control was impossible."[116] In 1978, the British ambassador observed that public criticism in Bulgaria was now flourishing as grassroots grievances were encouraged and some (lower) officials were fired; for him, this was far from real liberalization, but part of a strategy so that the Party would maintain control.[117] The spirit of public criticism was evident in official cultural production, as well. In 1977, the newspaper of the Komsomol (Communist Youth), *Narodna mladezh* (People's Youth), published a dialogue between Ralin and cartoonist Boris Dimovski that criticized aspects of the political regime.[118] These episodes demonstrate that nonconformity was selectively tolerated. Yet, one shift was clear in the late 1970s: with the rise of more visible dissent elsewhere in Eastern Europe, Western media now tended to imbue oppositional and nonconformist episodes with a new, clear-cut dissident meaning across the entire region.[119]

In February 1977, the Viennese newspaper *Die Presse*, based on information provided by a putative Bulgarian Committee for the Defense of Human Rights, reported that four Bulgarian writers had been arrested for their refusal to condemn the Czechoslovak oppositional advocacy group Charter 77. Kamen Kalchev, Hristo Ganev, Gocho Gochev, and Valeri Petrov all denied that they had been arrested (yet did not deny they had been questioned), and Kalchev declared to the Bulgarian Telegraph Agency (BTA), "if I were ever repressed, that was by the fascist authorities thirty-two years ago."[120] Likely under pressure, the four published a denial in the French newspaper *Le Monde* in early March, while other writers appeared on the radio, denying that intellectuals were unable to express critical opinions in Bulgaria.[121] Later in 1977, Blaga Dimitrova gave an interview to the French magazine *Nouvelles Litteraires* and discussed the challenges of maintaining one's creative and civic position in socialist society. The French journalist rather naively speculated about the existence of a dissident organization in Bulgaria, demonstrating the careless Western attitude that caused complications for Eastern European intellectuals who were working in precarious environments.[122] Finally, in March 1978, a document titled "Declaration 78" was slipped under the door of Western embassies in Sofia (Dutch, German, and British). The longer Bulgarian text was accompanied by a shorter, and rather sloppy, English translation, which included a call for the end of human rights violations in Bulgaria and demands for freedom of expression, religion, travel, and independent trade unions. Despite the discrepancy between the two texts and their unclear authorship, the Western press was buzzing with news about a "Bulgarian Charter 77."[123] For both the Western press and Western diplomats, the search for Bulgarian dissidents was on.

This shift in the West also had domestic repercussions. In 1977, the Sixth Division of the Committee for State Security started to obsess about dissidents and "potential dissidents" in Bulgaria and began compiling files of intellectuals to watch.[124] Still, the conclusion of the operatives was that "currently, there is no imminent danger of the creation of a dissident movement and there is no clear public figure that could lead it," demonstrating that the vigilant secret police, whose raison d'être was the existence of enemies to the regime, did not find the situation alarming.[125] At the same time, official propaganda campaigns to undermine any Western claims of Bulgarian dissidents began, especially after a number of high-profile defections, including the trusted correspondent of Bulgarian television in Paris, Vladimir Kostov, who received asylum in France in summer 1977 and joined RFE shortly thereafter. In its foreign broadcasts, Radio Sofia called reports of dissidence "Western slander" and charged that dissidents were "political renegades" and "people sick with their unfulfilled ambitions" who sought "profitable jobs" in the West. Further, such broadcasts reassured listeners that in socialist societies "constructive criticism is not punished, but encouraged."[126] Zhivkov proactively tackled the issue. In December 1977, he appeared at the annual Conference of Young Writers to describe dissidence as "the fastest way . . . to be forgotten." He branded dissent as a "phenomenon of conjuncture" (koniunktura) created artificially from abroad and insisted that "dissent does not exist in Bulgaria" because that required opposition to the political system, something that did not occur. In Bulgaria, there were no dissidents, which were a fantasy of the West, but only nonconformists, or as Zhivkov called them, "otherwise thinking individuals" (inakomisleshti).[127] In the late 1970s, the official position was that the West was "inventing dissidents in Bulgaria" to create a sensation because in its observation of human rights and its social policies, "Bulgaria had outstripped the West."[128]

The biggest blow to the image of the Zhivkov regime, however, did not come from within. Throughout the 1970s, Georgi Markov, as a correspondent of the BBC in London and a collaborator of RFE in Munich, published and broadcast profusely against the regime and Zhivkov personally.[129] Bulgarian diplomats protested Markov's employment, as well as that of fellow journalists Vladimir Kostov and Petar Semerdzhiev, calling them "defectors and traitors of the motherland" and foreign commentators who disseminated "lies" and "false commentaries" against Bulgaria.[130] State Security branded Markov as "the main loudspeaker of anticommunist and anti-Bulgarian propaganda and active perpetrator of ideological sabotage against our country."[131] Markov fell ill in London on 7 September 1978 and passed away on 11 September; a poisoned pellet had been injected into his leg with an umbrella (the notorious "Bulgarian umbrella"), creating speculations about KGB (the Soviet Committee for State Security) involvement but pointing to the unquestionable targeting of the author for political reasons.[132] The Western press exploded with the news. From the Bulgarian perspective, "lies and gossip against our country" proliferated, at exactly the same time that Bulgarian diplomats were promoting a new image of their country through culture.[133] In the words of British diplomats, "For once, the Bulgarians have reached front-page attention in the British press—and they don't like it."[134] As Bulgarian reports from London put it, the "anti-Bulgarian campaign" in Great Britain became "dissolute and malicious" in insisting that the Bulgarian government had ordered the murder. British journalists "exposed the corruption in Bulgarian leadership" and presented Bulgaria as "a country that does not observe the most basic democratic rights and freedoms of individuals."[135]

Hostile publications in the Western press snowballed. Bulgarian diplomats in France now frantically reported "anticommunist propaganda" that presented selective information and glorified Soviet and Eastern European dissidents. Prominent French leftists condemned the human rights abuses in the Soviet bloc and the Soviet Union, which they said were "full of concentration camps and psychiatric wards."[136] Once a friendly destination, France had become uncertain terrain, as had Austria. There, attacks on the Zhivkov clan became personal. In an article titled "Zhivkov on the Eve of His Fall," the Viennese magazine *Internationale Politik* criticized the lavish lifestyles of his daughter ("the princess") and his son-in-law ("the playboy") and contrasted their shopping sprees, fashion statements, and expensive restaurant choices to the modest lifestyles of ordinary Bulgarians.[137] In another article, the same outlet criticized the building of NDK to celebrate the 1300th anniversary events (and the Twelfth Congress of the BKP), labeling the structure "Liudmila's palace."[138] Although it had started with human rights and dissidents, the Western press was now dredging up the depravity of the Bulgarian power elites and the responsibility of the Zhivkov clan for the direction of the country.

Zhivkov remained confident in his ability to preserve his power and disarm domestic and international challenges. When a new British ambassador presented his credentials in September 1980, Zhivkov, "relaxed, jovial, [and] confident," joked that ambassadors liked to see the countries in which they served in the news. He then assured the diplomat that Bulgarians were "easy-going people" and "hard workers," and there were no dissidents, "not because everything [in Bulgaria] is perfect," but because the Bulgarians did not want to "shame" their country and "embarrass" their families.[139] Up until the mid-1980s, while the Western press and Bulgarian émigrés would keep looking for dissidents in Bulgaria, the regime remained secure in its control of the cultural sphere. Famously, in 1985 the literary journal *Puls* (Pulse) published an acrostic poem, "Down with Todor Zhivkov," but Zhivkov confidently dismissed the incident as a "trifle." The intellectuals, the most likely source of dissent, had been mostly tamed.[140] There were some "otherwise thinking individuals," but no dissidents threatening the core of the regime (at least not until the late 1980s).

What is the explanation for this lack of a more organized dissident movement? In the interpretation of a number of scholars, it was the velvet prison of material benefits and the calm personal attitude of Zhivkov that persuaded many Bulgarian intellectuals not to pursue the path of dissidence.[141] Further, if, as Hristova claims, dissidence required Western sanction to acquire legitimacy, then the West's failure to embrace any Bulgarian intellectual except Markov also played a role.[142] While "a small part of the cultural intelligentsia showed a clear tendency toward disagreement with the regime," ultimately it was "Zhivkov's style" (*zhivkovata atmosfera*) of personally engaging with the "otherwise thinking individuals"—as eloquently described by Markov himself—that undercut the effects of "potential Solzhenitsyns" in Bulgaria.[143] In her work, Gigova similarly describes "the transformation of [Bulgarian] writers into an obedient, materialistic, and nepotistic administrative body." With active state investment in culture, the slippage between cultural producers and cultural bureaucrats erased the possibility of dissent.[144] This situation is not without parallel elsewhere. Czechoslovak playwright Milan Uhde explained that it was the "mechanisms of ostracization" after 1968 that had led him down the path of dissent: "If they had only treated me a little bit better, they would have had me," he confessed.[145] Zhivkov apparently knew better than Gustáv Husák, and instead of firing and imprisoning intellectuals, he invited those who grumbled to lunch, listened to their grievances, promised cooperation, and then evaded or watered down his promises, while reassuring the public of the success of developed socialism.

The Normalization and Nationalization of Late Socialism

The features of late socialism that emerge out of this analysis of the long 1970s in Bulgaria are full of contradictions. The consolidation of Zhivkov's political regime was not the result of political repression; instead, he promoted new faces and reform programs, leaving the illusion of change while solidifying his position. Further, relative economic stability, rising living standards, and the social accommodation of the population undermined the allure of protest and facilitated the silent acceptance of Zhivkov's "benevolent dictatorship." As Zhivkov played off adversaries against each other, promoted loyalists, and disarmed dissidents, society grumbled, but did not revolt. The question remains, were the 1970s the period of the great boredom of monotonous state-produced propaganda or a golden time of state socialism before the collapse of its legitimacy in the mid-1980s? One might answer that it was both.

The cultural policies analyzed here allow engagement with this question as they involved elites, regular citizens, and international representatives in multilayered discussions about the values, traditions, historical lessons, and future directions of the country. The 1300-year jubilee, as the focus of these policies, played a critical role in the promotion and cementation of (cultural) nationalism as a strategy adopted by the Bulgarian regime for its legitimization during the period of developed socialism. Given the apathy of the population vis-à-vis worn-out ideological clichés, it was ultimately the national rhetoric that awakened the collective sentiment of Bulgarians and created an emotional bond that brought together the people and the state around shared national ideas and values. Katherine Verdery has demonstrated the similar functioning of national ideology for the legitimization of the Ceausescu regime in Romania.[146] In Bulgaria, too, cultural events often promoted national narratives, which appeared as sophisticated and universal, yet their patriotic charge clearly sought to mobilize and unify the population. This observation demonstrates the role of official culture in the perpetuation of the authoritarian regimes in Eastern Europe; while some citizens of developed socialism brushed off these activities as propaganda, for many others such national campaigns had value and impact.

Anniversary celebrations played an important role in inserting nationalism into socialist public debates elsewhere in Eastern Europe, as well. In 1966, the Polish regime organized a celebration of the Polish millennium, which similarly charted a continuum of the Polish nation throughout the centuries, from the Christianization of the Polish people in 966 to the socialist revolution in 1946, and similarly served the purpose of legitimization.[147] In Romania, too, the Ceausescu regime orchestrated the 1980 celebration of the 2050th anniversary of "the unified Dacian state of Burebista" as a precursor of contemporary Romania and charged intellectuals with rewriting national history to serve this goal.[148] In her comparative analysis of Bulgaria's 1300-year jubilee and East Germany's celebration of 750 Years Berlin, Elitza

Stanoeva analyzes those two celebratory occasions as the "search for positive instruments for mass mobilization." As far as the GDR is concerned, this trend involved the invention of an East German socialist nation, but the desire to engage the masses was paramount.[149] As shown by Emil Dimitrov, in Bulgaria the use of "national mythologies" in times of crisis had the function of creating a "positive national ideal in the sphere of culture, not politics or war."[150] In the precarious 1970s, cultural policies ultimately provided a positive national ideal that could unite a dispirited society around shared values.

The focus on "the national" (*natsionalnoto*) and its elevation to "fate" (*sâdba*) was at the core of the conceptualization of Bulgaria's 1300th anniversary, which embraced the euphoria of national triumph. The 1300th anniversary eulogized the spiritual strength of the Bulgarian nation and put national pride at the center of what Ivan Elenkov describes as an officially promoted "national cult."[151] At the same time, the global dimensions of the jubilee reinforced the Bulgarian longing for reassurance that, indeed, "we have also given something to the world," as Ivan Vazov, modern Bulgaria's most prominent literary figure, put it in verse. In the end, the promotion of (cultural) nationalism, both at home and abroad, provided a safety valve for the regime. In its most sinister version, this nationalism was also responsible for the suppression of the Turks in Bulgaria during the "rebirth" campaigns that began in 1984 with name changes and the prohibition of Turkish-language use and Muslim practice and culminated in the forced expulsions carried out in 1989. But for the period of the 1970s, patriotism was a strategy for positive reinforcement of a normalized developed socialist society that would otherwise be dominated by apathy and disappointment, and possibly tempted by dissent.

Chapter 2

Goodwill between Neighbors

In 1975, negotiations were underway between experts from Bulgaria and Yugoslavia regarding an exhibition, *Prehistoric Art in the Bulgarian Lands*, soon to open at the Belgrade History Museum. The museum director expressed concern about the title because "there is a difference between the Bulgarian and Serbo-Croatian meaning of [the word] 'lands'" and required clarification about "which lands you refer to—the present or the past." He worried—not without reason—that in Bulgarian scholarship, the term was used to refer to all the historical kingdoms that extended beyond the current Bulgarian borders. The Bulgarian representative, trying to defuse tensions, "answered jokingly that most probably there would be no artifacts from Macedonia," pinpointing the exact reason for the misgivings of his Yugoslav colleague.[1] In a compromise, the exhibition premiered in Belgrade under a new title, *Prehistoric Art in Bulgaria*.[2]

The contested place of Macedonia in the historical repertoires of Bulgaria and Yugoslavia caused much controversy once Bulgaria launched its international cultural offensive because it triggered rival interpretations of the past in the two countries. In October 1977, the Croatian journal *Oko* published a dispatch from New York City reporting on Bulgaria's *Thracian Treasures* exhibition that had just opened at the Metropolitan Museum of Art. The article lambasted the exhibition catalog, which featured a map that incorrectly showed the Balkan borders. "Based on this map, the unaware visitor may conclude that Macedonia is a separate country [and not a part of Yugoslavia]," sarcastically stated *Oko*, and concluded, "This must have been the intention." The report further fumed: "Do [the Bulgarians] think they can change the borders of Yugoslavia according to their wishes? Are they not aware that Yugoslavia is a country whose citizens are free to travel, including to New York, which was the case with our indignant readers who brought the catalog to us?"[3] In addition to Bulgarian and Yugoslav officials zealously reporting on each other's cultural events, Yugoslav travelers had to police Bulgaria's cultural activities, as well. In November 1979, Bulgarian diplomats in London wrote long dispatches about the Days of Macedonian Culture that the Yugoslav embassy had organized. They even launched a complaint with the Foreign Office, insisting that featured books and talks "misrepresented Bulgarian history." When the British hosts unequivocally responded that they would not "censor a cultural event," to counteract "the anti-Bulgarian focus" of the Macedonian Days, Bulgarian diplomats proceeded to organize their own Days of Bulgarian Culture in 1981.[4]

This chapter traces Bulgarian cultural efforts among its Balkan neighbors during the long 1970s to examine the intersection between political, national, and cultural factors in the conceptualization and execution of these policies. A profound tension existed between the projects of internationalism, socialism, and nationalism that shaped these programs. As officials launched their programs associated with the 1300th anniversary of the establishment of the Bulgarian state in 681, they encountered the rival historical interpretations of their neighbors. While the embrace of cultural nationalism had positive legitimacy-boosting effects at home, it complicated international endeavors, especially in the Balkans. Whether concerning ancient ancestry, medieval glory, the Ottoman legacy, or more recent historical dynamics, the ambitious Bulgarian projection of its allegedly unique role at the crossroads of civilizations caused annoyance and even alarm among its neighbors. In addition to defusing national tensions, Bulgarian officials also had to carefully consider the distinction between socialist and capitalist countries, which constrained their cultural repertoires further. In the end, Bulgarian officials organized 542 cultural events in the Balkans between 1977 and 1982, many of them dedicated to the 1300-year jubilee; this is a striking number given the small size of the countries and their various priorities. This investment in international cultural programs served clear reputational purposes, highlighting Bulgaria's use of cultural diplomacy to project a new image domestically, regionally, and globally. In the Balkans, Bulgaria's goal was to cultivate regional cooperation and enhance its own national goals, while also dispelling Soviet mistrust in these new overtures. That proved to be a difficult balance to strike. Yet, in some cases, cultural contacts facilitated fruitful regional dialogues, demonstrating how soft power projects could lead to tangible hard power outcomes.

Bulgarian and Yugoslav officials rarely reconciled their Macedonian agendas, and that continued to be the focus of Bulgaria's campaigns in the region. Yet, in other cases the Balkan neighbors were able to defuse their disagreements. In November 1981, the Turkish embassy in Sofia requested a meeting at the Committee for Culture (KK) to express observations about two films widely shown in Bulgaria during the 1300th-anniversary celebrations. In the opinion of the Turkish emissary, the films—*The Goat Horn* and *Notes on the Bulgarian Uprisings*—"do not create an appropriate atmosphere on the eve of the upcoming state visit of President Evren." He noted that the films—one depicting the rape of a Bulgarian woman in Turkish hands and the other showing massacres during the 1876 April Uprising—contained "imprecisions concerning the Muslim faith." Clearly, Bulgarian interpretations of the Ottoman period had touched a nerve. The Bulgarian official, however, insisted that *The Goat Horn*, made fifteen years prior, was an award-winning film with "humane and ethical content," while *Notes on the Bulgarian Uprisings* was based on the work of Zahari Stoianov, "an eyewitness account of our national liberation that has become a literary classic." Importantly, the latter film distinguished between "the Turkish irregulars and the Turkish army" while it also showed "some negative sides of the Bulgarian population, including participants in the uprising." Despite the polemical topic, this conversation, carried on in French, was conducted in a "friendly, calm tone."[5] Clearly, some historical disputes were better handled than others.

The Bulgarian cultural programs in the Balkans did not follow a straightforward ideological or national logic. Cultural engagements often defied the primacy of Cold War geopolitical divides and sometimes overcame the legacy of old national tensions. Perhaps surprisingly, the most successful cultural campaigns occurred in Greece, a NATO member that in the past had held a long list of national(ist) grievances against Bulgaria. Even the measured Turkish cooperation in cultural matters was striking, given the opposing geopolitical agendas of the two states and their long-standing conflicts on national issues (especially related to the Turks in Bulgaria). These breakthroughs with capitalist states make the huge obstacles Bulgaria faced in socialist Romania and especially Yugoslavia, two "brotherly" countries that actively and deliberately undermined Bulgaria's cultural agenda, even more remarkable. These mixed results highlight the volatile function of cultural diplomacy: while in some cases it could become the first step in charting new political visions, as it did in initiatives with Greece, in others it could prove counterproductive, as clear in the case of Yugoslavia. International cultural outreach could not please all Bulgarian partners, so officials had to carefully consider their national, regional, and global priorities.

What was the role of the 1300th anniversary in this complex situation? Similarly to all other case studies I discuss, culture became an opportunity for fleshing out or reiterating larger state priorities. In the Balkans, the goal was regional cooperation, and cultural exchange became the strategy for arriving one step closer to it. Bulgaria had established cultural relations with all Balkan states, based on cultural cooperation agreements signed on reciprocal grounds. Beginning in 1977, the country launched a clear cultural offensive connected to the 1300 Years Bulgaria celebrations. Embassies drafted detailed "jubilee plans" based on the specific country's context, diplomats organized "complex events," and national celebration committees strove to secure high-profile representatives for the "culmination" of the celebrations in fall 1981. These events sought to project a certain image of Bulgaria for regional and global consumption: based on their unique historical experience and current socialist reality, the Bulgarian people were proud to showcase their accomplishments, in the past and today, and fearlessly pursued an even better future for themselves, the socialist community, their Balkan neighbors, the European continent, and humanity in general. This message necessitated convoluted attempts to reconcile political, ideological, national, and cultural priorities, a tension that became a permanent feature of Bulgaria's cultural programs not only in the Balkans but also throughout the world.

To explain the interplay between politics, nationalism, and culture in the framing and execution of Bulgaria's cultural programs in the Balkans, I offer an overview of Balkan political developments during the long 1970s to highlight the ideological complexity and political fluidity of the region during the late Cold War. Next, I outline the nature of the national controversies between Bulgaria, Yugoslavia, Romania, Turkey, and Greece to demonstrate that tensions over lands and people endured in the post–World War II period, creating cleavages between geopolitical partners. Finally, I present a series of microanalyses detailing how the Bulgarian cultural offensive unfolded in four contexts in order to reconstruct the meticulous work involved in cultural cooperation. In the end, a balance between current political agendas, long-lasting historical controversies, and the global context of the 1970s determined the parameters of Balkan cultural outreach on the eve of Bulgaria's

1300-year jubilee, which led to some breakthroughs in Bulgaria's regional position, notably vis-à-vis Greece.

The Cold War in the Balkans

Bulgaria occupied a complicated position in the Cold War Balkans, as it bordered two NATO members, Greece and Turkey, to the south, and two idiosyncratic socialist states, Yugoslavia and Romania, to the west and north. The place of the Balkans in Cold War diplomacy has produced a lively literature. In the late 1940s, the Balkan peninsula emerged as a prime area of contestation between the superpowers in the looming Cold War. Yet, in the 1970s, with international attention focused on central and east-central Europe in the context of détente, it occupied a more peripheral place in European and world diplomacy.[6] Still, the Balkan states kept the superpowers on their toes because the variety of political systems and ideological positions complicated a neat delineation of spheres of influence among the two blocs.[7] In their totality, the Balkan states offered a striking case of political diversity and ideological unpredictability, which made drawing geopolitical lines difficult.[8] In this context, culture offered an additional strategy for Balkan politicians who sought to further regional cooperation and overcome their international isolation, an issue at the forefront of Balkan politics in the 1970s.

The large variety of political and ideological positions among the Balkan socialist states defied all Cold War assumptions about the existence of a unified socialist bloc. Bulgaria, Yugoslavia, and Romania each held a unique geopolitical position and developed their own brand of state socialism. Ever since its split with the Soviet Union in 1948, Yugoslavia had pursued a distinct path to socialism outside of the Soviet bloc's economic and military structures, the COMECON (the Council for Mutual Economic Assistance) and the Warsaw Pact. Yugoslav leader Josip Broz Tito developed a close relationship with the United States, which ultimately led the Soviet Union to soften its position so as not to further push Yugoslavia toward the West. To advance its international standing, the country actively maneuvered on the global scene and became a founding member of the Nonaligned Movement in 1961.[9] From the 1960s on, Romania also strove to assert its independence within the Soviet sphere of influence, which became a point of friction because its leader Nicolae Ceausescu maintained warm relations with China following its conflict with the Soviet Union in the early 1960s. In 1968, the Romanian leader opposed the Warsaw Pact invasion of Czechoslovakia following the Prague Spring (also sharply criticized by Yugoslavia). In 1969, U.S. president Nixon visited Romania, the first such visit to a Warsaw Pact country.

Romania continued its position of independence within the socialist bloc throughout the 1970s, defying Warsaw Pact decisions while never leaving the organization.[10] Even more independent was the course pursued by Albania, which also developed a close relationship with China in the 1960s. Unlike other Eastern European states that pursued contacts with the West, Albania remained isolationist. Its commitment to Stalinist policies put it at odds ideologically with the rest of the socialist states, so the country remained a separate phenomenon within world socialism.[11] Despite the vast distinctions between the Balkan socialist states, the rhetoric and practice of socialist internationalism could moderate their differences; this trend was evident in the fraught but continued Soviet relations with both Yugoslavia and Romania, which in turn influenced Bulgaria's choice of Balkan "friends."[12]

Bulgaria continued to be perceived internationally as the closest Soviet ally in the region. There was truth to this opinion: Todor Zhivkov regularly consulted with Soviet leader Leonid Brezhnev over matters of foreign policy. Yet, a closer examination of the historical record allows us to conclude that this relationship entailed much more than a blind subservience. Bulgaria carefully balanced the Soviet position, which opposed the development of a regional bloc in the Balkans that might facilitate Romanian and Yugoslav independence, with the assertion of its own interests, which entailed the gradual normalization of political relations with its neighbors and the resumption of active contacts in other spheres to overcome Bulgaria's regional isolation.[13] Zhivkov passionately explained to Brezhnev: "Regarding our policy in the Balkans, I would like to state that we coordinate all our steps with the Soviet Union . . . [but] we would like to be understood well. If we approach these questions with prejudice and we . . . do not to participate in any common Balkan initiatives, we shall become isolated from the other Balkan states. And this will not be in our common favor."[14] In the end, despite Soviet suspicion, Bulgaria pursued a lively Balkan policy, which demonstrates the ability of a small state to navigate complex geopolitical contexts to advance its own goals.

While socialist bloc solidary remained unattainable, the two NATO states, Greece and Turkey, also showed little cohesion along ideological lines. The independence of Cyprus in 1959 added fuel to disputes in the 1960s. Greece was under a military junta between 1967 and 1974, which fueled anti-Americanism because of the popular assumption that the United States supported the colonels. This situation determined Greece's more independent course within NATO, especially in the post-junta period. Periodically, Greek politicians threatened to remove American military bases while in 1974 the country withdrew from NATO's military command following the Turkish invasion of Cyprus. Trying to redefine their previously close relations to the United States, Greek politicians secured European Economic Community (EEC) membership in 1981.[15] All these developments helped to determine the active Greek involvement in Balkan politics. Turkey, while a NATO member, sporadically turned to the Soviet Union for economic and technical assistance in the 1960s. Its 1974 invasion of Cyprus put tremendous pressure on NATO because now American officials had to confront the vocal Greek demands for sanctions (thus the United States imposed a brief arms embargo on Turkey). Further, the country experienced a number of military coups— in 1960, 1971, and 1980—that destabilized it domestically and made it a wild card internationally.[16] In the southern Balkans a capitalist, democratic bloc was just an illusion.

This deviation from core political and economic alliances in the Balkans led to political fragmentation during the late Cold War that transcended the strict ideological parameters of both the Soviet and U.S. camps. In 1970, U.S. president Nixon visited Yugoslavia to offer support for its political independence, followed by a visit from Soviet leader Brezhnev a year later to encourage the country's socialist direction. For Turkey, "participation in NATO was in no way an obstacle for the development of certain relations . . . beyond the pact," and the country benefitted from economic and technical assistance by the Soviet Union in the 1960s and 1970s.[17] Romania, finally, sought to improve its relations with the United States, and under the American "differentiated approach" to Eastern Europe, reaped economic benefits when the status of most favored nation was bestowed on the country in 1974.

This political volatility of the Balkan states complicated the positions of the superpowers. The Soviet Union carefully courted Yugoslavia and tried to limit further Romanian deviation from the socialist line; Soviet leaders opposed multilateral relations in the Balkans because they suspected that Romania and Yugoslavia might try to develop an anti-Soviet bloc. At the same time, the Soviets wished to curb Western influence in the area. Thus, they encouraged Bulgaria to develop bilateral relations with its neighbors across ideological lines because they were interested in further distancing Greece and Turkey from NATO. This Soviet strategy explains why the United States carefully cultivated the southern flank of NATO, especially after Turkish-Greek acrimony deepened following the 1974 events in Cyprus. American diplomats, similar to the Soviets, also distrusted multilateralism because they worried about the development of anti-American feelings among their allies, which was a particular concern in post-junta Greece. Both superpowers were suspicious of the real motives of the Balkan states and the development of "secret diplomacy" that they would not be able to control.[18]

Despite the suspicions of the superpowers, the Balkan leaders pursued various projects of regional cooperation. Bilateral cooperation between the Balkan states had already begun to intensify in the 1960s. Between 1960 and 1964, Bulgaria and Greece resolved their most contentious issues and normalized their relations, culminating with the reopening of diplomatic posts in both countries. Even during the Greek junta between 1967 and 1974, Greece and Bulgaria remarkably maintained active relations. Bulgaria and Turkey similarly signed a series of agreements in 1964–1968 that opened up the channels of communication. Romania and Yugoslavia continued their closer cooperation, especially after the 1968 Warsaw Pact invasion of Czechoslovakia, which was opposed by both states. Romania in particular appeared as the staunchest supporter of Balkan cooperation.[19]

This trend became even more obvious after the signing of the Helsinki Final Act of 1975, which explicitly encouraged cooperation between countries from different socioeconomic and political systems.[20] From the mid-1970s on, there was systematic pursuit of multilateral initiatives, which the superpowers distrusted and opposed. In the summer of 1975, the first post-junta Greek prime minister, the conservative Konstantinos Karamanlis, visited Romania, Yugoslavia, and Bulgaria to urge the convening of a multilateral conference on Balkan cooperation, a step that has been described as the "Greek Ostpolitik." While Romania and Yugoslavia were supportive of the idea, Bulgaria was more careful due to Soviet pressure against the initiative, and tried to limit the mandate of the meeting to economic cooperation. In January and February 1976, the first multilateral meeting of Balkan leaders at the level of vice ministers for economic development occurred in Athens. Regular visits of Balkan heads of state followed: in the summer of 1976, Ceausescu, Zhivkov, and Tito all visited Athens and continued conversations on regional cooperation. British diplomats observed: "the tempo of relations in the Balkans [has] quickened. . . . [including the] exchange of high visits, . . . a whole host of visits and meetings at lower, more practical levels, . . . [and the issuance of] declarations, communiqués, and statements of policy." Taken together, these efforts had the effect of "reducing tension in the Balkans."[21] In the mid- to late 1970s, all of these states negotiated a series of bilateral agreements pertaining to economic cooperation, customs regulations, transportation, the common use of water resources, environmental issues, tourism and travel, and other matters.[22] In 1979, a second multilateral meeting in Ankara discussed the possibility of developing a Balkan framework for cooperation in the spheres of transportation and telecommunication. Other multilateral meetings followed in Sofia (1981), Bucharest (1982), and Belgrade (1984), culminating in a meeting of foreign ministers in Belgrade in 1988.[23]

In this context of expanding regional cooperation, Bulgaria pursued more robust relations with its neighbors through a "steadily proliferating number of bilateral and multilateral commissions, sub-commissions, unions, and associations." Bulgarian leaders now spoke about their country as a "good neighbor . . . working for peace, security, and cooperation."[24] Cultural exchange played an important role in these initiatives, as friendship societies and cultural associations helped frame and deliver the expression of goodwill between the Balkan states. In the 1970s, under existing cultural cooperation agreements with their neighbors, Bulgarian officials began to organize a growing number of exhibitions, book fairs, conferences, performances, art shows, and folk and classical music concerts, which fit with the general spirit of expanding cooperation between countries of different political systems after Helsinki. Increasingly in the late 1970s these events were dedicated to the celebration of the 1300-year jubilee, and there was a clear increase in the cultural activities of Bulgarian diplomats who now persistently requested the active involvement of their Balkan neighbors in these initiatives. Yet, as Bulgarian officials organized these events, their visions of history clashed with the national agendas of their neighbors, underlining the tensions between political and national considerations in Bulgaria's cultural message.

The Enduring Power of Nationalism

The complex national agendas of the Balkan neighbors, combined with the legacy of older irredentist confrontations, critically shaped the execution and reception of Bulgarian cultural events in the region.[25] Because the programs often embraced historical topics, the 1970s saw a series of heated exchanges among Balkan politicians, cultural experts, and scholars over the meaning of history from the perspective of their respective national interpretations; these debates spanned the entirety of the historical experience, from the ancient and medieval to the Ottoman and contemporary periods. Diplomats and other state officials on all sides often acted as national guardians defending their country's "true history." To understand the nuance of those debates, it is necessary to explain the function of nationalism under socialism and to outline the key national controversies at play.

In recent scholarship there is much debate about the relationship between nationalism and communism.[26] A number of theories explain the palpable revival of nationalism in Eastern Europe from the 1950s on. These include the need for political legitimization of the communist parties, the doctrinal similarities between communism and nationalism, the characteristics of the planned economy that required isolation from foreign influences, or pressures from below directed against national minorities. Historian Tchavdar Marinov offers yet another convincing explanation, particularly suited for the Bulgarian case: the state-building orientation of the communist regimes led to the rehabilitation and eventual embrace of nationalism as a form of "patriotism" that allegedly had nothing to do with "bourgeois chauvinism" but embraced the main postulates of interwar policies and ideologies.[27] Yannis Sygkelos illustrates the willingness of the BKP to adopt national rhetoric and symbolism and shows that even immediately after World War II, Fatherland Front politicians presented their political takeover not only as a socialist revolution but also as a "national liberation movement" that saved the country from a "national disaster." National rhetoric became a "central factor in legitimizing [the] regime."[28] By the 1960s, this reinvented Bulgarian "socialist" nationalism had "matured" in a way that led to a series of heated confrontations with its neighbors.

The resurgence of nationalism in Bulgaria manifested itself in two ways. First, domestically, since the late 1950s but especially during the 1960s, a campaign of "patriotic education" involved the open public discussion of national topics, the celebration of patriotic holidays (such as 24 May), and the adoption of irredentist historical analyses in academia and in the education of young Bulgarians.[29] The 1300th jubilee fit nicely within this trend, as it embraced the national narrative and channeled cultural nationalism among the entire population. Second, internationally, after years of restraint, the Macedonian controversy with Yugoslavia erupted again, initiating heated exchanges in the press of both countries. Bulgaria and Greece reconciled their disagreements in 1964 when Bulgaria rescinded all territorial and national claims on its southern neighbor, but Greek fears of Slavocommunism continued to color relations between the two countries. This period also saw shifts in Bulgarian and Turkish policies vis-à-vis the Turkish population in Bulgaria, a question that underpinned conversations between the two sides. At the same time, Bulgaria and Romania were obsessed with recovering "ancient ancestors" and competed over the role of indigenous ancient peoples in their history.[30] Bulgarian cultural events in the Balkans were viewed with suspicion because Bulgaria's neighbors believed that they often misrepresented history and functioned as tools of a cleverly disguised "Great Bulgarian chauvinism." Cultural nationalism was a double-edged sword: while effective at home, it caused complications abroad. For Bulgaria's neighbors the question was whether cultural nationalism might pave the way for more aggressive policies and demands in the future (which ultimately happened in the mid-1980s with the renewal of anti-Turkish and anti-Muslim campaigns in Bulgaria).

The most contentious issue in the 1970s remained the conflicting views on Macedonia in Bulgaria and Yugoslavia. The two countries disagreed about the presence of a Macedonian minority in Bulgaria while they also disputed each other's interpretations of key historical events.[31] This dispute was based on the complex pre–World War II history of irredentist contestation between Bulgaria, Greece, Serbia (later Yugoslavia), and Romania in this formerly Ottoman province; the Macedonian question of the late nineteenth century and the way it shaped military conflicts, political coalitions, and population politics among the Balkan neighbors remains one of the most contentious questions in the historiography of each state.[32] Immediately after World War II, in the context of discussions about a possible Balkan federation between Yugoslavia and Bulgaria, the BKP recognized the existence of a Macedonian minority in the region of Pirin Macedonia within Bulgaria and guaranteed the region's cultural autonomy. Following the Yugoslav-Soviet split of 1948, however, Bulgaria closed Yugoslav-sponsored institutions and expelled instructors sent by Skopje, causing a rift in Bulgarian-Yugoslav relations. In the early 1960s, the Soviet Union pressured Bulgaria to initiate rapprochement with Yugoslavia, a process that developed in fits and starts, as the two states pursued economic cooperation and reconciled some political disagreements. Yet, following the "patriotic" turn, Zhivkov's position hardened in national matters, leading to polemical national discussions throughout the 1960s and 1970s.

In 1963, at a special plenum of the Central Committee of the BKP, Zhivkov personally spelled out the main tenets of the Bulgarian position: Macedonia was "the crucible of Bulgarian history," the Macedonian revolutionaries of the late nineteenth century had a "Bulgarian consciousness," and the language spoken in Macedonia was a Bulgarian "dialect" based on western linguistic forms.[33] Zhivkov emphasized that Pirin Macedonia was a part of the Bulgarian nation, therefore no Macedonian minority lived there. This proclamation led to polemical press releases over the language, history, and identity of the population in Macedonia in the past and today in both Bulgaria and Yugoslavia (especially in the Socialist Republic of Macedonia, or SRM). In 1966, the Yugoslav government started advancing the opinion that a Macedonian minority in Bulgaria was being "subjected to assimilation, persecution, and internment."[34] As a response, in 1967, the Politburo of the BKP formulated four principles to support the argument for a centuries-long Bulgarian presence in Macedonia: (1) in the medieval and National Revival periods, Macedonia was a part of Bulgarian history, and there existed no Macedonian nation; (2) Macedonian national identity started forming with the establishment of SRM after World War II; (3) Pirin Macedonia in Bulgaria was a part of the Bulgarian nation and had no Macedonian population; and (4) those within Yugoslav Macedonia who considered themselves Bulgarians should be allowed to do so. At the same time, Yugoslav officials and especially representatives of SRM increasingly framed their own insistence on the presence of a Macedonian minority in Pirin Macedonia as a human rights issue, accusing Bulgaria of not allowing Macedonians to express their national consciousness. They demanded that Bulgaria include a Macedonian national category in its censuses and allow cultural autonomy in Pirin Macedonia. In the 1970s heated press exchanges that centered on historical interpretations occurred regularly. This polemic escalated in 1978 when Bulgaria celebrated the centennial of the establishment of the modern Bulgarian state with the Treaty of San Stefano, which had created a Great Bulgaria that also included the territories of Ottoman Macedonia (most of it now in Yugoslavia and Greece). On this occasion, Yugoslav accusations of "Great Bulgarian chauvinism" and territorial claims on Yugoslav Macedonia proliferated, despite Bulgarian assurances that it considered the question of borders in the Balkans resolved.[35]

Bulgaria and Greece had been involved in similarly contentious questions over territories and populations since the late nineteenth century when the national agendas of the two states clashed in the borderlands of Macedonia and Thrace. Bulgaria and Greece were in opposing camps during the Second Balkan War and the two world wars; a contested population exchange and minority controversies after the Great War determined the strained relations in the interwar period. The Bulgarian occupation of Greece during World War II caused particular acrimony, and the two countries broke off relations in 1941. After the war they were unable to settle their territorial and financial claims, so no formal diplomatic relations existed until 1954 when consultations began for their reconstruction.[36] After ten years of negotiations (the most contentious issue being the settlement of World War II reparations), a series of agreements between 1960 and 1964 led to the full resumption of diplomatic relations, marked by the opening of embassies in 1964 (consulates in Thessaloniki and Plovdiv opened in 1973). As a part of the process, Bulgaria rejected interwar and postwar revisionism and recognized the current borders between its neighbors as permanent.[37] While Greek fears of Slavo-communism and "invasion from the north" remained alive and suspicion permeated policy circles, in the 1970s, in contrast to Yugoslavia, Greek and Bulgarian politicians avoided historical issues and focused on current affairs.

The conflicting Bulgarian and Greek national claims, however, were evident in subtler ways, connected to larger historical narratives considered fundamental to the identity of each state. A contested issue remained the role of the ancient Thracians in Bulgarian ethnogenesis. As analyzed in vivid detail by Tchavdar Marinov, in the context of Greek classical studies the archaeology of Thrace occupied only a marginal role, while Greek scholars tended to subsume the historical developments in the area under the assertion of its thorough Hellenization following the arrival of Greek colonists and their intermingling with the indigenous (illiterate and thus uncultured) populations. By contrast, in Bulgaria in the late 1960s the Thracians were acknowledged as one of the three elements of the Bulgarian nation (the other two being the Proto-Bulgarians and Slavs) and elevated to the status of ancestors. With the "patriotic turn," Bulgarian academic circles now systematically promoted the science of Thracology, that is, the study of the indigenous non-Greek population of ancient Thrace. In 1972, Alexander Fol, a professor of ancient history who would become a close associate of Liudmila Zhivkova, became the director of the newly established Institute of Thracology affiliated with the Bulgarian Academy of Sciences. Soon thereafter, the promotion of Bulgaria's Thracian heritage became a central aspect of the international cultural outreach pursued by the regime (as evident in the *Thracian Treasures* exhibitions). As exhibitions and scientific events on the topic proliferated in the late 1970s and early 1980, Bulgarian and Greek (but also Romanian) scholars often found themselves at odds in debating the scientific evidence related to the Thracians.[38]

For Romania and Bulgaria, the historical importance and population composition of the region of Dobrudja, a borderland area that had put the two countries in opposite alliances throughout their post-Ottoman history, was a controversial topic. Following the Romanian incorporation of Dobrudja during the Second Balkan War in 1913 and the repeated Bulgarian accusations of minority rights violations in the interwar period, a 1941 agreement for the cession of southern Dobrudja to Bulgaria, accompanied with a population swap, offered the compromise solution of essentially splitting up the region between the two states. With the revival of nationalism in the 1960s, Bulgaria and Romania now sparred about historical truth in Dobrudja, which was also connected to the question of the role of Slavic populations in Romanian history.[39] Bulgarian and Romanian scholars also clashed about the presence of ancient indigenous populations—the Thracians and the Dacians (who were a branch of the Thracians)—as the "forefathers" of the Bulgarian or Romanian nations, respectively.[40]

These questions became particularly contested when Ceausescu transformed nationalism into a permanent feature of Romanian life in the 1970s. Scholars have shown the link between the revival of nationalism in Romania and its appeal to national self-reliance in the context of its more autonomous political position in the Soviet bloc in the 1960s and 1970s.[41] In 1973, Ceaus-escu promulgated a number of theses, which introduced a nativist agenda that rejected foreign influences. This development led to the articulation of the idea of protochronism, which claimed that Romanian literary and histor-ical developments anticipated foreign and especially Western ones. This view denied any foreign influences in Romanian history and resurrected interwar theories of the Dacian origins of the Romanian nation; the Romans, the for-eigners, were now demoted while the indigenous population, the Dacians, were promoted in Romanian ethnogenesis. According to Lucian Boia, with this "shift from the contemporary towards origins," in the end "ancient his-tory became even more politicized than contemporary history."[42] Through-out the 1970s, Romanian scholars were promoting theories associated with an "independent, centralized Dacian state of Burebista," which they interpreted as the precursor of contemporary Romania. Boia suggests that "Burebista offered Ceausescu the supreme legitimization" as a symbolic affirmation of the uninterrupted existence of the Romanian state since antiquity.[43] The independent state of Burebista anticipated the Great Romania of 1918, but also Ceausescu's current independent position in world politics. Yet, the state of Burebista included current Bulgarian territories, causing tension between the two neighbors. Distrust escalated in the late 1970s when Ceausescu's regime decided to celebrate the 2050th anniversary of the establishment of the state of Burebista in 1980, a year before Bulgaria's 1300th anniversary.[44] Anniversary wars now became an aspect of Bulgarian-Romanian relations.

Finally, relations between Bulgaria and Turkey were shaped by the policies the Bulgarian state followed in regard to the Turkish minority in Bulgarian territory. The period after World War II saw systematic attempts to assimi-late the Bulgarian-speaking Muslims, the Pomaks, including an assimilation campaign in 1973–1974 to change their names and other "patriotic" activities to distance the Pomak minority from the Turkish minority and incorporate them into the unitary socialist nation. Yet, it was mainly Bulgarian policies vis-à-vis its Turkish minority that caused tension with Turkey. After the emi-gration of some 155,000 Turks from Bulgaria between 1948 and 1951 under the provisions of an emigration convention, Bulgaria and Turkey pursued their own priorities. Turkey wanted the Bulgarian Turks to reunite with their "true motherland," but created logistical problems that hindered their inte-gration. Bulgaria needed agricultural labor and opposed mass emigration.[45]

Bulgarian policies toward its Turkish population fluctuated from restric-tions on cultural autonomy and language in the early 1960s (to facilitate build-ing the unitary socialist nation) to their relaxation in the late 1960s and the 1970s (when the focus shifted to the Pomaks). In this context, the emigration of the Turks was constantly on the agenda. Between 1968 and 1978, some 115,000 Turks emigrated from Bulgaria, based on a family reunification convention between Sofia and Ankara. By this point, Turkey did not want emigration, but prioritized the creation of Turkish national minority communities abroad, which required the active role of the Turkish motherland to help maintain their culture, language, religion, and traditions. Following the Cyprus invasion in 1974, Bulgarian officials were on alert: they worried about "troublesome demographic realities" among the Bulgarian Turks, discussed perceived dangers to the territorial integrity of their country, and proposed ideas of renaming the Turks on the Pomak model or encouraging their mass emigration. After another military coup in Turkey in 1980, relations between the two states came to a standstill as each side carefully watched developments across the border. Bulgarian-Turkish relations broke down in the mid-1980s, when Bulgarian officials began an uncompromising renaming campaign against 800,000 Bulgarian Turks in 1984, which was often accompanied by violence, and orchestrated the expulsion of 350,000 people in 1989.

The national agendas and overarching historical narratives of each Balkan state critically informed the parameters of their interactions. The shared past became a subject of claims and counterclaims as each side maintained the validity of its national agenda. The conflicting historical interpretations, often manifested in cultural events that engaged historical topics, regularly triggered intense debates about "historical truth" between representatives of the Balkan states. Foreign officers, cultural experts, and performers often acted as "professional patriots" with the mission of defending their country's "true history," straddling the fine line between defending national priorities and promoting nationalist visions. These national(ist) dynamics, combined with the Cold War political priorities of each country, determined the dimensions of the cultural relations between Bulgaria and each of its neighbors. A microanalysis of the exchanges in each country reveals the multilayered interplay between politics, nationalism, and culture in the execution of Bulgaria's cultural program in each state.

Romania: How to Fight Historical Revisionism

Relations between Bulgaria and Romania in the long 1970s were volatile: the leadership of the two states strove to highlight the shared goals of socialist internationalism, yet each side unapologetically acknowledged and maintained ideological and national differences. During this time, both Ceausescu and Zhivkov were at their peak, and both used national ideology to enhance their domestic and international legitimacy. Thus, rival anniversary celebrations—the 1300th jubilee in Bulgaria and the 2050th anniversary in Romania—and accusations of "historical revisionism" rendered relations between the two states even more colorful.

The two countries based their contacts on clearly defined positions: despite the recognition of differences in foreign policy and ideology, socialist internationalism dictated the continued dialogue between all socialist states. Zhivkov and Ceausescu met regularly after 1965; by 1980, they had exchanged more than twenty visits. But ever since 1968, Bulgarian leaders had been wary of "the peculiar line of the Romanian leadership," as evident in its refusal to coordinate action with the Warsaw Pact and its warm relations with China.[46] In fact, Zhivkov openly aired his frustration with Ceausescu to foreign dignitaries.[47] Despite these differences, the leadership of both states meticulously cultivated a public image embracing "the principles of Marxism-Leninism, international solidarity, equality, independence, national sovereignty, non-intervention in internal affairs, friendly cooperation, and the common good." The two countries signed a declaration in June 1980 to develop political, economic, scientific-technical, and cultural relations because "despite their differences. . . . the policies of Bulgaria and Romania remain policies of . . . cooperation in all spheres."[48] Yet, with the adoption of a national line in Romanian history that contradicted key Bulgarian historical assumptions, one more layer of suspicion was added between the two states, which influenced the development of cultural relations.[49]

Bilateral plans for cultural cooperation formed the basis of the two countries' cultural exchange along the lines of socialist internationalism, with a focus on the rather flexible notion of "friendship." In 1975, the two countries established Romanian-Bulgarian and Bulgarian-Romanian associations of friendship to oversee and coordinate cultural activities. According to the official vision for these associations, "The traditional friendship of our two neighboring peoples has deep roots in history—Bulgarians and Romanians have fought together for freedom, independence, and a just social system. . . . Especially after our liberation [from fascism], friendship between the two people developed further."[50] Based on the Plan for Cultural Cooperation for 1978–1980, for example, the two countries coordinated the celebrations of their centennials in 1978 (Bulgarian statehood and Romanian independence were both declared that year) and marked the thirty-fifth anniversaries of their respective socialist revolutions in 1979.[51] Despite the reassuring public rhetoric and the five-year plan for cultural and scientific cooperation signed in 1980, when the Bulgarians proposed a series of events associated with the 1300-year jubilee in the late 1970s, the Romanian response was negative: on national matters, friendship had its limits.

Following instructions from the highest levels of the Romanian Communist Party (Partidul Comunist Român, PCR), Romanian officials adopted a categorical position: they declined participation in Bulgarian commemorative activities and refused to form a 1300-year national celebration committee. This decision was connected to the parallel attempts of the Ceausescu regime to celebrate the 2050th anniversary of the establishment of the "independent and centralized Dacian state," which the Romanians considered to be the forerunner of their modern state.[52] Bulgarian diplomats meticulously reported that publications in the Romanian press offered historical interpretations that the Bulgarian side saw as wrong and provocative, such as the lack of Slavic presence in Romanian history or the national composition of Dobrudja.[53] In the Bulgarian opinion, Romania had emerged as a state in the fourteenth century, but the Ceausescu regime "charged Romanian scholars . . . with correcting this historical truth by proving the Getho-Dacian origins of the Romanians two thousand years ago." In the words of one ambassador, "It is obvious that the PCR wants to change Romanian history in line with Romanian nationalism. . . . The Romanian arguments do not have a scientific but only a propagandistic character."[54] The Bulgarian opinion held that Romanian historical interpretations were "dominated by a spirit of nationalism and attempts at historical revisionism."[55] When responding to Bulgarian requests to celebrate the 1300th anniversary, Romanian officials demanded the reciprocal celebration of their 2050th anniversary in Bulgaria. Bulgarian officials, however, felt that such an agreement would "give credence to the Romanian historical falsifications and Romanian nationalism, . . . and deliver a blow to historical truth."[56] The language of truth used here is striking. Despite obvious parallels between the two anniversaries, the Bulgarians saw the 2050-year jubilee as a "made-up anniversary" (izmislena godishnina).[57] They insisted that their own 1300-year jubilee, by contrast, "encapsulates the complexity of growth, resilience, and struggle for progress that Bulgaria has experienced during its 1300 years."[58] Anniversary wars and debates about "historical truth" thus framed cultural relations between the two countries in the 1970s, creating a series of uncomfortable encounters that are striking in their bluntness.

With the categorical Romanian position in mind, Bulgarian diplomats in Bucharest proposed alternative ways to celebrate the 1300th anniversary: based on the already ratified Plan for Cultural Cooperation, they would organize cultural activities on historical topics that would only indirectly address the jubilee. The embassy focused on "high-profile, effective activities that contribute to the brotherly relations between our two countries more generally," often described as "indirect propaganda."[59] Some of the "indirect" activities connected to the 1300-year jubilee included, first, the organization of an exhibition of Thracian art and culture (clearly designed to counter the Dacian theories) and visits of the Bulgarian National Theater and Opera to maintain active cultural connections. Second, the celebration of Bulgarian national holidays already ratified in the cultural plan provided an opportunity to showcase Bulgarian contributions to world civilization. Third, the publication of materials on historical topics in the Romanian press sought to clarify the Bulgarian position on key events.[60] The idea was to use every opportunity for public engagement to promote the 1300th anniversary message.

What is remarkable is the open hostility in these exchanges between supposed friends. There were verbal wars about truth between diplomats, academics, and cultural figures over the issue of competing anniversaries. Because of "big differences in historiography that our country cannot accept," historians engaged in highly dramatic encounters over scholarly interpretations.[61] History thus became an unambiguously political weapon. Take, for example, the Fifteenth International Historical Congress, held in Bucharest between 10 and 17 August 1980. In Bulgarian reports, the Romanian hosts took the presence of attendees from the United States, West Germany, France, Great Britain, Spain, Japan, South Korea, and Sweden as an opportunity to showcase the Romanian anniversary. Bulgarian delegates at the congress described an "overly nationalistic spirit and pompous celebration of the 2050-year pseudo-jubilee," which allegedly put off "Western scholars [who] either showed irony toward Romanian attempts to promote their non-scientific views on the origins of the Romanian state, or delicately stayed silent." Further, the Romanian organizers created logistical problems for the Bulgarian panel, which was scheduled at 7:00 a.m. in an uninviting faraway room. Still, according to diplomats, the Bulgarian presentation, appropriately dedicated to the 1300th anniversary, "positively impressed the participants with its modesty and strictly academic focus . . . in contrast to [Romanian] pomp." There was a vast difference, in the minds of the Bulgarians, between the "non-scientific" Romanian interpretations of their "pseudo-jubilee," on the one hand, and the "measured information" supported by objective, scientific interpretations of historical facts related to the "real" Bulgarian jubilee, on the other.[62] Excessive nationalism, in other words, would backfire, a warning that Bulgarian scholars also heeded during their international engagements elsewhere.

Romanian officials obstructed the Bulgarian cultural efforts, refusing to allow any 1300-year activities in 1981 while multiple publications in the press "twisted Bulgarian history." The Bulgarian embassy continued to use the strategy of indirect propaganda, organizing "events with good propaganda effect" even if they were not directly related to the 1300th anniversary.[63] There was a conscious attempt to have a concentration of events in September 1981, the month that Bulgarian officials had chosen for the jubilee's "culmination" internationally. The ninetieth anniversary of the establishment of the BKP (2 August), the seventieth anniversary of Todor Zhivkov's birth (7 September), and the thirty-seventh anniversary of the socialist revolution (9 September) all became occasions for celebrating the 1300th anniversary. As promised in the jubilee plan, the Bulgarian presence in Romania was "intensely felt" during that month.[64] Yet, the celebration of 1300 Years Bulgaria in Romania remained an indirect affair. To sum up its contradictory logic, the Bulgarian embassy concluded: "the execution [of commemorative activities in Romania] was significant, even if it did not necessarily involve commemorative events in all cases."[65]

The question remains, what were the consequences of Romanian officials' steadfast refusal to participate in Bulgaria's 1300-year celebration? Trying to avoid fallout from this boycott of the Bulgarian anniversary and its own international isolation, the Ceausescu regime carefully straddled the line between socialist internationalism and historical revisionism. In the end, the Romanian government sent a delegation to Sofia during the celebrations on 20 October 1981 when more than one hundred heads of state were present for the "all-people's celebration" of the 1300-year jubilee in the Bulgarian capital. Despite the public appearance of friendship, disputes over "historical truth" created layers of suspicion between the two neighbors that continued to color their relations throughout the socialist period.

Yugoslavia: Culture as Counterpropaganda

Rival historical interpretations similarly constrained the execution of Bulgarian cultural policies in Yugoslavia, but while Ceausescu and Zhivkov skillfully downplayed their disagreements, Bulgarian and Yugoslav officials often publicly challenged each other on the irreconcilable question of Macedonia. As a result, the encounters between Bulgaria and Yugoslavia on the occasion of the 1300th jubilee were unambiguously contentious and frequently dramatic. In this context, Bulgarian officials understood their cultural events to function as "counterpropaganda" to Yugoslavia's "hostile disinformation" about their country's history. Only occasionally were considerations of socialist internationalism able to defuse the notably confrontational tone of Bulgarian and Yugoslav representatives in cultural and historical matters.

In the 1960s, the Soviet Union urged Bulgaria to pursue constructive contacts with Yugoslavia and to adopt a compromise position on Macedonia, yet it did not take a strong position on the latter question, which the Soviets considered a bilateral issue. Thus, tensions between the two countries reemerged after 1966 when Yugoslavia insisted on the presence of a Macedonian minority in Bulgaria and Bulgaria unequivocally expressed its position on the place of Macedonia in Bulgarian history. In this context, cultural relations between Bulgaria and Yugoslavia in the 1970s developed in fits and starts, despite the fact that the two countries signed a Plan for Cultural Cooperation in 1974.[66] As in the relationship with Romania, debates focused on history and its relationship to politics, with each side maintaining that it held the monopoly over truth. Tensions grew in 1978 when Bulgaria celebrated the centennial of its modern statehood. Of particular concern to Yugoslav leaders was the elevation of 3 March, the date of the signing of the Treaty of San Stefano, to a Bulgarian national holiday, because the Bulgarian state created by San Stefano included the parts of Macedonia now in Yugoslavia. For the Yugoslavs, this anniversary was a sign of Bulgarian territorial claims vis-à-vis Yugoslavia and an expression of "Great Bulgarian nationalism." The Bulgarians insisted that they had renounced all territorial claims, but this did not placate their neighbors. The fact that several months later BKP Politburo member Tsola Dragoicheva published her World War II memoir did not help either because from the perspective of Yugoslavia, her take on the anti-fascist resistance in Vardar Macedonia constituted "the darkest anti-Yugoslav and anti-Macedonian slander written in Bulgaria in the last twenty years." The ensuing heated exchanges between the two countries engaged other touchy topics, notably the 1903 Ilinden Uprising and the nineteenth-century revolutionaries and national awakeners, with each side accusing the other in "twisting historical science."[67]

These passionate debates were not limited to cultural events in the Balkans because Yugoslav diplomats intervened in Bulgarian events organized outside of Yugoslavia, trying to correct Bulgarian historical interpretations about Macedonia. In the United States in 1979, Yugoslav diplomats attended a Bulgarian panel organized at the American Association for the Advancement of Slavic Studies (AAASS) on the occasion of the 1300th anniversary, questioned the Bulgarian presentations, and distributed literature "compliments of the Yugoslav embassy." They visited foreign embassies, pleading with diplomats to boycott the 1300-year jubilee celebrations in their respective countries, as the Bulgarians learned from their Cuban friends.[68] Yugoslav vigilance even led to the forced removal of books on historical topics from the Bulgarian stand at the Belgrade International Book Fair in 1979.[69] When

Bulgarian historian Hristo Hristov delivered a lecture on the historical development of Bulgaria at Columbia University in November 1980, the Bulgarian ambassador in Yugoslavia was summoned to explain attempts to "falsify history" and "undermine the existence of a Macedonian nation."[70]

These tensions over "open questions" continued around the 1300-year jubilee. The Yugoslavs directly refused to celebrate the 1300th anniversary and created obstructions when Bulgarian officials organized events on historical topics. During the negotiations regarding the Plan of Cultural Cooperation in 1980–1982, Yugoslav representatives declined to accept a provision obliging each country to celebrate historical anniversaries.[71] Throughout 1981, the Yugoslav side refused to participate in cultural events because of its "negative attitude to the 1300-year jubilee."[72] In the Bulgarian opinion, their neighbors were engaged in "anti-Bulgarian propaganda" to sabotage the celebration of the 1300-year jubilee: for example, the Yugoslav government declined to form a national celebration committee.[73] Considering all these complications, Bulgarian experts talked about the organization of cultural events in Yugoslavia as "counterpropaganda work."[74] Their explicit goal was to prove the veracity of Bulgarian historical claims while questioning the logic of Yugoslav assertions.

As they did in Romania, Bulgarian officials engaged in indirect strategies to celebrate the "big event" in Yugoslavia. For example, the KK issued instructions to the unions of Bulgarian writers, musicians, translators, and filmmakers, as well as Bulgarian radio, television, and the major newspapers, to establish contact with their respective counterparts in Yugoslavia.[75] As Bulgarian experts prepared for the Belgrade and Zagreb trade-industrial fairs in April and May 1981, they showcased Bulgaria's economic development "in the context of the 1300-year jubilee," including historical photographs and posters.[76] Some of the attempts to plan jubilee events bordered on the comical: when Circus Globus launched its Yugoslav tours, it included 1300-year themes in its program.[77] Yet, the Yugoslav side was vigilant. When the Bulgarian National Theater visited Belgrade in July 1981, only 2,000 out of the projected 3,500 tickets sold, ostensibly because of anti-Bulgarian propaganda in the press.[78] As they did in Romania, Bulgarian experts implemented indirect strategies, but in Yugoslavia they faced open anti-Bulgarian hostility in the press and outright refusal to participate in the jubilee. Thus, "complex events" organized in Yugoslavia focused on less contentious matters, such as the centennial of the establishment of the BKP or the celebration of the 1923 "anti-fascist uprising."[79] Socialist internationalism was the best way to disguise the rift between the two countries on national and historical topics.

Yet, unlike Romania where Bulgarian officials treaded carefully, the Yugoslav refusal to participate in the 1300-year jubilee reached the highest diplomatic circles, demonstrating the potent charge of the Macedonian question. In September 1980, Bulgarian diplomats, frustrated with the obstructions, suggested an official inquiry from MVnR regarding Yugoslav participation in the 1300th anniversary.[80] On 22 September, Deputy Minister of Foreign Affairs Mariĭ Ivanov summoned the Yugoslav ambassador in Sofia, Danilo Purić, and explained the importance of the 1300th anniversary for the Bulgarian people, informing him of the international resonance of the event and expressing hope that the anniversary would be welcomed in Yugoslavia, a country with "similar historical developments and shared contemporary objectives." Ambassador Purić responded that "each people has the right to celebrate its anniversaries" and suggested that, if the Bulgarian media refrained from using the jubilee to advertise open questions, the celebration would find a good reception in Yugoslavia.[81]

In January 1981, Ambassador Purić informed MVnR that the Yugoslav government would not participate in the 1300-year jubilee. He explained that Bulgarian officials had "appropriated the Macedonian people's history [and] voiced territorial aspirations" by characterizing the 1903 Ilinden Uprising as a Bulgarian revolutionary movement (the culprit was Liudmila Zhivkova herself). The "Great Bulgarian conceptions" that dominated the celebrations and denied the existence of a Macedonian nation breached prior Bulgarian assurances that the anniversary events would not touch upon open questions but focus on common issues, such as the struggle against the Ottoman Empire or fascism. In his response, Deputy Minister Ivanov tried to distinguish between political and historical arguments. He insisted that Bulgaria had no territorial aspirations toward its neighbors, however, "history remains history. It cannot be appropriated, twisted, or erased."[82] The conflicting uses of history and the open questions between the two countries remained insurmountable impediments.

On 24 February 1981, MVnR summoned Ambassador Purić yet again. Ambassador Ivan Ganev expressed concerns regarding publications in the Yugoslav media and events sponsored by Yugoslav institutions, which disseminated "numerous materials with anti-Bulgarian character." Specifically, the Bulgarian diplomat referred to the World War II memoirs of Svetozar Vukmanovic-Tempo, a member of the Central Committee of the League of Yugoslav Communists (SKJ) and a leader of the resistance movement in Vardar Macedonia in 1943–1944, which in the Bulgarian interpretation were full of "rude attacks against the BKP and its leaders [and] crude falsifications of historical truth." Ganev remarked, "Bulgaria has existed for 1300 years, and we do not ask for anyone's condescending admission to recognize this historical fact." Asking why the Yugoslav government tolerated this anti-Bulgarian campaign, Ganev concluded that "if the goal is to silence Bulgarian science, this has no future."[83] History had moved to the center of the Yugoslav-Bulgarian controversy.

The following day, at a meeting with the minister of foreign affairs, Petar Mladenov, Ambassador Purić explained why the Yugoslav government was refraining from participation in the 1300th anniversary: he cited specific articles and lectures by Bulgarian scholars, which he qualified as "not historical but political [writings] that contain various strange statements." Mladenov emphasized that the two countries should follow the prior agreement between Zhivkov and Tito "to seek what unites us while our disagreements should not be an impediment to good neighborly relations." He also commented on the relationship between history and politics, stating, "I am not a historian and study the facts from a political perspective." He insisted that historians should engage in the "conscientious study of facts," but "what historians write, whether true or not, is their personal opinion." Mladenov further charged members of the Central Committee of the SKJ with publishing polemical works, raising the question of "how to separate the historian from the politician." This was an insincere attempt to mask the fact that many Bulgarian historians tended to be in service of the "patriotic turn," while accusing Yugoslav scholars of the same sin. In the end, Mladenov concluded that the decision to participate in the 1300-year celebrations was "your sovereign right. We do not ask you, do not insist." But he warned that Bulgaria would resolutely counter any attempt by Yugoslav diplomats to sabotage its 1300th anniversary by visiting embassies and contacting international jubilee committees.[84]

The Yugoslav government ultimately reached a compromise decision: Yugoslav representatives would participate in the Twelfth Congress of the BKP in April 1981 but abstain from the 1300-year jubilee celebration in October.[85] Yet, Zhivkov "arranged to have the last word: At the concert at the Congress on 2 April, the second item on the program was a symbolic poem entitled 'Vardar' [an important river in Yugoslav Macedonia]." The Yugoslav ambassador made a formal protest. The Bulgarians answered that the Vardar Rhapsody, by composer Pancho Vladigerov, was written in 1922, at a time when a Macedonian nation (or state) did not exist.[86]

Despite these tensions, after Tito's death in May 1980, the Bulgarian side observed changes in the Yugoslav position regarding Bulgaria, which led to the expansion of economic relations as a first step toward the resolution of the "open questions." With the mounting internal problems in Yugoslavia, its leadership softened its position, despite repeated attempts throughout 1981 to minimize the effect of Bulgarian events dedicated to the 1300th anniversary.[87] Ultimately, on 17 October 1981, three days before the official celebration of 1300 Years Bulgaria on 20 October, Ambassador Purić contacted Bulgarian diplomats "on short notice" with the statement that, following a meeting between the foreign ministers Mladenov and Vrhovec in New York, he would be present at the 1300-year jubilee, although he asked for assurances that the celebration "would not be targeting any Balkan state."[88] Following the emotionally charged controversies surrounding the interrelationship between politics and history, in which each side had categorically spelled out its position, socialist internationalism came to the rescue. Yet, debates over the place of Macedonia in the historical interpretations of Bulgaria and Yugoslavia continued to trigger heated political tensions and historical debates between the two countries.

Turkey: The Importance of Reciprocity

In contrast to these dramatic exchanges, Bulgarian officials maintained a measured tone in their encounters with their Turkish partners. Turkish politics during this time—including the 1974 Cyprus invasion and a 1980 military coup—was a constantly shifting terrain, and Bulgarian diplomats adopted an anticipatory position. In this context, cultural cooperation agreements presented little risk as they dutifully followed the rules of reciprocity. Thus, regular if not particularly robust or novel cultural programs managed to navigate the political and national priorities of each state without causing major problems. The early 1980s marked a short period of relaxation between the two countries, which the resumption of nationalist pressures on the Bulgarian Turks in 1984 put to an end, reviving the sharp nationalist rhetoric on both sides.

In the 1970s, Turkey found itself at the center of Cold War debates because of two major international crises: its invasion and occupation of northern Cyprus in 1974 and the Iranian Revolution of 1979 (the two countries share an extensive border).[89] During this time, attempting to undermine the southern flank of NATO, the Soviet Union was also cultivating good relations with Turkey. The Soviet position shaped relations between Bulgaria and Turkey, as "big brother" requested that Bulgaria temper its controversies with its southern neighbor. In 1975, reflecting the Helsinki spirit, the two countries signed a Declaration for Good Neighborly Relations and Cooperation, which framed their interactions for the rest of the decade. Yet, the status of the Turks in Bulgaria and their emigration to Turkey remained an unresolved matter.[90] After the invasion of Cyprus of 1974, Bulgarian politicians watched their southern neighbor closely as they feared "Cypriot scenarios," especially after Prime Minister Bülent Ecevit spoke during his visit to Sofia in 1978 about the presence of a Turkish national minority in Bulgaria.[91]

Despite the enormous political and economic ramifications of the latter question, the two countries maintained a surprisingly measured tone in their encounters, in direct opposition to the emotionally charged exchanges Bulgaria had with Romania and Yugoslavia. The late 1970s and early 1980s were a time when Bulgaria had tempered its pressures on its Turkish population domestically, so that it was not a burning issue in the same way Macedonia and the Dacian question were for Yugoslavia and Romania. Once in a while there were disputes between Bulgarian and Turkish officials involving historical interpretations. Bulgarian diplomats continued to review and compile instances of "anti-Bulgarian propaganda" originating in "former Bulgarian citizens" of Turkish origin who had emigrated and now in Turkey spoke of the "miserable existence" of the Bulgarian Turks.[92] When negotiations were underway in 1979 about the future of cultural relations, the Turkish side declined to include provisions about visits by historians because Turkish archives were not open to foreign researchers.[93] The preferred Bulgarian historiographical term "Ottoman yoke" also caused periodic reactions from the Turkish embassy in Sofia because of its "political nuance."[94] Yet, in contrast to Romania and Yugoslavia, these disagreement were handled calmly and diplomatically.

In talks between Bulgaria and Turkey, political factors related to the new spirit of regional cooperation seemed to be paramount, easing Bulgarian fears of "pan-Turkish, anti-Slavic, and anticommunist" tendencies in Turkey. From the Bulgarian perspective, "maybe for the first time since the death of Ataturk, Turkey [was] seeking contacts with the socialist states, and especially its Balkan neighbors," because it wished to overcome its isolation after the Cyprus crisis. In this context, Bulgarian diplomats believed that "cultural exchange and relations" were "the most fruitful way" to advance cooperation.[95] When Zhivkov visited Turkey in June 1976, Bulgarian functionaries organized a series of events in Turkey whose goal was to showcase Bulgarian socialist culture: these included opera and ballet performances, pop music concerts, and the *Contemporary Bulgarian Art* exhibition.[96] The years between 1975 and 1979 marked a period of growing cultural contacts between the two countries that, adopting the language of Helsinki, used cultural exchange "to strengthen good neighborly relations" in the spirit of peaceful coexistence.[97] The two governments signed a two-year Agreement for Scientific and Cultural Cooperation in 1976, which was renewed every two years, including

1980–1981 cycle that was critical for the Bulgarians as it included provisions related to the 1300th anniversary.[98]

Yet, in the late 1970s Turkey experienced growing political instability. When Bülent Ecevit became prime minister in 1978, a series of new administrative appointments across ministries complicated the execution of existing agreements.[99] Following an increase in political assassinations and confrontations between left- and right-wing youth groups, early 1979 saw the imposition of a state of emergency in nineteen provinces of the country. This situation complicated cultural programs; in the opinion of the Bulgarians, "under the mask of goodwill, the Turkish side used every possible means to slow down or cancel our initiatives" while Turkish politicians systematically "utilized Turkish culture . . . [as] an instrument of political means."[100] In September 1980, a military coup put an end to civilian rule and placed severe limitations on freedom of the press, further frustrating Bulgarian efforts in Turkey.[101] A series of shifts in the administrative structures by General Kenan Evren created "an atmosphere of instability and even fear" and complicated Bulgarian plans on the eve of the approaching anniversary. Bulgarian officials continued to insist on the execution of existing cultural plans for 1980–1981 and especially the reciprocal celebration of anniversaries.[102]

The two countries had traditionally celebrated their anniversaries under conditions of "strict reciprocity." In 1973 and 1974, state delegations participated in the celebration of the fiftieth anniversary of the Turkish Republic (1923) and the thirtieth anniversary of the socialist revolution in Bulgaria (1944).[103] In the late 1970s, sensing the reserved attitude of the Turkish side toward the 1300th anniversary (Turkish diplomats were unsure whether a national celebration committee was appropriate), the Bulgarian side promoted the possibility of coordinating the centennial of Ataturk's birth (1881) with the celebration of the 1300-year jubilee.[104] Bulgarian diplomats resorted to (highly selective) historical arguments to convince their Turkish counterparts, pointing out that "the two countries should seek out those moments and events in their past that would be the basis for . . . cooperation today and in the future." Ataturk, for one, had had "a friendly attitude toward . . . Bulgaria, contributed greatly to progress in Turkey, and had a clear desire for all people to live in peace and understanding."[105] When the Turkish embassy in Sofia moved to a new building, which occupied a site where Ataturk had rented a room in 1913, Bulgarian officials offered to place a plaque as "a sign of the respect of the Bulgarian people for the great son of the Turkish people."[106] These plans were included in the Plan for Scientific and Cultural Cooperation between the two countries for the period 1980–1981, in which the 1300-year jubilee and the centennial of Ataturk were linked.[107]

After the military coup in September 1980, however, the paralysis in the country severely limited the execution of the 1300-year jubilee.[108] The Turkish side, for example, insisted that jubilee events "be spread out throughout the year," undermining the Bulgarian plan for a clear culmination.[109] The celebration of the 1300th anniversary in Turkey was thus a subdued affair due to the complicated internal situation and lack of cooperation from Turkish authorities. Due to its political and economic instability, the country never formed a national celebration committee for the 1300-year jubilee. In June, diplomats opened a Week of Bulgarian Film in Ankara while in September they hosted a reception at the embassy dedicated to the 1300th anniversary. Yet, irregularities limited the scope of the most high-profile event, the *Contemporary Bulgarian Art* exhibition in December.[110] In the end, the Turkish side reluctantly sent a delegation to the celebrations in Sofia in October and issued a modest state gift for the jubilee, "to match the spirit of relations between the two states."[111] In December 1981, as a sign of appreciation, Bulgaria organized a photo exhibit on Ataturk to mark the centennial of his birth, fulfilling its reciprocal cultural obligations.[112] Diplomatic formalities and insistence on reciprocity dominated the two anniversary celebrations. Even though those events were hardly groundbreaking, the fact that they took place at all is remarkable, and they marked a relatively high point in Bulgarian-Turkish relations before the tense encounters of the mid- to late 1980s related to the escalating persecution of the Bulgarian Turks by the communist regime.

Greece: How to Stage a Successful Jubilee

Given Bulgaria's tensions with its other neighbors, the dialogue that developed between Bulgaria and Greece in the 1970s was perhaps unexpected. Yet, Zhivkov meticulously cultivated friendship with both conservative and socialist Greek partners while Greek policy circles warmed up to their northern neighbors despite ideological and national differences. The Bulgarian cultural program in Greece presents an eloquent example of the interconnection between soft and hard power. Cultural links between the two countries steadily grew in the 1970s, and Bulgaria organized a 1300th-anniversary celebration in Greece that served as a model for international cultural events elsewhere; importantly, official culture facilitated the rapprochement that paved the road for the "Athens-Sofia axis" of the mid-1980s.

Opposing political orientations and a long history of national(ist) tensions should have prevented this rapprochement. As historian Nikolai Todorov, who served as the Bulgarian ambassador in Athens in the early 1980s, notes, "history . . . has left a contradictory legacy in the relations between the two states. The moments of tensions between the two peoples have been more than the moments of common struggle, friendship, and cooperation. The vast majority of Greeks up until today consider . . . that Bulgaria was created through the violent capture of sacred Hellenic land. Events in our century also did not contribute to the neutralization of anti-Bulgarian and anti-Slavic moods, but exacerbated the existing hostility."[113] Yet, the second half of the 1970s saw accelerated improvement in the relations between the two countries, including cultural contacts. Factors included the realism of both states' leaders and their willingness to work "across different economic and military-political formations" in the spirit of Helsinki, transforming "relations between Bulgaria and Greece [into] an axis of stability in the Balkans." For Bulgarian diplomats, the improvement of relations between the two countries "exerted a huge influence on the general political climate in the Balkans where the political picture remained multidimensional and relations between various parties complicated."[114]

Bulgaria and Greece only fully resumed diplomatic relations in 1964. The two countries continued contacts during the military junta (1967–1974), but the late 1970s offered new possibilities for rapprochement because both countries adopted the Helsinki spirit of cooperation across political and socioeconomic lines.[115] In July 1975, when Prime Minister Konstantinos Karamanlis, a conservative and pro-European politician, visited Bulgaria as a part of Greek Ostpolitik, Todor Zhivkov referred to him as "a very strong and brave man" because with his visit, he had demolished years of distrust and hostility between the two countries.[116]

This goodwill at the highest level percolated down to other sectors, too. In late 1975, the Greek-Bulgarian and Bulgarian-Greek associations for friendship emerged in Athens and Sofia.[117] From 1976 on, cultural exchanges provided, in the Bulgarian view, "unlimited opportunities for mutual acquaintance . . . of the two neighborly peoples."[118] When Zhivkov visited Greece in April 1976, the leadership of the Greek-Bulgarian Association hung several hundred Bulgarian flags in the Greek capital and provided photographs of both leaders to passersby.[119] In July 1976, when Liudmila Zhivkova embarked on an official state visit (followed by a reciprocal visit of the Greek minister of culture Konstantinos Tripanis in October), she provided a positive view of post-junta Greece. She pointed out the "general goodwill" of the cultural intelligentsia, despite the politicians' "partial restraint" and "attempts to avoid concrete commitments."[120] Cultural contact thus played an important role in building mutual trust between political elites. In 1978, Bulgarian experts declared, "The period of accidental exchange of specialists is over," and characterized cultural exchange between Bulgaria and Greece as

FIGURE 14. Meeting of Todor Zhivkov and Greek prime minister Konstantinos Karamanlis. Undated. Source: Aleksandâr Fol et al., eds. *Bâlgariia prez vekovete: Ochertsi* (Sofia: Nauka i izkustvo, 1982), held in the National Library, Sofia.

"dynamic [and] well-organized." In the late 1970s, film festivals, cooperation between Greek and Bulgarian radio and television, and visits of librarians and classical musicians created a lively exchange of cultural events.[121]

In the late 1970s, the Bulgarian embassy in Athens embarked on planning the 1300-year jubilee events in Greece. Diplomats maintained that "conditions in Greece are peculiar" because of the "conflicting legacies" and disagreements between the two countries on many historical questions. Based on their experiences with Romania and Yugoslavia, diplomats proceeded carefully. Yet, unlike Romania and Yugoslavia, Greek politicians and public figures tactfully refrained from any discussion of controversial topics, such as their conflicting views on Macedonia and Thrace, but focused on recent developments between the two countries. The overarching logic was "to avoid as much as possible references to the past and to focus on events that bring us together, especially in our contemporary history—the building of socialism, which is also the period of normalization and development of Bulgarian-Greek relations."[122]

In late 1979, Zhivkov appointed a new Bulgarian ambassador to Greece—the historian Nikolai Todorov—whose mandate, among other aspects of reinvigorating relations between the two countries, was to organize the 1300-year jubilee celebrations in Greece.[123] Once in charge of this mission, Todorov put scholars and experts at the center of the commemorations because he believed that only by enlisting the support of the Greek academic and artistic community could he cultivate a "benevolent climate" for the celebrations.[124] In defiance of the consistently ambitious and top-down jubilee agenda of the NKK in Sofia, Todorov adopted a "realistic" approach without "maximalist tendencies" by deciding to organize "only a handful [of] effective jubilee events."[125] A first step was the establishment of a national celebration committee, an attempt that had failed elsewhere in the Balkans. Todorov's choice of a chairperson was unusual if not controversial: Panaiotis Kanelopoulos was a former Greek prime minister who had opposed the junta, but politically stood on the right. Under his leadership, the Greek committee organized a number of high-profile events that served as a public breakthrough in Greek-Bulgarian relations.

The intersection between culture, history, and politics in these efforts was paramount. In spring 1980, Bulgarian exhibitions of ethnographic and artistic objects opened in Athens and Piraeus in the presence of the mayors of the two cities; the printed invitations specifically stated that they were dedicated to the 1300th anniversary. As a historian, Todorov did not shy away from engaging the contested history of the two countries. Two joint symposia in Thessaloniki gathered scholars from both countries to debate Bulgarian-Greek cultural relations during the Middle Ages and the Ottoman period. The goal was to initiate dialogue on topics that Greek and Bulgarian scholars could agree on and stay away from more contentious recent disputes.[126] In Todorov's mind these symposia "promised the failure of all efforts to undermine [the 1300th anniversary] because the group that we may expect to attack the jubilee [i.e., Greek historians] has been implicated so thoroughly in its celebration." Todorov was still alert: "Let's not be naïve, we will face many difficulties because the Greek side creates many obstacles."[127] Yet, he believed that the only way to overcome obstacles to the celebration of a historical anniversary was scholarly professionalism. Once the positive tone of the Bulgaria-Greek cultural encounter was set, Todorov took political steps: he initiated contacts with members of the Greek cabinet, seeking official involvement in the anniversary celebrations as instructed by Sofia. In response to the Bulgarian requests for a Greek parliamentary resolution, diplomats bluntly stated, "some things are impossible."[128] Yet, the Greek government officially recognized the jubilee, unlike Yugoslavia and initially Romania. Positive reviews of Bulgarian events emerged in the press, again unlike the rest of the neighbors, including a major article in the popular daily

Vima (Step) from February 1981 under the title "The Bulgarians Value Their Past."[129] A variety of cultural events were celebrated in Athens in spring 1981, always under the aegis of the 1300th anniversary.[130] There was an undeniable and clear momentum in the development of Greek-Bulgarian cultural contacts.

This is not to say that everything went smoothly. The Bulgarian general consul in Thessaloniki, for example, had suggested with nationalist pathos that the 1300-year events in Greece should "disseminate information about the contributions of our country to the international world cultural treasury, countering Greek insinuations that Bulgaria had only consumed Greek values without lending anything to it."[131] Greek nationalist organizations similarly "accused Kanelopoulos [and others Greek public figures] of selling themselves to the Bulgarians."[132] When the Greek ambassador in Sofia proposed the organization of an *Aegean Civilization* exhibition in 1981, "as a greeting to the Bulgarian people for their jubilee," there were suspicions that the goal was to overshadow Bulgarian contributions to ancient civilization, demonstrated in the blockbuster *Thracian Treasures* exhibition that toured the world at the same time.[133] Yet, these disagreements were handled

FIGURE 15.   Meeting of historian Nikolai Todorov, ambassador to Greece in 1981, and the former Greek prime minister Panaiotis Kanelopoulos, who chaired the Greek National Celebration Committee. Source: Nikolai Todorov family archive.

carefully, unlike the case of Romania and Yugoslavia where exchanges were blunt. Kanelopoulos, for example, urged the parties to "look to the past and seek not so much these elements that pitted us against each other, but those that united us during the difficult centuries of common obstacles."[134]

The mostly academic focus of the 1300th anniversary that Todorov initiated did not please the overseers of the jubilee celebrations at home. In a January 1980 meeting, MVnR officials recommended "limiting the unsystematic and frequently private contacts of Bulgarian scientists with Greek ones working on issues related to Bulgarian history and culture." While the publicly expressed apprehension was that "our hyperactivity could cause the suspicion and restraint of Greek authorities and could have undesired consequences," diplomats were clearly annoyed with the growing professional contacts between historians from both countries.[135] The NKK, noting that "the jubilee activities in Greece have a predominantly scientific and cultural character," recommended the "broadening of the [audiences of the] jubilee celebrations" and the inclusion of Greek Communist Party members.[136] But Todorov lashed out at bureaucrats who showed little regard for local conditions and stuck with his plans.[137]

From the Bulgarian perspective, the jubilee celebrations in Greece received a boost in May 1981 from the visit of Zhivkov and his meeting with Prime Minister Karamanlis, which was covered well in the press and created a sense of continuity between cultural and political agendas.[138] Yet, with their parliamentary elections coming up, the Greek side "categorically" requested that Bulgaria avoid any 1300th anniversary events during the preelection period that began in September.[139] For that reason, Todorov moved the "culmination" of the anniversary celebrations in Greece, as mandated in the jubilee plans required by the NKK in Sofia, to February 1982.[140] Even though the Greek government declined to offer an official statement on the 1300th anniversary on the eve of the elections, at the 9th September reception celebrating the national holiday of Bulgaria a telegram from Karamanlis "included one sentence about 1300," a victory for Bulgarian public relations efforts. The Greek government also decided to offer a state gift—a replica of an ancient sculpture—that would be delivered after the elections.[141] Ultimately, as a result of Bulgarian flexibility, the 1300-year celebrations in Greece were a success. The Greek leaders Konstantinos Karamanlis and Andreas Papandreou, the latter newly elected in late 1981, each delivered official greetings to the Bulgarian people for the 1300th anniversary, despite earlier indications that an official Greek declaration would be impossible.[142] Then in February 1982, Ambassador Todorov dazzled Greek audiences with two of Bulgaria's most coveted public relations resources, now available after the end of the jubilee frenzy: the Pirin Folk Ensemble and the Bulgarian astronaut Georgi Ivanov. Greece, an ideological adversary and national enemy, had become a model for celebrating the 1300th anniversary outside of Bulgaria.

From Cultural Cooperation to Political Breakthrough

Bulgaria's neighbors had conflicting views on a number of historical interpretations that Bulgaria used as a part of its international cultural repertoire, which complicated the execution of its 1300-year jubilee in the Balkans. This observation shines a light on the double-edged function of cultural nationalism, which helped domestically but complicated matters internationally, especially among the country's neighbors. But cultural exchange could also create goodwill, or the conditions for fruitful cooperation that might bridge the ideological and national differences among the Balkan states. Soft power projects went hand in hand with hard power objectives, facilitating a number of regional initiatives with lasting effects. In April 1981, during the Twelfth Congress of the BKP, Zhivkov spoke about the need to establish "a code of good neighborly relations," and for some Balkan states, culture became the way to test this proposition.[143] This breakthrough potential of cultural diplomacy was obvious in the dynamics between Bulgaria and Greece, where cultural cooperation provided an opportunity to advance political dialogue and regional cooperation in a variety of practical ways.

The complex relationship between culture and politics, and the role of the 1300th anniversary in bringing them together, was evident during the highly publicized "all-people's celebration" of the 1300-year jubilee in Sofia in October 1981. In attendance were heads of state and international figures from more than one hundred countries, including most Balkan neighbors (with the exception of Albania). Zhivkov spoke about the need for regional cooperation: "only a policy of peace and understanding, of friendship and cooperation corresponds to the interests of the Balkans' people." He then announced Bulgaria's new major international initiative: to secure "the gradual transformation of Europe into a continent free of nuclear arms" by creating a nuclear-weapons-free zone (NWFZ) in the Balkans together with all willing neighbors.[144] The proclaimed goal was to make the Balkans "an area of peace and security."[145]

Having built goodwill among its neighbors during the past decade, including through culture, Bulgaria was now ready to deliver tangible political results with the help of its Greek friends. In late 1981, with the new Greek prime minister, the socialist Andreas Papandreou, in office, Greece and Bulgaria began consultations related to the possibility of establishing the

NWFZ. This prospect, in turn, caused trouble for NATO because of its political implications concerning the cohesiveness of the organization and the increasingly sensitive question of U.S. deployment of missiles in Germany.[146] For Papandreou, this was a strategy to renegotiate the future of U.S. military bases on Greek territory, but the very fact that Bulgaria and Greece were involved in talks related to nuclear arms was indicative of how far their relationship had come.[147] Despite NATO reservations and pressures associated with EEC membership, cooperation between Bulgaria and Greece expanded further during the years of the Panhellenic Socialist Movement (PASOK) (1981–1989). In 1986, the two countries signed a Declaration of Friendship, Good Neighborliness, and Cooperation. Soft power projects had paved the road for tangible hard power achievements.

This dynamic suggests that in the late Cold War, official culture provided a set of opportunities to test regional cooperation beyond the ideological standing of the Balkan neighbors. The fact that Bulgaria achieved the most successful regional rapprochement with Greece, its ideological and national enemy to the south, while it could not coordinate its agenda with its socialist "friends" Romania and Yugoslavia, is telling. This development is especially striking if one contrasts this situation with the initial stages of the Cold War in the Balkans in the late 1940s, which was characterized by sharp ideological confrontation between the socialist and capitalist camps. By the 1970s, however, it was not the ideological commitment within the two blocs, but the ability to enter political dialogue and moderate historical controversies that determined the framework for regional cooperation in the Balkans. This shift, in turn, complicated the policies of both superpowers who could not rely on the consistency of their allies. Culture had served as an important tool in this process of regional realignment.

CHAPTER 3

Culture as a Way of Life

In July 1973, Radio Sofia declared that cultural exchange between East and West had become extremely important in the context of détente. Due to the "new political climate and shift from confrontation to coexistence," a Bulgarian cultural "breakthrough" (*probiv*) abroad could showcase the achievements of "real socialism" (*realniiat sotsializâm*).[1] Castigating the Western strategy of "silencing the success of socialism" by creating an "information vacuum," Bulgarian experts now started organizing "cultural-propaganda events" to promote their ideas of state and society in the West.[2] From the Eastern European perspective, the Western focus on the free exchange of people and ideas after the signing of the Helsinki Final Act in 1975 reflected attempts "to infiltrate socialist societies" and attack the socialist "way of life" (*nachin na zhivot*). Why else would the Western press eulogize a "handful of Czechoslovak counterrevolutionaries" (Charter 77) while ignoring acute problems at home?[3] Clearly, Western support for "the so-called dissidents" served "to undermine socialist society."[4] Otherwise, why did the West not allow the flow of ideas from East to West, which would mean publishing Eastern European authors supportive of state socialism, and not only dissidents? Even more urgently, why did Western media discuss human rights in Eastern Europe, but ignore U.S. violations in South Africa and Latin America?[5]

This chapter examines Bulgarian cultural contacts with Western Europe and the United States to explain the role of cultural exchange in the 1970s.

Between 1977 and 1982, Bulgarian officials organized 7,420 events in capitalist countries, showcasing the best of Bulgarian culture.[6] Despite the cultural shortages associated with the celebration of the 1300th anniversary worldwide, the best Bulgarian cultural products were dispatched to the West. Even though this cultural project served an undeniably ideological rationale, its content was somewhat surprising—"representative" exhibitions on historical topics and classical events embracing universal human values played a central role in this program. From the *Thracian Treasures from Bulgaria* exhibit to *1000 Years of Bulgarian Icons* to *Medieval Bulgarian Civilization* to *Contemporary Bulgarian Art*, these high-profile events promoted not only the image of socialist modernity, but also of Bulgaria as "one of the oldest states of Europe." Bulgarian representatives now embraced their European identity as a cornerstone of their cultural campaigns in the West. These exhibitions were the perfect choice for officials: curated by the best archaeologists and historians, they possessed the aura of professionalism without projecting explicit political content. These events fit with the "patriotic line" that showcased Bulgaria as one of the cradles of European civilization. But they also subtly highlighted the attention that the socialist state gave to national heritage. By using trusted cultural experts to organize these exhibitions, their message could be meticulously tailored. Pitchers, amphorae, jewelry, and icons remained silent to provocative questions, while they could be packaged with glossy brochures that talked up the success of real socialism in Eastern Europe. The tension between ideological and universal messages was at the core of Bulgarian cultural diplomacy in the West, which sought to advance the prestige-making agenda of the communist regime and promote a new image for Bulgaria abroad based on civilizational claims related to Europe's common heritage.

At the same time that Bulgarian functionaries were staging their most ambitious cultural programs in the West, they were anxiously trying to limit the spread of Western culture in their own country. In June 1980, the same year that *Thracian Treasures* premiered in Munich and Cologne, the West German ambassador arrived at the Ministry of Foreign Affairs (MVnR) to register his complaint that an exhibition of books from the Federal Republic of Germany (FRG), taking place at the National Library in Sofia, did not attract the anticipated number of visitors due to the lack of advertisement. The ambassador explained that no exhibition posters were visible in town, no announcements had been printed in the press, and no flyers were available at bookstores, making it impossible for the citizens of Sofia to find out about the exhibition.[7] This exhibition had been a subject of controversy in the months before its opening due to the contested use of the term "German" in the originally proposed title. The Bulgarians had insisted on clearly distinguishing between German and West German, in line with Soviet bloc policies in support of the German Democratic Republic (GDR), and given the sensitivity of the issue, it is likely that when the exhibition finally opened at the National Library, the organizers found ways to make the suspicious books invisible to the Bulgarian audience.

In fact, Bulgarian diplomats had sought the advice of their Hungarian colleagues about the Days of the FRG held in Hungary the previous year. To neutralize the "propaganda of West German life and politics," the Hungarians had declined to facilitate any events with a mass character, such as the sale of books and vinyl records or meetings with young people, and only allowed the showing of prescreened films. Most importantly, they warned their Bulgarian colleagues, it was imperative to guarantee the "lack of any coverage in the media"; there were no posters or articles about the Days of the FRG in Hungary, so that "events can go unnoticed."[8]

This encounter points to the continued importance of socialist internationalism, which sought to maintain a united Eastern European cultural front vis-à-vis the West during the 1970s.[9] Cultural attachés from the "socialist community" regularly met, sought advice, and coordinated action. As explained by Radio Free Europe (RFE), what the Soviet Union and its allies wanted after Helsinki was the "political, military, and economic relaxation of tension—and nothing more." They continued to have reservations about Western ideas related to the flow of people, information, and ideas, and after 1975 domestic propaganda renewed its "struggle with western ideological influences, hostile propaganda, ideological aggression, and similar perils." Any Western mention of cultural and informational ideas, not to mention the new focus on human rights and dissidents, was countered as an "attempt to interfere in internal affairs." In 1977, Bulgarian representatives spoke of a "coordinated ideological campaign in the West [against the East], wrapped up in the slogans of Helsinki."[10] Thus, Bulgarian diplomats—like their Eastern European colleagues—frequently summoned foreign ambassadors to convey their dissatisfaction with the coverage Bulgaria received in their country, and remained unsatisfied "with the famous statement about the freedom of the press" in Western democracies.[11]

But while Bulgarian representatives were busy organizing exhibitions and other high-profile events, their Western partners often insisted on more mundane, face-to-face cultural contacts through film showings, book readings, and informal meetings. At the heart of this tension were different understandings of the role of culture, which the East saw as a state-directed project of cultural exchange, and the West understood as a more spontaneous process of cultural interaction.[12] Because of these conflicting views of culture, some urgent questions dominated the efforts of small Bulgaria and its Western partners. If in the Eastern view culture was the flip side of ideology, what was the most effective way to carry out cultural exchange in the West? From the Western perspective, would allowing more Eastern European culture in the West only serve the propaganda goals of communist elites? Or did cultural exchange provide a window into the way of life in the West that could destabilize Eastern European regimes? The way West and East interpreted the role of culture reflected their competing ideas of state, society, and human rights. Ultimately, as Bulgarian elites promoted their cultural ideas, they sought to advance their ideas of state, which explains the critical importance of culture in the contacts between East and West in the context of détente.

For the Bulgarians, the goal was to organize their own cultural breakthroughs abroad, while limiting Western events at home, a common strategy of all socialist states. When Western culture came to Bulgaria, it tended to be classical: English watercolors, French tapestries, Roman treasures from the Rhine, or Celtic art from Gallia. But mass culture was frowned upon: books and films remained suspicious, as did meetings at Western embassies that could provide access to unwanted print materials. This distinction between real culture and mass culture remained at the heart of Bulgarian (and state socialist) ideas of the functions of the cultural front during developed socialism. Bulgarian experts used the phrase "true arts" (istinsko izkustvo) to promote their vision of culture, which was essentially seen as high culture aimed at the masses, as opposed to culture in the West, which they saw as split between elite culture reserved for the rich, and cheap, vulgar mass culture. As a result of this fundamentally different conception of culture, distrust and vigilance in regard to Western cultural events remained the norm. At the same time that Bulgaria sought access to the best exhibition spaces and performance halls in the West, requested more publicity in the media, and expected political recognition of its cultural efforts at the highest levels, officials zealously policed what type of Western culture could be shown in Bulgaria.

As I show in this chapter, there was a dynamic interplay between culture, ideology, and propaganda in the way Bulgaria staged its cultural presence in the West; indicatively, Bulgarian functionaries continued to speak about "cultural-propaganda events." But there was a slippage in the use of those terms. While internally the Bulgarian cultural events in the West were spoken about as an aspect of propaganda and described as an "ideological breakthrough," once on foreign ground the Bulgarian organizers muted their ideological message, focused on culture, and embraced a universal, humanistic vocabulary. I stress that Bulgarian cultural cooperation with the West was a state-sponsored initiative conceived and executed at the highest level of the political and intellectual bureaucracy, and ideology remained an important part of it. Yet, the success of these events depended on the local endeavors of Bulgarian officials—and the cooperation of their Western European and American hosts—which created a space for the interaction of cultural practices from both sides of the ideological divide. The end result of this engagement was a dynamic cultural affair that spoke the language of universal human values and the common European historical heritage. Through this project of self-fashioning, a small socialist state meticulously cultivated an international image that promoted universal ideas.

East and West in the 1970s: From Détente to the New Cold War

To understand the logic of Bulgarian cultural engagement with the West, it is necessary to outline the key developments in East-West relations during this time, which became a reference point for the Bulgarian power elites making cultural decisions. The 1970s was a decade of economic upheaval, domestic political shifts, social tensions, and cultural contradictions, yet in a global context it marked the period of the mature Cold War when the two blocs continued to normalize their relations. The process of détente included a variety of political strategies aimed at East-West reconciliation, which emerged out of concerns over the unsustainability of the Cold War escalation following the Cuban missile crisis. The 1960s had already seen an increase in the exchange of ideas between the East and the West. By the 1970s, political elites on both sides had embraced the idea of "antagonistic cooperation" with the goal of decreasing the likelihood of direct confrontation and establishing a process of negotiating differences.[13] This stabilization allowed for the lessening of Cold War political tensions after the intense confrontation of the previous period, and was accompanied by the expansion of both elite and bottom-up opportunities for contact that allowed for the "imagining [of] a less fractured European future."[14]

The German question remained at the heart of East-West relations during the entire Cold War. While most evident during the Berlin crises of 1948–1949 and 1961, the unresolved international situation of the FRG and GDR continued to cause tensions between the Soviet Union and the United States. Thus, a breakthrough in the German question was instrumental for the evolution of détente. West German Ostpolitik was a game changer, as Chancellor Willy Brandt, a Social Democrat and a former mayor of West Berlin, adopted an *"active* strategy of engaging . . . communist neighbors."[15] After his emotional visit to the Warsaw Ghetto Uprising Memorial in 1970, treaties signed with Moscow and Warsaw in 1970 de facto recognized the intra-German and the German-Polish borders. The Quadruple Agreement over Berlin in 1971 guaranteed Soviet consent in facilitating cross-border contacts. In 1973, the United Nations recognized and admitted the FRG and GDR as sovereign nations, and soon afterward treaties with Prague, Budapest, and Sofia restored diplomatic relations between the FRG and the rest of the Soviet allies. That same year, Brandt received the Nobel Peace Prize.[16] Advancing the cause of reconciliation, German and Polish religious leaders, journalists, and activists creatively used this new opportunity for communication to promote "peaceful change through . . . human contacts." This West German engagement with the East "transformed the global environment of the Cold War" by demonstrating the viability of political, economic, and cultural contacts among ideological adversaries.[17]

The restored lines of communication between West Germany and its neighbors contributed to the eventual multilateralization of East-West cooperation. The process culminated in the signing of the Helsinki Final Act in August 1975, following three years of negotiations at the Conference on Security and Cooperation in Europe. The provisions of Basket One—which included the inviolability of frontiers and non-intervention in internal affairs—carried an important political significance for the Soviet Union by recognizing the post–World War II European borders. But for the West, the most important accomplishment was the inclusion of the language of personal freedoms and human rights in the Helsinki Accords, which provided a pretext to push for reforms in the Soviet bloc. The provisions of Basket Three—which pertained to travel, family reunification, educational cooperation, and "the free flow of information"—sanctioned further increase in East-West communication. In the view of Sarah Snyder, the role of Basket Three was to "'unfreeze the situation' in Eastern Europe by exposing people to new influences" and "open the Iron Curtain through human contacts" on a new scale.[18] The process agreed upon in Helsinki—even though only functioning as a "declaration of intention"—bound Eastern European and Western elites to negotiate differences and maintain contacts across ideological divides for the rest of the Cold War.

Yet, more cynical interpretations present the rapprochement between West and East as a strategy of political legitimization by ruling elites following the profound domestic challenges that both Western and Eastern politicians experienced during the protests of the late 1960s. In the analysis of Jeremi Suri, "After two decades of Cold War rivalry, policy makers felt that they understood their foreign enemies and could rely on their consistency and pragmatism."[19] In other words, the enhanced East-West contacts could boost the credentials of political leaders without much risk. This analysis of détente as a conservative reaction by political elites who wished to reinforce the status quo certainly explains the willingness of communist leaders to embrace it. During this exact time period in the early 1970s, Bulgarian power elites expanded their contacts with the West through both cultural and economic cooperation, justifying their new partnerships with their previous ideological enemies in the language of détente. The Bulgarian case confirms that the period of late socialism in Eastern Europe was a time of gradual elite reorientation toward the West, which would fully crystalize in the 1980s.[20]

What was the West to Bulgaria in the 1970s? While the terms West and Western remained frames of reference in diplomatic correspondence and media coverage in the 1970s, the Bulgarian choice phrase was "developed capitalist states" (*razviti kapitalisticheski strani*), which also included Japan and Australia, while the term Western itself was largely reserved for the United States and Western Europe. At the same time, in the 1970s there was widespread recognition that the United States and its Western European allies diverged on key issues, ranging from the economy to arms control, especially after Thatcher's and Reagan's renewal of Cold War rhetoric; similar to the Western "differentiated approach" to Eastern Europe, which treated each communist regime based on its domestic reforms and international contacts, Bulgarian officials were sensitive to the differences between their Western partners. While the rhetoric of "Western imperialism and capitalism" persisted, the Bulgarian approach to the developed capitalist states was emphatically nuanced, and policies toward the specific states varied widely.

When questioning the coherence of a Western bloc during the Cold War, no other state stands out more than Austria, a neutral country since the reconstitution of the Austrian Republic in 1945. Austria played the role of "mediator in the relationship between East-West" and maintained active cooperation with socialist states.[21] The Socialist Party of Austria was in power throughout the 1970s, pursuing further expansion of political, economic, and cultural contacts in the context of détente. Its leadership constantly "warned [other] Western European leaders not to play along with American . . . politics."[22] For Bulgaria, "the importance of Austrian-Bulgarian relations lies in the fact that Austria combines the advantages of being technologically and economically a Western state with those of having a neutral status and being both geographically and in its political and cultural traditions closer to the Balkans than other neutral countries like distant Sweden or somewhat isolationist Switzerland." For Austria, Bulgaria was an important partner due to its strategic location. In the words of one Austrian politician, "the Austrians regard all people who border on the Danube as their neighbors."[23] The "goodwill" between the two countries had steadily built up since the 1960s, with high-profile visits, expanding economic ties, growing tourism, and visa-free travel.[24] When, in May 1975, Austrian chancellor Bruno Kreisky (1970–1983) visited Bulgaria, the two countries found common language in the Helsinki vocabulary of "peaceful coexistence between states of different social systems."[25] In the early 1980s, state visits covered a range of topics, from ski lift construction to family reunifications.[26]

France was also an important Bulgarian partner due to its aspirations to serve as an intermediary between the Cold War superpowers. Based on the priorities set under Charles de Gaulle in the 1960s, France wished to overcome the bloc mentality of the Cold War and create a counterweight to the two-superpower reality. Its leadership pursued a "firm dialogue" with the Soviet Union and the rest of the Eastern European countries through cultural contacts and political consultations. France held first place in cultural exchange with Eastern Europe because of its policies of "building bridges" with the Soviet Union since the 1960s. The French goal was to counterbalance U.S. hegemony and cement its reputation as "the third most important power" globally.[27] In April 1976, nine months after Helsinki, when Foreign Minister Jean Sauvagnargues visited Bulgaria, international observers noted "the excellent if modest" relations and the absence of "divergences or disagreements" between the two countries.[28] Bulgaria remained, in the French opinion, a loyal Soviet ally, but political contacts with the smaller Eastern European countries were helpful from a French perspective as they gave indications of Soviet intentions. Due to the traditional French involvement in the Balkans, its interest in Bulgaria remained solid.[29] From the Bulgarian perspective, in the late 1970s relations with France were "warmer than those with any other Western country except perhaps the FRG."[30]

Throughout the 1970s, relations with West Germany were also steadily improving.[31] Bulgaria and the FRG only established diplomatic relations in December 1973, as a part of Chancellor Willy Brandt's (1969–1974) Ostpolitik offensive. For the Bulgarians, the "realism" of the Social Democrat Brandt promised the desired "transition from the Cold War" to "lasting coexistence."[32] Similarly to France, West Germany also used culture "to build bridges" with Eastern Europe, so this line of gradual rapprochement was appealing to political elites in both countries.[33] Further, relations between Bulgaria and the FRG were not burdened with the emotional cost of the Polish and Czechoslovak historical experiences, not to mention the competing agendas between the FRG and the GDR.[34] Trade relations, tourism, the transit of German Turks through Bulgarian territory, and terrorism in the aftermath of the Munich Olympics brought the two countries together in the mid-1970s.[35] Tourism and trade increased, turning West Germany into Bulgaria's most important economic partner by the late 1970s. Cultural, scientific, technological, sports, and tourist exchanges also proliferated, overtaking those with the French. The visit of Chancellor Helmut Schmidt (1974–1982), also a Social Democrat, in May 1979—during which Zhivkov and Schmidt joined a much-publicized folk dance in the streets of Varna— "kept the détente ball rolling."[36]

Given the improving relations with Austria, France, and West Germany, the indifference of Great Britain and the United States to Bulgaria were conspicuous, pointing to their different priorities in Europe. The Bulgarian leadership wished to expand its contacts with Great Britain, one of the traditional European powers, but treated the country with caution because it saw it "as being too close to the USA; lacking the independence and initiative of France . . . and not having the same immediate interest in and commitment to détente as the FRG."[37] In the Bulgarian opinion, British foreign policy in the 1960s and 1970s was best understood "in light of lost imperial glory and a substantial decrease in economic and military might," which made it dependent on the United States and NATO.[38] British diplomats admitted that their "inactivity [in Bulgaria] contrasts with the activity of our allies," as the Labour government of Jim Callaghan (1976–1979) had repeatedly declined Bulgarian invitations for state visits.[39] Matters worsened when Margaret Thatcher (1979–1990) came to power in May 1979; in the Bulgarian view, hers was "one of the most ring-wing, reactionary, and conservative governments after World War II." Thatcher maintained that the West should unite against the East because, almost five years after Helsinki, the Soviet bloc had done nothing on human rights, while it had benefited politically and economically from détente; thus, she only reluctantly cooperated with Eastern European states.[40]

In terms of the United States, contacts between the two countries had been minimal since a breach in diplomatic relations from 1950 to 1959.[41] Normalization of relations began after the end of the U.S. military involvement in Vietnam in 1973 and sped up when Bulgaria signed the Helsinki Final Act in 1975. In June 1977, during the presidency of Democrat Jimmy Carter (1977–1981), the two countries concluded an agreement for cultural cooperation, and in 1978 negotiations at the level of deputy foreign ministers and visits of U.S. senators to Bulgaria resumed.[42] Liudmila Zhivkova's two visits to the United Nations in New York City, in 1977 and 1979, paved the way for more talks. During those visits, she met informally with President Carter and Secretary of State Cyrus Vance; despite the unofficial character of these meetings, they were publicized in Bulgaria as a political breakthrough, demonstrating the charged propaganda potential of any contact between East and West.[43] When the Republican Ronald Reagan arrived in the Oval Office in 1981, however, the tempo of contacts slowed down. For U.S. policymakers, the lack of political crises or dissident activities confirmed the cliché of Bulgaria being "the Soviet Union's most obedient partner," and so the country remained on the margins of U.S. interest.[44] Given the reserved attitude of the White House, the Bulgarian strategy was to extend invitations to U.S. senators and representatives, typically Democrats who opposed Reagan's foreign policy agenda, to participate in political talks during their European trips.[45] This strategy seemed to work: in 1979 Senator Adlai Stevenson argued on the floor of the U.S. Senate that Bulgaria did not deserve its reputation as "one of the most repressive nations in Eastern Europe" and emphasized that the American "misperception" was due to "neglect."[46] As is clear, Bulgaria's international reputation in the 1970s was becoming more nuanced and moving away from the perception that the country was a ruthless dictatorship and the Soviet master satellite.

Despite the advancement of East-West dialogue, international crises in 1980 associated with the Soviet invasion of Afghanistan in December 1979 and the Polish events surrounding the establishment of Solidarity in August 1980 created new tensions.[47] These developments transformed the dynamics of East-West rapprochement, leading to the perception of the beginning of a new Cold War. During his visit in June 1981, Austrian chancellor Kreisky gave a talk at Sofia University titled, "Is the Policy of Détente a Policy of Illusion?," which criticized the Soviet invasion of Afghanistan.[48] That summer, when the socialist François Mitterrand became the new French prime minister, he began to act as a champion of human rights by criticizing the situation in Poland and condemning the Soviet intervention in Afghanistan. Every so often, he expressed the opinion that real socialism in the Soviet bloc resembled totalitarianism.[49] Even West Germany, the "bridge-builder," chose to join the U.S. boycott of the Moscow Olympics in the summer of 1980.[50] In July 1981, when Foreign Minister Hans-Dietrich Genscher visited Sofia, he sent a message to the entire Warsaw Pact, which had just convened in the Bulgarian capital, warning that "the West will not intervene in Poland and no one else should."[51] In response, and likely speaking for the Soviets, Foreign Minister Petar Mladenov declared that Poland was a sovereign state, but indicated that events there were of "vital importance to the entire socialist community." He then cautioned that "the liquidation of everything positive achieved during the 1970s" was possible because "détente is greatly endangered" by the Western position.[52] From détente without illusions, the two sides had reverted to the illusion of détente.

The Framework of Cultural Exchange with the West

What was the role of culture in the evolving East-West dialogue of the long 1970s? With the advent of a new Cold War stalemate in 1980, cultural cooperation remained a steady channel of communication between East and West that allowed political rapprochement to survive in the 1980s. Similarly to their Polish, Hungarian, or Yugoslav colleagues, Bulgarian officials were promoting the notion of a common European heritage as a cornerstone of their cultural activities in the West.[53] Shared visions of European history and identity continued to bring political opponents together in a cautious yet determined exchange of ideas for the rest of the Cold War.

Throughout the Cold War, both East and West heavily invested in cultural diplomacy to convince the world of the superiority of their political and economic models.[54] If "the Cold War was, in its essence, a struggle between ideas," cultural relations structured the ideological content of the broader framework of political, economic, and military relations through the "transmission of ideas and values." In this interpretation, exporting culture was "an offensive strategy designed to propagate the successes of the . . . system and attract new adherents and sympathizers."[55] In many ways, culture functioned as a proxy for propaganda; in East and West alike, the goal of official cultural programs abroad was to "pour . . . ideas and values into the minds of foreign public[s]."[56] Yet, the process was seen as a matter of compromise and mediation because both sides facilitated "access to the other side's society in return for the granting of corresponding access to one's own."[57] The idea of reciprocity thus became the guiding principle of official Cold War cultural contacts. Finally, while cultural cooperation led to the exchange of ideas and values, it also functioned as an instrument to advance political and economic dialogue: cultural relations often became the first step in establishing or expanding relations between countries in other spheres. Soft and hard power went hand in hand throughout this period, as culture served the overall policy agenda of the state.

Cultural relations between the Soviet Union and the West expanded under Nikita Khrushchev (1953–1964), who opened the country to foreign visitors, initiated cultural contacts with the West, and adopted internation-alism as an aspect of Soviet foreign policy.[58] The United States joined the battle to win hearts and minds by initiating its own cultural programs across the globe, including in Eastern Europe.[59] After 1956, both the Soviet Union and the United States created a rigorous institutional framework for scien-tific, technical, educational, cultural, and athletic cooperation, often explic-itly referred to as "exchange" (obmen in Russian). In Eastern Europe, the thaw after 1956 contributed to the internal cultural liberalization and more independent international involvement of Warsaw Pact members. Much of Eastern Europe experienced extensive transborder contacts, including the expansion of travel, experimentation with Western cultural ideas, and new consumer practices in the context of the global 1960s.[60]

Cultural exchange between East and West acquired new importance in the 1970s when Soviet leader Leonid Brezhnev (1964–1982) continued rap-prochement with ideological opponents, but also granted more autonomy to his Eastern European allies. In the context of Ostpolitik, cultural contacts functioned as a diplomatic tool of reconciliation between West Germany and Poland.[61] After the signing of the Helsinki Final Act in 1975, cultural diplomacy continued to be an important arena of interaction between world leaders because many of the new ideas associated with Helsinki were tested out in the cultural sphere. In particular, Basket Three of the Helsinki Final Act, with its insistence on the free flow of ideas, information, and people, became the target of Eastern European attacks. According to the Bulgar-ian Telegraph Agency (BTA), after Helsinki the West unleashed a "Fourth Basket" against the East—a "basket of lies and slanders, of fabrications and accusations, of base intrigues."[62] Because capitalist states "utilize[d] inter-national cultural cooperation to intervene in the internal affairs of other states under the pretext of . . . freedom of creativity and information," the organization of "cultural-propaganda events" became an important aspect of Bulgarian (and other Eastern European) foreign policy.[63] Despite these concerns, and even with the advent of the new Cold War in the early 1980s, cultural exchange continued to function as an important (and less politically charged) arena of interactions between East and West.

Bulgaria entered the Western cultural scene in the early 1960s, but due to financial constraints its initial cautious exploration had a limited impact.[64] When Liudmila Zhivkova became in charge of culture in 1975, she launched a number of ambitious projects at home and abroad. Cultural exchange with the West was a particularly obvious aspect of her policies. Zhivkova, an Oxford alumna, personally directed many of these projects. But a new generation of power elites, many within Zhivkova's circle, also saw cultural exchange as an exciting opportunity and used their newly cultivated Western contacts as leverage against the older generation in charge. As a result, throughout the 1970s Bulgarian culture went to the West and Western culture came to Bulgaria on a regular basis.

The political importance of Bulgarian cultural projects in the West is clear from the institutional arrangements for cultural cooperation. Cultural exchange with the developed capitalist states closely followed political mandates from the Central Committee of the BKP, coordinated with the Ministry of Foreign Affairs (MVnR). Cultural relations with Western states were outlined in bilateral agreements for cultural cooperation, usually renewed every two years, which included a preamble containing political declarations and a detailed plan of specific cultural events.[65] By the early 1980s, Bulgaria had cultural agreements with sixteen capitalist countries in Europe, North America, Australia, and Japan.[66] These agreements were the subject of heated discussions between diplomatic representatives. Generally, cultural attachés were in charge of the execution of cultural programs abroad, but due to their importance, ambassadors actively participated in the process of negotiating and overseeing these events. In Bulgaria, the Committee for Culture (KK) sought the endorsement of the Cultural Department of the Central Committee of the BKP and worked with MVnR on the specifics in each country, but also consulted with creative organizations, museums, theaters, and other cultural agencies on the concrete events in the official plan. After the 1300th anniversary became the centerpiece of these cultural campaigns in 1977, the National Coordinating Committee 1300 Years Bulgaria (NKK) oversaw the conceptualization and execution of the jubilee celebrations. Bulgarian representatives sought reciprocal commitments with Western governmental agencies such as the United States Information Agency (USIA, later USICA), which handled U.S. cultural cooperation across the globe and worked in cooperation with the State Department. Yet, given less centralized functioning of culture in the West, they also pursued contacts with independent cultural organizations—academic institutions or libraries, private museums or performance halls, and individual artists or performers—and often entered separate agreements with them. Cultural institutions and media outlets such as the Institute Français, the Goethe Institute, and the British Council also served as Bulgarian partners; while these institutions were funded publicly, they had independent programming, which made them attractive to the Bulgarians. Finally, left-wing activists, trade union leaders, and branches of the communist parties in the West maintained contact with the representatives of Bulgaria for their own reasons.[67]

The expansion of cultural relations with the West in the late 1970s created new dilemmas for Bulgarian cultural bureaucrats. One problem was how to deal with the issue of reciprocity that had been the guiding principle of Cold War cultural exchange since its inception. According to this principle, partner countries had to strive for "balanced export [and import]" of cultural products of reciprocal quality and impact.[68] As representatives of a small state with limited resources that often experienced cultural shortages, Bulgarian officials had to make careful decisions about how to distribute the available cultural products to allow for a balanced cultural program both abroad and at home. Debating what sort of events were best suited for the Western context, officials decided that, given the high propaganda stakes and the anticipated prestige effects of cultural events, cultural exchange with the West should emphasize quality rather than quantity. The rich cultural scene in the large Western capitals, such as Paris and London, created problems of visibility: Bulgarian events were simply not noticed, and so the Bulgarians had to present their best cultural products. This strategy generated heated discussions because when the best performers and artists were sent to the West, it was difficult to maintain internal momentum, which created a lackluster cultural scene at home and in the socialist countries.[69] Nevertheless, Bulgarian officials continued to expand cultural contacts with the West, with the understanding that it was "better to plan fewer events but to organize them well."[70]

The best solution to these dilemmas was meticulous and coordinated planning, which provides the perfect example of state management of culture under total mobilization of the state apparatus. Similarly to elsewhere, once the 1300th anniversary became the focus of Bulgarian efforts abroad, cultural functionaries and diplomats in the West designed detailed "jubilee plans," which were vetted by the MVnR and the NKK and required a final "general report" detailing their execution. In this context, Bulgarian officials throughout the world were in competition over cultural resources. As certain countries and institutions were prioritized over others, access to cultural resources became an aspect of the power struggles within a state bureaucracy operating under cultural shortages. The fact that the most acclaimed and ambitious Bulgarian exhibitions, folk ensemble tours, classical concerts, and publishing enterprises took place in the capitalist countries was indicative of the key role allocated to cultural exchange in the West. Only the activities in India and Mexico, the topic of chapter 5, were comparable.

Given the showdown between East and West after Helsinki, ideology remained an important justification for cultural contacts with the West. As evident from the rationale of officials at the KK, cultural activities in capitalist countries were based on the "class-party approach adjusted to the concrete socioeconomic conditions [in each state]."[71] Events in the West were supposed to follow an "uncompromising, coordinated ideological line" that emphasized the superior cultural practices in the "socialist community."[72] Culture was not the end goal, but the tool. Bulgarian officials constantly spoke about "cultural-propaganda work" whose objective was to showcase the "wide-ranging achievements of building mature socialism" and the Soviet bloc's commitment to "the end of the arms race and preservation of world peace."[73] Because hard-liners objected to cultural outreach to the West, this ideological framework was used for domestic justification of the rapid expansion of cultural exchange with the capitalist world. For example, in 1980 the KK opined that Bulgarian-U.S. cultural cooperation, coming from "diametrically opposing ideological, political, social, aesthetic, and moral perspectives," should be based on "the primacy of the communist party, proletarian internationalism, and peaceful mutual coexistence."[74] Similar ideological rhetoric permeated official state correspondence throughout the period.

The ideological reasons for cultural cooperation with the West, however, went hand in hand with broader reputational objectives that necessitated flexibility. The global Bulgarian cultural expansion was, ultimately, a campaign of self-fashioning, so Bulgarian cultural experts embraced humanistic and civilizational ideas that would be attractive to Western audiences. Thus, in the West, officials avoided the Marxist-Leninist vocabulary and adopted a universal tone that focused on Bulgaria's European identity: the goal of cultural exchange was "to emphasize the significant contribution of the Bulgarian people to the cultural-historical development of Europe."[75] Ambitiously, experts spoke about "enhancing the Bulgarian contribution to the spiritual treasury of humanity." In this view, "cooperation in the spiritual sphere inevitably should contribute to the elevation of the human being, the enrichment of original national cultures, [and] the mutual acquaintance of peoples and nations."[76] In this universal spirit, exporting culture to the West served to emphasize the Bulgarian contribution to European civilization and human progress.

The 1300-year jubilee became the centerpiece of this cultural offensive. For Zhivkova, the jubilee celebrations had to highlight the unity of past, present, and future and to express that today's Bulgaria, on the triumphant path of building communism, was the proud heir of an equally glorious past. The objectives of the cultural events associated with the 1300th anniversary were twofold: to "display the real contribution of Bulgarian culture to the development of human civilization" and to "stimulate [international] political, economic, cultural, and social relations, with a focus on the advantages and superiority of real socialism."[77] Official culture, carefully curated by Bulgarian officials, would help satisfy ideological, national, and reputational considerations, while also serving as an instrument for advancing political reconciliation and expanding economic relations with the West.

Culture, Not Propaganda: Bulgaria in the West

Bulgarian cultural cooperation with the West did not develop uniformly in each country, but had a common logic and followed directives from the top, like the events organized in the Balkans. Detailed plans, meticulous coordination between institutions, painstaking reporting, and competition over resources defined these engagements. While adjustments were made in individual countries to meet local conditions, the core message—and the cultural products used to channel that message—remained the same.[78] The expectation for Bulgarian cultural events in the West was that they would emphasize "the significant contribution of the Bulgarian people . . . in the cultural-historical development of Europe," advertise "the achievements of real socialism in our country (the social and material benefits of the population, peaceful foreign policy, high level of culture)," and enhance Bulgaria's image "as a country with a modern economy."[79] This refined vision of cultural-propaganda work relied on culture, not ideological arguments, to highlight the achievements of contemporary Bulgaria. Under the wise guidance of its current political leaders, a modern nation was saluting its past.[80]

The centerpiece of cultural efforts in the West was the organization of "prestigious events" (*prestizhni meropriiatiia*) and "representative exhibitions" (*predstavitelni izlozhbi*) that showcased the best of Bulgarian culture during its 1300-year development. In 1973, the Central Committee of the BKP approved an ambitious project: experts from the Institutes for Archaeology and Thracology gathered over eight hundred golden and silver artifacts from more than twenty-three museums to put together a spectacular exhibition to display the best of Thracian archaeology. *Thracian Culture and Art*, later known internationally as *Thracian Treasures from Bulgaria*, opened in Paris in 1974, went to Moscow, Leningrad, Vienna, London, and New York City in 1975–1977, and eventually toured all major European capitals.[81] In 1976, another high-profile exhibition began its career. Showcasing artifacts from the ninth to the nineteenth centuries, *1000 Years of Bulgarian Icons* highlighted the role of "orthodoxy as part of national history," which was somewhat of a surprise for the West, and emphasized the achievements of Slavic culture in European civilization. This exhibition premiered in the Soviet Union and France and also made a tour of famous museums, collecting overwhelmingly positive reviews.[82] *Medieval Bulgarian Civilization*, *Treasures of the Rila Monastery*, and *Ethnographic Treasures of Bulgaria* followed. Because of their reputational purposes, these exhibitions were usually organized on the occasion of national holidays and anniversaries, such as the thirtieth anniversary of the socialist revolution in 1974 or the centennial of the Bulgarian state in 1978. Later, most events in the West were explicitly dedicated to the 1300-year jubilee.

The core message of these exhibitions, consistent with the "patriotic turn" and embrace of cultural nationalism in the 1970s, was to display the glorious history of Bulgaria, one of the oldest European states, established in 681. Charting the centuries-long history of today's Bulgaria, these exhibitions proudly showcased Thracian civilization, the pre-Greek, indigenous populations in the Bulgarian lands. They highlighted the rich Bulgarian medieval tradition, especially emphasizing the Bulgarian role in the preservation and dissemination of the Slavic alphabet and literacy. Icons emphasized the link between religion and nationality, an important marker of Bulgarian national identity. Folk objects showed the authenticity and longevity of the Bulgarian

FIGURE 16.   A banner for the exhibition *Thracian Treasures from Bulgaria*, Metropolitan Museum of Art, New York City, June 1977. Source: TsDA, f. 405, op. 9, a.e. 667, l. 145a.

spirit and traditions since times immemorial. Modern art pieces demonstrated the commitment to remain in the cultural avant-garde of humanity. No doubt, these were messages that pursued ambitious civilizational claims. Yet, while conceptualized around historical themes, these exhibitions tried to avoid a "nationalist overdose" in a refined and professional attempt to showcase the historical trajectory of "one of the oldest states of Europe." But there was a (not so) subtle ideological nuance in this promotion of Bulgarian culture to the West. At the opening of *Thracian Treasures* in Vienna in March 1975, Liudmila Zhivkova delivered a message of national pride by claiming that "in some respects [Thracian culture] is superior to Greco-Roman culture," but she also, rather deceptively, described the Thracians as "a newly discovered culture only studied under the people's rule."[83] Only under the care of the current socialist regime—and thanks to the "achievements of real socialism"—was the full glory of history being properly recovered, preserved, and displayed. A careful balancing of culture and ideology was underway.

The treasures concept seemed to resonate in the West. In 1976, Western journalists covered Bulgaria's "most glittering cultural treasures, such as icons and ancient Thracian ornaments" in detail and praised their "successful tours of western capitals."[84] When *Thracian Treasures* opened in London, British Museum experts opined that it would "rival the Tutankhamen exhibition" that had attracted 1.6 million visitors; the première of a lavish European civilization that predated the Greeks and the Romans was certainly attractive.[85] In 1978, when Zhivkova visited France to sign the new cultural exchange agreement, she spoke about her country as "one of the oldest European states and a country of rich ancient culture."[86] Echoing this language, in 1981 UNESCO issued a resolution "recognizing the contribution of one of the oldest states of Europe . . . to the development of world historical processes" and recommending to its member states to "mark this anniversary in a suitable manner."[87] The civilizational rhetoric stuck: during his visit to Bulgaria in 1979 FRG chancellor Schmidt called the upcoming 1300th anniversary "a remarkable jubilee of the Bulgarian people and European civilization."[88] After the opening of the *Medieval Civilization* exhibition in Paris in 1980, *Figaro* emphasized how its five hundred artifacts "lifted the curtain from medieval Bulgaria," revealing the vast territories of the Bulgarian empires and their continuity since 681.[89] Such high-profile events emphasized the European credentials of a country what wished to claim its rightful place in the past, present, and future of the old continent. As Bulgarian elites had hoped, small Bulgaria was now proudly emerging as an important contributor to European civilization.

There was nuance in the choices that Bulgarian officials made in expanding cultural contact with their concrete Western partners that depended on the respective framework of political relations with each country. In the case of France and Austria, cultural relations in the 1970s built upon extensive prior contacts, both from the interwar period and the beginning of Bulgaria's "opening" in the 1960s. A cultural agreement between France and Bulgaria was signed in 1966 and included events in the spheres of music, film, art, theater, and literature. Bulgarian and French performers, musicians, artists, and public figures regularly exchanged visits.[90] For a small country trying to make its international debut with a splash, the allure of Paris, "one of the largest, if not the largest, centers of Western culture," was irresistible.[91] When in 1973 the Central Committee of the BKP approved the first major Bulgarian international overture, the *Thracian Treasures*, its first showing, from May to August 1974, was at the Petite Palais in Paris.[92] In March 1976 the "very beautiful" *1000 Years of Bulgarian Icons* exhibition also opened at Petite Palais, drawing large crowds.[93] In 1978, *Contemporary Bulgarian Art* marked the Bulgarian centennial in Paris.[94] Cooperation further developed with UNESCO, also stationed in Paris, including events associated with the International Year of the Child in 1979 and the 700th anniversary of the medieval Orthodox Christian composer Ioan Kukuzel (Jean Coucouzèle) in 1980.[95] In 1980, much to Bulgarian satisfaction, a French diplomat declared that "the average Parisian was used to and expected Bulgarian cultural events" because "small Bulgaria is represented better than many larger states."[96]

Austrian-Bulgarian cultural contacts followed a similar upward trajectory: building on already established networks, the 1970s turned into a time of "all-encompassing dynamism," as Bulgarian officials were pleased to note.[97] In 1975, Vienna was the fourth world capital to show *Thracian Treasures*, after Paris, Moscow, and Leningrad; more than 110,000 Austrians visited the exhibition at the Museum of Applied Arts (Museum für angewandte Kunst or MAK).[98] The same year, the Bulgarian government purchased Haus Wittgenstein, an early example of architectural modernism in Vienna, and renovated it to house the Bulgarian Cultural-Informational Center that opened in 1977, the first such institution in a capitalist state. In February 1977, the *1000 Years of Bulgarian Icons* exhibition opened, also at MAK. Throughout 1978, the embassy marked the centennial of the Bulgarian state with various events, including a Bulgarian National Gallery exhibition at the Albertina.[99] In 1979, Schallaburg Castle, an hour away from Vienna, became the stage for *7000 Years of Arts and Culture in Sofia*, an exhibition that attracted more than 110,000 visitors.[100] Austria's small size made Bulgarian events visible, attended, and expected. Between 1978 and 1981 there were 150 Bulgarian

cultural events in Austria, including concerts, art exhibits, academic conferences, publishing events, movie screenings, poetry readings, and meetings
at the embassy and Haus Wittgenstein, with an estimated attendance of
250,000.[101] Austria became one of the preferred destinations for official Bulgarian culture.

In the case of the FRG, the development of cultural and political relations
went hand in hand. Two cultural events framed the reestablishment of political relations between Bulgaria and the FRG. In January 1972, in the midst
of diplomatic activity behind the scenes, an exhibition of West German artists opened in Sofia. For the Bulgarians, "this exhibition is still another step
toward the further expansion of cultural relations between the two countries
and will contribute toward their knowing each other better." For the West
Germans, "this is a premiere, which will be followed by a number of other
manifestations in that direction."[102] The official establishment of diplomatic
relations between the two countries occurred in December 1973. In February 1974, another exhibition, *Architecture, Urbanization, and the Restoration of
Cities in the FRG*, opened in Sofia.[103] Once set in motion, culture played an
important part in the normalization of relations. The federal structure of the
FRG presented advantages as it allowed the organization of events without
the pitfalls of demands for reciprocity. In 1979 and 1980, *Thracian Treasures*
toured Cologne, Munich, and Hildesheim to great acclaim. At the exhibition
opening in Cologne, Zhivkova met with Chancellor Schmidt. Some 197,500

FIGURE 17. The exhibition *1000 Years of Bulgarian Icons* in Vienna, 1977. Source: *Bulgaria
Today*, no. 11, 1980.

people visited the exhibition in Cologne, which made it the second most visited *Thracian Treasures* showing ever, following the record of 360,000 visitors at the British Museum (which charged no entrance fee).[104]

Matters developed differently in Britain and the United States where tenuous political relations, especially after the elections of Thatcher in 1979 and Reagan in 1981, determined a different approach to culture. Given the lack of productive political relations, cultural cooperation played important public relations functions for the Bulgarian power elites because it provided substance in the official attempt to pursue contact with the West. In this case, the personal interests and choices of Zhivkova, who had written a thesis on Bulgarian-British diplomatic relations during her time at Oxford, played a large role.[105] Despite the indifference or even hostility of British politicians and the press, Zhivkova's associates pushed to organize the *Thracian Treasures* exhibition at the British Museum in London in 1976. The exhibition generated good press coverage and attracted a record number of visitors, while the visit of Queen Elizabeth II, even though completely coincidental, gave it the desired "official" stamp.[106] Following this success, during the centennial year 1978 Bulgaria prepared to show *1000 Years of Bulgarian Icons* at the Courtauld Institute of Art in London, followed by the Edinburgh Festival.[107] Yet, the assassination of émigré writer Georgi Markov a few weeks before the opening dampened the British public's enthusiasm for Bulgarian culture. Despite the openly hostile atmosphere, Bulgarian officials persisted with the organization of cultural events in Britain.

In the United States it was difficult for a small country to make its cultural events visible, so the Bulgarians were thinking in terms of "a large breakthrough representative of our culture."[108] The signing of a cultural cooperation agreement in June 1977 led to the intensification of contacts, which were facilitated by two appearances by Zhivkova at the United Nations in 1977 and 1979. In a highly publicized speech she made in 1979 on the occasion of the International Year of the Child, she passionately explained Bulgaria's hosting of the Banner of Peace International Children's Assembly.[109] The *Thracian Treasures from Bulgaria* exhibition visited the Metropolitan Museum in New York City between June and October 1977; it then went to the Boston Museum of Fine Arts. Other events followed. A Week of the Bulgarian Book at the Martin Luther King Memorial Library in Washington, DC, in March and April 1977 showcased Bulgarian fiction.[110] The Library of Congress and the Bulgarian National Library concluded a cooperation agreement including book exchanges and librarian visits.[111] The Pirin Folk Ensemble toured the United Stated for three months in 1979, including concerts at Carnegie Hall in New York City and the Kennedy

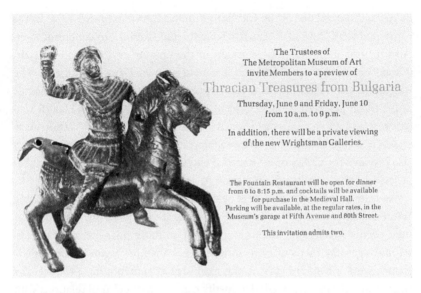

The Trustees of
The Metropolitan Museum of Art
invite Members to a preview of

Thracian Treasures from Bulgaria

Thursday, June 9 and Friday, June 10
from 10 a.m. to 9 p.m.

In addition, there will be a private viewing
of the new Wrightsman Galleries.

The Fountain Restaurant will be open for dinner
from 6 to 8:15 p.m. and cocktails will be available
for purchase in the Medieval Hall.
Parking will be available, at the regular rates, in the
Museum's garage at Fifth Avenue and 80th Street.

This invitation admits two.

FIGURE 18. Invitation to the opening of *Thracian Treasures from Bulgaria* at the Metropolitan Museum of Art. Source: TsDA, f. 405, op. 9, a.e. 667, l. 143.

Center in Washington, DC.[112] From the Bulgarian perspective, these events constituted a true breakthrough in their relationship with their prime ideological adversary.

As Bulgarian elites expanded their cultural contacts with the West, they took advantage of new global trends connected to the more rapid circulation of ideas and technologies in the 1970s. To maximize the effect of their programs abroad, officials used new cultural tools, such as the format of "complex events," which combined cultural events with the distribution of printed materials and the broadcast of radio and television programming to create a concentrated Bulgarian presence in the country of choice. Often, cultural events were combined with economic initiatives, such as Bulgarian tourism days or economic fairs. During the *Thracian Treasures* exhibition in London in 1976, officials also organized an academic conference on Thracology and supplied the BBC with a film on Thracian art in Bulgaria. As a result, "the [British] press published many materials . . . with the most positive reviews on Bulgarian archaeology . . . and Bulgaria in general."[113] In New York City in 1977, too, experts innovated with technologies of cultural dissemination: the *Thracian Treasures* exhibition was accompanied by a conference at the Archaeological Institute of America, the screening of films, the distribution of print materials, and the broadcast of radio and television programs.[114] As time went on, these events became more complex. When *1000 Years of*

Bulgarian Icons opened at the City Museum in Munich in March 1978, it was combined with Days of Bulgarian Tourism and Cuisine, an economic symposium, and an agricultural seminar; in the opinion of Bulgarian officials, it was "practically" as if Munich had held its own Days of Bulgaria. The Bulgarians also used new strategies to encourage attendance at their events: at the *Bulgarian Icons* exhibition in Munich, the 20,000th and 40,000th visitors received a free seven-day tour of Bulgarian monasteries.[115] While these endeavors were indicative of overreaching attempts at central planning, they also revealed the ability of communist elites to take advantage of new global processes and use cultural innovation to spread their ideas of state.

As Bulgarian cultural experts perfected their methods for approaching Western audiences, they continued to moderate the ideological framing of their events. Over time, ideology gave way to more nuanced, even universal messages: the focus was on culture, rather than propaganda. Ideological clichés were inevitably part of the extensive documentation produced by Bulgarian officials who needed to justify expansion of cultural relations with the West. But as cultural functionaries pursued contacts with any Western partners willing to accommodate their priorities, they put aside the ideological language for the sake of a more universal civilizational message. When the *Thracian Treasures* went to New York City in 1977, the official goal of the exhibition was to "familiarize the American public with the ancient roots of Bulgarian culture, to underscore the attention our country gives to our heritage, [and] . . . to acquaint the Americans with contemporary Bulgarian socialist culture and art."[116] But in its execution, the focus was on the glorious ancient past rather than the success of socialist Bulgaria. This was an exhibition for educated, cosmopolitan audiences who wished to find out more about "the obscure circumstances of the ancient and rugged Thracian culture" and marvel at "the significant art of 'barbarian' peoples who have contributed far more to the advanced civilizations of Greece, China, India, and Persia than previously was recognized."[117] In the end, ideology was muted to emphasize universal historical contributions, a strategy that attracted large Western audiences to Bulgarian exhibitions throughout the world.

In effect, different languages were used internally and externally to promote the Bulgarian cultural presence in the West: domestically, the focus was on propaganda, while internationally, the emphasis was on culture. In November 1980, noted Bulgarian poets and close associates of the Zhivkov clan Liubomir Levchev and Georgi Dzhagarov read their work at the Library of Congress. These two came with impeccable political credentials—Dzhagarov served as vice chair of the State Council while Levchev was the chairperson of the Union of Bulgarian Writers. As noted in official correspondence, their presence served to demonstrate "our desire to continue the policies of détente and the development of cultural ties [with capitalist countries] during a period of renewed pressures against socialism."[118] But the actual presentations adopted an apolitical, universal language. As the U.S. coverage of the visit remarked, "Bulgarians and Americans may live in different corners of the world, but good poetry, which speaks to universal emotions, will unite those from different cultures."[119] On the global cultural scene, there was a dynamic relationship between ideology and culture in the execution of Bulgarian cultural programs in the West.

"A Remarkable Jubilee": 1300 Years Bulgaria in the West

As 1981 approached, Bulgarian representatives in the West began celebrating the 1300th anniversary, as in the rest of the world, by organizing prestigious events dedicated to the jubilee. In France in June 1980 the *Bulgarian Medieval Civilization* exhibition opened in the Galeries du Grand-Palais. In October, Days of Bulgarian Culture at the Georges Pompidou Center featured photography, book exhibits, films, and musical performances.[120] In Austria in October 1980 *Treasures of the Rila Monastery* opened in the building of the Vienna Town Hall (Rathaus). In February 1981, some 5,000 Viennese residents participated in a ball at Hofburg Castle dedicated to the jubilee.[121] In the FRG, the *Thracian Treasures* exhibitions that opened in 1979–1980 were dedicated to the 1300-year jubilee.[122] Celebrations were more subdued in the United States and Great Britain where the Bulgarians were still working to organize high-profile events. This was particularly the case in Great Britain where "incessant anti-Soviet and anticommunist propaganda" after Markov's assassination undercut the Bulgarian plans.[123]

The establishment of national celebration committees in each Western country, consisting of sympathetic intellectuals, public figures, and politicians, was a priority. These committees would serve as organizational hubs for the 1300th anniversary celebrations. By the end of 1980, fourteen Western European countries, the United States, and Canada had established national committees honoring the 1300-year jubilee.[124] For the French committee, the Bulgarians successfully recruited the president of the National Assembly, the Gaullist Jacques Chaban-Delmas, as chair.[125] In the FRG, due to demands to include West Berlin, Bulgarian diplomats bypassed plans at the federal level and established subcommittees in Baden-Württemberg, Saarland, and Hamburg.[126] The British Committee of Honor for the Celebration of the 1300th Anniversary was chaired by Goronwy Owen Roberts

(Lord Goronwy-Roberts), deputy leader of the Labour Party opposition in the House of Lords.[127] In the United States, the National Jubilee Committee included prominent U.S. politicians and academics, from senators John Fulbright and Adlai Stevenson to the writers John Updike, Erskine Caldwell, and William Styron, and scholars of Balkan studies including John Bell, Frederick Chary, James Clarke, Charles Gribble, John Lampe, and Philip Shashko.[128] Karl Blecha, the deputy chief of the Austrian Socialist Party and member of parliament, served as chairman of the Austrian Jubilee Committee, which sponsored a meeting of the representatives of national jubilee committees from nineteen Western European countries in Vienna in February 1981.[129]

According to the plans of Bulgarian cultural bureaucrats, the celebration of the 1300th anniversary in each country had to contain a clear "culmination" during the jubilee year, preferably executed before the peak of domestic events in October 1981. In Austria, the culmination occurred on 14 June 1981, when 1,400 guests, including President Rudolf Kirchschlaeger, were present at the Vienna Opera House for the official celebrations (Zhivkova was in attendance as well). During a visit to Sofia in May 1981, Chancellor Bruno Kreisky had promised Austria's "political engagement and preparedness, at the highest levels, to popularize the 1300-year jubilee."[130] Elsewhere, the celebratory events were less glamorous but still solid. In April 1981, the Days of Bulgarian Culture in the FRG opened in Stuttgart and then continued in Saarbrucken, Munich, Wolfenbüttel, Hanover, and Oldenburg.[131] *Treasures of the Rila Monastery* visited Stuttgart, where exhibitions, performances, and book readings were also held. Exhibitions of Bulgarian books opened in Munich, Mannheim, Freiburg, and Münster.[132] Considering the upcoming presidential campaign in France, smaller events were held at the embassy in March 1981. Advertised as Days of Bulgaria, they featured lectures, concerts, photo exhibits, and film screenings.[133] In September 1981, diplomats held Bulgarian Days at the UNESCO headquarters.[134] In the United States, Bulgarian representatives organized a number of complex events dedicated to the 1300th anniversary: an ethnographic exhibition accompanied by folk concerts in Pittsburg; scientific symposia at Ohio State University and the University of Pittsburgh; and a Week of Bulgarian Culture in Los Angeles.[135] The mayors of New York City and Los Angeles sent congratulatory telegrams to the Bulgarian people for the anniversary, giving the desired official stamp to the events.[136] Despite Washington's official snub, the jubilee events in the United States were considered a triumph of Bulgarian culture abroad. By contrast, in Great Britain, the Days of Bulgarian Culture were a subdued affair because of a controversy with the British hosts.[137] The *Contemporary Bulgarian Art* exhibition, supposed to open at the Royal Festival

Hall in London, was envisioned as the centerpiece of the celebrations, but in June 1981 Svetlin Rusev, a close associate of Zhivkova's, pulled the artworks because the organizers had offered "only a hall" (*koridor*) for the showing.[138] Despite these uneven results, Bulgarian cultural products steadily flowed to the West throughout the anniversary year.

In the end, Bulgarian officials considered the 1300-year celebrations in the West a great success: small Bulgaria had achieved its goal of advertising its contributions to European and world civilization. Bulgarian cultural experts boasted: "There is hardly a world capital—from Washington to London, from Paris to Tokyo—that has not been engaged in an exciting opportunity to experience the extraordinary traditions and accomplishments of our people in culture and art."[139] As a result of the jubilee, for example, "hundreds of thousands of Austrians became acquainted with the glorious history of the Bulgarian people, its rich traditions and spiritual heritage, and its high contemporary achievements in all spheres of material and spiritual life."[140] In 1983, the new chairperson of KK, Georgi Iordanov, expressed the view that as a result of the 1300th anniversary celebrations, "the world, literally, 'rediscovered' the culture of old and new Bulgaria."[141] From the perspective of Bulgarian power elites, their focus on culture paid off as the 1300th anniversary extravaganza had fulfilled its reputational goals, solidifying Bulgaria's image as an important player in Europe's past, present, and future.

Propaganda, Not Culture: The West in Bulgaria

Because Cold War cultural exchange was based on the premise of reciprocity, the Bulgarians also had to open their domestic cultural scene for Western events. But bringing more Western culture home created the dilemma of how cultural organizers might control "cultural invasion" and "ideological aggression," reviving the ideological language for domestic consumption.[142] In the opinion of Bulgarian cultural functionaries, capitalist countries used "cultural exchange . . . to impose the capitalist way of life."[143] Thus Bulgarian officials diligently tried to control the spread of Western culture in Bulgaria and neutralize its "propaganda effects." For Bulgarian officials in charge of culture, the goal was to stage their own cultural offensive abroad, while limiting Western events at home, a strategy that caused Western irritation because Western cultural events took on a very muted form. Often, this was a matter of financial priorities: the Bulgarians exercised "disproportionate use of resources" to sponsor "an active program of cultural events . . . making the world conscious of the Bulgarian heritage."[144] State management of culture thus created an uneven cultural field. In 1978, RFE observed that

Bulgaria, "like East Europe in general, exports more of its culture to West Germany than Bonn does to Bulgaria."[145] In the view of the West Germans, the solution was to "insist that our artists and ensembles can perform in the East, too, and that we do not simply act as hosts to theirs."[146] Debates about cultural exchange thus became an important arena of communication in the context of East-West dialogues in the 1970s.

In their international cultural engagement, Bulgarian officials insisted on a distinction between "true arts" and mass culture, attaching an emphatically negative value to the latter. Liudmila Zhivkova proudly declared that she "abhors 'primitive aspects' of Western culture such as rock and avant-garde art" and, in line with her policies regarding beauty, insisted: "[In Bulgaria], we want to educate our people to beauty, to evolve a new consciousness which in itself will eliminate negative influences. . . . As to these primitive arts, the extremes of pop art, jazz, it is not art anymore and doesn't aid man's development . . . this desire for the more primitive behavior toward culture will die by itself."[147] "The jungle of mass culture" in the West, which was preoccupied with sex and violence, had nothing of value to offer, in contrast to "culture for the masses" in the East, which focused on vital social issues. Strolling the streets of Hamburg in 1978, encountering cheap books from kiosks and vulgar movies, a Bulgarian journalist condemned "the omnivorousness of culture" in the West: "the entrance to the true arts is reserved for the vanguard, for the elite [in the West] while the omnivorousness is left to the masses. This results from the nature of capitalism and deepens still further the spiritual crisis of the doomed world."[148] Western attempts to export "primitive arts" to the East were to be curtailed because mass culture was of no value for the socially engaged socialist citizens.[149] Instead, Bulgaria offered and wished to be exposed to the "true arts"—or one might say "real culture"—that encapsulated the best of humanity.

But while the Bulgarians insisted on prestigious exhibitions, classical music concerts, and folk ensemble visits, for the West cultural exchange had another mission, underlining the tension between the cultural projects pursued by East and West. The deputy foreign minister of Great Britain explained that "less spectacular but no less important, are the constant flow of specialist visitors, researchers and students, the organization of symposia and courses and the exchange of information in all spheres which together make up the day-to-day substance of the programme. Exchanges of this type make a valuable contribution by enabling our two peoples to become more closely acquainted with each other's history, culture, and way of life."[150] It was exactly those spontaneous aspects of cultural exchange that caused headaches for Bulgarian officials because they were unable to fully control them. After Helsinki, Western academic institutions provided stipends, scholarships, and internships to young academics and high schoolers, a new development that Bulgarian power elites interpreted as "careful but purposeful ideological aggression aimed at Bulgarian youth." The fear was that such exchanges would lead to the "systematic ideological indoctrination, not only of the participants but also their families, based on the stories [they would tell] after their return to Bulgaria."[151]

Throughout the 1970s, as they were expanding their cultural presence in the West, Bulgarian cultural functionaries were also trying to limit the exposure of their publics to Western art and culture, and especially popular music, books, and films. When exhibitions or concerts happened, the Bulgarians had ways to neutralize their "propaganda effects" by keeping the audiences small. As noted earlier, there were no announcements in the press or posters when the exhibition of FRG books opened at the National Library in November 1979, which coincided—completely by chance as the Bulgarian experts claimed—with a GDR exhibition on the Brothers Grimm at the same venue.[152] During the *Age of Shakespeare* exhibition in February 1979, the British organizers also wondered why slideshows and films were not projected as agreed upon and none of the 250 posters provided was seen on the streets of Sofia.[153] In February 1977, during a British poster exhibition in Sofia, the Bulgarian hosts demanded the removal of poster 85 (*Think Metric*) because it contained two Soviet stamps with images of Lenin and Stalin that were seen as politically "subversive." Despite British assurances that the poster had "no political meaning," even the British ambassador agreed that it was "tactless" to include an item that could be construed as "deliberately provocative."[154] Culture remained a politically charged affair, as East and West navigated their different conceptions of the role of international cultural contacts.

The Bulgarian authorities carefully filtered what aspects of cultural cooperation would be developed and who would be able to take advantage of them. In March 1978, the U.S. embassy extended an invitation to the KK to attend a screening of the film *Star Wars* at the embassy; after much deliberation a list of fourteen attendees, including political commissars, translators, and a technical team, was vetted.[155] Informal encounters between Western and Eastern youth were also carefully policed. In 1981, at a reception for former holders of the German Academic Exchange Service (DAAD) scholarship at the FRG embassy in Sofia, participants came across a journal, *Skala* (Range), that included information on the building of the Berlin wall and a biography of Lev Kopelev, a political activist and samizdat author whose Soviet citizenship had been revoked during a cultural exchange visit to the FRG. An extensive correspondence ensued after this incident, despite the insistence of West German diplomats that this was a "moderate publication" and no insult was intended to the Bulgarian attendees.[156] Vigilance and ideological screening remained the norm in the early 1980s, as cultural exchange could lead to unintended consequences.

The Bulgarians were highly suspicious of any exhibition proposed by USICA, their main conversation partner in official cultural exchange matters with the United States. Even a neutrally titled exhibition, *The Artist at Work in America*, seemed to have political overtones as it came with a library that contained undesired books (thus visitors had to be monitored) and audiovisual effects that were no match for Bulgarian technological abilities (emphasizing the superiority of American culture).[157] The topic of another exhibition proposed in 1982, *The American Museum: An Experience in Community*, also caused frantic correspondence because it envisioned the projection of films and the presence of U.S. curators.[158] Instead of having to deal with such treacherous cultural media, the Bulgarians wanted a "reciprocal event" on the scale of the *Thracian Treasures* exhibit at the Metropolitan Museum of Art in 1977. Bulgarian representatives thus proposed an exhibition of one hundred paintings from the Metropolitan to tour Bulgaria in 1979. Firmly committed to securing an apolitical exhibition, officials declined to accept a third photo exhibit, as proposed by USICA.[159]

When Western culture came to Bulgaria, it tended to be classical and universal, hence politically neutral. In 1976, Bulgarian officials boasted that their publics had been able to marvel at "Persian miniatures, Old Flemish art, English watercolors, contemporary Italian artists, and French Gallic art."[160] In 1978, Western cultural events organized in Bulgaria included French medieval sculptures from Bordeaux and the Vienna Burgtheater's performance of Goethe's *Ephigenia*.[161] In 1979, the *Age of Shakespeare* exhibition came to Sofia. Huge lines in front of ticket counters revealed a public hungry for Western cultural products.[162] The emphasis on the universal values of European civilization ultimately led to the convergence of the core message of Bulgarian and Western cultural presentations. As one of the "oldest states of Europe," Bulgaria now provided opportunities for other European states to showcase their "true arts," as well.

In November 1979, the opening of the exhibition *Leonardo da Vinci and His School* at the Crypt of the St. Alexander Nevski Cathedral marked one of the high points of this cultural flirtation with the West. This event was a part of the programs focused on "multifaceted personalities" that became a priority for Bulgarian cultural functionaries under Zhivkova.[163] The organization of this exhibition required coordination with a number of Western institutions and tested the abilities of Bulgarian cultural officials to deliver a world-class event. In the end, the exhibition showed loans or facsimiles of Leonardo's artwork and notes from British institutions, including the Victoria and Albert Museum, the National Gallery, and the British Museum, but also a copy of the *Mona Lisa* from the Louvre and other artworks from French and Italian museums. Sir Robin Mackworth-Young, treasurer at the Royal Library-Windsor, attended the opening of the exhibition while the British cultural attaché noted the long lines in front of the Crypt, "something that all major museums would envy."[164]

Encouraged by their ability to handle the organization of Western culture at home, in November 1980, Bulgarian officials sponsored a Cultural Week of the FRG. When the proposal for this event was first received, it caused a ripple of panic at MVnR because "we have never had a Days of Culture for a capitalist country."[165] The event opened under the aegis of FRG foreign

FIGURE 19. Poster for the exhibition *Leonardo da Vinci and His School* at the Alexander Nevski Crypt, November 1979. Source: *Bulgaria Today*, no. 2, 1980.

minister Genscher and Bulgarian culture minister Zhivkova; in the catalogue, both spoke of "continued dialogue" as the result of détente and "the common heritage of European culture" shared by both East and West.[166] This event featured the exhibition *Roman Treasures from the Rhine District* at the Archaeological Museum in Sofia; but also film screenings; ballet, theater and musical performances by top West German artists; a joint seminar of Hamburg and Sofia Universities; and meetings of former students of the Humboldt Foundation. In many ways, this was a West German "complex event" in Bulgaria. Learning from past experiences, the FRG embassy, together with Goethe Institute, took advertising into their own hands; it published advertisements in newspapers, held a press conference at the embassy, contacted journalists with interview opportunities, and posted five hundred posters in the central parts of the Bulgarian capital.[167]

Седмица на култypата
на Федерална република
Германия
в Народна република
България
17–23 ноември
1980 г.

FIGURE 20. Cover of the West German brochure published for the Cultural Week of FRG in Bulgaria, 17–23 November 1980. Source: TsDA, f. 405, op. 9, a.e. 593, l. 34.

The Bulgarian public was hungry for Western culture, so these were extremely popular events that attracted large crowds. Despite suspicions, Bulgarian officials had to accommodate the cultural demands of their population. At the end of the Cultural Week of the FRG, German officials admitted that "sometimes the Bulgarians surprised" them because they had sanctioned a disruption in the GDR's cultural domination in Eastern Europe.[168] Even in official Bulgarian interpretations, such cultural events were evaluated as beneficial because "the Bulgarian people wishes to live in peace, cooperation, and understanding with all peoples of the world, to broaden and enrich its horizons through communication with the cultural and spiritual achievements of other peoples." According to the laws of beauty envisioned by Zhivkova, culture was an "active means for the development of the individual and society, [and] a bridge to the future . . . in the name of peace and progress for our planet."[169] In the end, "true arts," even if they came from the West, had won a place in Bulgarian society.

Despite the dangers of ideological infiltration, Bulgarian officials continued importing Western culture. In 1981, the BTA talked about "a year of brisk cultural contacts."[170] That year, a photography exhibition from the British Museum, *Personal Views*, was shown in Sofia. There was a major exhibition of the British abstract sculptor Henry Moore in the prestigious Shipka 6 Hall in June; even though Moore was unable to attend due to poor health, he gifted "to the Bulgarian people" an original work of art dedicated to the 1300th anniversary.[171] In 1981, preparations continued for the exhibition *Egyptian Treasures from the British Museum*; conversations were underway to allow the Gospels of Ivan Alexander, a fourteenth-century manuscript of the Second Bulgarian Empire held at the British Museum, to tour Bulgaria.[172] In 1983, after years of trying to organize a "balanced" American cultural event, the Bulgarians finally secured an exhibition that lacked "propaganda effect": the *American Impressionists*, with sixty oil paintings from the Metropolitan Museum, was coming to Bulgaria.[173] The same year, the National Gallery in Sofia hosted *Five Centuries of Masterpieces*, "one of the finest private collections in the world," owned by Armand Hammer, the chief of Occidental Petroleum. The showing of Rubens, van Gogh, Monet, and Rembrandt, among others, drew 110,000 visitors.[174]

With all the perils of Western contact, in the early 1980s top Bulgarian officials insisted that "cultural, scientific-technical, tourist, and athletic exchanges contribute to the positive development of contacts and political dialogue, . . . the better acquaintance of the two peoples, and especially improvement in economic relations."[175] In 1982, Georgi Dzhagarov, the poet and vice president of the State Council, speaking at the Bulgarian embassy in

Paris, emphasized that Bulgaria's "historical fate [is] closely intertwined with the culture and interests of all peoples in Europe." In return, Minister of Leisure André Henry praised the accomplishments of "a state that has been at the crossroads of civilizations, at the crossroads of clashes in Europe."[176] This exchange is an eloquent example of the convergence of politicians in both East and West around shared notions of European identity. From the perspective of Bulgarian power elites, through cultural cooperation with the West, small Bulgaria had reclaimed its rightful place in European civilization.

Culture, Ideology, Propaganda: Conflicting Ideas of the State and Ways of Life

In the complex climate of the long 1970s, what was the role of culture in East-West dialogue? The insights of cultural diplomacy discussed earlier allow us to understand East-West cultural contacts as a battle for hearts and minds that ultimately focused on the different ways of life in East and West. In the Eastern European conception, official culture and its export to the West served ideological purposes whose goal was to emphasize the superiority of state socialist ideas. As anticommunist propaganda in the West embraced the human rights rhetoric of Helsinki from the mid-1970s on, official culture was able to create a more neutral image of the Eastern European way of life to disseminate in the West. Bulgarian officials were thus walking a fine line between culture, ideology, and propaganda, while also anticipating a similar slippage in the meaning of Western culture in Bulgaria.

Seeing culture as the flip side of ideology explains why the Bulgarians handled culture in the West in terms of propaganda and counterpropaganda. In the words of the BTA, the goal of Western propaganda was "to predispose people to the capitalist manner of living and most of all to the celebrated 'American style of life.'"[177] The notion that East and West followed different ways of life was based on different interpretations of the ideas of state, society, and human rights. As Benjamin Nathans has shown, there was a profound difference between the Eastern conception of human rights, based on social rights, and the Western conception, based on political rights.[178] In the West, the Bulgarians claimed, legal equality masked social inequality because the rhetoric of rights and freedoms was the product of "the right and freedom of the minority of monopolists to exploit the vast majority of working people."[179] In the same fashion, "freedom of the press in the West [wa]s a myth" because the media there were "tools of monopoly capitalism."[180] Eastern European criticism of the Western way of life was particularly sharp when directed against the United States. According to a BTA dispatch from

1977, in the United States American capitalists were free to "prohibit people with progressive sympathies" from occupying political positions, but "every criminal in Eastern Europe becomes the hero of the day." The Bulgarians vocally castigated the Americans: "In the 'freest country,' the USA, every citizen . . . has many other rights: to unemployment, to lower wages for equal work, to becoming the object of a notorious 'witch-hunt,' to keep consolation in films of violence, pornography, and drugs."[181] This was a struggle to claim the superiority of real socialism over Western pseudo-democracy. The Western obsession with human rights sought to distract from the root causes of capitalist exploitation, which celebrated political freedoms but neglected the basic social rights of its citizens.

This link between Bulgarian culture and ideology explains the palpable tension between Eastern and Western understandings of the role of international cultural contact during this time. From the Eastern European perspective, the goal of exporting culture to the West was to advertise real socialist ideas of state and society while limiting the access of Western propaganda to Eastern European societies. Soon after Helsinki, hard-liners at the Bulgarian Ministry of the Interior decried the spread of "hostile [Western] propaganda" as a result of the renewed contacts between East and West and appealed for "revolutionary vigilance."[182] This need for vigilance explains why the ideological language never disappeared from justifications of Bulgarian cultural events abroad. Because the West was involved in anticommunist "reactionary propaganda" against "the socialist social system," Bulgaria would "organize multifaceted, mass, and complex cultural-propaganda events" that would showcase "the achievements of real socialism in all spheres of material and spiritual life" and emphasize "the peaceful policy" of the Bulgarian government.[183]

Given the ideological function of culture, why did the West continue to engage in cultural contact with the East? Bulgaria's Western partners often objected to the use of cultural events for propaganda purposes: in November 1980, during a meeting of the Mixed Commission for Cultural Cooperation in Washington, a U.S. representative asked for an oral declaration that "the celebration of the [1300th] anniversary would not be accompanied by communist propaganda." In indignation, the Bulgarian ambassador threatened to leave the negotiation table.[184] But other Western experts recommended a less confrontational approach. Lord Goronwy-Roberts, the British deputy foreign minister overseeing Eastern Europe, explained the Western strategy: "Western democracy should not and need not challenge the totalitarian system as its centre, e.g., by crude and strident attitudes in human rights. We must roll up the flanks—by exploiting the attractions of the facts of western life to which individuals, especially the young, are so susceptible. The methods are clearly the proliferation of contacts and exchanges at all levels."[185] Other diplomats also agreed that "by pressing the regime to open more windows to the West, and keeping them open on our side, we can contribute a small impetus towards those changes and help to ensure that, if and when Moscow allows any more radical developments, Bulgaria (and particularly its young people) is ready to adopt them."[186]

With the disagreement between East and West over global priorities in the 1970s, cultural exchanges functioned as a way "to keep the temperature from cooling too noticeably."[187] The different perceptions of culture in East and West notwithstanding, by the mid-1970s culture had become the universal method of communication across ideological divides. Remarkably, this trend continued after the revival of Cold War tensions in 1980. In the summer of that year, a British diplomat advised: "take the hand and shake it . . . rather than slap it."[188] Knowing your enemy was the only alternative to constant Cold War confrontations. Culture remained a reliable strategy to bring East and West together in a shared European vision.

CHAPTER 4

Forging a Diaspora

On 1 September 1981, a "gathering [*sâbor*] of Bulgarians from abroad," dedicated to the 1300th anniversary, opened in Sofia. Some four hundred Bulgarians residing outside of the country—"regardless of ideological influences and nuance in political orientation or social status"—spent ten days visiting historical sites and monuments, participating in concerts and celebrations, and meeting with officials and Bulgarian citizens. Many of them, having been away from the motherland for years if not decades, "cried with pride and tender emotion [*umilenie*]" and "admired . . . new socialist Bulgaria." A group of twenty-three "activists" also met with Todor Zhivkov, who celebrated his seventieth birthday on 7 September, while on 9 September the visitors were offered the opportunity to attend the public celebrations of the national holiday, the day of the socialist revolution. In its evaluation of this event, the Slavic Committee, the organization in charge of Bulgarians abroad, concluded that this gathering "strengthened the national consciousness, self-esteem, and . . . dignity of our compatriots."[1] To further cultivate contacts between the state and émigrés, in 1982 the committee, freshly renamed the Organization for Bulgarians Abroad, drafted a "Program for Work with the Bulgarian Colony in Non-Socialist States"; its goal was "to embrace the Bulgarians living abroad," utilize their "patriotic-emotional feelings . . . for the benefit of our country, [and] showcase the thirteen-centuries of Bulgarian history and culture among our compatriots and the other peoples of the world." The organization compiled detailed plans for approaching Bulgarian communities in Western countries. Regarding the 12,000 Bulgarians in West Germany, who were described as "in the large majority . . . of patriotic orientation," officials envisioned work with existing cultural associations; educational exchanges for the second and third generation; the organization of Bulgarian language courses; the circulation of Bulgarian printed materials; the organization of lectures, film screenings, excursions, and summer camps in Bulgaria; and the celebration of appropriate anniversaries.[2]

This self-congratulatory take on the events notwithstanding, some Bulgarians living abroad were skeptical of the endeavors of the People's Republic of Bulgaria (NRB). On Christmas Eve 1982, an anonymous émigré in West Germany composed an open letter to the Slavic Committee, published in *Luch* (Ray), a publication of the Association of Bulgarian Writers and Artists in Exile, stationed in Los Angeles:

> Thank you for the vinyl record. Thank you that you remembered me at all. What really surprised me, however, is the way you addressed me in the enclosed message. Since when have we become "dear compatriots"?!? [*sic*] Up until yesterday we were "criminals," "enemies of the people," and "traitors of the motherland," and suddenly [we have become] "dear compatriots." How did you decide this? . . . Do you think anyone would believe you? And does this change your criminal acts of censoring our correspondence and listening in on our telephone calls?

Castigating the communist regime in charge of the country, the writer continued: "I am one of the thousands of Bulgarians whose family cannot travel abroad because of my 'flight' [*biagstvo*]. But why do you not allow the rest of the 'equal' [*ravnopravni*] Bulgarian citizens to travel? What are you afraid of?"[3] For this person, the attempts of the Bulgarian state to approach émigrés was nothing but the publicity stunt of a regime desperate to cover up its crimes against its own people.

This chapter explores how Bulgarian officials handled their interactions with emigrants to the United States and the Federal Republic of Germany (FRG), which adds one more layer to the complicated matrix of Bulgarian cultural engagements in the long 1970s. The execution of the cultural program that Bulgarian power elites launched during this time involved many considerations: political, ideological, reputational, national, and financial. The 1300th anniversary of the establishment of the Bulgarian state also became an occasion for renewed contacts between official Bulgaria and the Bulgarian diaspora. Attracting émigrés to these events had been an important aspect of the jubilee celebration since its initial conceptualization. Early on, Bulgarian officials had studied the role of the organization Polonia during the Polish millennium in 1966 to similarly involve émigrés in the 1300-year jubilee. Yet, these contacts created many complications: while Bulgarian officials often successfully secured the participation of "loyal" Bulgarian emigrants in the 1300th anniversary celebrations, they also encountered others "hostile" to the official Bulgarian agenda because of their anticommunist stance. Thus, attracting the loyal while silencing the hostile émigrés became an important issue in the execution of Bulgarian programs in the West.[4]

New research on Cold War refugees complicates our understanding of the role of postwar émigrés as their treatment became embroiled in the conflicting understandings of freedom and rights between East and West. Melissa Feinberg has demonstrated that political exiles often elaborated on their stories of persecution and overstated the facts surrounding their interactions with the state authorities that they had fled; these stories of totalitarian terror and complete control were then enhanced by Radio Free Europe (RFE) and Voice of America (VOA) analyses that portrayed an unambiguously oppressive picture in their country of origins.[5] The realities on the ground were more complicated, especially during late socialism. With enhanced mobility in the 1960s and 1970s, as more Eastern Europeans defected and as Western authorities started worrying about "so-called refugees," exiles had to strategically manage their public profiles. As Tara Zahra argues, in the 1970s, exactly when the West proclaimed its commitment to human rights, including the right to emigration and family reunification, it also started enforcing limitations on immigration from Eastern Europe, which naturally influenced the behavior of individuals.[6] Further, the socialist regimes actively pursued relationships with their diasporas abroad, generating a new layer of considerations that émigrés had to navigate. In his examination of transnational movements in Yugoslavia, Ulf Brunnbauer analyzes emigration as an "object of political intervention" that often involved the "promotion of cultural definitions of the nation" by the state in order to mold "the ideal body politic."[7] This analysis mirrors the dynamics in socialist Bulgaria where similar endeavors to cultivate a "Bulgarian community abroad" through cultural policy based on a national message was underway in the 1970s. In this context, complex new alliances between émigrés and official Bulgarian representatives developed.

The interactions between Bulgarian officials and émigrés exposed the tensions between political, national, and international factors in the conceptualization and execution of cultural programs, which had already caused complications in the Balkans and the West. The conflicting forces of nationalism and socialism were most evident here: while Bulgarian officials wished to cultivate the patriotism of the Bulgarian community abroad, to accomplish their international missions they had to compromise with political mandates that postulated the primacy of ideology in the context of developed socialism. Thus, awkward silences in the face of politically charged public appearances and twisted arguments trying to reconcile the agendas of all participants informed those interactions. In the end, the diaspora-building endeavors of Bulgarian power elites took precedence, as they were trying to cultivate the "collective identity" of the Bulgarians abroad.[8] The desire to promote cultural definitions of the nation (per Brunnbauer) and to unite all loyal compatriots behind the mission to celebrate Mother Bulgaria led to the victory of national considerations, which overshadowed clear-cut political priorities. Thus, the role of national ideology under socialism is manifested once more in the use of cultural nationalism to forge a Bulgarian diaspora.

When examining the contacts between Bulgarian officials and émigrés, I focus on their public behaviors as evident mostly through official records. What we often witness in these contacts is the collision between different "worlds" that spoke, quite literally, different languages or, as I call them, different types of "speak." This interpretation borrows from Jonathan Bolton's analysis of the "worlds of dissent" in post-1968 Czechoslovakia and the various "spokesvoices" of individuals confronting the state.[9] I extend this analysis to the different "worlds" that interacted in Bulgarian activities abroad—those of Bulgarian officials, the allegedly loyal and hostile émigrés, and local actors—and examine the various types of "speak," or style of public behavior, of the various actors. This approach allows me to engage how different players performed on the global scene, without claiming to uncover their exact motivations, which are more difficult to gauge through the available sources.

The public voices or different types of "speak" I discern include the bureaucratic language of Bulgarian officials, which could be infused with ideological jargon ("party-speak") or national(ist) rhetoric ("nation-speak"); the stylized, simplistic, and sometimes stiff vocabulary of second-generation émigrés who often used pre–World War II orthography and phraseology ("exile-speak"); the anticommunist rhetoric of political émigrés who wished to unmask the propaganda of official Bulgaria ("anticommie-speak"); and the strategies of recent defectors who resorted to the Western language of dissent to insert their voices into public debates ("dissi-speak"). I am not suggesting that these were fixed voices with only one purpose or tone: the five types of "speak" shifted and overlapped, while individuals could use different versions of "speak" over time to address their own agendas in the most suitable vocabulary. As the five styles of "speak" interacted, collided, and compromised, a series of awkward encounters unfolded between Bulgarian officials and their émigré audiences.

This chapter charts the contacts between official Bulgaria and Bulgarian émigrés on several levels. First, I outline Bulgaria's shifting policies relative to its diaspora and describe the immigrant organizations in the West most active during this period. Second, focusing on the Bulgarian "colonies" in West Germany and the United States where the most visible communities resided, I tackle their reactions to the reinvigorated outreach of the Bulgarian state in the context of the 1300th anniversary. Next, I look at two towns in the United States and the FRG to reveal the messy logic of global cultural encounters at the local level. Finally, I analyze the public behaviors of three individuals to show the multiple considerations of persons straddling political, national, professional, and personal choices. The tension between the projects of building real socialism and nurturing patriotism remained a permanent feature of Bulgaria's international cultural program, yet in the encounter with émigrés, nationalism reigned supreme.

Bulgarian Policies toward the Colony

Throughout the socialist period, the Slavic Committee was the official organization in charge of Bulgarians living abroad. The committee was founded in Moscow in August 1941 by Bulgarian exiles who sought to bring together all antifascist groups fighting against Nazi Germany. Its activities, focused on strengthening "comradeship and cooperation with all Slavic peoples," continued in Bulgaria after the Fatherland Front came to power in September 1944. In 1961, the functions of the committee expanded and it began to emphasize "ideological-political and propaganda activities among Bulgarian emigrants abroad." The organization supported Bulgarian culture, language instruction, and associational life abroad and published the magazine *Slaviani* (Slavs). In the 1970s, parallel to the expansion of the Bulgarian international agenda more generally, the Slavic Committee pursued contacts with "progressive" Bulgarian associations, clubs, and editorial boards by supplying them with books, textbooks, records, printed materials, and radio and television programming while it also organized cultural events abroad and hosted visits and meetings in Bulgaria. At the same time, the committee embraced a more patriotic turn with the mission of cultivating the Bulgarian national identity of a global diasporic community. The magazine *Slaviani* spearheaded this campaign by publishing patriotic appeals, folk craft ideas, and photographs of joyful gatherings of Bulgarians abroad alongside amnesty announcements, legal advice, and news from the country.[10] This shift became codified with the latest administrative change in 1982, which renamed the Slavic Committee the Organization for Bulgarians Abroad and stated as its explicit goal "to nurture the patriotism of our compatriots abroad [and] attract them to projects benefiting Bulgaria."[11] A Bulgarian diaspora was now in the making.

The terminology that Bulgarian officials used to refer to Bulgarians abroad varied. When describing Bulgarians who worked or lived in the Soviet Union or the rest of the socialist camp—even if they were in mixed marriages or had permanently moved to those countries—they often employed a term that one could render in English as "community," or perhaps "collective of fellow countrymen/women" (*zemliachestvo*), which implied coherence, egalitarianism, and retaining strong connection with their country of origin. But when talking about the Bulgarians in the West (including Western Europe, North and South America, and Australia) who had permanently moved to their new places of residence and had often severed their relationship with their country for an extended time period, the term of choice was "emigrants" (*emigratsiia*). By the mid-1970s, in line with the attempts to build a united Bulgarian community, the preferred term was the more flexible and inclusive "colony" (*koloniia*), which nicely captured the diaspora-building attempts of the regime. The Bulgarian colony, as envisioned by officials, was comprised of several groups: according to one report from 1977, the term included "those of Bulgarian origins with foreign citizenship . . . and their

FIGURE 21. Bulgarians living abroad visiting the city of Bansko and the monument of Paisii of Hilendar, likely in 1981. Source: Georgi Dosev and Stefan Zhelev, eds., *Bâlgariia, 40 godini po pâtia na sotsializma* (Sofia: Sofiia Press, 1984), held in the National Library, Sofia.

first, second, and third generations; Bulgarian citizens with the legal status of permanent residents in another country; Bulgarian citizens temporarily residing abroad with legal documents; Bulgarian citizens who left the country illegally or those who traveled legally but refused to return in the specified time frame."[12] In this vision, the colony consisted of disparate groups that now had to be molded in a single Bulgarian community abroad.

Among the colony in the West, there was a further differentiation between various groups, but most notably, from the 1960s on, between the loyal and the hostile. The term "hostile emigrants" (*vrazheska emigratsiia*) emerged in the mid-1950s to describe two separate groups—the "traitors" (*izmennitsi*) who had fled Bulgarian territory after 1944 and the "non-returners" (*nevâz-vrashtentsi*) who had found themselves outside of Bulgaria in 1944 but chosen not to return due to the political change in the country. Originally, the characterization was broad, referring to all "counterrevolutionary elements" who had refused to participate in the building of new Bulgaria after World War II, imbuing the term with unambiguous ideological implications. By the 1960s, however, the term hostile had been refined and narrowed, and it now included, more explicitly, only those who actively participated in anticommunist political activities.[13]

Political considerations connected to the domestic credibility and international reputation of the Zhivkov regime determined how Bulgarian officials treated specific émigré groups. Some organizations that were seen as particularly harmful to the cause of socialist Bulgaria included the Bulgarian National Committee of the former Agrarian Party leader G. M. Dimitrov in Washington and New York City (which published the newspaper *Svobodna i nezavisima Bâlgariia* [Free and independent Bulgaria]) and other branches of the Bulgarian Agrarian National Union (BANU) in exile; the National Front, a disparate group of monarchists, nationalists, and legionnaires originally established near Munich but with branches in Australia, Austria, Canada, England, the FRG, and the United States (which published the magazine *Borba* [Struggle] in Chicago); and the Bulgarian National Council, formed in New York City in 1960 to coordinate the activities of all Bulgarian anticommunist organizations. The Bulgarian Social-Democratic Party, with members residing in Austria, France, the FRG, the United States, and elsewhere, became more active in the 1970s when its leadership transferred to Vienna (where Stefan Tabakov published the ardently anti-Zhivkov newspaper *Svoboden narod* [Free people]). The staff of the Bulgarian sections of radio stations such as RFE, VOA, BBC, or Deutsche Welle were considered to be particularly hostile to the Bulgarian cause, and their actions were often described as "ideological sabotage." As new organizations emerged and became more active in the 1970s—such as the Bulgarian Committee for the Defense of Human Rights in Paris (led by Kiril Yanatchkov)—their attacks on the Zhivkov regime also earned them the classification of hostile.[14] In these cases of unambiguously hostile organizations, Bulgarian officials' party-speak and the emigrants' anticommie-speak collided as the two sides vocally presented rival interpretations of the political situation in Bulgaria.

Yet, national(ist) considerations could moderate the treatment of techni-cally anticommunist yet otherwise patriotic émigrés by following a tortuous logic of compromise by necessity. In the 1970s, Bulgarian officials started treating discrete groups of émigrés who had fled the country after 1944 due to their (at the time) anticommunist agenda more favorably. One notable example were the members of the pro-Bulgarian Macedonian Patriotic Orga-nization (MPO) in the United States and Canada who continued to nurture

FIGURE 22. The cover of the magazine *Borba* (Struggle), November 1981, published by the Bul-garian National Front in Chicago, featuring an unambiguously anticommunist message. Source: Library of Congress, LCCN—2007222911.

anticommunist feelings but engaged in "Bulgarian propaganda." In line with the "patriotic turn" and embrace of national ideology, now officials deemed the MPO useful for the Bulgarian cause at a time when Bulgaria and Yugoslavia were engaged in a showdown over the Macedonian issue. The MPO was established in 1922 by pro-Bulgarian Macedonian activists who advocated for "an independent Macedonian republic within its geographical and economic boundaries," but it underwent multiple transformations that paralleled the tumultuous history of the Macedonian question. Eventually based in Geary, Indiana, and having branches throughout the Midwest, Northeast, and Canada, by the 1970s the MPO focused its work on defending the Bulgarian national identity of the Macedonians. As a result, its leaders sought contacts with Bulgarian diplomats in order to counter the Yugoslav campaigns cultivating Macedonian language and identity in the United States.[15] As both sides were seeking allies, when interacting with members of the Macedonian diaspora Bulgarian officials tried to reconcile their political and national agendas. Thus, the pro-Bulgarian (but anticommunist) Macedonian émigrés became the core group of supposedly loyal emigrants that Bulgarian emissaries tried to approach.[16] In official Bulgarian interactions with MPO activists, nation-speak replaced party-speak permanently.

Another contentious issue was the role of religion in the contacts between the Bulgarian state and the émigrés. This tension was due to the generally ambiguous attitude of the communist regime to religion: on the one hand, communist officials maintained an atheist stance, yet on the other, they recognized that the Orthodox Church had played an important role in Bulgarian history (one of the "representative exhibitions" during this time was *1000 Years of Bulgarian Icons*). Thus, contradictions colored the relationship between the Bulgarian authorities and the Eastern Orthodox clergy working in the Bulgarian communities abroad. Since the 1930s, the Bulgarian Diocese of North America and Australia had functioned under the umbrella of the Bulgarian Orthodox Church (then an exarchate), but self-financed its activities, which gave it independence from the Bulgarian state. This situation allowed its continued existence after 1944 when the diocese was constantly trying to strike a balance between the communist state apparatus and anticommunist émigrés who criticized the regime vocally. When in 1953, with the support of the communist authorities, the Bulgarian Orthodox Church became a patriarchate, a compromise was reached between the state's aspiration to control church institutions and the church's desire to maintain its functions.

Yet, this arrangement did not satisfy all émigrés, and especially those who continued to nurse anticommunist feelings. In 1963, fourteen Bulgarian dioceses in North America (led by the archbishop of Pittsburgh and Western Pennsylvania), supported by the MPO, the Bulgarian National Council, and BANU in exile, split from the Synod in Sofia; in 1977, they transferred to the Orthodox Church of America and established a Bulgarian diocese stationed in Toledo, Ohio. In the 1970s, the Bulgarian Diocese of North America and Australia, which remained under the Patriarchate in Sofia, was divided into two dioceses, stationed in New York City and Akron, Ohio, respectively. This situation created a complicated relationship between representatives of the Bulgarian state, the archbishops dispatched by the Synod in Sofia, the clergy under the jurisdiction of the Orthodox Church of America, and the immigrant communities these churches served, many of whom had anticommunist or pro-Macedonian sympathies.[17] Still, when making their appearances in the West, Bulgarian officials had little choice but to communicate with the Eastern Orthodox priests who were ubiquitous at events organized by the Bulgarian communities. Together with nationalist organizations, religious representatives (who generally sympathized with the national cause) joined the loyal émigrés, as defined by Bulgarian officials. Here, nation-speak allowed the conflicting views of Bulgarian representatives and the Orthodox clergy to publicly reconcile.

In the 1970s, as contacts with émigrés of various backgrounds expanded, Bulgarian officials acquired a flexible and inclusive understanding of the Bulgarian colony and used the term "loyal" (*loialni*) to describe anyone willing to work with them (at the same time, "anti-Bulgarian" became an umbrella term for anticommunist and pro-Yugoslav émigrés). As a result, Bulgarian diplomats now actively courted the entire cohort of second-generation Bulgarians whose families had left Bulgaria in the late nineteenth and early twentieth centuries for economic reasons and who tended to have neutral political positions.[18] In 1980, the Politburo instructed the Slavic Committee to use the 1300th anniversary as an occasion to forge more sustained contacts with the Bulgarian colony and outlined the main groups to be approached: "Bulgarians who had left the territory of contemporary Bulgaria [for economic reasons]; persons who feel Bulgarian despite the fact that they were born outside of the Bulgarian borders; persons of partially Bulgarian origins; and persons of non-Bulgarian origins but residing . . . in Bulgaria and loving this country as their motherland."[19] As a result of this mandate from the highest levels, in 1982 the Slavic Committee designed plans to engage the different generations of Bulgarians and to reach out to different geographical locations according to specific conditions. Cultural approaches played an important role in these plans, whose goal was to promote "organized patriotic models of life in the colony . . . through literature, films, exhibitions, performances, souvenirs, etc., [to direct] the individual consciousness of our compatriots toward pride in our motherland and a desire to help its future development."[20] The Bulgarian state was now actively cultivating a Bulgarian diaspora through culture.

Given the complex composition of the Bulgarian community and the apolitical position of most emigrants, it was the explicitly political organizations that worried Bulgarian authorities. Officials kept detailed records of hostile émigrés. In 1966, in the estimates of the Politburo, there were 5,933 "traitors" and 372 "non-returners."[21] In the late 1960s and early 1970s, the number of hostile émigrés grew, largely because the number of Bulgarian escapees to the West increased, including more "young people, specialists with higher education, who are under Western influence and seek an easy way of life."[22] While these young, educated people were assumed to be economic and not political emigrants, as asylum seekers they tarnished the image of the country and were considered harmful to the Bulgarian cause. Even more worrisome were the number of high-profile defections of previously loyal intellectuals who now worked for foreign radio stations and became vocal and popular critics of the Bulgarian regime in the West. While Georgi Markov, a contributor to the Bulgarian section of the BBC, was the main target of the Bulgarian secret police, others closely followed by the regime included Asen Ignatov, editor in chief of the Bulgarian section of Deutsche Welle, and Dimitar Bochev and Vladimir Kostov, who both worked at the Bulgarian section of RFE in Munich. Those individuals, due to their visibility, were often attacked personally as being allied with "the reactionary powers" (*reaktsionnite sili*) and committing "ideological sabotage" (*ideologicheska diversiia*).[23] The use of this straightforward ideological jargon, or party-speak, persisted throughout the long 1970s.

Maintaining contacts with the diaspora remained a highly controlled and carefully monitored endeavor. In an attempt to have a clearer idea of the number, activities, and potential loyalty of all emigrants, the Bulgarian embassies adopted new methods in the 1970s. Diplomats started encouraging the "registration" (*registratsiia*) of Bulgarians permanently residing in their districts so that the emigrants were better informed of changing legislation, including a number of amnesties that directly benefitted them. At the same time, archival documents indicate that diplomats also used "a catalog system" (*kartotekirane*) of those who had chosen not to register by compiling "files" (*dela*) for each individual.[24] As a result of this work, by 1980 the regime had a clearer view of the colony. The minutes of a Politburo meeting from 7 July 1980 claimed that the Bulgarian community abroad comprised 300,000 individuals (including second-generation Bulgarians). The vast majority of these Bulgarians were not of concern because only 11,000 had left the country "illegally" after 1944 and only 600 were involved in "active hostile activities." Because the vast majority of the émigrés were apolitical, officials considered as loyal even those who had left Bulgaria most recently for economic reasons; the goal was to make sure that there were more friends than enemies among the Bulgarian colony.

On balance, it seems that "patriotic," national(ist), diaspora-building factors won out over political or religious reservations when Bulgarian officials approached the "Bulgarian community abroad." Reflecting the importance of national ideology, nation-speak remained a permanent feature of how Bulgarian representatives communicated with the vast majority of emigrants. The goal was to nurture the patriotism of the émigrés through cultural policy so that a more robust Bulgarian diaspora might emerge. In the words of the Slavic Committee, "every nation seeks its roots—the roots of its historical, cultural, and spiritual essence—and every nation has things to be proud of. . . . [The Bulgarians too] are the heirs of a great and heroic people, a people that has given something to the world."[25] Yet, in a developed socialist society marching toward the inevitably bright future of communism, party-speak persisted. Thus, the Politburo continued to mandate rigorous actions vis-à-vis the hostile emigrants, seeking to "limit and neutralize" their work while pursuing their "political, ideological, and organizational degradation."[26] These conflicting priorities concerning the Bulgarian émigrés shaped the actions of Bulgarian officials when they entered the cultural scenes of the United States and West Germany.

1300 Years Bulgaria and Émigrés in the United States and West Germany

Contacts between Bulgarian authorities and émigrés intensified with the expansion of Bulgarian international cultural activities in the 1970s and especially during the celebration of the 1300th anniversary of the establishment of the Bulgarian state that dominated the cultural calendar in 1977–1981. While mobilizing the diaspora behind the 1300th anniversary became a permanent feature of Bulgarian international cultural events, dealing with emigrants, especially in the West, was a complex task. Bulgarian representatives carefully navigated the situation, swinging between nation-speak and party-speak while engaging with their émigré audiences.

When the Bulgarian embassy in Washington, DC, started preparing for the 1300 Years Bulgaria celebrations in the United States in 1978, its detailed "jubilee plans" included a section dedicated to Bulgarian emigrants in the

United States; diplomats saw the 1300th anniversary as the ideal occasion for "unifying the emigrants and strengthening our influence [among them]," and they included many politically neutral yet patriotically oriented events in their plans.[27] Despite this early enthusiasm, another report, likely from 1980, outlined the challenges ahead of Bulgarian diplomats as they approached the diaspora. From the official Bulgarian viewpoint, the first generation of economic emigrants was growing old and had withdrawn from active public life while their children "had Americanized" and showed little interest in Bulgarian activities. Many "otherwise positively oriented" folks avoided any organized activity whatsoever, whether political, cultural, or religious, because they did not want to become involved in politics. While waning, the "undermining influence of hostile political organizations" associated with the anticommunist émigrés alienated still others. Further, Yugoslav-affiliated organizations cultivated Macedonian, rather than Bulgarian, allegiances. Finally, some church congregations split from the Bulgarian Orthodox Church, because they saw it as a communist "agent," recognizing instead the American Orthodox or Macedonian Orthodox churches.[28]

With these divisions within the community in mind, Bulgarian diplomats in the United States concentrated their efforts on recruiting loyal émigrés through four sets of closely interconnected actions. First, officials designed cultural-educational activities that would reach out to "as many Bulgarians as possible" among the politically neutral, "patriotic" émigrés, with the goal of "strengthening their Bulgarian national consciousness [and] patriotic spirit." They concentrated on supplying already active cultural-educational organizations and churches in Pittsburgh, Toledo, Los Angeles, and Washington, DC, with high-quality historical materials and helping with Bulgarian language and folk-dance instruction. Second, diplomats continued collecting information about the activities of "anti-Bulgarian" organizations such as the Bulgarian National Front and the Bulgarian National Council, while carefully avoiding public confrontations. Third, they maintained contacts with Bulgarian clergy in certain dioceses, such as Akron and New York City (but not the splinter groups based in Toledo), including providing legal aid in the struggle to retain property claimed by the Macedonian or American Orthodox churches. Further, officials thought it imperative to provide financial support to specific churches in Indianapolis, Detroit, and Lorain, Ohio, whose membership included "strong Bulgarian elements." Finally, diplomats carefully approached the MPO, which, while ideologically anticommunist, "ardently defends the Bulgarian national consciousness of the Macedonians [and] criticizes the anti-Bulgarian campaigns of the Yugoslav leadership and the distortion of our history by the Skopje chauvinists." While "politically delicate," officials concluded that in the current situation Bulgaria had an interest in "finding appropriate ways for maintaining contact" with the MPO in order to neutralize the influence of the "hostile and anti-Bulgarian oriented emigrants . . . and the activities of the Skopje groups."[29] Clearly, patriotic considerations won out in the rationale of Bulgarian officials who proactively used cultural and educational activities to cultivate relations with the émigrés.

The embassy suggested specific cultural strategies for uniting the colony, such as reaching out to the younger people in New York, Pittsburgh, Toledo, Detroit, Akron, Chicago, Milwaukee, Indianapolis, Saint Louis, Los Angeles, and Washington; organizing more frequent visits of folk and other performers—"the most efficient means for patriotic influence and a strong weapon against hostile propaganda"; sponsoring group and individual émigré visits to Bulgaria, including free charter flights for the 1300th anniversary events; and continuing the distribution of high-quality materials to Bulgarian clubs, radio and television stations, and churches.[30] In the long run, these endeavors would help create a strong group of loyal Bulgarian émigrés in the United States while undermining the influence of the politically hostile. The 1300th anniversary provided the perfect opportunity to unite the patriotic efforts of the Bulgarian state and the diaspora through cultural means. As demonstrated in the mass turnout of émigrés during the concerts of the Pirin Folk Ensemble and the Alexander Nevski Quartet in 1979, many Bulgarians in North America were willing to participate in emotional, patriotic, high-quality cultural activities that lacked political messages but still, in official evaluations, "drew [the émigrés] to the People's Republic."[31] The Slavic Committee organized, to great acclaim, a number of patriotic performances, in New York City and elsewhere, under the title "For Sacred Bulgaria" (Za teb Bâlgariio sveshtena), which were received enthusiastically by the Bulgarian communities in those cities.[32] In the end, nation-speak dominated the diaspora-building efforts of Bulgarian diplomats among the émigré communities in the United States, as they concentrated on bringing together all "patriotic" emigrants in a united "Bulgarian community abroad."

Inspired by those experiences, diplomats kept lists of loyal émigrés and engaged in regular, friendly correspondence with certain well-disposed Bulgarians abroad.[33] Moved by the patriotic message but likely also pursuing their own goals, individuals contacted the embassy with various ideas about commemorating the 1300-year jubilee. Liliana Popova from California, after visiting her native country, proposed a "massive campaign for the popularization of Bulgaria" through the sale of Bulgarian folk art in the United States during the Christmas shopping season.[34] Stefan Saklarian, an American artist

FIGURE 23.   A performance of folk ensembles from the Midwest in New Lexington, Ohio, in June 1978. Source: TsDA, f. 405, op. 9, a.e. 668, l. 289.

born in Bulgaria, wished to commemorate the 1300th anniversary by establishing an annual prize fund for art students in Bulgaria.[35] An art enthusiast, Dimitar Batoev, wanted to show his work during a visit to Bulgaria, despite the objection of the Union of Bulgarian Artists (which did not approve of the quality of the artwork), and wrote to Zhivkova personally to lobby for his exhibit.[36] Some Americans, with the urging of their Bulgarian friends, also visited the country and started writing media dispatches and travelogues on Bulgarian topics.[37] As is clear from these examples, the nation-speak of official Bulgaria had resonance among some members of the colony in the United States. As celebration of the 1300th anniversary ignited national pride and Bulgarian diplomats provided organizational and financial resources, grassroots reactions revealed that a Bulgarian diaspora, united through nation-speak, was now in the making.

In the FRG, Bulgarian diplomats similarly studied the émigré community and designed elaborate plans for approaching it. According to diplomatic estimates, in 1982 there were between 10,000 and 14,000 Bulgarians in West Germany, with the largest communities concentrated in Munich, Hamburg, Stuttgart, and Frankfurt am Main.[38] More than 95 percent of these Bulgarians were "non-returners" who had either left Bulgaria illegally or had refused to return to Bulgaria after legal travel to West Germany. Relations between Bulgarian diplomats and the émigrés were based on mutual neglect until 1975, when "the party and the government changed its attitude to the patriotic, loyal, and neutral non-returners and [Bulgarians] illegally residing [in Germany]." In other words, after 1975 being "illegal" did not make one automatically hostile. At that point, embassy officials started organizing consular meetings to assist individuals with personal issues and encouraged the registration of the Bulgarians living in Germany.[39] The goal was to "isolate the hostile emigrants" by creating incentives for "neutral" Bulgarians to reestablish relations with state authorities, even if they had the status of "illegals."[40] In 1981 alone, more than 130 émigrés visited Bulgaria for the first time since their "illegal emigration."[41] As in the United States, the overall objective was to court and recruit the politically neutral émigrés.

However, the situation in West Germany presented Bulgarian diplomats with persistent political challenges: in the words of officials, the country had "the largest number of hostile oriented emigrants who actively attempt to undermine the organization of our official events while at the same time designing their own activities during Bulgarian holidays . . . [which often] are covered in the local mass media better than our official events."[42] For example, Munich was the home of organizations with an anticommunist orientation that published materials criticizing the position of the Bulgarian government strategically timed to coincide with high-profile state visits.[43] Of particular concern were the activities of radio stations, such as Deutsche Welle and especially RFE, broadcast from German territory, whose Bulgarian sections were staffed by anticommunist émigrés. The rhetoric of RFE, also stationed in Munich, emerged as the mirror image of official Bulgarian discourse, due to its clear-cut, programmatic anticommunist message. RFE contributors often published press materials lambasting Bulgarian policies against dissidents and disclosing the existence of "special psychiatric clinics" for political opponents.[44] This rhetoric was anticommie-speak at its purest. On such occasions, the Ministry of Foreign Affairs (MVnR) summoned the FRG ambassador to explain whether particular broadcasts reflected the views of the West German government, despite the habitual answer that Western governments had no control over media programming.[45] Sparring over ideology was a constant feature of Bulgarian exchanges with Western representatives, in which each side used its own Cold War jargon in a formalistic, slogan-like way. The only response to anticommie-speak was persistent and straightforward party-speak.

Turmoil erupted in the West German media in September 1978 following the assassination in London of Georgi Markov and the attempt on Vladimir Simeonov, both contributors to the Bulgarian section of the BBC.[46] By contrast to the United States, where the assassinations were reported in passing,

European media covered the case extensively. Given the fact that many RFE contributors resided in Munich, the "umbrella murder" resonated deeply. In the aftermath of the assassination there were numerous publications in the West German press with strongly worded materials implicating the Bulgarian regime. In spring 1980 local television stations in Munich, Hamburg, and Cologne broadcast a film about the assassination, written and directed by émigrés.[47] In 1979 and 1980, these media campaigns complicated the organization of cultural activities in West Germany; this was particularly true regarding the 1300th anniversary celebrations focused on the opening of the *Thracian Treasures* exhibitions in Cologne and Munich because what people in those two cities heard was the anticommie-speak of vocal RFE contributors.

To counter these hostile voices, Bulgarian officials used cultural strategies to rally the "patriotic, loyal, and neutral" émigrés by focusing on national goals and resuming, in even more forceful ways, their diaspora-building activities. Diplomats maintained regular contact with existing émigré organizations and established new friendship societies and cultural associations that included well-disposed Germans and members of the Bulgarian colony. Emissaries now sought out organizations that they had previously deemed suspicious, such as the Peio Iavorov Cultural Association in Stuttgart (established 1941) and the Dr. Petar Beron Academic Association in Heidelberg (established 1965). On the occasion of the 1300-year jubilee, diplomats also coordinated the establishment of new cultural-educational associations in Essen, Darmstadt, Hamburg, Hanover, Munich, Mannheim, and Frankfurt am Main.[48] In Munich and Frankfurt am Main, the explicit goal was "to isolate the hostile emigration" that was trying to sabotage the jubilee celebrations or portray them as communist propaganda. This strategy had some success because when the *Thracian Treasures* exhibit was shown in Cologne and Munich, the associations in Essen and Stuttgart organized museum visits that many émigrés received enthusiastically.[49] Using cultural policies and proactive nation-speak was working to unite the colony.

Diplomats' ultimate objective was to create a politically neutral space for interaction with Bulgarian émigrés that emphasized their patriotic mission: they proposed "organiz[ing] regular events with Bulgarians so that they can maintain their national consciousness and be informed about cultural and other events in the People's Republic."[50] Embassy officials considered the celebration of 24 May, the Day of the Slavic Alphabet and Bulgarian Literacy, as the most appropriate occasion for uniting the community. In 1977, the embassy organized a series of celebrations to mark the holiday. A reception for three hundred people in Bonn and academic events in Cologne and

Saarbrucken were infused with patriotic symbolism and rhetoric.[51] Diplomats also suggested an annual ceremony of placing wreaths at the memorial plaque of St. Methodius in Ellwangen.[52] Another strategy for fostering interactions, despite the delicate nature of such encounters, was approaching the Bulgarian religious communities in Hamburg, Stuttgart, and Munich.[53] It is difficult to judge the success of these efforts, but, as indicated in official reports, unlike previous years when there were virtually no contacts between diplomats and émigrés, a growing number of Bulgarians in West Germany now attended embassy events and made donations in money and kind to mark the 1300th anniversary.

The ways in which the patriotic focus of diplomatic activities bore fruit is evident in the interactions of Bulgarian diplomats with the Dr. Petar Beron Academic Association in Munich, which pursued cultural and educational activities among the Bulgarians in West Germany and funded publications on Bulgarian topics. The bylaws of the association explicitly stated that it did not engage in political actions, but some of its most prominent members were RFE employees, including the founder Stefan Popov, who was the head of the Bulgarian section (and at one point a private tutor of the Bulgarian king in exile Simeon). In 1975, Bulgarian officials had characterized this organization as "anticommunist . . . with a negative attitude toward contemporary socialist Bulgaria," but had also expressed readiness to "cooperate with the association in certain aspects of its activities." The leadership of the organization automatically placed it in the hostile camp, yet, Bulgarian diplomats now coordinated celebrations of historical events, anniversaries, and the 1300-year jubilee in West Germany with its members.[54] Here again, national factors won out over political considerations.

In the end, by 1981, both in the United States and West Germany, nationspeak appeared as the most effective strategy for Bulgarian officials in their cultural efforts among emigrants. In a memo outlining the long-term plan for work with Bulgarians abroad from 1982, Bulgarian officials listed as their main goal the "unification of the Bulgarian colony on a patriotic basis, [and] the preservation and further development of its Bulgarian national consciousness . . . [to show] the real place and contribution [of Bulgaria] in the development of human civilization and culture."[55] The creation of a Bulgarian community united around a patriotic mission required the abandonment of political divisions and the full embrace of a national message centered on the core ideas of 1300 Years Bulgaria. "Patriotic policies that support the Bulgarian cause" became the focus of official policies toward the colony as an eloquent example of the embrace of cultural nationalism by the late socialist regimes in Eastern Europe.[56] Cultural activities connected to the 1300-year jubilee helped in one more aspect of the official state priorities regarding international cultural projects: by beginning to forge a Bulgarian diaspora.

Sites of Encounter: New Lexington, Ohio, and Ellwangen, (West) Germany

Official records of contacts between state authorities and émigrés can only take us so far as they tend to minimize the conflict underlying these interactions. To explain the multilayered nature of the encounters between diplomats and representatives of the diaspora, it is worth reconstructing these contacts at the local level. By paying attention to the dynamics of these interactions at the community level, it is possible to reconstruct what anthropologist Anna Lowenhaupt Tsing calls the "messy and surprising features of encounters across difference." Focusing on two small towns—New Lexington, Ohio, United States, and Ellwangen, Baden-Württemberg, West Germany—this section seeks to expose the contradictory experiences of these global contacts and uncover "the productive friction of global connections."[57]

New Lexington, Ohio, is a town of five thousand inhabitants located sixty miles from the state capital Columbus. The town was the birthplace of Januarius MacGahan, a late nineteenth-century American journalist who traveled to Europe in the 1870s to report on events in France, Russia, and Central Asia. In 1876, MacGahan traveled to the Bulgarian lands under Ottoman rule to witness and condemn the infamous Batak Massacre, which brought the Bulgarian national question to international attention. His dispatches for the liberal *Daily News* (London) played a major role in turning British public opinion against the Ottoman Empire. During the Russo-Turkish War of 1877–1878, MacGahan traveled with the Russian Army and reported from many of the major battlefields in present-day Bulgaria; he was also present at the signing of the Treaty of San Stefano on 3 March 1878, which reestablished the modern Bulgarian state.[58] MacGahan died in Istanbul in 1878, but his body was exhumed and reburied in New Lexington in 1883. In 1911, local residents erected a monument bearing the inscription "MacGahan. Liberator of Bulgaria." In the 1970s, when a citizen committee began annual celebrations of MacGahan's death, Bulgarian emigrants from across the Midwest started to frequent New Lexington each June to pay their respects to the "Liberator of Bulgaria."[59]

In Bulgaria, 1978 was the year of the centennial of the Bulgarian liberation from the Ottoman Empire following the Russo-Turkish War. Bulgarian officials republished MacGahan's dispatches from Batak in Bulgarian and erected a monument in Batak to celebrate his contribution to the Bulgarian cause.[60] Across the Atlantic Ocean, when the local committee in New Lexington prepared to celebrate the centennial of his death, it invited members of the Bulgarian communities in New York, Toronto, Chicago, and various places in Ohio to pay their respects.[61] As grassroots efforts to honor the journalist intensified, the Ohio House of Representatives declared the week of 3–9 June as the Week of Januarius MacGahan.[62]

In the summer of 1978, a Bulgarian television crew filming a documentary on MacGahan visited New Lexington and encountered "Bulgarian emigrants hostile to our socialist system." To neutralize "anti-Bulgarian (against the current system) episodes," the delegation recommended to the Committee for Culture that they gift a replica of the commemorative bust of the American journalist that had recently been erected in Batak to New Lexington.[63] This monument was eventually placed in the New Lexington cemetery next to the 1911 monument of MacGahan.

In the meantime, Bulgarian émigrés from Toledo and Akron, Ohio, most of them with an anticommunist orientation, spearheaded an alternative project to commemorate MacGahan. In the late 1970s Dr. Tabakoff, a physician from Akron, established the Bulgarian-American MacGahan Association

FIGURE 24. The celebration of the centennial of Januarius MacGahan's death in New Lexington, Ohio, in June 1978. Source: TsDA, f. 405, op. 9, a.e. 668, l. 288.

FIGURE 25.   MacGahan's original monument at the New Lexington cemetery (right) and the replica of the monument from Batak, Bulgaria (left). Photo by author.

with the explicit goal of celebrating this anniversary. But his agenda was highjacked by representatives of official Bulgaria who in 1978 showed up in New Lexington for the centennial events and proposed donating the replica of the Batak bust. Dr. Tabakoff approached other émigrés in the area to coordinate action. Quite auspiciously, a Bulgarian defector, the sculptor Liubomir Dalchev, had just settled in Cleveland, Ohio, after seeking asylum in the United States during an exhibition in Vienna. A well-known monumental artist, Dalchev's high-profile defection had personally offended Zhivkova, providing a perfect occasion for the anticommunist émigrés who sponsored Dalchev's exhibition in Akron in 1980 and commissioned a monument of MacGahan.[64] The full-size sculpture, executed in the unmistakable style of state socialist monumental art, was eventually placed across from the New Lexington City Hall.

Throughout the 1980s, the annual memorials organized during the month of June on the occasion of MacGahan's death became the site of unlikely encounters in the context of the new contacts initiated by the Bulgarian state, which brought together representatives of communist Bulgaria, recent anticommunist émigrés, second-generation Bulgarian heritage folk ensembles, U.S.-based Bulgarian Orthodox priests, and the local American inhabitants of

FIGURE 26. The statue of MacGahan by Bulgarian sculptor Liubomir Dalchev, who defected in 1978 and immigrated to the United States. Photo by author.

New Lexington.[65] In a manifestation of "productive friction," official Bulgarian cultural objectives intersected with local community interests and émigré national sensibilities. The representatives of the NRB had to participate in awkward cultural encounters involving Orthodox priests and Bulgarian émigrés. Still, New Lexington became one of the main destinations for official Bulgarian visits to the United States. One can only imagine the thoughts of Bulgarian representatives when encountering the MacGahan sculpture erected by the defector Dalchev whose work they no doubt recognized. The new global encounters pursued by Bulgarian officials in their desire to foster a Bulgarian diaspora led to unlikely interactions and contradictory outcomes.

Such odd confrontations were not limited to the United States. Ellwangen is a town of 23,000 in (then West) Germany, located in the southwest state of Baden-Württemberg. Established in the seventh century, in 870 the town became the residence of Methodius, the Byzantine monk and scholar who together with his brother Cyril had codified the first Slavic alphabet, the Glagolitic, which captured the unique features of the Slavic languages. Following a mission among the Slavs in Moravia (today in the Czech Republic), Cyril and Methodius had become embroiled in conflict with the bishops of the Holy Roman Empire who claimed religious jurisdiction over these Slav-populated territories. After Cyril's death in 869, Pope Adrian II named Methodius the archbishop of Sirmium with jurisdiction over Great Moravia and Pannonia, angering the bishop of Passau who, following a trial in Regensburg, imprisoned Methodius in Ellwangen between 870 and 873 (some of these facts are debated in medieval scholarship). After the death of Methodius in 885, his disciples, persecuted by the Germanic bishops, arrived in the medieval Bulgarian Kingdom where they designed the Cyrillic script, which gradually replaced the Glagolitic and led to the "golden age of Bulgarian culture" during the reign of King Simeon the Great (893–927).[66]

In 1885, to commemorate the millennium of Methodius's death, the city of Ellwangen placed a memorial plaque on the outside wall of the Saint Vitus Basilica, featuring scenes of Methodius's trial that had led to his exile in Ellwangen. In 1970, to mark the 1100th anniversary of his exile, the city named a central square Methodiusplatz and unveiled another plaque on the Saint Vitus Basilica in the presence of members of Stuttgart's Peio Iavorov Cultural Association and Bulgarian diplomats. In 1975, with the support of the Bulgarian government, a Bulgarian sculptor, Velichko Minekov, designed another bronze plaque, featuring Methodius holding a scroll with the first five letters of the Bulgarian alphabet, which was placed on the basilica as well. In 1987, the Bulgarian government and the Bulgarian Orthodox Church further oversaw the building of a small chapel named after Methodius. (There are also Slovak and Macedonian plaques honoring Methodius on the wall of the cathedral, added later on, emphasizing the scholar's central place in the national imagination of several Slavic nations.) Ellwangen thus became one of the magnets for Bulgarian emigrants and visitors in Germany, who came to town for the annual celebration on 24 May, the Day of Bulgarian Culture and Slavic Literacy.[67]

FIGURE 27.   The bas-relief of Methodius *(right)* at the cathedral of Ellwangen, Germany, next to the original memorial plaque *(left)*. Wreaths placed by members of the Iavorov Cultural and Educational Society in Stuttgart are visible. Source: *Slaviani*, no. 2, 1981.

Similarly to New Lexington, Ellwangen became the site of "productive friction" and contested encounters between representatives of official Bulgaria and loyal or hostile émigrés while the intrinsically religious site added one more layer to these already loaded contacts. In 1977, during a wreath-laying ceremony at Methodius's memorial plaque, members of the "hostile emigration" brought their own wreaths and distributed flyers with an anticommunist message (the embassy duly attached a copy of the flyer to its report, but it is missing from the archival records).[68] The actions of such organizations were thus always on the mind of Bulgarian officials as they organized their "patriotic" celebratory activities.

The uneasy coexistence between Bulgarian diplomats, loyal members of Bulgarian communities, and hostile émigrés became a feature of Bulgarian meetings in Germany, too. During the New Year's celebration in Stuttgart, attended by three hundred people, the "hostile emigrants" were "moved by the beautiful, typically Bulgarian atmosphere" and "delighted with the enthusiastic performance of Bulgarian and Russian folk songs." In Darmstadt too, at a concert organized for the occasion, BANU members tried to distribute their magazine *Bâdeshte* (Future) and flyers with "provocative content, but they were isolated and left the performance hall before the end of the concert." Despite such uncomfortable confrontations, the national focus of these events tended to erase the political divisions within the audience. In the opinion of the Bulgarian embassy in Bonn, "the majority of Bulgarian citizens nurture love and respect for our motherland, greet with interest and attention everything related to our country, and support . . . our cultural initiatives."[69] In the early 1980s, all sides learned how to accommodate each other's positions so as to avoid embarrassing "Mother Bulgaria." In the end, nation-speak served as the universal language of bridging difference and reconciling "the messy and surprising features" of global encounters.

Prosopographies: Émigré "Voices" from the United States

In addition to paying attention to local sites of interaction, it is also important to analyze the actions of concrete people involved in these global contacts. The international cultural program of the Bulgarian state created fresh opportunities for some individuals who either enlisted themselves in support of the new cultural programs, vocally opposed the official cultural agenda, or used international exchange to pursue their own purposes. By juxtaposing three public figures who prioritized different professional, political, or personal choices in their interactions with Bulgarian representatives (or their avoidance of any official contact), this section charts the "messy encounters" between the Bulgarian state and Bulgarians abroad on one more level. Here, I focus on the voices of these individuals, uncovered through an analysis of official and personal records that deal with their public-facing activities, or different types of "speak." The emphasis is on performance rather than motivation, as I seek to relate the (strategic) uses of national and political rhetoric in specific contexts.

Some of the most visible groups of "loyal" émigrés in the United States to adopt the nation-speak of Bulgarian officials were the people involved in the Tamburitzans Folk Dance Ensemble at Duquesne University in Pittsburgh, Pennsylvania, one of the most renowned Eastern European folk troupes in the United States. The passionate deputy director of the ensemble, Patricia French, was a second-generation Bulgarian who was enthusiastically involved in the promotion of Bulgarian (and Macedonian) cultural life in Pittsburgh. She and her husband, Walter Kolar, and her brother, Nicholas Iordanoff, had been previously involved in cultural exchange with the Soviet Union. Yet, once contacted by Bulgarian officials in the 1970s, Penka French, as she fashioned herself for Bulgarian audiences, seemed to have found her voice. She regularly traveled to Bulgaria to study techniques of folk dancing and secure costumes and instruments for the troupe. She paid visits to the Slavic Committee and discussed opportunities for Bulgarian-U.S. cultural exchange with the KK. During these visits, she knew well what was admissible and what non-negotiable: she avoided any talk of politics and kept her conversations focused on cultural cooperation and national solidarity, seamlessly in line with the nation-speak of Bulgarian officials.[70]

When Bulgarian diplomats in the United States launched their "jubilee plans" for the 1300th anniversary, they naturally enlisted Penka French in their activities. French was instrumental, through her influence in the local Bulgarian-Macedonian Cultural Association, in organizing one of the first Bulgarian "jubilee events" in the United States, the Month of Bulgarian Culture in Pittsburgh in spring 1979, a much-advertised "complex event" that included a concert by the Pirin Folk Ensemble, the showing of twelve Bulgarian films, photo and ethnographic exhibitions, and academic and public lectures. Characteristically, the Bulgarian ambassador and KK representatives also met with Bulgarian émigrés and participated in a local television program, titled *The Bulgarians—The Wonderful People of Pittsburgh*.[71] When the embassy embarked on the task of assembling a national celebration committee for the 1300th anniversary, Penka French (together with her brother and husband) became one of the executive directors of the committee, which featured a handful of émigrés, in addition to U.S. senators, academics, and cultural figures.[72] In 1981, the anniversary year, she helped organize two academic symposia in Pittsburgh and Columbus, Ohio, as well as a Bulgarian folk festival dedicated to the 1300-year jubilee in Pittsburgh. For all these activities, she received an honorary 1300th anniversary medal in the company of senators Adlai Stevenson and John Fulbright.[73] For her, the 1300-year jubilee was an opportunity to both reconnect with her roots and to further her professional interests in folk art and music, so she did not hesitate to work with the representatives of communist Bulgaria to keep the channels of communication open. Throughout these interactions, she adopted the nation-speak of the Bulgarian officials, while her own exile-speak, with its archaic Bulgarian and organic, amateur (*samodeen*) enthusiasm, appealed to Bulgarian officials who were in search of authentic and soulful compatriots in their diaspora-building endeavors.[74]

Authentic exile-speak, however, did not guarantee loyalty, as evident in another émigré woman of the same generation, Dora Gabensky, whose anticommie speak was typical of the strategies of the hostile anticommunist activists who, once Bulgarian cultural activities began proliferating in the United States, saw it as their mission to remind the U.S. public about the perils of communism.[75] Dora Gabensky, the wife of a Bulgarian diplomat in Italy, had emigrated to the United States in the late 1940s together with her husband, Ivanko Gabensky, who became an RFE contributor in the United States (they first resided in New York City). After a series of unrewarding experiences with various anticommunist groups (the family was engaged in extensive communication with activists of the National Council, National Front, and the various BANU splinters), Gabensky decided to withdraw from leadership positions in political organizations. That being said, her sympathies aligned with the Bulgarian National Front, a nationalist, monarchist organization: she contributed to its newspaper *Borba*, printed in Chicago, and was close to its leader, George Paprikov. She maintained regular correspondence with Bulgarian émigrés from Latin America, Australia, Canada, Europe, and Israel, nurturing a solid transnational network of anticommunist sympathizers. She regularly spoke of herself as living "in exile" (*v izgnanie*), and her conscious mission was to preserve the experience of the Bulgarian "emigrants in exile" (*emigratsiiata v izgnanie*). Her anticommunism was somewhat organic, growing out of her personal experiences as the wife of a diplomat-turned-RFE-contributor (she meticulously, almost frantically collected "information about communism, ideology, [and] tyranny"). Yet, her work also had a more moderate public face. Gabensky was the editor of *Luch*, the magazine of the Association of Bulgarian Artists and Writers in Exile that she and her husband established in 1960 due to "deep, principled disagreements" (*dâlboki, printsipni razlichiia*) with the existing Bulgarian political associations, and especially the Bulgarian National Council, a royalist organization in New York City. *Luch* provided a forum for émigrés who wished to connect to other "Bulgarians in exile" in an alternative, non-political format. Through this work, Dora Gabensky maintained correspondence with émigré women who cherished her publications on Bulgarian traditions and customs and wrote to her in their archaic Bulgarian using pre–World War II orthography, nurturing solid diasporic links based on exile-speak.

Yet, as time went on, and especially after Gabensky moved from New York to California following the retirement of her husband, Dora Gabensky's exile-speak became more infused with anticommie-speak. From the 1970s on, even though (or perhaps exactly because) détente was still on the agenda, Dora Gabensky embarked on a campaign to undermine what she saw as Bulgarian "communist propaganda" in the United States (this activism seems to coincide with the death of her husband in 1976). Gabensky became an activist in the renewed Captive Nations Committee, an anticommunist advocacy group of émigrés from throughout Eastern Europe that experienced a renewal in the late 1970s. She was one of the rare women to participate in the annual Captive Nations Week, dominated by men, using this occasion in her campaign to publicize informational materials about Bulgaria under communist control (featuring, for example, the inevitable map of "forced labor camp Bulgaria" [*kontsentratsionna Bâlgariia*]). She was an active member of the Federation of Republican Women and, quite appropriately as a resident of California, she actively campaigned and fundraised for Ronald Reagan, whose uncompromising Cold War rhetoric she appreciated. During these years she even established a Bulgarian-American Republican Club. When the Bulgarian government organized a series of 1300th anniversary events in Los Angeles in 1981, she vocally protested the mayor's involvement in what she saw as communist propaganda. By 1983, she had formed the organization BACKPAC, or Bulgarians against Conciliative Kakistocracy Political Action Committee. This organization vocally protested the Week of Bulgarian Culture held on the UCLA campus in May 1983, calling it a "deplorable event." In her strongly worded correspondence, Gabensky passionately urged the governor not to allow taxpayer money to fund the activities of a "terrorist organization" (i.e., the BKP).[76] In an endeavor to create an alternative commemorative agenda among the Bulgarian community in North America, she participated in the commissioning of a memorial for the victims of totalitarianism that anticommunist émigrés inaugurated in 1983 on the outskirts of Toronto on the grounds of the Bulgarian Orthodox Church of SS. Cyril and Methodius.[77]

If these two women represented the two extremes of loyal and hostile émigrés, a third person's story demonstrates the more nuanced choices of other more recent exiles who attempted to maintain a low public profile for private reasons. Atanas Slavov was a Bulgarian writer, poet, scholar of semiotics, and professor of English literature at the University of Sofia. A widely published academic and author, he participated in the official cultural activities of the Bulgarian state of the 1970s, which had become an unavoidable, obligatory part of the public profile of Bulgarian intellectuals. Yet, Slavov became one of the handful of defectors among the cultural intelligentsia, together with the sculptor Liubomir Dalchev. Slavov decided not to return to Bulgaria during a cultural exchange visit to London in early 1978 when he walked into the U.S. embassy and requested asylum.[78] He first arrived in Chicago but then went to Washington, DC, and finally California. A member of the Union of Bulgarian Writers and a professor at the University of Sofia, he fit the perfect Western image of the heroic, romantic, idealistic anticommunist dissident who not only abandoned Bulgaria leaving his family behind but also smuggled a manuscript on the underground literary movement out of Bulgaria. Slavov could have claimed a dissident status, if he wished, but his actions were subtler. He was in contact with other prominent Bulgarian émigrés (including Georgi Markov in London, Petar Semerdzhiev in Israel, Asen Ignatov in Munich, and Tzvetan Todorov and Julia Kristeva in Paris), seeking their advice. He had extensive prior contacts with American academics and prominent American writers, such as Kurt Vonnegut (which may explain why he chose to defect to the United States). But once in the United States, he had a disappointing experience trying to find a trade publisher for his smuggled book, a potential blockbuster dissident narrative because it narrated the political predicaments of the literary world in communist Bulgaria (he eventually published the work with a reputable academic press).[79]

As the rejection letters kept piling up, in a situation of frustration and despair he turned to Dora Gabensky to publish some of his work in *Luch*; this strategy would not only generate income but also help him establish his name in California where he had moved. Slavov started writing for a magazine that could be construed as anticommunist based on the affiliations of its editor, but his texts were unambiguously neutral. However, after Georgi Markov was assassinated in London in September 1978, he withdrew from all politically associated organizations, including *Luch*, and maintained a low profile. Yet in his correspondence, he continued to caustically criticize American intellectuals who did not support him publicly because they did not wish to tarnish their relations with official Bulgaria.

In the end, Slavov had to shift his strategy. After swallowing the fact that his smuggled manuscript on Bulgarian underground literature was too narrow a topic for the United States, he tried to launch "a journal of Eastern European émigré literature," *Meridian*.[80] Trying to stay away from the dissident brand, he conceived it as "a journal of personal opinion" that would include authors from both communist and noncommunist Eastern Europe. For example, Turkey, Greece, Cyprus, and Finland were included; the pilot issue contained Czeslaw Milosz's Nobel lectures, work by Odysseas Elytis and Isaac Bashevis Singer, and contributions from Milan Kundera and Georgi Markov, among others. Slavov claimed that the journal's "interest lies in the field of artistic expression in which . . . politics and ideology play only a secondary role." Instead of being a dissident publication, *Meridian* declared its commitment to "pluralism, tolerance, [and] non-attachment." As he was writing to publishing houses, academic institutions, and foundations in his quest for funding, resorting to subtle dissi-speak proved unavoidable, especially after his collaborator wrote in despair, "Magazines on East Europe are proliferating like mushrooms!" In 1981, Slavov started advertising *Meridian* as the forum for "East European writers in exile" whose goal was "the stimulation of the democratic cultural traditions of the area." In the end, he was unable to find financial support for his "niche" magazine (he envisioned an initial circulation of 8,000 in both the United States and Europe). Eventually, Slavov had to focus on finding a stable employment. Ideally, he wanted a position at a university, library, or cultural institution. Yet, in the end, he took a job that he had initially tried to avoid because he did not want to be stereotyped, namely a position in the Bulgarian section of the VOA in Washington, DC. A defector from Eastern Europe, he only "made it" when he reconciled himself to following Western expectations of Eastern European intellectual asylum-seekers. As a VOA contributor, he entered the world of anticommunists and technically became one of the hostile émigrés, even though he had tried hard to disassociate himself from political activism and never publicly claimed dissident status (after 1989, Slavov returned to Bulgaria).[81] In the late 1970s, anticommie-speak was unescapable for émigrés from Eastern Europe who wanted to start a new life in the West.

A Bulgarian Diaspora in the Making

In their encounter with émigrés during the 1970s as they were trying to nurture a Bulgarian diaspora, officials meticulously tried to divide up the colony into loyal and hostile members, sorting out people according to a straightforward Cold War logic that saw either friends or enemies. Perhaps that made sense for people whose jobs were based on political loyalty and who reported on their activities in the ideological jargon of late socialism. Thus, a core group of hostile émigrés was ever-present in the correspondence of Bulgarian representatives. Yet, officials also knew that people did not automatically fit into the clear-cut categories of anticommunists versus patriots. It is true that there were some committed, hostile activists, but the anticommunist organizations were disorganized and divided into splinter groups that bitterly accused each other of various sins. Further, some of them could be used for the purposes of official Bulgaria, notably the anticommunist but "patriotic" pro-Bulgarian Macedonian activists who became the core of "loyal" émigrés. Even "illegal" economic emigrants could potentially become allies if approached through a patriotic strategy. Many of the allegedly loyal émigrés, however, being neutral, also tended to be unreliable—most of them did not mind showing up at the occasional folk concert or museum exhibit, but they did not pursue formal contacts with the country that they had left. Some remained suspicious of official Bulgarian attempts to approach them, but others were simply not invested in their Bulgarian identity enough to participate in regular activities. Ironically, then, some of the hostile émigrés were also the most reliable contacts for official Bulgarian representatives because they were actively invested in their Bulgarian connections. This observation fits James Clifford's classic definition of diaspora as a community of people who maintain "a memory, vision, or myth about their homeland" and see "the homeland as a place of eventual return, when the time is right."[82] In the end, despite the ever-present obsession with classifying people into hostile or loyal, a messy and thus flexible logic informed the approach of Bulgarian officials toward the Bulgarian colony that they were trying to cultivate.

Considering the diaspora-building goals of the Bulgarian cultural policies of the 1970s, it is not surprising that nation-speak, or the persistent use of national rhetoric, infused the contacts between representatives of official Bulgaria and the Bulgarian community abroad. Ultimately, while trying to balance domestic political concerns, international ideological considerations, and an overarching preoccupation with patriotic objectives, Bulgarian officials resorted to cultural nationalism—as evident in the promotion of cultural definitions of the nation—as the most reliable guiding force in articulating priorities and carrying out policies. This observation allows us to link global Bulgarian cultural outreach back to domestic priorities, which similarly used the patriotic language of official culture as a strategy of legitimatization. As in the internal situation in Bulgaria, the normalization and nationalization of the late socialist way of life became intertwined, emphasizing the importance of national ideology in the rejuvenation and perpetuation of the communist regimes in Eastern Europe. National rhetoric was indispensable in fostering a global Bulgarian community through approaching individuals of different political, socioeconomic, or generational backgrounds and forging their patriotism. As émigrés resumed contacts with Bulgaria in the context of the 1300th anniversary extravaganza, the nation-speak of official Bulgarian representatives ultimately normalized the communist regime in the eyes of many Bulgarians abroad. A Bulgarian diaspora united behind national values and historical traditions was now in the making.

CHAPTER 5

Like a Grand World Civilization

In 1980, 308 delegates from 82 Bulgarian-Indian Friendship Societies—representing over 150,000 dues-paying members and an estimated 300,000 total supporters of Bulgaria—gathered at a convention in New Delhi to discuss the activities of their organizations.[1] The members of these societies tended to be affiliated with the Communist Party of India (CPI), but many were members of Indira Gandhi's ruling Congress Party.[2] Typically, the organizations took part in meetings with Bulgarian diplomats and collected a small subsidy to organize events for Bulgarian holidays. From the Bulgarian perspective, these societies "fulfilled a noble task—to acquaint [the Indian population] with the history, culture, economy, life, and activities of the Bulgarian people, and their struggle and labor to build a new, happier life."[3]

Many society members were excited to learn about the accomplishments of the small Balkan state. Celebrations of 9 September, the national holiday marking the socialist revolution in Bulgaria, often featured Indian officials from the state or federal levels who wanted to find out more about the transformations in the country.[4] In 1977, at the meeting of the friendship society in the city of Hyderabad, the state minister for budget and economic planning, Narsa Redi, gave a speech about his 1973 visit to Bulgaria, declaring that "Bulgarian agriculture is the best in the world" and India had much to learn from it. The chairperson of the society, Radjesvar Rao, explained that under the new cultural exchange agreement signed between the two countries in 1976, three Indian students had the opportunity to study in Bulgaria free of charge, an announcement that caused much enthusiasm among the fifty attendees.[5]

Excitement about cooperation between Bulgaria and India was also evident at the highest levels. In November 1981, in the midst of the Bulgarian celebrations of the 1300th anniversary of the establishment of the medieval Bulgarian state in 681, Prime Minister Indira Gandhi visited Bulgaria. In her speech, she declared: "We must strengthen our bilateral relations through greater exchanges of commerce and culture. But it is even more important that we work to deepen the feelings of fellowship among our peoples."[6] This project of creating fellowship was already underway, if we are to judge from the activities of the Bulgarian-Indian Friendship Societies, which organized numerous celebrations of the Bulgarian 1300-year jubilee in India.

Such fond exchanges were not unique to Bulgaria and India. In March 1981, a centrally located boulevard and a square in Mexico City acquired the names Bulgaria and Georgi Dimitrov, respectively, while in the city of Puebla, a street near the beloved main city park was named Sofia, after the Bulgarian capital. A Bulgarian journalist in attendance was elated: "You need to be away from your motherland to feel the true power of the word 'Sofia' written with still-wet blue paint on the otherwise short Sofia Street in the city of Puebla with its millions of residents!"[7] The gesture was even more meaningful for the Bulgarians given the fact that the current Boulevard Bulgaria used to be called Boulevard California. These ceremonies occurred in the presence of Bulgaria's first lady, Liudmila Zhivkova, the minister of culture and daughter of the Bulgarian leader Todor Zhivkov, who was attending celebrations in Mexico dedicated to the 1300th anniversary. The events included the opening of the *Medieval Bulgarian Civilization* exhibition, in the presence of President López Portillo, who had just been awarded the highest Bulgarian honor, the Dimitrov Prize, in recognition of his contributions to Bulgarian-Mexican friendship.

This chapter explores Bulgarian cultural involvements in India and Mexico to demonstrate that the pursuit of global connections was at the heart of the socialist project, leading to the development of vibrant interactions between junior members of the Soviet bloc and some developing states well into the 1970s. Together with the next chapter, which explores Bulgarian notions of development in Nigeria, this analysis seeks to highlight the existence of alternative global geographies beyond the East-West and North-South contacts that dominate historical studies. My goal is to advance a "pericentric" perspective, which emphasizes the importance of the global periphery in the Cold War. In this analysis, Sofia, New Delhi, and Mexico City were important actors that cooperated fruitfully outside of the shadows of Moscow, Washington, London, Paris, Vienna, or Bonn. India and Mexico had their own reasons for pursuing contacts with the socialist states of Eastern Europe; however, here I reverse the question to ask why a small Balkan state sought new allies outside of Europe and invested in international cultural activities in the developing world. In this sense, this is a Bulgarian-centered approach based predominantly on Bulgarian archival records. In the 1970s, Bulgaria was rather successfully cultivating relationships outside of the East-West trajectory in the Global South, and both the East and the West were noticing these attempts to chart new East-South relations. By presenting the perspective of a state on the margins—a state that was also assumed to be the Soviet flag-bearer—I show that interactions among actors on the periphery "gave the Cold War the character it came to have."[8] This analysis contributes to the new scholarship that emphasizes the role of East-South relations through the examination of socialist globalization, or the uniquely socialist ideas of global cooperation that functioned as an alternative to Western notions of development and global integration during the Cold War.[9] By focusing on culture, rather than economics or politics, topics that dominate studies of the relationship between the Second and Third Worlds, I show that the Cold War interactions between "peripheral" actors did not follow a single logic.[10] By extending the analysis into the early 1980s, I demonstrate that relations between Eastern Europe and the Global South remained robust longer than usually assumed; up until 1982, if not longer, India and Mexico were among the most important international partners of small Bulgaria.[11]

There is a larger picture to this cultural extravaganza in the Global South. Between 1977 and 1981, according to official statistics, Bulgarian officials organized 15,413 cultural events in Asia, 3,442 in the Arab countries, 2,973 in Latin America, and 1,170 in Africa. Not even the 7,420 cultural events in capitalist countries, a clear priority of the prestige-making agenda of the regime, matched the scope of this cultural offensive in the developing world.[12] Why were the Bulgarians cultivating such distant and seemingly unusual cultural relations? Bulgarian international cultural outreach outside of Europe was consistent with the logic of Bulgarian cultural policies since the mid-1970s that have been examined so far: the same ideological, political, reputational, and national(ist) factors determined the decision to stage elaborate cultural programs in a variety of states in the developing world, as well. Economic objectives further shaped the choices of Bulgarian elites who sought hard currency and new markets in the fragile 1970s, so often economic and cultural cooperation went hand in hand (as is clear in the case of India). Yet, in some places in the Global South, culture played an independent role as a key driver of relations between states (as obvious in Mexico). In this chapter I advance debates on alternative global connections during the Cold War by emphasizing the role of culture in the new partnerships emerging along an East-South axis, which allowed actors on the margins to articulate alternative cultural geographies on a global scale.[13]

Beyond the global scale, however, key domestic factors shaped events, demonstrating again the interrelationship between local and global considerations in the conception and execution of these cultural programs. A special logic distinguished the way Bulgarian officials organized events in India and Mexico from their approach to cultural exchange with their Balkan or Western partners. Most importantly, the choice of the two countries as a main destination of Bulgarian culture was the result of the priorities of Bulgarian power elites, and particularly those of Liudmila Zhivkova, whose idiosyncratic personality and personal interests in Eastern philosophies and esoteric thought determined the scope of Bulgaria's policies. Through the 1970s, Zhivkova developed her interests in theosophy, meditation, yoga, and the paranormal, and often during her official trips she traveled to historical and archaeological sites, visited with gurus, experimented with foods, and participated in informal gatherings whose scope was often clouded in mystery.[14] Largely because of her influence, India and Mexico (and Japan, not discussed here) accounted for most of the Bulgarian cultural involvement outside of Europe during this time.[15] In the conditions of "cultural shortages" associated with the celebrations of the 1300th jubilee, the best Bulgarian cultural products were dispatched to these faraway countries (as well as the West), as a clear sign of the two main priorities of the regime.

Traveling to distant countries presented Bulgarian officials with unexpected opportunities to craft a distinct cultural message in front of global audiences without much prior knowledge about the country, unlike their Balkan neighbors or Western partners. This situation allowed Bulgarian cultural forays in India and Mexico to acquire a peculiar flavor. Unlike the cultural events organized among neighbors where national stakes were high, or those in the West where ideological considerations were paramount, in India and Mexico Bulgarian officials promoted often extravagant civilizational claims. There were two aspects of this civilizational message. On the one hand, Bulgarian officials operated under the assumption of their own uncontested Europeanness, unlike in the West where they often had to explain or defend their European identity, yet, on the other, they continuously asserted the image of Bulgaria as an equal peer of other "grand world civilizations" such as those of ancient Mexico or India. Because the Bulgarian message was not scrutinized in the same way as it was in the Balkans or the West, cultural activities often took on exaggerated, even pompous dimensions, in order to emphasize the unique role of small Bulgaria at the crossroads of civilizations.

To explain the unique character of the Bulgarian cultural encounters with India and Mexico, I engage the historical narrative at multiple levels. First, I situate events in the context of the multipolar Cold War that saw a variety of interactions between the West, East, and "the rest." Second, I show that Bulgaria had a variety of reasons to pursue contacts with actors outside of Europe. While political and economic considerations often prevailed, ideological, public relations, and national(ist) factors also informed those choices. Third, singling out the intense cultural relationship that developed among Bulgaria, India, and Mexico, I emphasize the importance of culture in cultivating new relationships between the Second and Third Worlds. In this case, the civilizational rhetoric portraying Bulgaria as one of the oldest European and world civilizations determined the nature of these relationships. Finally, I conclude by emphasizing that culture allowed Bulgaria to project its own civilizational ideas to a global audience, contributing to the creation of alternative cultural imaginaries along an East-South axis.

The Multipolar Cold War: A Bulgarian Perspective

There is a growing literature on the global Cold War that has insisted on the importance of the Third World in the evolution of the conflict between West and East. The emergence of the newly sovereign states and their high-profile, indigenous leaders challenged the bipolar political model of West versus East because the "rise of the rest" provided an alternative to Cold War polarization. Adopting this perspective, historians have made it clear that various configurations of power between the West, the East, and "the rest" created a complex system of global interconnections. As David Engerman argues, inserting the perspective of the postcolonial world into Cold War histories allows us to see the Cold War "as a fundamentally multipolar conflict, with the superpowers constantly responding not just to each other but to their allies and adversaries in the Third World."[16] This multipolar Cold War perspective is at the center of my analysis.

In 1952, French economist Alfred Sauvy coined the term Third World to denote the newly independent, postcolonial states in Asia and Africa. Seeking the possibility of a "third way" distinct from both American capitalism and Soviet state socialism, he contrasted the Third World to the "first world," or the West with its traditions of imperialism and capitalism, and the "second world," or the (rhetorically anti-imperialist) Soviet Union that was building a Soviet empire in Eastern Europe. The concept of "Third World" took hold after the Bandung Conference of African and Asian peoples in 1955, and many newly independent states embraced it as a term of common identity.[17] It is not coincidental that this conference paved the way for the Nonaligned Movement, officially launched in 1961, whose explicit goal was to create an alternative political path between the two blocs in the Cold War.[18]

The term Third World enjoyed wide usage in the 1960s with the growing consciousness that post-independence Africa, Asia, and the Caribbean shared a common cause and required a common action. The states of Latin America also became associated with the Third World, even though they had been independent since the early 1800s. Despite their different historical trajectory, U.S. control in the Americas helped link Latin America to the rest of the Third World through the frameworks of "dependency theory" and "structural imperialism."[19] During the 1960s and 1970s, economic issues moved to the center of discussion.[20] Instead of dividing states politically between East and West, the differences between the prosperous North and impoverished South—a taxonomy that used the latitude of the Mediterranean to distinguish between developed and developing nations—was emerging as a new demarcation in the global community. Various proposals were advanced for reordering the international economic system to alleviate the gap between rich and poor. By the late 1970s, the terms Third World, South, and developing countries were used as synonyms for "poorer countries." Only in the 1980s did the power of Third World solidarity begin to wane, a process that accelerated in the aftermath of 1989.[21]

Many of these debates centered on the concept of development.[22] Despite the active role of the United States, many Third World leaders did not pursue a strictly Western model of development based on free market practices. In fact, for some newly independent countries the Soviet model of development was attractive because it represented a repudiation of Western economic exploitation and political domination.[23] The Soviet Union emerged as a prominent actor in the Third World under Nikita Khrushchev (1954–1964), and this involvement continued under Leonid Brezhnev (1964–1982).[24] Soviet leaders believed that their opposition to imperialism and track record of rapid economic development would be appealing to the newly independent states. The Soviets generously provided aid to countries whose governments had socialist credentials, such as China, Cuba, Ethiopia, and Mozambique. But many recipients of Soviet aid—including India, Indonesia, Egypt, Algeria, Iraq, Syria, and Ghana—were not Marxist but rather nonaligned states that adopted selected elements of state socialist economic development.[25]

The multipolarity of the Cold War is especially obvious in the involvement of Eastern Europe in the Third World, which charted unique East-South connections outside of the immediate Soviet orbit. Several trends are emerging out of the growing literature on the topic.[26] Soviet allies played an important role in projects of international development in the Third World, but often they pursued their own priorities over Soviet bloc solidarity. Many of them, such as Czechoslovakia and the GDR, were more developed than the Soviet Union, so Third World leaders often preferred their expertise over Soviet advice. Further, the socialist states had the appeal of not being super-powers dictating geopolitical terms, but states that acted as equal partners. The involvement of Soviet allies in the Third World—sometimes acting as Soviet proxies but sometimes pursuing their own interests—created a condi-tion that Young-Sun Hong has aptly called a "bipolar (dis)order."[27]

Based on their examination of these contacts, scholars of Eastern Europe have been advancing a discussion about the existence of alternative notions of globalization, or multiple globalizations, during the Cold War. In her study of United Nations debates about the New International Economic Order (NIEO) in the 1960s and 1970s, Johanna Bockman has demonstrated the global appeal of "socialist globalization" focused on state intervention rather than free trade. Addressing concerns specific to the postcolonial world, UN circles articulated the idea that "developed countries"—which did not necessarily mean capitalist countries—should assist developing countries in their efforts to speed up progress. This strong preference for "cooperation and solidarity" was only erased from the historical record in the late 1980s after the triumph of capitalism at the end of the Cold War.[28] But these new visions were not limited to economic ideas. In his work on Eastern Euro-pean architects working outside of Europe, Łukasz Stanek prefers to use the term mondialization to point to the overlapping international projects of the Cold War, questioning the master narrative of the gradual triumph of glo-balization as homogenizing Americanization; socialist internationalism and the Nonaligned Movement provided a viable—and welcome—alternative to Western development projects well into the 1980s.[29] Finally, in their strong defense of the existence of multiple globalizations, James Mark, Steffi Marung, and Artemy M. Kalinovsky speak about "different and competing models of globalization" to emphasize "the plurality of cultural, social, political and economic projects within this 'global condition'" that devel-oped from the 1950s on. In this analysis, which insists that "globalization can only be thought of in the plural," the character of socialist globalization is also seen in the major role of the state in determining those global choices.[30] As this chapter shows, Bulgarian diplomats and specialists also participated in networks of foreign experts who competed in providing expertise for devel-opment projects in Nigeria during the long 1970s. In the Bulgarian case, culture, in addition to economics and politics, infused those contacts.

The question remains, in what ways did Bulgarian elites think about their place in the global order of the 1970s? By pursuing this question, I am able to present the perspective of a small state on the functioning of the world, inserting nuance into the distinction between First, Second, and Third worlds that dominates current scholarship. Bulgarian officials tended to refrain from the Three Worlds model that used the designation Second World to refer to the Eastern European socialist states as second to the West. Diplomats occasionally used the categories of North and South, especially when in conversation with their new partners in Africa. Yet, the Bulgarian term of choice was "developing countries" (*razvivashti se strani*), and the objective criterion for this classification was a large agricultural population, industrial underdevelopment, and a desire for modernization. This definition allowed Bulgaria—and the Soviet bloc states in general—to assert their credentials as recently developed socialist states vis-à-vis the "developed capitalist states" (*razviti kapitalisticheski strani*), and offer an alternative model of modernization to developing states to help them avoid the evils of capitalism. This understanding of development saw the process as natural and inevitable, achieved through a stable political system, industrialization, urbanization, high literacy rates, and high levels of public involvement, all criteria that fit the socialist bill.[31] Having adopted the identity of a recently developed state, Bulgaria was now prepared to lend a hand to friendly developing states interested in speedy socioeconomic transformation.[32] A small state, in other words, had a distinct role to play in this world system, as imagined from the periphery.

To accomplish this mission, Bulgarian officials exalted a special Bulgarian cultural model, which placed their country on an equal level with other world civilizations—such as the Aztecs, Mughals, and Hindus—but also articulated an unquestionably European template of development rivaling the legacies of the ancient Greeks and Romans. This was supposed to be a subtle message: ancient and modern, Balkan, European, and of the world, Bulgaria could provide a unique example for countries that wanted to defy traditional (Western) civilizational claims and superpower (neo)imperial projects by adopting an alternative template of modernization. In the larger context of the global Cold War, Bulgaria's ideas of development were expressed not only through economic or political cooperation, but also via practices of cultural exchange infused with civilizational rhetoric.

Discovering the Developing World

In the mid-1970s, as a part of the prestige-building endeavors of Bulgarian elites in the context of developed socialism, Bulgaria took on a new international role by refocusing its attention regionally (on its neighbors in the Balkans), but also globally (on selected developing countries). What were the reasons for this active global overture of a small Eastern European state during the precarious 1970s? Reputational considerations were at the heart of this project: according to the British Foreign and Commonwealth Office (FCO), "Bulgaria is seeking a new role. It is tired of being type-cast." Trying to defy the stereotype of the "Soviet flag-bearer," Bulgaria was now pursuing a more independent role on the world stage.[33] Yet, unique domestic conditions facilitated these choices, as well. Unlike the heads of other socialist states (particularly Poland and Czechoslovakia) that had internal political challenges, Bulgaria's Todor Zhivkov, wishing to be seen as a great statesman and enhance the prestige of his country, became "the most travelled East European leader."[34] Zhivkov's travel record was impressive: in 1976, he engaged in state visits to India, Libya, Tunisia, Iran, and Iraq and accepted visitors from Ethiopia, Tanzania, Somalia, Angola, Mozambique, Egypt, Vietnam, Laos, and Mexico.[35] Africa, in particular, was emerging as a new item on the Bulgarian agenda, prompting British diplomats to condescendingly talk about "Bulgaria's jungle offensive."[36] Reaching out to these states was part of a general Warsaw Pact campaign for involvement in the developing world; there is little doubt that Zhivkov coordinated these efforts with Soviet leader Brezhnev, who had established a ritual summer meeting of Soviet bloc heads of state in Yalta. Yet, a complicated set of motives determined the Bulgarian drive toward international contact, including ideological and political needs, economic objectives, prestige-making goals, and national(ist) aspirations, as well as the personal choices of the political leaders in charge of the country. To understand the role of cultural exchange in these endeavors, it is necessary to outline the broader context of Bulgaria's global reach.

Ideology played an important role in the Soviet bloc's outreach to the developing world. The Soviet turn toward internationalism occurred under Nikita Khrushchev beginning in 1956. In the 1960s the Soviet Union abandoned attempts at "revolutionary transformation" in the developing world and adopted the principle of "peaceful coexistence": instead of working only with socialist states, the Soviet bloc now sought to create "a broad coalition of progressive forces standing in opposition to the powers of imperialism."[37] In the 1970s, but especially after the signing of the Helsinki Final Act in 1975, the concept of "peaceful coexistence between different socioeconomic systems" also became the cornerstone of Bulgarian foreign policy. The Bulgarian commitment to "proletarian internationalism" continued to drive contacts with countries whose governments had socialist credentials, notably Vietnam, Mozambique, and Angola. Yet, the rhetoric of "anti-imperialism" and "anti-neocolonialism" (focused on the developing world's rights over its economic resources) resonated with a broader group of potential allies who may not have shared the Bulgarian commitment to the Soviet political model, but were attracted by the notion of peaceful coexistence.

In 1976, on the eve of the Bulgarian Communist Party's Eleventh Congress, a publication in the BKP's daily, *Rabotnichesko delo* (Workers' deeds), explained the parameters of Bulgarian foreign policy in the developing world after Helsinki. Condemning "racism and apartheid" and proclaiming support for the "national liberation movements" of the "peoples struggling against imperialism and colonialism," Foreign Minister Petar Mladenov declared that Bulgaria would provide help to the young states in Africa, Asia, and Latin America "to stimulate revolutionary transformations" in their societies, framing cooperation with the developing world broadly.[38] Bulgarian politicians used anti-imperialism and anti-neocolonialism, in particular, as umbrella terms that appealed to a variety of postcolonial states. In 1978, during his visit to Nigeria, Zhivkov spoke of his full support for "the final eradication of colonialism in Africa and the victory of true economic independence of the free African countries."[39] This ideological framing of Bulgaria's outreach to the developing world remained a constant during this period.

Ideological and practical factors, however, went hand in hand, and economic interests infused these efforts. In the spirit of proletarian internationalism, Bulgaria had robust economic relations with a number of African states with a socialist orientation, including Mozambique, Angola, Ethiopia, and Tanzania, where treaties of friendship and cooperation charted in detail the terms of Bulgarian economic involvement.[40] But elsewhere, purely economic factors shaped the contacts, as the Bulgarians tried to procure hard currency through specialist exchange, find markets for their industrial or processed food goods, or secure access to natural resources such as oil. Iraq, Syria, Tunisia, Libya, and Algeria were some of the places that benefited from Bulgarian economic investment and specialist exchange in the fields of engineering, construction, and medicine. Similarly, in Nigeria, the most populous African country, Bulgaria competed for an economic niche in the construction, industrial, and agricultural sectors of the newly independent state (1960), which was astutely navigating Soviet bloc and Western military and economic aid.[41] The practical inclinations of Bulgarian elites critically shaped their choice of partners in the Global South.

High-profile overseas events also served reputational strategies with the goal of "play[ing] up Bulgaria's international role."[42] Leaders were sensitive to Bulgaria's reputation as the most loyal Soviet ally and skillfully used these contacts to project an image of independence, sovereignty, and international status. According to British diplomats, Zhivkov personally showed "considerable satisfaction to project himself as an elder statesman of the Communist world in an arena in which . . . Bulgaria seems to have a distinct role to play."[43] Further, these endeavors served well the domestic legitimization purposes of communist elites in the 1970s as for ordinary Bulgarians, involvement in Third World countries came to signify "that Bulgaria carries some weight in international affairs."[44] Both among elites and the population at large there was a new level of excitement at the prospect of a small state entering the global scene and establishing a tangible presence outside of the geopolitical parameters of the mainstream Cold War divide between East and West.

In this context, a growing number of Bulgarian officials, supported by Zhivkova, thought that culture could play a key role in Bulgaria's involvement in the developing world. In 1977, a Bulgarian Cultural-Informational Center opened in New Delhi, and plans were underway for the opening of similar centers in Mexico City, Lagos, and Algiers. In 1979, Bulgarian friendship societies existed in Syria, Iraq, Yemen, the Arab Emirates, Lebanon, Jordan, India, Bangladesh, Sri Lanka, Pakistan, Indonesia, Nepal, Algeria, Nigeria, and Sudan; there were Bulgarian educational-cultural associations in Uruguay and Argentina.[45] Between 1977 and 1982, Bulgarian officials organized close to 23,000 cultural events in the developing world.[46] This extensive cultural outreach outside of Europe is striking, given the size of Bulgaria and its limited economic and cultural resources.

National(ist) motivations in line with the "patriotic turn" in Bulgaria no doubt informed these choices to invest in culture in the Global South. Interweaving domestic and international considerations in a fashion that had emerged as a defining feature of Bulgarian culture in the 1970s, officials projected Bulgaria's unique role in the world's cultural treasury through these campaigns. Basically, Bulgarian elites promoted the idea that cultural heritage elevated their country to the level of other civilizations such as the Aztecs, Mughals, Egyptians, ancient Greeks, or Romans. This was a message specifically molded for a global consumption: Bulgaria was a "grand nation" that provided a unique template for other nations that wished to elevate their international position while charting an independent role for their states in world affairs. In Zhivkova's words, cultural contacts served to "display the tangible contribution of Bulgarian culture to the development of human civilization."[47] State investment in culture paid off because it became a tool for the assertion of the prestige of a small state—one of the "cradles of European civilization"—on the world stage. Thus, the new encounters between Bulgaria and the developing states, being ideologically sound, politically beneficial, economically profitable, nationally affirming,

and culturally rich, became an opportunity to promote the special civilizational model that Bulgaria could offer to the world outside of the shadows of
better-known (typically Western) civilizations. A small state on the margins
used official culture to carve out its unique place in the world.

Resolving Contradictions: Bulgaria in India and Mexico

India and Mexico were Bulgaria's two most important international partners from the mid-1970s on, establishing "parallel histories" 10,000 miles and
eleven times zones apart.[48] Both India and Mexico saw nearly the same string
of Bulgarian political and economic delegations, agricultural experts, exhibition commissars, artists, performers, and folk troupes. In terms of cultural
relations, Bulgarian leaders often combined their trips to the two countries in
a desire to showcase their contacts with two states that, at first glance, shared
few commonalities.[49] Bulgaria established diplomatic relations with India in
1954. In 1967, newly elected prime minister Indira Gandhi visited Bulgaria,
followed by Todor Zhivkov's visit to India in 1969. In the 1960s and 1970s
regular if not particularly robust communication developed along economic
lines. From the mid-1970s on, culture added a new dimension to these contacts. Mexico, however, was an entirely new phenomenon in Bulgarian diplomacy. Bulgaria only established relations with Mexico in 1974 and opened
an embassy in 1975. The "sudden upsurge" of Mexican-Bulgarian contacts,
including a state visit by Mexican president José López Portillo in 1978, was
"something of a mystery" to foreign diplomats.[50] What brought Bulgaria,
India, and Mexico together in such unlikely friendships? Only the examination of Indian and Mexican archives could address the motivations of those
two states in sufficient nuance, yet here, having worked exclusively with Bulgarian records, I offer a pericentric perspective. My analysis confirms other
observations that socialist elites were extremely flexible with their political choices in the Global South, cultivating vibrant relationships even with
oppressive political regimes.[51] As seen in Bulgaria during the 1970s and 1980s,
political flexibility and the search for new allies, combined with the personal
choices of the power elites in each state, determined the fond relationships
with authoritarian India and populist Mexico.

From a Marxist perspective, there was much to criticize in the internal
affairs of Bulgaria's new partners: Bulgarian diplomats often used the term
"contradictions" (*protivorechiia*) to describe both countries. A Bulgarian
study from 1981 concluded: "There are numerous political struggles, social
conflicts, and religious tensions," including lasting "feudal remnants" or

"atavisms" (*otzhivelitsi*) in India. Poverty rates were at 40 to 50 percent, adult illiteracy was rampant, and rapid population growth impeded improvements in the standard of living, all factors making India a risky partner from an ideological perspective.[52] Mexico was problematic as well, as the "big bourgeoisie" connected to "American export capital" dominated political life.[53] To address the acute political and social problems after the economic crisis of 1973, the "ruling class" employed "traditional capitalist schemes: [appeals to] calm, national unity, sacrifice, patience, and trust."[54] While similar dynamics would have been the basis of a sharp critique of the government's choices elsewhere (especially in the West), in memos concerning India and Mexico these contradictions were duly noted but then carefully ignored.

Political compromise was the basis of the successful global romance between the three states. As far as India was concerned, Bulgarian officials maintained contacts and often praised the Communist Party of India (CPI), whose members periodically visited Bulgaria, but ideological commitment was never a priority in expanding contacts in the country.[55] In fact, the Bulgarian leadership had extremely good relations with Indira Gandhi's Congress Party; despite the "bourgeois" credentials of the congress and Gandhi's imposition of a "draconian" state of emergency in 1975–1977, Zhivkov and his daughter visited India in 1976. In the opinion of Bulgarian diplomats, Gandhi was a better, "less right-wing" alternative to other political parties, even though she was likely to continue using "authoritarian" methods to maintain her rule (which ultimately cost her the election in 1977). When Gandhi returned to power in 1980, the growing dynamism and enthusiasm of expanding economic and cultural contacts were paramount.[56] In Mexico Bulgarian diplomats also worked with the party of "financial oligarchy," the Institutional Revolutionary Party (PRI), which had held power since 1929 and had a "practical monopoly" on political life.[57] The same party had overseen the Tlatelolco Massacre during the 1968 student protests in Mexico City and the suppression of left-wing insurgents in the state of Guerrero in the early 1970s. Bulgarian diplomats, however, found the PRI's populist program focused on the rural and urban poor acceptable, and decided that the progressive if bourgeois agenda of the party made it a solid political partner.[58] In both India and Mexico, following a tortuous logic, Bulgarian officials sought to erase or downplay politically and socially inconvenient internal developments to justify growing relations. The new global entanglement between the three states was undeniably based, first and foremost, on their elites' willingness to resolve contradictions.

Although the expansion of contacts was rapid, their extent should not be overstated. Given the distance between the countries, they were limited

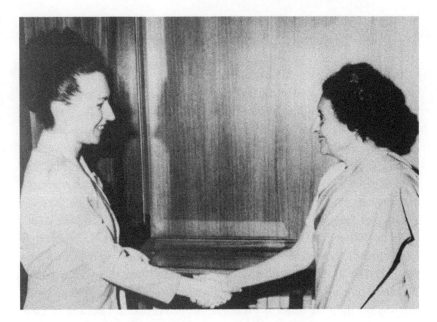

FIGURE 28.   Meeting between Liudmila Zhivkova and Indira Gandhi in New Delhi, 1976. Source: Elena Savova, Zdravka Micheva, and Kiril Avramov, eds., *Liudmila Zhivkova: Zhivot i delo (1942–1981); Letopis* (Sofia: Izdatelstvo na Bâlgarskata akademiia na naukite, 1987).

to highly ranked political leaders, party functionaries, diplomats, and their families, plus a growing number of exchange specialists, scholars, artists, and performers. The strong personal relations that developed between political leaders at the highest level was instrumental.[59] A close friendship flourished between Gandhi and Zhivkova, both daughters of leaders who had taken their countries in radically new directions. Their personal patronage played an important part in the intense, cordial relations between the two countries that developed from 1976 on. The two female politicians often made comparisons between the post-1944 socialist period in Bulgaria and the post-1947 independence period in India whose common goals were modernizing their countries and lifting their peoples out of poverty. In the words of Gandhi, "we have pursued different paths but the goal is the betterment of our people's lives."[60] In addition, both Zhivkova and Gandhi had an affinity for the use of history in their narratives of political success: while Zhivkova visited museums and historical sites and spoke about the mysterious Thracians and tenacious Slavs, Gandhi visited Hindu temples and used rituals and symbols, including those of Durga, the Hindu mother goddess, to mobilize national(ist) sentiment as a strategy of legitimization.[61] Their view of the transformational role of their families' political choices and the common use of historical rhetoric bound the two women together in their determination to pursue the "betterment" of their respective nations, both heirs of ancient civilizations.

In Mexico, the personal engagement of two presidents, Luis Echeverría (1970–1976) and his political ally and successor, José López Portillo (1976–1982), both of the populist and authoritarian PRI, were indispensable. The two actively facilitated contacts with small Bulgaria as described in the memoirs of the Bulgarian ambassador who was dispatched to cultivate those relations. Highly placed women played an important role, too. In 1975, Zhivkova visited Mexico in her capacity as chairperson of the Committee for Culture, the same year the new Bulgarian embassy first opened. In 1976, she attended the inauguration of President López Portillo, in a highly symbolic gesture, and visited again in 1978 and 1981. During those visits, First Lady Carmen Romano de López Portillo hosted receptions, museum openings, and ceremonies honoring Zhivkova; she also paid a visit to Sofia in 1977 and met with a host of Bulgarian officials.[62] The growing fondness between the two women paved the way for the state visits of President López Portillo in 1978 and of General Secretary Zhivkov in 1979.[63] While rhetorically portrayed as the rapprochement between the Mexican and Bulgarian people, the relationship had

FIGURE 29. President José López Portillo honoring Liudmila Zhivkova, 1978. Source: Elena Savova, Zdravka Micheva, and Kiril Avramov, eds., *Liudmila Zhivkova: Zhivot i delo (1942–1981)*; *Letopis* (Sofia: Izdatelstvo na Bâlgarskata akademiia na naukite, 1987).

a certain royal flavor because it was so obviously based on the personal connections between the political families in charge of the two countries.

The closeness between Zhivkova, Gandhi, and Romano attracted international attention, prompting the press to speculate about the characteristics of Bulgaria's "red dynasty" in comparison to those in the GDR,
Albania, and Romania.[64] Zhivkova was often referred to as the "Bulgarian
princess," the protégé of a regime that enjoyed "a high degree of family
management."[65] But through these unexpected and somewhat exotic foreign
contacts, Zhivkova was thought to be bringing something fresh to the international scene. Western observers were fascinated by the fact that "few men,
let alone women, are able to . . . effortlessly sprinkle their press conferences
with references to ancient Sanskrit philosophy."[66] In Bulgaria, many shared
the opinion that the spectacular expansion of Bulgarian cultural contacts
with India and Mexico was due to Zhivkova's personal interests in Eastern
philosophy, meditation, and yoga, which made these new contacts unique
and exciting.[67] Ironically, these idiosyncrasies gave Zhivkova some legitimacy
internationally because she was seen as introducing new approaches to a
sphere previously dominated by ideology. In the late 1970s the foreign press
overwhelmingly evaluated her efforts as a "brilliant success as an exercise of
international public relations [that put] this small, obscure Balkan country
on the western world's cultural map."[68] From the perspective of Bulgarian
elites, the decision to invest in culture in faraway places paid off in terms of
prestige-making.

Political and Economic Cooperation:
An East-South Perspective

To explain these contacts solely as the wishes of the "Bulgarian princess,"
however, does not take into consideration the wider Bulgarian interests in
the developing world. Furthermore, India and Mexico pursued contacts with
the socialist countries for their own reasons.[69] In the 1970s both India and
Mexico had emerged as important voices in support of the newly independent postcolonial states, making them key players in the global Cold War.
At different times and for different reasons, their governments sought to
assert their political neutrality and disentangle their economic infrastructure from former colonial masters (India) or diversify political and economic
contacts beyond their immediate powerful neighbor to the north (Mexico).
Looking for alternatives, both countries turned their attention to the socialist
states, including smaller states like Bulgaria. Taken together, the political
and economic cooperation that developed between the three states serves

as an example of the alternative models of global interconnectivity that accelerated in the 1970s. This East-South axis highlights the limits of theories that explain globalization as a process of westernization only, as in this case, dynamic global contacts in the political, economic, and cultural spheres developed outside of the East-West and North-South frameworks well into the 1980s. Here, again, I offer an analysis of those contacts mainly from the perspective of small Bulgaria.

Since its independence in 1947, India had actively navigated the realities of the Cold War under the leadership of Jawaharlal Nehru (1947–1964). Once its regional adversary Pakistan entered into an alliance with the U.S. military in the mid-1950, the country initiated contacts with the Soviet Union (whose rapid industrialization Nehru admired) and sought advice from a range of international players (including experts from socialist Poland).[70] A former anticolonial leader and a moderate socialist with an Eton education and Cambridge law degree, Nehru sought the middle way. Domestically, the country was a parliamentary democracy, winning U.S. admiration, yet to modernize its economy it implemented economic planning, including five-year plans on the Soviet model. Internationally, India's neutrality was most evident in its key role in the Nonaligned Movement established in 1961. Indian relations with the United States were necessary yet cautious because the Kennedy administration provided substantial economic aid in the 1960s, yet Nehru despised U.S. racism, which he saw as a legacy of colonialism, and criticized American ideas of development as one-sided. Indian relations with the Soviet Union were selective and self-serving: Nehru secured the building of a Soviet steel plant in 1955 and sought further technical and economic expertise in the 1950s and 1960s, but he criticized the Soviet political system and was suspicious of Soviet support for the CPI.[71]

Once in power in 1966, Indira Gandhi was also determined to pursue an independent role for India vis-à-vis the main Cold War players. In the 1970s, to counterbalance U.S. economic and military aid, she increased Indian economic ties with the Soviet Union and other socialist states, not least in the context of the "green revolution" through which she sought to secure agricultural self-sufficiency. Gandhi also asserted India's international role through a successful war against East Pakistan in 1971 (which led to the creation of Bangladesh) and through the testing of a nuclear weapon in 1974. In the mid-1970s, in the context of détente and discussions of peaceful coexistence after Helsinki, India saw its role as expressing the interests of countries that did not commit to the Western or Eastern blocs. In the aftermath of the 1979 Soviet invasion of Afghanistan, Gandhi did not unequivocally condemn the Soviets in an attempt to counterbalance U.S. influence in the region, as evident in U.S. support for Pakistan. Domestically, she paid a heavy price for a state of emergency she imposed between 1975 and 1977 by losing the 1977 elections, so when back in power in 1980, Gandhi continued to proclaim commitment to neutrality and nonalignment to boost her legitimacy.[72] In this context, reinvigorated contacts with the smaller Eastern European states were a safe choice.

Mexico similarly held the position of a "middle power" in the context of the Latin American Cold War due to its ability to balance the superpowers. The country maintained its international reputation through neutrality, nonintervention, and non-participation in international organizations such as OPEC and the Nonaligned Movement.[73] While courting their powerful northern neighbor economically, Mexican governing elites were ambiguous political partners, as they committed to "Third Worldism" and maintained active (and generally supportive) relations with Cuba. Mexican relations with the Soviet Union were cautious yet generally tolerant: the PRI allowed the existence of a Communist Party at home (even if it harassed and disappeared its members) while in 1980 Mexico refused to participate in the U.S. boycott of the Moscow Olympics.[74]

What Gilbert Joseph calls "the Janus-faced policies of Cold War Mexico" were also obvious in its internal affairs. While Mexico was one of the few states to preserve its civilian government during the era of military dictatorships in Central and Latin America in the 1970s, the PRI, consistently in power since 1929, experimented with a range of authoritarian, repressive, and populist policies. In the 1970s, presidents Echeverría and López Portillo presented themselves as technocrats able to deal with the political and social instability after the 1973 crisis that had erased the success of the Mexican miracle from the previous decade, so they expanded the role of the state in the economy (especially agriculture), increased spending for school construction and housing projects, and made peace with young people by investing in education. The discovery of oil in the mid-1970s funded this state investment in social policies. Yet, at the same time, Mexico led quiet dirty wars against revolutionary groups and indigenous populations, while the social polarization between the middle class and the poor remained sharp.[75] For Mexico too, maintaining relations with a range of international actors, including the small socialist states, was a useful exercise.

In following a pericentric perspective it is important to analyze the logic of the Bulgarian officials pursuing connections with India and Mexico, despite their problematic political allegiances and dubious social credentials. In a global context, when Bulgaria chose international partners far from home, the bar was rather low: close contacts with India and Mexico were possible because their internal and foreign policy agendas were "not objectionable." Given Bulgaria's distance from these countries and general lack of knowledge about them, Todor Zhivkov's overtures in these two far-off states presented little political risk while potentially increasing his legitimacy at home and his reputation as an international player abroad. Thus, small Bulgaria actively cultivated East-South relationships, boldly advancing novel global contacts in the context of the 1970s.

There was a systematic expansion of contacts with India, in particular. Under the leadership of Indira Gandhi, who followed her father's principles of peaceful coexistence, India embraced détente, supported disarmament, proposed more contacts along North-South lines, and encouraged cooperation with the socialist states. The two countries avoided discussions of their political disagreements and focused on what bound them together. Further, despite its capitalist economy, Indian modernization projects provided opportunities for cooperation with the socialist states because Indian political elites experimented with forms of state planning and agricultural development.[76] Bulgarian diplomats believed that their presence in India served to undermine the traditional Western role in the postcolonial world while it gave substance to the official position that "the socialist states are the natural ally of all nonaligned states."[77]

With its population of 320 million and vast natural resources, Latin America also emerged as a region of interest for Bulgaria in the 1970s. Bulgarian diplomats were willing to work with all "democratic, progressive, and revolutionary forces" that would pursue cooperation outside of U.S. influence.[78] Venezuela, Colombia, and Mexico were the focus of Bulgarian diplomatic efforts because the three countries had preserved their civilian governments in the 1970s. In Mexico, the ruling PRI party followed "progressive" policies: it maintained close contacts with the social-democratic parties of Latin America and Western Europe and severed relations with Chile after the junta in 1973.[79] Together with Venezuela, Mexico established the Latin American Economic System (SELA) in 1975 to promote economic cooperation in the entire region, including with Cuba. Mexico was also willing to expand its relations with other socialist states, such as Hungary and the Soviet Union.[80] Establishing a presence in the region through involvement in Mexico suited the interests of Bulgarian policymakers.

Economic considerations were also an important motivation in fostering contacts with the two states, especially India. According to Bulgarian estimates, in the late 1970s, about 20 percent of the Indian economy (including 40 percent of industry) was under state control and Indian elites were still interested in pursuing alternative methods of modernization.[81] In 1973, an Indo-Bulgarian Joint Commission was established to coordinate matters of economic interest, and Bulgarian correspondence suggests the Bulgarian representatives made systematic efforts to be perceived as a "desired economic partner."[82] By 1976, Bulgaria had built eight food, pharmaceutical, and chemical factories in India and expanded its reach in the spheres of agriculture, electronics, machine building, metallurgy, and light industry. By 1981, four more Bulgarian plants had opened in the country.[83] During the same period the Bulgarians established their presence in Indian electronics by winning contracts for the import of computers and computer software.[84] Bulgarian specialists also extended help in setting up agricultural-industrial complexes: in 1976, when Zhivkov visited India, he inaugurated a Bulgarian complex in Bangalore. In 1980, when Gandhi came to power again, trade turnout between Bulgaria and India was double what it had been in 1970.[85]

In the late 1970s, Bulgarian leaders also pursued economic cooperation with Mexico. The PRI was particularly interested in the Bulgarian agricultural experience, and especially in setting up agricultural-industrial complexes similar to the projects already underway in India.[86] President López Portillo had come to power promising "efficiency and productivity" in agriculture.[87] After his visit to Bulgaria in 1978, upon his request, Bulgarian specialists established two agricultural-industrial complexes and food processing plants in the state of Guerrero that employed 2,100 peasants.[88] The Bulgarians also investigated the possibility of opening refineries and petrochemical plants with Mexican help.[89] But negotiations proceeded slowly, and besides the Guerrero complex, overall economic relations between Bulgaria and Mexico remained "unsatisfactory" from Bulgarian perspective.[90]

As is clear, despite the questionable political and social records of the ruling elites in India and Mexico in the long 1970s, the Bulgarian regime readily cultivated relations with two countries whose policies were characterized as no more than "not objectionable." Socialist elites were rather comfortable pursuing cooperation with authoritarian capitalist states. These dynamics highlight the fact that while East-South relations might have served to counterbalance the competition between the superpowers and to provide examples for alternative global possibilities, they were riddled with unresolved tensions that should not be ignored. Yet, in addition to politics and economics, culture played a role in charting these new ideas of cooperation and friendship between the Second and the Third Worlds.

From Technical-Scientific to Cultural-Educational Cooperation

Along with architects, engineers, chemists, textile and agricultural specialists, and technical personnel, Bulgaria also dispatched to India and Mexico scholars, artists, writers, folk and jazz musicians, archaeologists, and moun-taineers. The close connection between hard power and soft power is clear here: "technical-scientific cooperation" went hand in hand with "cultural-educational propaganda," emphasizing the role of culture, alongside econom-ics, in the projection of Bulgaria abroad. In February 1981, All India Radio broadcast a program titled "Growing Relations between India and Bulgaria," which intertwined economic and cultural themes. The broadcast noted that "Bulgaria is a small country. . . . [It] also has now highly developed modern industry and large-scale mechanized agriculture." But it was "the field of knowledge, culture and science" that "may open new vistas of understanding between two of the most ancient civilizations."[91] As Zhivkov put it, culture was "the trailblazer on the way toward broad and productive political and economic cooperation."[92] Confirming this opinion, in 1981 observers com-mented that "the name Bulgaria, which six years ago was almost unfamiliar in the land of the Aztecs, today is well known as a country . . . with rich culture and ancient history [as well as] an advanced and modern economy."[93] It is striking that culture played such an important role in contacts between Bul-garia and its two new partners: while in the case of India, the longer history of political relations and parallel development of economic cooperation might explain the role of culture, in Mexico, virtually identical cultural programs happened despite the rather rudimentary state of political and economic con-tacts, pointing to the ability of culture to support new global entanglements.

How can culture's important role be explained? These new international visions nicely supplemented the domestic agendas of the three states, dem-onstrating once more the inextricable link between local and global consid-erations in cultural exchange. Mexican and Indian ideas of solidarity and national unity as articulated by elites bore a striking resemblance to the BKP's own reinvigorated use of class and national rhetoric in the 1970s. President Echeverría's reforms, supported by "progressive intellectuals," involved more state investment in education and support for indigenous cultures in order to "transform education and culture from the monopoly of a minority to an achievement for the entire people."[94] His successor López Portillo, too, in his attempts to "manage abundance" after the new oil discoveries of the mid-1970s, attracted intellectuals by investing in museums and universities and used cultural outreach to the countryside, in addition to the building of schools and clinics, as a key channel for political legitimization.[95] Ever since Indian independence in 1947, the projection of a national past through museums and art exhibitions had been a preoccupation of Nehru's in his nation-building projects. Through its cultural role, the state "staked claim to history-making . . . and reaffirmed modern India's connections to the first civilizations in South Asia."[96] Under Indira Gandhi Indian cultural policies similarly sought to preserve the country's cultural heritage, yet they also acquired a social character, as Gandhi wanted to end illiteracy, raise the cultural level of the masses, and support the development of local artistic production to counter Western influences, while at the same time promoting Hinduism as the essence of Indian national identity.[97] From the perspective of Bulgarian power elites, these were progressive agendas oriented toward the people and the nation that showed appreciation for both past and future, akin to Liudmila Zhivkova's vision of Bulgarian culture in the 1970s. Domestic agendas and international priorities reinforced each other, allowing small Bulgaria to seamlessly connect its own visions of the nation to those of India and Mexico.

In diplomatic correspondence frequently mentioned commonalities between the three countries involved references to culture and history, emphasizing the importance of the civilizational rhetoric in this new rapprochement between the three countries. The ancient cultural heritage of the three states and their desire to preserve the legacies of Aztec warriors, Thracian kings, Mughal princes, and Hindu sages was a recurring theme. In the words of All India Radio, "Like India, Bulgaria has a hoary past and a chequered history. Both believe they have a cultural mission to fulfill and they kept up the fighting spirit even when they were down and under."[98] Mexican president López Portillo, too, pointed out that his first and most memorable impression of Bulgaria was the fact that "Bulgaria is truly a country with a rich ancient culture."[99] During the Bulgarian exhibitions, Mexican newspapers profusely praised "the glorious history of the Bulgarian nation."[100] Bulgarian and Indian leaders mentioned as a point of comparison their relatively recent independence: 1947 for postcolonial India and 1944 for socialist Bulgaria. Bulgarian and Mexican leaders spoke about the shared social justice agendas of the Mexican revolution of 1910 and Bulgaria's "socialist revolution" of 1944. This desire to establish historical connections—and use the past to justify current political choices—explains the importance of culture in the contacts between the three states. In the context of profound anxieties about domestic and global stability during the 1970s, historical and cultural arguments provided reassurance that, as grand civilizations of the past, the three countries would persevere in the face of adversity and succeed in their future goals. Ultimately, these ideas allowed a "peripheral" actor, Bulgaria, to chart new global imaginaries and project an active role from the periphery of the global Cold War.

Opening New Vistas of Understating: Bulgarian Culture in India

What was the scope of the cultural exchange between Bulgaria and India? The history of cultural relations between Bulgaria and India dated from the interwar years when Rabindranath Tagore, the Indian artist, novelist, and first non-European Nobel Prize winner, visited Bulgaria. During this time, thirty-four Indian authors were published in Bulgarian translation. After 1944, the communist regime resumed these contacts: book publications, exhibitions, and academic exchanges continued at the state level. In 1955, the first Indian films were shown in Bulgaria, and became a popular entertainment throughout the socialist period. In 1956, Vice President Sarvepalli Radhakrishnan was awarded an honorary doctorate from the University of Sofia during his visit to Bulgaria. The Punjabi writer Amrita Pritam wrote a travelogue about her visit to Bulgaria and translated Bulgarian prose, poetry, and folk songs.[101] This solid basis for Indian-Bulgarian cultural relations led to the signing of the first cultural cooperation agreement between Bulgaria and India in 1963, which recognized higher education diplomas and set up frameworks for language education in addition to other already established forms of cultural exchange.[102]

However, a new, dynamic expansion of cultural contact with India began after Liudmila Zhivkova became the chairperson of the Committee for Culture (KK) in 1975 and pursued systematic cultural cooperation with South and East Asia that mirrored her personal interests. In February–March 1976, Zhivkova toured North Korea, Vietnam, Burma, and India.[103] After her return, the KK discussed the possibilities for expanding relations with India. Despite the anti-neocolonial orientation of Bulgarian international outreach, official evaluations of Indian cultural life bore a condescending tone: "It will be difficult for us to reach the many millions of Indian people at this stage of their development through culture and arts, due to their misery and illiteracy and the lack of exposure to any culture whatsoever." Therefore, cultural exchange with India would be a middle-class endeavor targeting the educated, progressive bourgeois strata: "Our cultural events are aimed at the more or less educated circles in cities, which vary from those who simply have the habit of going to the movies to the upper classes with a taste for fine arts. India also has a large army of intellectuals, highly specialized technical personnel, and active university youth, a powerful element, which should become the main object of our cultural activities."[104] Such statements reveal Bulgaria's belief in the superiority of their cultural model in relation to postcolonial India, ironically echoing attitudes that the country otherwise criticized.

During the cultural agreement talks in 1976, the Bulgarian experts learned firsthand about the key Indian priorities in cultural exchange. Specialists from the Indian Ministry of Education, Social Policy, and Culture inquired about the Bulgarian experience with mass culture, illiteracy, and especially the Bulgarian "reading clubs" (*chitalishta*). The Indians were also interested

FIGURE 30. A meeting of the Indo-Bulgarian Friendship Society in the state of Andhra Pradesh, most likely in 1978 on the occasion of the Bulgarian centennial. Source: TsDA, f. 405, op. 9, a.e. 620, l. 116.

in collaborating with Bulgarian specialists in the arts and folklore and sought help with the preservation of ancient archaeological sites.[105]

In May 1977, a Bulgarian Cultural-Informational Center opened in New Delhi, in the middle-class neighborhood of Golf Link, to "popularize the achievements of building new life in our country."[106] The center published a glossy monthly magazine, *News from Bulgaria*, to present snapshots of Bulgaria's political, economic, and cultural way of life and emphasize common endeavors between Indian and Bulgarian specialists.[107] Diplomats worked to establish Indian-Bulgarian friendship societies, which were supposed to function as hubs of Bulgarian activity in India.[108]

Given that few Indians were familiar with Bulgaria, scholarly cooperation was another way of pursuing cultural contacts. Delhi University established a Bulgarian language professorship in 1977, enrolling seventeen majors for the study of Bulgarian language, history, and culture. These students became the vanguard of the Bulgarian presence in New Delhi: they performed at the Bulgarian Cultural-Informational Center and at the embassy, moving their (mostly Bulgarian) audience with recitals of Bulgarian literature on the occasion of the Bulgarian centennial celebrations in March 1978 or International Women's Day.[109] Indian and Bulgarian scholars discussed common

FIGURE 31. Reading of Bulgarian poetry by students at Delhi University. Source: *Bulgaria Today*, no. 5, 1980.

strategies in the study and preservation of ancient cultures, proposing joint research projects focused on ancient civilizations, and especially cooperation between Bulgarian specialists in Thracology and Indian specialists in ancient Indian cultures.[110] Civilizational agendas were at the core of this cultural partnership.

The number of Bulgarian events in India grew. By December 1980, Bulgarian diplomats had held 76 exhibitions, organized 242 film showings and 56 celebratory meetings, and distributed 628,000 copies of books and magazines; there were altogether 420 visits of a cultural character between Bulgaria and India. Fifty-two Indian students pursued a Bulgarian language degree. Indian children participated in the International Banner of Peace Assembly in 1979. Throughout the early 1980s, Bulgarian artists, jazz musicians, folk dance performers, and writers visited India regularly.[111]

In the spirit of reciprocity, the number of Indian cultural events in Bulgaria also grew, featuring visits of Indian scholars, translations of Indian literature, the showing of Bollywood films, and performances of classic Indian dance. In 1979, author Amrita Pritam, who translated Bulgarian literature, was awarded the Vaptsarov Prize for her contribution to the dissemination of Bulgarian culture in India; her works were in turn translated into

Bulgarian.[112] Two exhibitions showcased India on the Bulgarian scene: *Contemporary Indian Art* opened in Sofia in March 1979, followed by a showing of the paintings of Rabindranath Tagore in June 1981.[113] In the meantime, Bulgarian curators were tasked with the acquisition of Indian art: when the Gallery of International Art opened in Sofia in 1985, it featured a large collection of ancient Indian artifacts that Bulgarian publics could now admire.[114]

Despite the discrepancy in size, tiny Bulgaria exported far more cultural products than did much larger India; the reason lies in Zhivkova's influence. Even when the country experienced cultural shortages in the midst of the 1300th jubilee she was willing to commit huge state resources to this ideologically justified cultural extravaganza that also fulfilled her personal interests. During her official visits, she typically took free time to explore archaeological sites and meet with Indian gurus. Official reports claimed that her visits were the best possible propaganda for real socialism, but the Bulgarian cultural presence in India looked like the fulfillment of the personal aspirations of the daughter of the communist dictator.

Culture as the Main Element of International Relations: Bulgaria in Mexico

Given that Bulgaria and Mexico's political and economic relations were in a nascent stage, culture gave substance to the fresh political romance between the two countries. Bulgarian diplomats spoke of culture as the "obligatory and main element of international relations," because "political and economic relations are not enough to address the larger framework of our future peaceful mutual development."[115] The two Mexican presidents of these years, Echeverría and López Portillo, seemed to agree that international cultural exposure could only enhance their reputation as great statesmen. Culture thus became the cornerstone of relations between Bulgaria and Mexico, and not simply a side effect of political and economic priorities— an expression of the distinct shape of global connections outside of a North-South or East-West trajectory.

Conditions in Mexico impeded Bulgarian cultural expansion among the Mexican people due to "the high percentage of illiteracy among the population, the chaotic migratory processes, the distance of the largest ethnic groups from general progress, [and] the broad masses' lack of access to professional culture." Their impeccable Marxist credentials notwithstanding, Bulgarian diplomats found commonality with the Mexican elites on national(ist) and civilizational grounds. After all, Mexican cultural elites had the "ambition to rebuild the reputation of the country that had given humanity the culture of the Maya,

Aztecs, [and] Toltecs [and] created the geniuses of [José Clemente] Orozco, [David Alfaro] Siqueiros, [and Diego] Rivera."[116] Given the fact that Bulgaria also wished to promote its ancient roots while displaying its contemporary progress, Bulgarian and Mexican cultural aspirations converged. Much like in India, the Bulgarians' main conversation partners and audiences were the "progressive intelligentsia" from the "bourgeois class" such as university students, professors, and the directors of state cultural agencies and museums.[117]

Bulgarian cultural efforts in Mexico were not as wide-ranging as in India, given the fact that they began practically from scratch in 1976. To impress their hosts, the Bulgarians relied on the "prestigious" exhibitions that had

Una vista de la exposición pictórica

FIGURE 32. Audiences at the *Contemporary Bulgarian Art* exhibition held in Mexico City, 1977. Source: TsDA, f. 405, op. 9, a.e. 676, l. 22.

already successfully toured the world. In March–April 1977, the *Thracian Treasures from Bulgaria* exhibition came to Mexico City after it had concluded its visit to the British Museum and before it headed to the United States.[118] Another exhibition that had become a worldwide sensation, *1000 Years of Bulgarian Icons*, came from Paris in March 1978 to commemorate the centennial of Bulgarian statehood.[119] In 1979, *Contemporary Bulgarian Art* opened on the eve of Zhivkov's visit to Mexico City.[120] As they were new to Mexico, the Bulgarians were relying on quality rather than quantity, displaying their "representative" cultural products that had already attracted significant international attention.

Mexican culture came to Bulgaria, too. The opening of a Mexican embassy in November 1976 was accompanied by the *3000 Years of Mexican Art* exhibition, which Todor Zhivkov visited "with all the attendant publicity."[121] When President López Portillo came to Sofia in 1978, an exhibition of the folk artist and cartoonist José Guadalupe Posada opened in the prestigious Shipka 6 Gallery. Other events that year included the *Art of the Aztecs* exhibition and a week of Mexican film.[122]

To put these cultural contacts in perspective, during this time Bulgaria was preparing to celebrate its 1300-year jubilee throughout the world, while experiencing severe shortages of cultural products that it could use for the anniversary celebrations abroad. Access to cultural resources became a part of the power struggles within the state bureaucracy and especially the diplomatic corps. In these conditions of cultural shortage, practically every Bulgarian ambassador was requesting the same exhibitions and performers, but not every country was prioritized when the state bureaucracy decided where to send the Bulgarian folk ensembles, classical musicians, and archaeological treasures. Still, during 1977–1981, the best of Bulgarian culture came to Bulgaria's newest ally, Mexico. This fact demonstrates the new priority given to Mexico at the highest levels of the cultural and state bureaucracy.

A Momentous Year: 1981

As 1981 approached, more demands were put on embassies worldwide to organize events commemorating the 1300th anniversary of the establishment of the Bulgarian state. This "jubilee fever" was also apparent in India where the Indian-Bulgarian friendship societies, for example, started to celebrate the anniversary at their meetings. Bulgarian diplomats in India similarly engaged in numerous activities to fulfill their "jubilee plans" through "complex events" and the establishment of national celebration committees. The Bulgarian Cultural-Informational Center organized celebratory talks, roundtables, symposia, exhibitions, and public discussions in New Delhi, Calcutta, Madras, Hyderabad, Guntur, Vijayawada, and other cities. Bulgarian mountaineers held a meeting dedicated to the 1300th anniversary at the end of their Himalayan expedition. In early 1981, at Indira Gandhi's urging (no doubt after intervention by Zhivkova), Satyanarayana Rao, general secretary of the Congress Party and member of parliament, inaugurated a national celebration committee for the 1300-year jubilee to coordinate celebratory events between the two governments.[123]

Despite the lack of any prior cultural connections, Mexico became the first foreign country ever to establish a national celebration committee for the 1300-year jubilee. In January 1978, at Zhivkova's request, First Lady Carmen Romano agreed to chair the committee, which also included ministers and mayors.[124] A Week of Bulgarian Culture on the National Autonomous University of Mexico (UNAM) campus, dedicated to the 1300th anniversary, featured film screenings, readings of Bulgarian translations, and theatrical performances. Photo exhibitions toured Sahagun, Cuautla, and Mexico City.[125] In a grand gesture, Mexico gifted 1300 art works by 280 Mexican graphic artists to commemorate Bulgaria's jubilee in 1980.[126]

But the culmination of both celebratory programs was the parallel opening of two of the most prestigious Bulgarian exhibitions in New Delhi and Mexico City. In February 1981, Zhivkova arrived in India to open the world-renowned exhibition *Thracian Treasures from Bulgaria* at the National Gallery of Modern Art in New Delhi.[127] Zhivkova spoke about the strong links between India and Bulgaria in historical, cultural, and civilizational terms:

> Here, on Indian land, Thracian art feels more at home than anywhere else outside of Bulgaria. Here one can tangibly feel the parallels, the similarity, and the organic closeness in the symbolic nature of Thracian and Indian art . . .
>
> There is no doubt that the Indian and Bulgarian people, heirs of rich culture and civilization, bearers of centuries-old life experience, having survived the tests of life and fate, . . . and having preserved intact their quest for perfection, will work and cooperate even more closely and conscientiously towards . . . Fraternity and Beauty.[128]

Indira Gandhi paid a visit to the exhibition. Following a complex event—an academic symposium and literary meetings in New Delhi—celebrations dedicated to the 1300th anniversary were held in Lucknow, Bangalore, Hyderabad, Madras, and Aurovil. At these events, Zhivkova met with governors and mayors, impressing her hosts with her intimate knowledge of Indian philosophy and history.[129]

FIGURE 33.   Liudmila Zhivkova at the opening of the *Thracian Treasures* exhibition at the National Museum in New Delhi, 1981. Source: Elena Savova, Zdravka Micheva, and Kiril Avramov, eds., *Liudmila Zhivkova: Zhivot i delo (1942–1981); Letopis* (Sofia: Izdatelstvo na Bâlgarskata akademiia na naukite, 1987).

Following a twelve-hour stay in Sofia to visit with her children, Zhivkova flew to Mexico to open the *Medieval Bulgarian Civilization* exhibition at the National Anthropological Museum in Mexico City.[130] At the ceremony, President López Portillo remarked that "this is one of the most beautiful exhibitions ever shown in Mexico." Presenting the president with a high state honor, the Dimitrov Prize, Zhivkova spoke about the remarkable development of Bulgarian-Mexican relations, again using a civilizational and spiritual vocabulary to reflect on the common historical heritage and future choices of the two states:

> Our two peoples are peoples with ancient history and rich culture, heirs of important and rich civilizations. Overcoming the challenges of time, they have preserved alive the flame and fire of their freedom-loving and strong spirit, or if we are to express this symbolically, the flame of Quetzalcoatl and the light of Orpheus. This is why there is a strong desire among our peoples to travel upward, toward light, to move forward, toward progress, and to perfect themselves.[131]

Zhivkova then participated in a number of celebrations honoring the jubilee in Mexico City and Puebla.[132] First Lady Carmen Romano hosted a concert at the Mexico City Philharmonic and a private dinner for Zhivkova.[133] In essence, the 1300-year jubilee in Mexico became a celebration of the two families in power.

In July 1981, Liudmila Zhivkova died in the midst of the jubilee celebrations in Bulgaria that had been her brainchild. Rumor had it that the two long, exhausting trips to India and Mexico, which included meetings with gurus and clairvoyants in addition to high officials, precipitated her death.[134] Her unexpected death generated wide international media coverage that ranged from praise of her international impact to condemnation of her use of culture for the purposes of the communist regime. Because of the unclear circumstances of her death, there was even talk of KGB involvement. Yet, many ordinary Bulgarians and international observers also sympathized with the visibly grief-stricken Todor Zhivkov while others speculated about the future of Bulgaria and its opening to the world after her death.[135]

Both Indira Gandhi and Carmen Romano honored Zhivkova in their countries. In Mexico City on 4 September 1981, elementary school 229 was given Zhivkova's name to celebrate her personal role in the development of Bulgarian-Mexican contacts.[136] In November 1981, Indira Gandhi, honoring her close associate, visited Bulgaria in the midst of the 1300-year jubilee celebrations, in a highly symbolic gesture.[137] Gandhi spoke passionately at a state dinner: "I came to your land of roses from my land of the lotus," she said, and congratulated Zhivkov for the "remarkable progress [of Bulgaria] under your dynamic leadership." Gandhi then announced the establishment of the Liudmila Zhivkova Professorship in Bulgarian Studies at Delhi University.[138]

Alternative Geographies of Global Contact

The intensity of the cultural encounters between Bulgaria, India, and Mexico stands out in the context of the already extravagant international cultural program that Bulgarian officials initiated in the late 1970s. Despite the cultural shortages that the bureaucracy experienced, the best Bulgarian cultural products were dispatched to those two states, in addition to the West. The Bulgarian presence in Japan, where Bulgarian officials organized many of the same "representative events," closely parallels that in India and Mexico, and like in India, the relationship also fulfilled ambitious economic objectives.[139] In all of these cases, the focus on cultural convergences and civilizational commonalities made possible the articulation of new global imaginaries, which linked a small country on the margins of Europe with some of the most prominent world civilizations. Ultimately, these linkages, as seen

in the rhetoric and practice of official cultural exchange, charted alternative cultural geographies that challenged dominant narratives centered on
Western civilization while inscribing the importance of Bulgaria's ancestors, the Thracians and the Slavs, into a global, rather than just European,
civilizational context. In effect, Bulgarian power elites were pursuing several
global models at once: in the West, they claimed to be European, while in
the Global South, they belonged to the whole of humanity. These endeavors
were no doubt rooted in national(ist) aspirations, yet this national agenda
had an impact because it followed universal models and pursued global partnerships. While domestic and international factors consistently intersected
in the articulation of Bulgarian cultural projects, in India and Mexico the
pursuit of alternative global connections was at the core of the cultural programs envisioned by Zhivkova and her associates. In the end, many of the
newly forged connections outlived Zhivkova, as apparent in the continued
economic and cultural cooperation between Bulgaria and India (as well as
Japan) throughout the 1980s and after the end of the Cold War.[140] Soft power
could become the launchpad for hard power projects as well.

Ultimately, this analysis highlights the importance of the "peripheral"
Eastern European players during the Cold War, demonstrating why the pericentric approach advocated earlier is necessary. Importantly, the Bulgarian
cultural overtures underlined the ability of a small socialist state to make
some independent international choices. The patriotic and civilizational
message of Bulgarian cultural outreach often clashed with Soviet expectations: increasingly, Moscow seemed annoyed with the apparent unorthodoxy
of its most loyal ally portraying itself as the first Slavic civilization in direct
contradiction to foundational Soviet historical narratives of the role of Rus'
in the development of the Slavic peoples. As far as the 1300th anniversary,
which was the cornerstone of these cultural efforts, Western observers heard
"rumours . . . that Moscow expressed a wish to see the anniversary played
down because of fears, which turned out to be justified, that it would mag-
nify the role of Bulgaria's pre-1944 heroes at the expense of the Party."[141] As
a result of these cultural involvements, foreign representatives came to question whether the Bulgarians were acting purely as a Soviet proxy or were pursuing a level of independence through culture. For British diplomats, these
projects demonstrated that "little brother is growing up and is sometimes
resentful of big brother's [Soviet] air of superiority." A manifestation of this
attitude was the "disproportionate use of [state] resources" to sponsor "an
active program of cultural events . . . making the world conscious of Bulgarian heritage."[142] In the end, Bulgarian cultural contacts with the developing
world make clear that, while political agendas and economic decisions might

have followed a predetermined role in the Soviet bloc, culture allowed more autonomy to the smaller Eastern European states.

It is perhaps striking that small Bulgaria felt that it could participate in these conversations on an equal—if not superior—footing in relation to these two much larger states because of their imagined shared values and historical similarities as grand world civilizations, which bound them together in a past-present-future continuum. Here, the "advantages of smallness" are clearly visible: Bulgarian cultural efforts in the Global South highlight the ability of a small state to influence the cultural imagination of the 1970s by pursuing unlikely channels of communication and contacts beyond the East-West competition for the global order. Such alternative global connections actively shaped the world from the margins, creating mental geographies outside of East-West or North-South considerations, to craft new global visions along an East-South axis instead.

Cultural engagement with India and Mexico allowed Bulgaria to project its own civilizational self-definition to the world, highlighting the existence of multiple geographies of global cultural contact in the context of the 1970s. Yet, there were also uniquely state socialist notions of development—emphatically merging economic and cultural objectives—that determined the scope of the relationship between Bulgaria and the developing world, which is the focus of the next chapter, centered on Nigeria.

Chapter 6

Culture under Special Conditions

In September 1980, in the city of Kano, the capital of the State of Kano in North-Central Nigeria, Bulgarian representatives opened a photo exhibition organized around three distinct themes: 1300 Years Bulgaria to mark the upcoming jubilee; Bulgaria-Africa: Solidarity, Friendship, Cooperation, to express support for the African states in search of political and economic independence after decolonization; and Bulgarian Agriculture, the Bulgarian Chemical Industry, and Children in Bulgaria, to showcase the successes of the Bulgarian state in raising its citizens' living standard through economic and social policy. At the event, the state minister of health, Sadik Vali, who had recently visited Bulgaria, spoke about Bulgarian hospitality and Bulgarian achievements in the spheres of economics, science, culture, and, especially, medicine. At the end of the week-long exhibition, the Bulgarian diplomats planned to donate children's books and vinyl records to the local library.[1] Such exhibitions occurred with some regularity in Nigeria in 1980 and 1981: in those two years, Bulgarian diplomats traveled to the states of Ogun, Oyo, Kwara, Ondo, Edo, Imo, and Rivers, all within a day's drive from the capital Lagos, but they also ventured to more distant destinations such as Benue, Plateau, Bauchi, Kaduna, Niger, Kano, and Sokoto, which required days of intense travel (the distance between Lagos and Kano is over 660 miles). These exhibitions inevitably combined economic and cultural messages, in addition to the compulsory boilerplate reassurances about

Bulgaria's commitment to the struggle against imperialism, colonialism, neocolonialism, and racism. According to Bulgarian records, they resonated among their intended Nigerian audiences, who were eager to learn about the rapid transformation of small Bulgaria over the last thirty-five years. In 1980, the governor of the state of Imo enthusiastically agreed that "a people should value and preserve its historical monuments."[2] The same year, during a visit to the state of Rivers, which produced half of Nigeria's oil, Ambassador Ivan Atanasov met with Governor Milford Okilo, who had visited Bulgaria in 1975, had "good impressions of the successes of socialist Bulgaria," and had joined the Nigerian National Celebration Committee for Bulgaria's 1300th anniversary. After the two officials paid tribute to the jubilee, the talks focused on possible Bulgarian contributions to electrification, water supply management, public transportation, and housing projects in the booming oil state.[3] A similar merging of cultural and economic objectives was evident during a visit to the state of Ogun in November 1981, when Bulgarian diplomats distributed pins marking the 1300th anniversary to all attendees during talks regarding the possibility that Bulgarian specialists would get involved in procuring water supplies, building a glass factory, and starting an agricultural processing plant in the state.[4]

This chapter continues the analysis of the multiple geographies of global contacts and exchange of ideas that communist power elites actively pursued with a range of actors during the 1970s. Charting Bulgaria's presence in Nigeria, I explore the distinctive state socialist notions of development—which combined economic and cultural elements in a holistic understanding of modernization—that underpinned small Bulgaria's projects in the large African state. Undeniably, the Bulgarian priorities in Nigeria had to do with economic opportunities in the booming petro-state, which had been implementing an ambitious program of economic and educational reforms since the early 1970s. Yet, instead of presenting a straightforward narrative of state-led economic modernization as the alternative to the Western free market model, Bulgarian officials also talked about ancient khans, Thracian treasures, and medieval fortresses during their travels in Nigeria, while they also sought to celebrate the 1300th anniversary of the Bulgarian state with jubilee events. Partly, this persistent combination of cultural and economic messages followed the general logic of Bulgarian international projects of this time, which contained obligatory cultural components—exhibitions, concerts, film screenings, book presentations, academic conferences, or cultural exchange visits—linked to the celebration of the 1300-year jubilee of the establishment of the Bulgarian state in 681. "Jubilee plans," "complex events," and national celebration committees were the focus of Bulgarian diplomats everywhere. Yet, unlike the extravagant cultural efforts in India and Mexico, the programs in Nigeria had particular characteristics because the resources available to officials were extremely limited, unlike in the other two states, which saw the best of Bulgaria's cultural products. Thus, diplomats used different cultural forms adapted to local conditions—such as the traveling photo exhibition—to recruit Nigerian audiences. Talking about history and culture in tandem with modernization and development dominated the Bulgarian projects in Nigeria. This convergence had parallels in the programs of other socialist states that wished to promote progressive ideas of state- and nation-building at home or help the consolidation of world socialism abroad and emphasized the existence of uniquely state-socialist notions of cooperation and development infused with cultural ideas.[5] Importantly, such alternative visions of global integration between the East and the Global South were vibrant well into the 1980s, demonstrating that communist elites continued to actively pursue diverse global models of cooperation outside of East-West relations throughout the Cold War.

As in the case of India and Mexico, only research in Nigerian archives could fully illuminate the motivations of Nigerian elites for becoming involved in these cultural events. Therefore, I continue with the "pericentric" approach that puts the perspective of "peripheral," small Bulgaria at the center. Three observations help us frame the logic of Bulgarian economic and cultural cooperation with Nigeria. First, official Bulgarian rhetoric adopted the language of anti-imperialism and condemned Western racism and neocolonialism as a legacy of imperialism. Yet, Bulgarian diplomats often exhibited paternalistic and condescending attitudes toward the Nigerian population. In subtle references to "unusual" cultural habits, a "peculiar" work ethic, and unique "local conditions," the Bulgarians perceived themselves as civilized Europeans whose goal was to help develop and ultimately civilize a population that lagged behind.[6] Even though Bulgarian representatives stressed that their country had never pursued colonial expansion, a claim that was meant to legitimize their efforts in Nigeria, they adopted a note of superiority that was no doubt connected to racialized perceptions of their new partners.[7]

Second, even though ideological justifications were always a part of the Bulgarian rationale for expanding contacts with Africa, in the case of Nigeria, as with the general Bulgarian objectives in the developing world since the 1960s, "pragmatism, not ideology" dictated the Bulgarian choices.[8] This attitude was encouraged by similar Soviet pragmatism in West Africa, well documented in the cases of Ghana, Guinea, and Nigeria: a socialist model of development was not a requirement for Soviet aid in Africa after the mid-1960s.[9] "Peaceful coexistence between different socioeconomic systems" became the rhetorical cornerstone of Bulgarian foreign policy in the 1970s, allowing tremendous ideological flexibility in contacts with the developing world, and leading to unlikely alliances with authoritarian states, as seen in the case of India and Mexico.

Finally, and most importantly here, referencing history and culture made sense, because like the situation in Eastern Europe after the end of empires in the late nineteenth and early twentieth centuries, claiming and exalting the past became a natural part of the project of nation- and state-building in Nigeria after its independence in 1960. Andrew Apter highlights the fact that African elites framed modernization projects with narratives of historical unity as they built new states and new nations. In Nigeria, after the civil war of 1967–1970, a focus on national traditions and cultural products became an indispensable element of rebuilding the country.[10] As Łukasz Stanek shows, in neighboring Ghana, Eastern European architects proved their credentials to work in postcolonial Africa by emphasizing their experience in both state-led modernization after World War II and nation-building against foreign, "colonial" powers in the late nineteenth century. In 1961, a Ghanaian journalist had argued that after "five hundred years . . . under Turkish rule," the Bulgarians of today "understand the African and are sympathetic with her struggle for the liberation of [the] continent from foreign domination."[11] The choice of history to frame current modernization plans therefore fit the logic of both Eastern European specialists and their African hosts.

Ultimately, a study of Bulgarian cultural and economic cooperation in Nigeria highlights the value of the pericentric approach and contributes to debates about the multiplicity of global interconnections during the Cold War.[12] Multiple networks of "knowledge specialists" facilitated the exchange of a range of ideas between the Second and the Third Worlds well into the 1980s. In his research on Eastern European architects working outside of Europe, Łukasz Stanek documents the overlapping networks of specialists from different political contexts working in postcolonial Africa and the Middle East; these specialists both competed and collaborated on different projects, creating a cosmopolitan milieu that brought together experts from Eastern Europe, the West, and the rest of the world.[13] Yet, Eastern European specialists, as representatives of non-colonial small states, often had the upper hand. A pericentric approach that emphasizes the role of actors on the margins thus pays off. Kristen Ghodsee has shown how Bulgarian and Zambian women's rights activists designed common strategies for social and political mobilization that were specifically articulated in opposition to the West. In her analysis, these unlikely yet logical communication channels "had a real impact on the global discourse of women's rights as debated at the United Nations."[14] In Nigeria, too, Bulgarian representatives were trying to cultivate new economic and cultural connections with local elites, using appeals to culture and history to make their development projects attractive to their hosts.

To follow Bulgaria's tortuous steps in Nigeria, I first outline the general logic of Bulgarian outreach to a number of countries in Africa and the new production of knowledge about the continent in the 1970s that shaped the understanding of Bulgarian development projects. Next, I chart the political, economic, and national factors in Nigeria, informed by the need to rebuild after a bloody civil war, that allowed the development of a closer relationship with Bulgaria in the long 1970s. Official culture in the two states played a critical role in cementing this relationship, as both Bulgaria and Nigeria organized impactful international events and celebrated important anniversaries. Thus, when Bulgarian officials staged their cultural events in Nigeria, they found an audience that could relate to why historical topics framed the presentation of Bulgarian economic projects. Considering the overall logic of Bulgarian cultural endeavors in the Third World, it is clear that for Bulgarian elites, the use of culture helped project an image of progress and independence on the global scene.

Bulgaria in Africa: Confronting Backwardness with Cooperation

To understand the logic of the Bulgarian merging of history and culture with ideas of development and modernization in Nigeria, it is necessary to address broader issues of Bulgarian attitudes toward Africa and developing countries as a whole. Bulgaria was in many ways a newcomer in Africa. Bulgarian contacts with North Africa (Egypt, Algeria, Tunisia, and Libya) dated from earlier times (linked to the existence of Ottoman-era networks between the Balkans, the Middle East, and North Africa) but grew with the Soviet adoption of policies of internationalism after 1956. Throughout the 1960s, Bulgarian trade with the newly independent countries in Asia, Africa, and the Middle East increased steadily: while statistics are imperfect, Bulgarian exports to developing states grew from 23.4 million leva in 1960 to 117.0 million leva in 1968.[15] But subequatorial Africa was an entirely new phenomenon in Bulgarian diplomacy from the early 1960s on when the process of decolonization was in full swing. Bulgaria opened embassies in a plethora of African states—Ghana, Mali, Ethiopia, Tanzania—soon after their declared independence. In the 1970s, Bulgaria continued to build ideological and political coalitions with a number of African states with socialist credentials, including Mozambique and Angola. But in line with the pragmatic Bulgarian approach to the developing world, the range of allies was much wider.[16]

Western diplomats closely watched these Bulgarian endeavors, too. In the opinion of British officials, Africa was "increasingly a preoccupation" of Bulgarian foreign policy from the mid-1970s on when a string of African delegations visited Bulgaria: in 1976 alone, Bulgaria hosted state visits by the leaders of Ethiopia, Tanzania, Somalia, Angola, Mozambique, and Egypt.[17]

Bulgaria's expansion of economic and political relations with African countries generated the systematic production of new knowledge about Africa, which captures attitudes about the African continent in academic and policy-oriented circles. In 1966, the African Institute at the Soviet Academy of Sciences organized a conference of specialists from socialist states in Moscow to coordinate the advancement of African studies in the Soviet bloc. In 1967, the Bulgarian Scientific-Research Center on Africa and Asia (NITsAA), affiliated with the Bulgarian Academy of Sciences (BAN), opened on a Soviet model. The NITsAA started publishing monographs, mainly on economic and theoretical issues related to the nature of "capitalist exploitation" and "class formation" in developing states. These studies focused on the key question, "how to overcome economic backwardness," but also tackled issues related to "industrialization, social and demographic [dynamics], and cultural development," taking a comprehensive approach to generating knowledge and development ideas about Africa.[18]

An almanac of Africa prepared by the NITsAA for a general educated audience in 1973 compiled geographic, demographic, historical, political, social, economic, and cultural information on each African state. Based on the close reading of this book, I would argue that Bulgarian specialists saw the African continent through the prism of "economic and social backwardness [*izostanalost*]" which was "the result of their long colonial existence."[19] Intertwining historical and contemporary experiences, the essays analyzed Western intervention, usually dated to the beginning of the slave trade in the sixteenth century, as the key reason for current African problems. The Bulgarian Africanists used the terms colonialism and imperialism interchangeably to describe the fateful role of capitalism and to chart a long-term process of Western exploitation in Africa. Curiously, to translate that experience in terms comprehensible to the Bulgarians from their own history, scholars used the vocabulary of "slavery" (*robstvo*) and "oppression" (*gnet*)—a direct reference to the "five-century Ottoman yoke" interpretation of Bulgarian history—drawing parallels between the "multi-century foreign domination" in both areas.[20] Based on those interpretations, what Africa needed was "rapid [*uskoreno*] *economic and cultural development* [emphasis mine] . . . [which] required tangible and selfless help from the industrially developed countries, including the capitalist ones."[21] In this quotation, economics and culture went hand in hand, while Bulgaria was one of the industrially developed countries that offered selfless help. Africans were perceived as being "on a very different level of political, economic, and cultural development," which was often described by the idiosyncratic Bulgarian term "remnants from the past" or "atavisms" (*otzhivelitsi*). In the end, only the combined state-led development of the "national economy, education, and culture" could help "overcome backwardness."[22]

To facilitate the process of modernization in Africa, a growing number of Bulgarian specialists worked on the continent under agreements for scientific-technical cooperation. The goal of these programs was to advance "progress" and to help developing states "to gradually end their lagging behind in the spheres of science, technology, and manufacturing; . . . to organize the rational extraction of their national resources; to implement the advantages of social-economic progress in science, culture, education, [and] medicine; to enhance their economic potential; and to increase the living standards of their workers."[23] In the early 1970s, there were more than a thousand Bulgarian specialists in Africa. These experts "organized Tunisia's state policies in construction and public works, created the basis of public health policies in Guinea, established the first musical high school in Ethiopia and the first technical high school in Mali, helped Sudan to spray its cotton fields with chemicals using airplanes supplied by Bulgaria, [and] assisted the development of agriculture in Tunisia, Sudan, Ethiopia, Mali, and Tanzania." At the same time, about 360 African students came to Bulgaria each year on scholarships administered by their own states, bringing the number of Africans who pursued Bulgarian education in the period 1955–1970 to several thousand.[24] Overall, "cooperation" (*sâtrudnichestvo*) was understood to be helping African states develop their own resources and achieve self-sufficiency, in contrast to Western "aid" (*pomoshti*), which involved African states in capitalist schemes and was inherently exploitative; further, Western aid programs funded "propaganda campaigns" directed against socialist states working on the continent, which necessitated the commitment of resources on the cultural front, too.[25] This holistic definition of cooperation explains the central role of culture in development programs: the choice of an economic model was a civilizational choice as well.

Bulgaria in Nigeria: "The Odd Man" in Bulgaria's "Jungle Offensive"

In 1978, Todor Zhivkov embarked on a highly publicized tour of Nigeria, Angola, Mozambique, Ethiopia, and South Yemen (North and South Yemen unified in 1990) to convey support for the post-independence development of these states. As advertised at home and abroad, Zhivkov's visit demonstrated the essence of Bulgarian foreign policy, "aimed at strengthening world peace and security, at creating friendship among the people, [and expressing] solidarity and support for the peoples fighting against imperialism, colonialism, neocolonialism, [and] for freedom, independence, and social progress."[26] Given the socialist credentials of the governments of Angola, Mozambique, Ethiopia, and Yemen, commitment to "proletarian internationalism" justified these contacts as Bulgaria had promised help to "safeguard and widen the socioeconomic achievements of their peoples" based on treaties of friendship and cooperation.[27] Yet, following the Soviet example of more a pragmatic attitude in Africa since the late 1960s, Zhivkov also wanted to show that "there is an element of flexible development possible even on 'the road to Socialism.'" In the words of British diplomats, "Bulgaria has been carrying a banner (and a pick and shovel)."[28] This pragmatic approach was most evident in the Bulgarian presence in Nigeria, "the odd man out" during Zhivkov's African tour of 1978, once again according to British diplomats; while the rest of the trip could be interpreted as the return of visits by left-leaning African leaders to Bulgaria in 1974–1977, Nigeria was "tacked on because of its growing economic importance."[29] The British were so unnerved by Bulgaria's African program that in 1980 they mockingly spoke about Zhivkov's "jungle offensive," making it clear that condescending, racialized attitudes were rampant among diplomats at the Foreign and Commonwealth Office (FCO).[30]

What brought Bulgaria and Nigeria together? In my interpretation, converging visions of state- and nation-building priorities allowed the development of this new global entanglement. When Nigeria, once a British colony, declared independence in 1960, the elites in charge of the country adopted a federal structure whose goal was to bridge regional and ethnic divisions among the more than 250 ethnic groups that constituted the population of the country. They divided up the country into twelve states, with the intention of distributing economic resources more equitably, but this political arrangement failed to create national unity because of the rampant regional economic disparity. The civil war between the federal government and the secessionist Biafran state in the east in 1967–1970 demonstrated the precariousness of this postcolonial arrangement.[31] After the civil war, like other postcolonial states, Nigeria pursued new global partnerships outside of its old colonial connections to seek knowledge about alternative state-building models.

Bulgaria established relations with Nigeria in 1964, four years after its independence.[32] Based on an agreement on economic, scientific, and technical cooperation, Bulgaria participated in construction projects and technical training of Nigerian students, but these forms of cooperation were initially limited. The civil war of 1967–1970 opened up a fresh economic opportunity, however. Because of the refusal of Great Britain and the United States to offer military support to either side during the war, the federal government in Lagos turned for help to the Soviet Union, which in turn involved Bulgaria.[33] The connections established by Nigerian and Bulgarian elites in the military sector paved the way for further expansion of economic cooperation, but relations between the two countries were not particularly robust until the mid-1970s. To understand the changing nature of those new relations along an East-South line, it is necessary to chart the developments in Nigeria in the post–civil war decade and to outline how Bulgarian diplomats adjusted to the shifting political realities in the country.

After the civil war ended in 1970, the military regime of General Yakubu Gowon (1966–1975) introduced new economic policies that sought to develop Nigeria's vast petroleum reserves and industrialize the country. By 1974, oil accounted for 82 percent of its revenue, and Nigeria became a vast petro-state that dispensed prosperity through kickbacks and the old patronage networks (a "spigot state," according to Frederick Cooper).[34] In the mid-1970s Nigeria was both the most populous and the wealthiest African country, with a population of 80 million and a rapidly expanding economy thanks to international demand for oil. Oil revenues allowed General Gowon and his political allies to supervise a huge state investment in vast infrastructure projects, the building of new educational facilities, and preparations for the Second World Black and African Festival of Arts and Culture (FESTAC 77) to project Nigeria's new role among its African peers.[35]

In the early 1970s, political relations between Bulgaria and Nigeria were tenuous because the military regime had eliminated all political parties, mass organizations, and parliament, making it difficult to establish contacts, while the governing elites pursued a foreign policy focused mainly on Africa.[36] The confident and assertive demeanor of Nigeria's leaders caused a lot of concern for the Soviets, too. In 1974, General Gowon visited the Soviet Union to convey his gratitude for Soviet help during the civil war, yet he defiantly stated, "I did not go to Moscow to be ideologized. I only visited the place to see what I can make use of in their system for the betterment of my country." Instead of intensifying his links with the Soviets, he was pursuing an "African style" of development that was difficult to predict.[37] In this context, pragmatism was the only way forward. The Nigerian elites' focus on modernization opened the door for specialists from Eastern Europe, who came from Bulgaria as well as the GDR, Poland, Yugoslavia, and the Soviet Union.[38]

FIGURE 34.   National Theatre in Lagos, construction in progress. Source: TsDA, f. 608, op. 6P, a.e. 6, Technoexportstroy catalog.

In 1972, following the visit of a Nigerian federal delegation, the Bulgarian state construction firm, Technoexportstroy, was chosen to build the new National Theatre in Lagos, on the model of the Palace of Culture and Sports in Varna, to host FESTAC 77. Completed in only two years, this monumental building at the heart of the Nigerian capital was a major accomplishment for a small state that wished to position itself as a development model for the newly independent African states.[39]

In 1975, Gowon's military regime was removed by General Murtala Mohammed who promised to transition the country to civilian rule. Following his assassination, General Olusegun Obasanjo came to power in 1976 and promoted three goals: eliminating corruption, encouraging national unity, and transitioning to democratic rule. While still maintaining military control, General Obasanjo purged corrupt officials from the civil service, police, and judiciary. A special commission worked to draft a new constitution and to prepare the country for state and federal elections in 1979. As part of his attempt to create a stronger national identity, General Obasanjo instituted the National Youth Service Corps and mandated that students perform one year of government service after graduation to aid in the development of a shared sense of patriotism among young people. He embraced plans to move the federal capital from Lagos to a new site in Abuja, in the center of the country, and created seven more states (bringing the number of federal states to nineteen) to improve access to state-managed resources for the entire population. This desire to project national unity culminated in the organization of FESTAC in 1977.[40] This reinvigorated nationalism certainly looked familiar to the Bulgarians who were pursuing their own "patriotic" projects at home during the same time. Global connections thus led to unlikely convergences in the ideas of state promoted by Bulgarian and Nigerian elites.

From the pericentric perspective of Bulgaria, General Obasanjo's reforms were a positive development. The Bulgarians considered the generals in charge of Nigeria to be of the "nationalist" and "patriotic" variety, whose "anti-imperialist" agenda made them good potential allies.[41] The Nigerian economy continued to be based on oil production: 93 percent of its exports involved petroleum. However, 80 per cent of the Nigerian population worked in agriculture, and that sector emerged as the priority during General Obasanjo's "green revolution." State oil income had already increased the role of the state in the development of infrastructure and industry; it also allowed the execution of social projects, such as the expansion of education and health services and investment in affordable housing. The transfer of the capital from Lagos to Abuja also promised to be a lucrative economic enterprise for those who secured contracts.[42] This situation created hope that the socialist states would carve out a new niche in the Nigerian economy, and especially in the area of new infrastructure projects. The Bulgarians' prior experience with the National Theatre in Lagos formed a solid basis for further collaboration.

The behavior of the Bulgarian leadership in the Global South demonstrates how the small Eastern European states actively inserted themselves into the global scene of the 1970s. General Secretary Todor Zhivkov traveled to Nigeria on a state visit in October 1978, during a year that also saw visits to Lagos by U.S. president Jimmy Carter and FRG chancellor Helmut Schmidt.[43] During his meeting with General Obasanjo, the Bulgarian leader expressed his support for the "national liberation struggles of the African peoples fighting against colonial masters" and emphasized that his country stood behind Nigerian condemnation of the apartheid regime in South Africa, the absolute priority in Nigeria's African agenda.[44] Nigerian foreign policy presented few problems for Bulgaria because the country was "unaligned, with an anticolonial and anti-imperialist agenda" while "a central place in her foreign policy is occupied by the situation in Africa," a platform that presented no ideological risks from the perspective of Bulgarian diplomats.[45] During his visit, Zhivkov stuck to broad but powerful and appealing political pronouncements, condemning imperialism and neocolonialism. But he also addressed the situation in Nigeria by assuring General Obasanjo that the

Bulgarian people fully supported "unitary, modern, and sovereign Nigeria" and its "dynamic socioeconomic development" with its goal of "increas[ing] the prosperity of the Nigerian people."[46] Cooperation required finding common rhetorical ground and recognizing the national choices made by the new Nigerian elites in charge of the country. Shared understandings of the role of the nation and the people provided that desired common ground between Bulgarian and Nigerian elites.

Despite such political pronouncements, economic possibilities were doubtless the prime motivation for expanding contacts with Nigeria, especially in the spheres of construction, machine building, and agriculture. In 1978 the Nigerians were experiencing an acute lack of skilled personnel and sought to diversify the education of their elites, who had traditionally studied in Great Britain. In that year, 320 Nigerians pursued their higher education in Bulgarian institutions. This number compared well to the 580 Nigerians studying in the Soviet Union during the same year.[47] Bulgaria exported heavy machinery, agricultural equipment, radios, batteries, pharmaceuticals, tomato puree, and frozen fish to Nigeria, and imported mainly cocoa.[48] The Bulgarians were also interested in Nigerian oil, but they wanted to barter rather than to pay hard currency for the resource, something the Nigerians were reluctant to accept.[49] About ninety Bulgarian specialists, mainly physicians, engineers, architects, and agronomists, worked in Nigeria; their number grew to 150 by the end of 1978. Instructors in the engineering fields were particularly sought after since Nigeria wanted to increase the number of higher education technical schools.[50] This number increased steadily to several hundred in the late 1970s (no firm statistics are available) as the Nigerians sought more lecturers for the growing network of technical colleges, teaching institutes, and other institutions of higher learning.

It is important to place the Bulgarian economic presence in Nigeria within the broader context of overlapping visions of modernity and progress during the global 1970s. During the mid-1970s, Nigeria's focus on economic development brought new opportunities for cooperation with the socialist states. Nigerian leaders, firm supporters of the reorganization of economic relations between the prosperous North and poor South in the context of global discussions about the New International Economic Order (NIEO), wanted to decrease the influence of their traditional economic partners in the West and diversify their economic contacts. This Nigerian propensity to discuss the world order in terms of "the poor south and the rich north" without making distinctions between capitalist and socialist countries created a new mental geography that facilitated the attempts of the small socialist states of Eastern Europe to chart new international agendas.[51] There were clear signs that Nigeria was moving in an independent direction. To undercut foreign influences, in 1976 General Obasanjo enacted policies of Nigerization that mandated Nigerian participation in each international enterprise operating in the country.[52] In 1979, Nigerian elites turned to the Soviet Union to build the Ajaokuta steel plant, which was seen as the "ultimate symbolic representation of true independence in the postcolonial age."[53] Most radically in 1979 Nigeria nationalized Shell-British Petroleum due to its sale of oil to Pretoria.[54] In the opinion of British diplomats, who closely watched their former colony, Nigerian elites were pragmatic: "Nigeria would seek the friendship of any country that was prepared to assist her development."[55]

Even though the United States, Great Britain, the FRG, and Japan continued to account for most of the economic activity in Nigeria, the role of socialist countries in the economy grew: in 1980, socialist states accounted for 3.5 to 4 percent of Nigerian foreign trade.[56] These states, such as Poland, Bulgaria, and the GDR, developed their relationships with Nigeria at a time when the Soviet Union struggled to maintain its position in this important African country. As shown by Maxim Matusevich, in addition to their political misgivings in regard to the Soviet Union, the Nigerians harbored doubts about whether the Soviets would be able to provide the most modern equipment and up-to-date technology. At the Ajaokuta steel plant, delays and inferior technology dampened Nigerian enthusiasm about collaboration with the Soviets.[57] These shifting Nigerian attitudes to the Soviet Union may explain why Nigerian elites increasingly sought development help, especially in technology and higher education, from the smaller socialist states. While in the context of overall Nigerian development the share of Eastern European states might seem miniscule, their presence in large Nigeria brought tangible economic results for them, as evidenced in the continuation of specialist exchange throughout the Cold War. New East-South global economic linkages were now actively and profitably in the making.

By the late 1970s, the political situation in Nigeria stabilized as political parties were resurrected on the eve of the state and federal elections of 1979, providing new avenues of contact for Bulgarian diplomats.[58] A democratically elected civilian administration took control of the country in October 1979, proclaiming the birth of the Second Republic. Nigeria now had a new constitution, a National Assembly, a president and vice president with broad federal powers, and state governors with extensive local control. President Shehu Shagari continued to promote national policies to forge a unified country and people.[59] He promised to elevate the standard of living of the population by focusing on agriculture, infrastructure, and education, in addition to industrialization. Another priority was the continued construction of the new capital Abuja, "a colossal site" heavily financed by the federal government.[60] Thus, the Second Republic saw another wave of large federal housing projects, the building of federal universities and colleges, and attempts to establish federal television and radio stations in each state.[61] Bulgarian diplomats held high hopes for future construction contracts, given their prior experience with the National Theatre in Lagos. Despite Nigeria's capitalist orientation, President Shagari wished to develop contacts with all countries because Nigerian elites wished to emphasize their neutrality in the Cold War while using the socialist countries' presence as a strategy to renegotiate better contracts with their traditional economic partners in the West.[62]

In many ways, the period 1979–1982 marked the high point of Bulgaria's presence in Nigeria, which seemed to have benefited both the leaders of Nigeria's Second Republic and Zhivkov's prestige-making and hard currency–generating efforts abroad, demonstrating the viability of East-South global visions in this particular juncture of the Cold War. While Bulgaria was just one small state operating in Nigeria, its presence in this large African state brought tangible economic results to both sides. When an oil glut hit the world markets in 1981 and oil prices dropped, Nigeria entered an economic recession and gradually turned to international borrowing, mainly from the International Monetary Fund and Saudi Arabia. This economic crisis destabilized the civilian government and led to the end of the Second Republic in 1983.[63] Yet, the Bulgarian state construction firm, Technoexportstroy, continued its involvement in governmental and public building projects throughout the 1980s, demonstrating the successful forging of lasting global contacts along an East-South axis.[64] Eastern European power elites continued exploring alternative global models through the end of the Cold War.

In this volatile situation in Nigeria during the long 1970s, Bulgarian representatives designed elaborate schemes to secure a new niche in the modernization plans of Nigerian elites, actively inserting their voices into a global network of development ideas.[65] Diplomats saw Nigeria as an "economically promising and strategically important African state" with "enormous potential" to become the leading force in the African continent, which explained their persistent endeavors to intensify contact with the country.[66] Yet, difficulties abounded due to "the inefficiency of the state apparatus, bad organization, and lack of cadres." Most frustratingly for Bulgarian diplomats— whose condescending tone is plainly visible in their correspondence—all projects were accomplished "very slowly" (*mudno*).[67] A fitting example of this sense of superiority are reports from 1978 that described Lagos as a "city of millions, very dirty, with long distances not covered by public transport, no possibility for foreigners to walk, [and] lack of culture or other entertainment." These were "specific conditions completely unlike those in Europe," which "affected one's nerves and psyche [and] one's general health," creating special challenges for the Bulgarian mission in Nigeria.[68] One strategy for overcoming these limitations was to combine economic and cultural goals, and to launch "informational-propaganda work" explaining why Bulgaria was a good choice for Nigerian development plans. Culture now became one more strategy for pursuing contacts—and contracts—in Nigeria.

From Contracts to Culture: From FESTAC 77 to 1300 Years Bulgaria

Given the constantly shifting political climate in Nigeria and the nascent state of relations between the two states, Bulgaria's attempts to create a cultural presence might appear as overkill. Bulgaria's efforts to marry economic and cultural endeavors in Nigeria dated at least to 1972 when Bulgarian architects and engineers took charge of the construction of the new National Theatre in Lagos. Ultimately completed in 1976, the theater contained an auditorium for 5,000, a conference hall for 160, two exhibition halls, two cinemas with 800 seats each, dressing rooms for 600 actors, and eighty offices. As the Bulgarian architect in charge of the project, Stefan Kolchev, saw it, the building—which exceeded the size of its Varna prototype by six times—represented "the symbols of a new life" and "the spirit and vitality of the African people in pursuit of modernity and free expression."[69] During the opening of the theater, Bulgaria participated in the Second World Black and African Festival of Arts and Culture (FESTAC 77), which Nigeria hosted in winter 1977. This development highlights the connection between economic and cultural contacts.[70] Massive federal funds financed this celebration of Nigerian and African culture, which centered on the National Theatre and the FESTAC Village and included theatrical and dance performances, conferences of Black scholars, and exhibitions of archaeological artifacts and contemporary art in the presence of delegates from the African states, the African diaspora, and select friendly countries. As Apter argues, FESTAC was an event of enormous importance for Nigeria, which used it as an occasion to emphasize its preeminent role in Africa, showcase the prosperity of the new petro-state, and promote visions of national unity after the civil war. FESTAC was "a spectacle of development" that advertised "the magic of Nigeria's oil-fueled modernity" while it also created a national master narrative based on the presumption of a common, indigenous, cultural essence of the Nigerian nation.[71]

FIGURE 35.   The National Theatre in Lagos, which was at the center of the FESTAC 77 celebrations. Source: TsDA, f. 608, op. 6P, a.e. 6, Technoexportstroy catalog.

In many ways, this cultural project, even though based on ideas of Pan-Africanism and Blackness, shared commonalities with Bulgaria's 1300-year jubilee in its attempt to use culture as political capital domestically and internationally. Apter's analysis is particularly helpful here, as it is based on fieldwork conducted in Nigeria during and after FESTAC 77. Like Bulgaria's state-sponsored celebrations of the establishment of the Bulgarian state in 681, FESTAC was a "national campaign" orchestrated by "an ideological state apparatus" led by "specialists" whose job was to promote "a cultured appreciation of national culture among the masses."[72] Just as Bulgarian officials emphasized the ancient past, Nigerian officials sought to highlight "the rich and ancient heritage which has produced our complex nation," as head of state General Mohammed declared in 1975.[73] Bulgaria's preoccupation with "representative exhibitions" was echoed by Nigerian cultural experts, who put together a spectacular exhibition, *2000 Years of Nigerian Art*, which toured internationally to showcase the unity of the Nigerian nation. The director of the Nigerian National Museum, Ekpo Eyo, explicitly used arts, archaeology, and culture as a tool for building a common national identity and conveying to the public the "underlying philosophical and psychological basis providing a common root" for all Nigerians.[74] This emphasis on state- and nation-building thus brought the two countries together in their common use of culture and history for larger political goals.

As shown by Sarah Van Beurden in her work on Congo/Zaire, the concept of "cultural guardianship"—or "a common set of strategies that legitimate political power through the stewardship of cultural heritage"—carried special significance for African nations after independence.[75] This was particularly true in Nigeria because the civil war of 1967–1970 had exposed the regional and ethnic fissures in the country, so the creation of a unified national identity through culture was an important priority for the Nigerian regimes both domestically and internationally. Apter notes that "the state's production of national culture took its place within a larger scheme of directed development and national renewal" after the civil war. Using culture as an international tool further projected Nigeria's "growing influence as the elder statesman of Africa" while also promoting the New International Economic Order and the possibility of preferential treatment for developing countries in international trade.[76] Lastly, this understanding of culture colored notions of development promoted in Nigeria. In the words of Flora Edouwaye S. Kaplan, Nigerian officials believed that local, "'African' cultural components can be made part of decisions for national economic and political development, taking into account what is indigenous and useful, and discarding what is not."[77] The focus on indigenization and Nigerization in economic projects certainly fits that paradigm.

Culture also operated in similar ways in Nigeria and Bulgaria. With the creation of the Department of Antiquities and the National Museum in Lagos, whose mission was to collect "representative" national culture from each state, the government monopolized control over cultural production.[78] In its attempts to control the dissemination of cultural and national ideas, on the eve of FESTAC in 1977 the Nigerian government bought the largest share of the two most influential Nigerian newspapers and placed television and radio under state control.[79] Culture thus was not a trivial matter in Nigeria as it served broader national and international agendas. The Bulgarians' own preoccupation with culture thus found an understanding audience in Nigeria in the late 1970s. Nigeria was preparing to celebrate the twentieth anniversary of its independence in 1980, so Bulgarians' obsession with the 1300-year jubilee in 1981 resonated with Nigerian representatives. The fact that Bulgarian diplomats combined economic and cultural talks during their tours of Nigerian states came as no surprise to their hosts because many of the states' governors were already involved in FESTAC, and invitations to participate in the 1300-year Bulgarian "jubilee events" made sense to Nigerian officials. Culture therefore became a logical core element of the greater Bulgarian mission to assist the process of nation-building and economic modernization in Nigeria. The common understanding of the role of culture in the master political and national narratives of the two states led to a surprising yet logical and productive relationship between ruling elites.

Despite these convergences, the Bulgarians struggled to determine how to approach their cultural missions in Nigeria. In 1979, the Bulgarian ambassador spoke of the "special cultural conditions" in Nigeria due to the "reserved attitude to any foreign ideological and cultural influence."[80] Adopting a paternalistic tone once more, he explained that the "great difficulties in the process of formation of a Nigerian nation and the lack of consolidated national Nigerian culture, a direct result of the many centuries of a colonial yoke, are the main reasons for the negativism and reserved attitude to foreign cultural events."[81] From the Bulgarian perspective, the lack of "progressive political parties to work as Bulgarian allies" and the "vast corruption of the political and journalistic circles" further complicated expanding cultural cooperation.[82] Given "the high illiteracy in the country, the weak social activism and political apathy of the masses, the bad communications, long distances, lack of exhibition spaces, high cost of living, and difficult climatic conditions," the ambassador recommended "highly selective planning of cultural events." Such events, organized around anniversaries and national holidays, would mainly involve educated young people and the mass media and pursue the broader goal of advertising "the success of real socialism."[83] The ultimate goal was to convince the Nigerians that Bulgaria could provide a model of economic and cultural development suited for their particular demands. Culture, in this view, would be an element of Bulgaria's greater mission to assist the process of nation-building and modernization in Nigeria.

Staging Culture under Special Conditions

With these assumptions about Nigerian culture in mind and based on a series of cultural cooperation agreements signed in the late 1970s, Bulgarian diplomats embarked on a cultural program tailored to Nigeria's "special" cultural conditions. They worked to establish contacts with the media, trying to secure the publication of materials and broadcast of radio and television programs about their country. They attempted to show films, a trusted and effective tool of cultural diplomacy, but found it difficult to secure appropriate content that would capture the attention of the audience. In the end, they settled for short documentaries about tourism and key economic sectors in Bulgaria. Due to the "temperament" of the Nigerians who "get bored quickly"—another not so subtle condescending, racialized reference—diplomats recommended the organization of pop music concerts rather than folk ensemble visits, a staple of Bulgarian cultural diplomacy elsewhere.[84] Diplomats wished to distribute more "propaganda materials" showcasing Bulgarian progress, but the lack of appropriate English-language printed materials remained a chronic problem.[85] Following Todor Zhivkov's visit in 1978, Ambassador Atanasov suggested the possibility of opening a Bulgarian Cultural-Informational Center in the capital of the largest African state to coordinate activities elsewhere in the region.[86] Yet, Nigeria was never a priority for the Bulgarian cultural bureaucracy in the way India and Mexico were, which explains why Bulgarian cultural resources were allocated to the country unevenly. For example, while negotiating with the director of the National Museum, the Bulgarian ambassador asked that a "prestigious" exhibition like *Thracian Treasures* or *1000 Years of Bulgarian Icons* (both of which had successfully toured India and Mexico) be dispatched to Lagos, but the Committee for Culture declined his request due to the "difficult climate" and the exhibitions' commitments elsewhere.[87] It was clear that the "special" conditions in Nigeria would require the creative adaptation of the usual Bulgarian international cultural practices for the African context.

To facilitate these evolving cultural contacts, Bulgarian representatives persistently recruited local allies among "progressive" public figures, trying to expand the circle of Bulgaria's friends.[88] Based on Bulgarian records, which likely skewed the importance and impact of such events, there was a clear momentum in the development of Bulgarian-Nigerian "friendship." In September 1979, a Nigeria-Bulgaria Friendship Society was established in Lagos, attracting 300 visitors to the opening reception.[89] Former Nigerian students in Bulgaria were invited to celebrate the 1300-year jubilee at the embassy so that diplomats could cultivate relations with people with direct knowledge of the country.[90] During a Lagos event in August 1980, titled *Children in Bulgaria*, the sale of Bulgarian folk objects benefited the Handicapped Children of Nigeria Fund, an organization created by Nigerian women's movement activists who were also in contact with the Bulgarian Committee for Women.[91] Nigerian children, who had visited Bulgaria as delegates of the Assembly of Peace meeting in Sofia in 1979, were invited to celebrate New Year's at the embassy in 1980 and given small gifts by an embassy official dressed as Santa Claus.[92] In early 1980, Nigerian trade union members, on their way to a forty-five-day seminar in Bulgaria, spoke about "the success of real socialism" and "the social equality typical for socialism" at another embassy reception.[93] Diplomats lent a hand to the Nigerian Labour Congress, another trade union that organized a celebration of 1 May for the first time in the history of Nigeria.[94] At the opening of the exhibition of Bulgarian artists at the Island Club in Lagos in April 1980, dedicated to the 1300th anniversary, Ambassador Atanasov appeared in a folk costume, rather than the obligatory diplomatic suit, to match the elaborate attire of his African hosts. Charting new paths for Bulgaria required being creative in "special" local conditions. All proceeds from selling prints of the artwork were allocated to help "victims in the oil spillage areas of Nigeria," an (in)direct critique of Shell policies.[95] Following an art exhibit by Stoian Stoianov, secretary of the Union of Bulgarian Artists, at the National Theatre in Lagos in May 1980, the Society of Nigerian Artists signed an agreement for cooperation, which included exchange of delegations and exhibitions.[96] These events combined ideological and cultural elements to build up alliances with a range of Nigerian actors who were believed to have a positive attitude to the socialist states.

Given the chronic lack of resources, the bulk of Bulgarian cultural activities involved the organization of traveling photography exhibitions—consisting of photo panels prepared by the Bulgarian international press agency, Sofia Press—usually combined with trips of an economic nature. The goal of these endeavors was to portray Bulgaria "as a stable and worthy partner in trade and economic cooperation" and to "present the famous historical past of our people."[97] The exhibitions combined different messages, depending on the audience and availability of materials during a specific time, but consistently portrayed a picture of triumphant—if somewhat linear—economic and cultural development in Bulgaria over the centuries and especially during the years of developed socialism. In May 1980, for example, at the Polytechnic School in Lagos Bulgarian diplomats presented a combined exhibition: *1300 Years Bulgaria*, *Bulgarian Electronics*, and *Bulgaria-Africa: Solidarity, Friendship, Cooperation*. In line with endeavors to organize "complex events," the two hundred students present at the event also saw a short movie about Bulgaria's Black Sea resorts and received folk art souvenirs.[98] The exhibition in Ibadan in the state of Oyo in July featured Bulgarian folk music and Bulgarian monasteries, in addition to showcasing the accomplishments of Bulgarian agriculture and electronics.[99] During a visit in the city of Akure in the state of Ondo in November, the guests were presented with an exhibition of Bulgarian folk objects, including ceramics, wood carvings, copper objects, and textiles, and shown films about Bulgarian ski resorts, Black Sea hotels, and the rose oil industry.[100] As envisioned by the Bulgarian organizers, all displays conveyed pride in the rich historical heritage and recent economic transformations of the country, invoking a preferred model of "development" (*razvitie*) that merged economic and cultural factors to emphasize the active involvement of the Bulgarian state in the welfare of its citizens.[101]

FIGURE 36. Photo exhibition and discussion held on occasion of the Twelfth Congress of the BKP and the 1300th anniversary in Lagos, April 1981. Source: MvNR, op. 38, a.e. 3817, l. 35.

It should be noted that Bulgarian representatives in Nigeria did not harbor a uniformly positive attitude about this extended cultural program, and conflicting ideas emerged regarding how to present Bulgaria's potential role in Nigerian development projects. Ambassador Atanasov expressed dissatisfaction with the materials dispatched by the Ministry of Foreign Affairs (MVnR), lamenting the lack of "a calm, information-based documentary film about Bulgaria, which in thirty minutes would depict the 1300-year history of our country in simple visual ways." In a memo to the vice minister of foreign affairs for cultural cooperation, Maria Zaharieva, he insisted that "in Nigeria they show no interest in our kings and khans, but in real socialism . . . [which] should be represented in a dignified manner."[102] The ambassador criticized "the emphasis on Bulgarian history, unnecessary for African conditions," and considered removing the historical part of the exhibitions to emphasize the contemporary period.[103] He also criticized the sluggishness of the state apparatus in sending appropriate printed materials to Nigeria. One delivery from Sofia Press, for example, contained "propaganda literature" in French and German; another delivery of books arrived six months late.[104] Despite this pushback, the embassy had a cultural plan to fulfill; while the paper trail is silent, most likely higher-ups in the MVnR decided to follow the plans for Nigeria that had already been approved.

As it did elsewhere, 1981 emerged as the key year for Bulgarian cultural endeavors in Nigeria, as the embassy in Lagos had a "jubilee plan" to follow. In February, diplomats organized the National Celebration Committee for the 1300th anniversary, which included Nigerian politicians at the federal and state levels. Ambassador Atanasov approached President Shagari personally, requesting that he take over the committee as "an expression of goodwill and a token for the future flourishing of the extensive relations between our two friendly nations in all spheres of life."[105] Ultimately, Dr. Olusoka Saraki became its chairperson. The speaker of the Senate and the rumored next president, he often spoke about the "rich accomplishments of the Bulgarian state in the spheres of economics and culture" and assured his audiences that relations between Bulgaria and Nigeria would continue to grow in the future.[106] In March, the Days of Bulgaria in Nigeria dedicated to the 1300-year jubilee opened at the cultural center of the Soviet embassy in Lagos; the use of Soviet facilities reflected the spirit of socialist internationalism that continued to inform cultural relations between socialist states. At the reception, diplomats distributed materials for the highly anticipated competition "Do You Know Bulgaria?" The prizes included free airfare on the Bulgarian national carrier, Balkan Airlines, and full board for a one-week Black Sea vacation, awards that particularly excited Nigerian university students, a key target group for the Bulgarians.[107] In December 1981, a regional branch of the Nigeria-Bulgaria Friendship Society opened in the city of Benin in the state of Bendel to prepare for celebrations of the 1300th anniversary.[108]

Various other initiatives also brought Nigerian culture to Bulgaria. In summer 1980, Nigerian artists arrived in Bulgaria for a retreat. Later that year, the Nigerian minister of social development, youth, sports, and culture, the director for culture, and the director of the National Museum visited Bulgaria, accompanied by Nigerian journalists.[109] In 1980, a Bulgarian television crew came to Nigeria to shoot a documentary about the twentieth anniversary of the country while a Nigerian crew visited Bulgaria and filmed *A View on Bulgaria* on the eve of the 1300-year jubilee.[110] In 1981, Bulgarian lecturers at the University of Nigeria in Nsuka began work on an anthology of Nigerian short stories, including the works of Chinua Achebe, Wole Soyinka, Kole Omotoso, Buchi Emecheta, Flora Nwapa, and others.[111] To the enormous delight of the ambassador, the director of the National Museum in Lagos confirmed the commitment of his government to send the famous exhibition, *2000 Years of Nigerian Art*, to Bulgaria in 1982, after it concluded its tours of the United States and the Soviet Union.[112] The common preoccupation of the two countries with deep history and national culture at this particular time allowed the unlikely convergence of the cultural efforts of two states with little prior contact.

In the early 1980s, Bulgarian diplomats continued to energetically traverse the large country, staging various events explicitly dedicated to the 1300th anniversary. Typically, these included the opening of a photo exhibit, accompanied by a brief speech, the screening of a film, and the distribution of printed materials, which presented a mix of information on Bulgarian history, famous historical monuments, the industrial and agricultural accomplishments of modern Bulgaria, and Bulgarian solidarity with the peoples of Africa.[113] During these events, diplomats—often dressed in folk costumes—conveyed specific Bulgarian notions of how the country could serve as a model of development for Nigeria. During his visit to the state of Sokoto in September 1981, Ambassador Atanasov tried to appeal to the key Nigerian focus on South Africa: "We condemn all imperialist forces who support the policy of international terrorism of the white racists [in Pretoria] . . . [and] we are rendering real, serious assistance in different forms and different means to the oppressed and fighting people [of South Africa]." Engaging in negotiations over technical and educational cooperation, including the building of a tomato puree factory in the state of Sokoto, the ambassador—who seemed to vacillate between embracing and dismissing the cultural message— explained to his audience: "Bulgaria is an ancient country, but at the same time also a young, recently developed state. We are old because this year we mark thirteen centuries since the foundation of the Bulgarian state. We are young because the real growth of our country began thirty-seven years ago after the victory of the people's revolution."[114] In this interpretation, similar to Nigeria whose cultural traditions went back millennia, Bulgaria was only able to fulfill its true historical mission recently, after the implementation of ambitious development plans by its progressive government. The reality of a rich cultural heritage and the possibility for rapid economic development clearly converged.

Cultural and economic goals continued to go hand in hand in Bulgarian endeavors as diplomats projected the possible role of their country in Nigerian development. According to Bulgarian records, this message resonated among Nigerians who wished to see improvements in standard of living through investment in agriculture, infrastructure, and education and welcomed the help of specialists from the socialist states.[115] During a visit to the city of Ilorin in the state of Kwara in January 1981, the economic talks were accompanied by photo exhibits dedicated to the 1300th anniversary and invitations to Nigerian officials to join the National Celebration Committee

FIGURE 37. Opening of an exhibition featuring Bulgarian art, December 1981. Source: MvNR, op. 38, a.e. 3845, l. 41.

for the Bulgarian 1300-year jubilee. The directors of the local newspaper and radio and television stations, as well as a number of state ministers, expressed their willingness to participate. Governor Ata, already a member of the committee, spoke about "the success of your people, especially during the last thirty-six years of your centuries-long history." Satisfied with the work of the 150 Bulgarian specialists who had built the sports facility in the city, he appealed for more cooperation in the spheres of agriculture, construction, tourism, and the exchange of university lecturers.[116] In February 1981, the embassy organized Days of Bulgaria in the state of Niger. Ambassador Atanasov gave a speech during his visit with the governor, Alhadji Ibrahim, also a member of the National Celebration Committee, which highlighted Bulgaria's "thirteen-century history, which reached the pinnacle of development in the last thirty-six years [since 1944]." The following day, five hundred students at the Mina Teachers' Institute listened to a lecture titled "Bulgaria during the Centuries," which was illustrated with a rich photo exhibit.[117] In March, the ambassador visited Abuja to see the construction site that was projected to move 900,000 people to the new capital by 1983. The project overseer, Mr. Rufai, was already a member of the National Celebration Committee for the 1300th anniversary and the Bulgarian-Nigerian Friendship Society, so the hope was to secure participation of Bulgarian specialists in this "massive project" of economic development.[118]

In the early 1980s, Bulgarian representatives in Nigeria constantly referred to history and culture as a justification for why their ideas of development and cooperation should be taken seriously in this modernizing African state that was building national unity and economic prosperity after its civil war. Thus, together with engineers, doctors, and university lecturers, the Bulgarians also brought to Nigeria books, folk objects, and photo exhibitions to show that history and culture could complement state- and nation-building projects. Like in India and Mexico, soft power approaches often pursued hard power goals: as mentioned previously, the state construction firm Techno-exportstroy built a number of impressive buildings in Abuja, Benin, Lagos, and Kano throughout the 1970s and 1980s, generating hard currency for the regime. In the end, efforts to marry economic and cultural arguments made sense to the ruling elites in both countries and ultimately allowed for the creation of vibrant East-South connections between small Bulgaria and large Nigeria, emphasizing the value of the pericentric approach that highlights the role of the global periphery.

East-South Visions of Development

In the 1970s, Bulgarian officials actively promoted the role of culture in international affairs, believing it could serve as the basis of new diplomatic overtures while also increasing the prestige of their country and asserting its independence on the global scene. While this larger objective is important, Bulgaria's intense cultural involvement in the developing world—and the vast amount of money and personnel committed to it—was in many ways astonishing during the precarious 1970s. What was the logic of Bulgaria's contacts with the Global South? No single solid, clear-cut criterion existed in determining the nature of these new relationships: ideological, economic, national(ist), prestige-making, and cultural factors all shaped Bulgarian choices. In some cases, such as Nigeria, economic motivations drove the urge for contact. In the case of India, economic and cultural factors were closely intertwined. Yet, in others, such as Mexico, high-profile cultural events were the only thing that provided substance in the new encounters.

A convoluted logic shaped these global entanglements; Bulgarian officials constantly sought to resolve the many contradictions in the policies they pursued. In all of these partnerships, anti-imperialist, anti-racist, and anti-neocolonial language was used to explain why Bulgaria saw its role as "the natural ally of the developing states." However, as seen in Nigeria, Bulgarians became involved in the Third World for a mixture of ideological and pragmatic reasons. While in some cases the promise of political influence was appealing, the possibility of establishing an economic presence and seeking alternative markets for Bulgarian goods was a strong motivation during the 1970s. Yet, despite the pragmatic attitude to such contacts, the holistic understanding of development outlined previously mandated the concurrent preoccupation with cultural programs. This might seem to be a stretch, but it is consistent with the Bulgarian civilizational objectives in India and Mexico analyzed previously. In Nigeria, Bulgarian representatives were even more willing to assert their Europeanness and their image as a "grand civilization." Thus, it is not surprising that while the anti-imperialist and anti-racist rhetoric persisted, officials often nurtured condescending, racialized attitudes toward their new partners in Africa, Asia, and Latin America because they saw the Bulgarian developmental model as superior to what they found in the Global South.

Civilizational rhetoric combined with the language of development thus infused the cultural programs that Bulgarian elites pursued in the developing world. Here, the integrated understanding of development typical of state socialist regimes that merged economic and cultural notions to pursue "a total transformation of social relations" explains the preoccupation with culture, as Artemy M. Kalinovsky had shown in the case of the Soviet Union.[119] Yet, as Frederick Cooper and David Engerman have argued, the language of development could also serve claims-making objectives.[120] This observation is typically examined from the perspective of those receiving development assistance, and not those providing it. However, there was much at stake for a small state such as Bulgaria in its participation in international development projects. Bulgarian officials had certain assumptions about what they were pursuing out in the world: their ideas of development fit a standard, one might even say a Western understanding of modernization that followed a linear, inevitable model based on Enlightenment ideas of standardization and rationalization. The model was of course understood to be socialist, as it followed the mandates of state planning, but development was also seen as basically European. Most importantly, the entire interaction between Bulgaria and the developing states was based on the assumption that Bulgaria actually constituted a developed state. This assumption of development explains the importance of discourse—and culture—in Bulgaria's global interactions. For a country to be considered developed, it had to be "generally recognized to be developed."[121] Therefore, discourse had to create reality. This logic explains the importance of culture as a strategy to assert a superior development model that the Bulgarians could offer.

In short, when Bulgarian officials went to Nigeria, India, and Mexico, and spoke about these countries as developing states in need of assistance—whether economic, military, political, or cultural—and when they offered their own experience as a template for a successful modern transformation, they tried to create perceptions of Bulgaria as a developed state that could provide that assistance. The language of development, based on notions of the inevitable convergence between the developed and developing states, allowed a small Eastern European state to claim superiority vis-à-vis both the Global South and the West. In this East-South logic, culture enabled the active global role of a small state on the margins.

Epilogue

The Socialist Past Today

         As I have shown throughout my examination of the international cultural programs organized by Bulgaria's power elites, multilayered considerations were at play in this global cultural extravaganza. A permanent feature of the encounters between small Bulgaria and the world was the close interrelationship between local and global dynamics in the policies pursued by the communist regime. Domestic factors shaped international choices while the global context determined the local implementation of Bulgarian decisions, creating a lively cultural program blending Bulgarian and universal messages that was unique in late socialist Eastern Europe. The events examined here capture the spirit of late socialism when an uneasy compromise was achieved between the Eastern European regimes and their citizens. For Bulgaria, this was the time of normalized developed socialism when Zhivkov's regime seemed to be in full control. But the events also reflected the uneasy worldwide attempts during the 1970s to reconcile the contradictory forces of East-West reconciliation, the growing influence of the postcolonial world, and the spread of global interconnectivity. From the perspective of small Bulgaria, the 1970s was a time of both limitations and opportunities, as economic and political constraints associated with Soviet influence went hand in hand with new possibilities for advancing novel global partnerships in the Third World. As experienced from the margins of Europe, the 1970s was a decade of measured optimism, accompanied by persistent efforts to resolve the contradictions of the new "global condition."

Another key feature of these cultural programs was the constant attempt to reconcile ideological, national, international, cultural, and global factors, as the agendas of socialism, nationalism, internationalism, cultural dynamics, and global forces collided, competed, and compromised. The Bulgarian regime envisioned programs that emphasized its communist aspirations and commitment to socialist internationalism. At the same time, the events were supposed to capture the national spirit of the Bulgarian people and its unique role in history. Yet, the unpredictable nature of cultural contact and its global dynamics necessitated constant finetuning of the official cultural message. Thus, a peculiar program ensued, which juggled conflicting priorities to showcase the idea that small Bulgaria was a committed builder of communism and socialist internationalism while also being a good Balkan neighbor, an appreciated European partner, and an active global player.

The existence of slippage between culture, propaganda, public relations, and nation branding is one of the insights from studying these cultural contacts, because crafting the public image of any state is bound to reflect diverse considerations. The focus on high-quality, meaningful culture with a universal message was paramount in the shaping of these programs, whether Bulgaria was showcasing its decisive role as "one of the oldest states of Europe," promoting its standing as a "grand civilization" separate from the ancient Greeks and Romans, or emphasizing the ability of state socialism to support the "real arts" and their classical, humanist content. During this time, official culture flourished indeed: Bulgarians partook in a rich cultural life at home and were able to explore other parts of the world, albeit selectively and under the watchful eye of the state. Yet, the ideological function of the cultural front under developed socialism never disappeared. Cultural contacts served to boost the legitimacy of the Zhivkov regime domestically while advancing its reputation and policy agenda internationally. The "cultural opening" of late socialist Bulgaria resulted from the aspiration of communist elites to reinvent themselves, reinvigorate the socialist system, and participate more actively in global developments related to détente and the expansion of global interconnectivity.

Not least, official culture served as a strategy of nation branding that followed the slippery slope of cultural nationalism. The focus of these events was a supposedly refined version of "patriotism" promoted through the 1300 Years Bulgaria events, which put the unique fate of Bulgaria at the crossroads of civilizations at the center of the celebratory programs. Bulgaria was both ancient and modern: the resilience and ingenuity of the Bulgarian people in the past paved the way for the noble endeavors of today's modern nation. Yet here again, official culture came full circle back to ideology, because the aspiration for unity of the past, present, and future laid out the only possible future: marching toward the bright horizons of communism. It is not coincidental that the regime spoke about "cultural-propaganda work" even as it adjusted its rhetoric to emphasize culture or ideology according to context.

Public relations campaigns are at their heart attempts at self-fashioning that often leave a meaningful imprint. Bulgaria actively used "the advantages of smallness" to redefine its reputation as the Soviet master satellite by asserting an image of national uniqueness. While the assurance of the eternal Bulgarian-Soviet friendship never disappeared, and the country's political, economic, and military policy followed Soviet mandates, in the sphere of culture small Bulgaria showed independence by sidestepping orthodox state socialist historical interpretations and cultural cannons, which frequently put the Soviets on alert. In the capitalist West, the idea that Bulgaria's forefathers, the Thracians, Proto-Bulgarians, and Slavs, helped shape a common European history and identity was gaining momentum. The important role of public diplomacy was obvious in small Bulgaria's encounters with a number of big states in the developing world, such as India, Mexico, and Nigeria, where lively contacts developed not only in the realm of culture, but also in economic, scientific, and technical exchange. Soft power strategies led to tangible hard power outcomes.

In the end, our understanding of the 1970s is richer if we include the experiences of "peripheral" actors while our knowledge of late socialism is fuller if we place it in a global context. At the same time local and global, executed in the spirit of socialist internationalism yet also pursuing new transnational directions, Bulgarian cultural contacts followed the logic of late socialism while they also reflected global trends of the 1970s. During this time, a small state on the margins of Europe was able to craft and assert a public image through its investment in culture, demonstrating that cultural diplomacy allows actors on the margins to create legitimacy domestically, make impact regionally, and gain visibility globally.

There are several important long-term consequences of the cultural extravaganza of the 1970s, which spilled over into dynamics outside of the scope of this book. The 1300 Years Bulgaria campaign and the cultural programs associated with it successfully boosted the legitimacy of the communist regime in charge of the country: up until the mid- to late 1980s, a normalized society, brought together in a common national vision, continued to tolerate many aspects of developed socialism and rarely voiced public criticism. The growth of dissent and protest only occurred in Bulgaria in the late 1980s when civic associations of an environmental nature gained visibility.

This situation in turn influenced the nature of the Bulgarian democratic transition, as communist reformers staged a palace coup against Zhivkov on 10 November 1989 with Soviet approval, and many members of the old state and party bureaucracy maintained their influence and power. One way of doing so was through international knowledge and contacts cultivated during the late socialist period.

The nature of nationalism in Bulgaria also underwent critical shifts during the 1980s. The cultural nationalism that crystallized on the occasion of the 1300-year anniversary in 1981 went hand in hand with growing assimilationist pressures on Muslim and especially Turkish minorities. In 1981, schoolchildren in Bulgaria went to see the film *The Glory of the Khan*, which showed events associated the establishment of the Bulgarian state in 681. In 1988, they went to see *Times of Violence*, which focused on the Islamization of the Rhodope region and featured gory scenes of torture, rape, and killing by Muslims. The patriotic pathos of the 1300th anniversary paved the road for the "rebirth" campaign of forced assimilation in 1984 and the expulsion of the Bulgarian Turks during the "great excursion" in 1989, which demonstrates how cultural nationalism can easily become highjacked in the service of ethnic cleansing.

Finally, the international contacts developed under socialism have shaped Bulgaria's current standing in the world. One example comes from the reinvention of political elites, some of whom pursued spectacular international careers, such as Irina Bokova—the daughter of a prominent Politburo member—who served as the head of UNESCO between 2009 and 2017. Bulgarian international relations underwent a transformation after 1989: in the 1990s and first decade of the twenty-first century, the focus of the state's political identity was on the return to Europe in the context of democratization, NATO membership, and EU accession, and thus a reorientation to the West occurred. Yet, other global partnerships continued: the presence of Bulgarian medical personnel, engineers, architects, and other professionals throughout the world and the military deals of state-owned companies with partners in the Middle East, Africa, and India all have Cold War roots. Recently, Bulgarian scholars have started asking questions about the role of foreign students in Bulgaria and the presence of Bulgarian specialists in the world. The global contacts established under socialism resonate in today's globalized world where the search for alternative global connections outside of Europe and the West is emerging as important.

The cultural policies of late socialism continue to be debated in contemporary Bulgaria. Thirty years after the end of communism, many Bulgarians think about the late 1970s as the time when culture mattered: supported by the state financially, culture was universally available at home while it boosted Bulgarian prestige in the world. Of course, any interpretation of this historical legacy is filtered through people's conflicting understandings of the socialist period. In memory wars related to the nature of Bulgarian communism, culture remains an important issue as it informs the very meaning of the state socialist project; here again, culture becomes a proxy for ideology, as in the Cold War.[1] Today, Bulgarians reflect on the socialist period from the position of their personal fate during the postsocialist transition. Similarly to elsewhere in Eastern Europe, nostalgia has a powerful impact on how people remember the recent past.[2] The issue of communist elites and their postsocialist reincarnation remains a contested matter.

Many Bulgarians are fascinated with the life and career of Liudmila Zhivkova, the daughter of communist dictator Todor Zhivkov, who made possible the country's cultural extravaganza. Her young age, interest in Eastern philosophies, eccentric attire, and colorful international career made her stand out. Her role in envisioning the International Assembly of Children in 1979 created fond memories for the children of developed socialism who came of age in the late 1980s and are today the builders of democracy and capitalism. Not least, the mysterious circumstances surrounding her death have led to speculation about Soviet complicity in her assassination. After 1989, a number of her associates—from her bodyguard and nurse to her personal friends and advisors—published memoirs about their time working with Zhivkova. Some of these works try to idealize her and disassociate her figure from the communist regime.[3] Other close collaborators have even promoted a non-conformist image of her as a person "who undermined ideological limitations, iron curtains, and Berlin walls."[4] Despite the critical work of historians, in popular thinking Zhivkova is often admired as an outlier from the system. Her spiritualism—including a close relationship with a clairvoyant, Baba Vanga—resonates among Bulgarians who after the fall of communism turned to psychics to predict their uncertain future. Her reputation as having initiated a "golden century" of Bulgarian culture, both domestically and internationally, remains her signature legacy. One post in the Facebook group "Memories from the People's Republic" described her as a remarkable woman whose "good and beautiful deeds cannot be erased or forgotten" because she "made Bulgaria famous worldwide."[5]

Zhivkova's legacy continues to be contested. In 2012, her daughter, Evgeniia Zhivkova, commemorated the seventieth anniversary of her mother's birth with an exhibition at the Gallery for International Art. Zhivkova had envisioned this museum as she purchased foreign art for Bulgarian collections (prompting accusations of the misuse of funds and the prosecution of art dealers after her death). Many close associates—including the former minister of culture Georgi Iordanov and the former chairman of the Union of Bulgarian Artists Svetlin Rusev—appeared at the opening, giving the gathering the flavor of a reunion of "Liudmila's circle." The exhibition featured photographs of Zhivkova's meetings with international leaders and public figures, from Leonid Brezhnev and Fidel Castro to Jimmy Carter and Indira Gandhi, but also publishing magnate Robert Maxwell, British sculptor Henry Moore, and Russian-Indian artist Svetoslav Roerich. According to the organizers, despite the "contemporary political polarization" about Zhivkova, her leadership of the cultural sphere had created "a hope for change" during difficult times. The project of forging a public hagiography of the late socialist power elites was underway.[6]

Later that year, an international academic conference on "the Bulgarian cultural opening to the world" at the University of Sofia tried to give a scientific stamp to the anniversary. The conference featured talks by close associates of Zhivkova's while her daughter reflected on her mother's contributions. But observers noticed in the audience the socialist-era head of State Security's Cultural Section, Dimitar Ivanov, a sinister reminder that any cultural opening under socialism was closely watched by the gatekeepers of the regime. Loud protests erupted at the event, accusing the organizers of rehabilitating the recent past and glorifying the communist elites. Critics insisted that Zhivkova was not "the minister of culture" but the "minister of dictatorship" (the words culture and dictatorship—*kultura* and *diktatura*—rhyme in Bulgarian). Exchanges in the press between historians of different political orientations debated the appropriateness of an event that idealized the doings of communist elites without nuancing the power dynamics involved in the process of "cultural opening."[7]

Socialist-era culture continues to provide a platform to fight out political disagreements regarding public spaces. In the center of Sofia a crumbling monument inaugurated in 1981 to commemorate the 1300-year jubilee for many years split architects, urban planners, cultural experts, and politicians over its possible removal or repair. This monument was installed in close proximity to the National Palace of Culture, built to host the Twelfth Congress of the BKP and the 1300th anniversary celebrations. Designed by a noted Bulgarian sculptor, Valentin Starchev, the monument embraced Zhivkova's core idea for the 1300-year jubilee: to show the unity of past, present, and future in the historical development of Bulgaria. The structure featured three seven-meter-high figures—the medieval King Simeon portrayed as a warrior and a scholar; a version of the Pietà or the mourning mother; and a worker shown as the creator—as well as a number of inspirational quotations from revolutionaries and writers. This monument became controversial early on.

Completed in eight months, its marble plaques began to fall shortly after its opening in 1981. Zhivkov expressed repeated displeasure with its modernist design.[8] After 1989, the monument fell into extreme disrepair; skateboarders and drug users utilized it, but the falling marble plaques compelled Sofia municipality to cordon it off to prevent a lethal incident.

Throughout the first decade of the twenty-first century various opinions in the press, public forums, and online discussions debated its removal and the reinstatement of the Fallen Soldier Memorial (built in 1934 and removed in 1981), its renovation, or its transformation into a modern outdoors facility featuring climbing walls and skateboarding ramps.[9] In the summer of 2017, despite the protests of cultural figures and campaigns to raise funds for its renovation, the municipal authorities embarked on a month-long removal process, using heavy machinery to take down the solid concrete structure. In November 2017, a small part of the interwar memorial to soldiers fallen in

FIGURE 38.   The 1300 Years Bulgaria Monument in ruins in 2016. Photo by author.

the Balkan and First World Wars—a lion holding a shield picturing San Stefano Bulgaria—stood in the middle of a small garden, awaiting the full reconstruction of the monument.[10] Postsocialist anticommunism had defeated
socialist-era cultural nationalism by resurrecting an explicitly irredentist
monument from the interwar years.

FIGURE 39.   The lion of the Fallen Soldier Memorial, installed in 2017 after the removal of the
1300 Years Bulgaria Monument. Photo by author.

Heated debates surround other socialist-era monuments, notably the Home Monument of the Party on Buzludzha, built on top of the Balkan Mountains to commemorate the ninetieth anniversary of the BKP, also in 1981. In the 1990s, this monument similarly experienced disrepair and was closed to the public because water leaks damaged the ceiling while vandals destroyed its mosaics and glasswork. The eerie structure has attracted journalists and thrill-seekers worldwide who enter the monument illegally with the help of local guides.[11] In summer 2019, a steady trickle of domestic and international tourists came to the summit (which also reveals breathtaking views) where the presence of an around-the-clock guard sought to discourage further scaling of the monument whose ceiling had started to collapse. That same year, Bulgarian and German architects won a Getty Foundation grant to design a conservation management plan to preserve the building "as an integral part of Bulgarian history" and explore options for the adaptive reuse of this "masterpiece of architectural engineering."[12] This fascination with the Home Monument of the Party highlights a tortuous logic regarding historical preservation, which allowed the demolition of a socialist-era monument—1300 Years Bulgaria in Sofia—that honored national history using modernist visual tropes, yet seeks to preserve a monument celebrating the deeds of the BKP in the ideological language of Marxism-Leninism.

Cultural debates within Bulgaria have international dimensions, too. In April 2015, an exhibition of Thracian archaeological artifacts from Bulgaria opened at the Louvre. The prime minister, minister of culture, and a flock of journalists were present for the ceremony in Paris, provoking unflattering comparisons in the press with the state management of culture in the 1970s.[13] There were heated discussions about the communist past when Prime Minister Boyko Borisov, a former bodyguard of Todor Zhivkov's, called the exhibition "a fulfillment of Liudmila Zhivkova's dreams."[14] The fate of Thracian treasures has been a sensitive topic for many Bulgarians because the longtime director of the National History Museum, Bozhidar Dimitrov, seemed to have cozy relations with oligarchs who mysteriously acquired spectacular Thracian artifacts for their private collections. Accusations emerged that by showing these treasures at the Louvre, Dimitrov had helped them legalize their shady deals. But Dimitrov's position remained unapologetic while the media discussions of the Louvre exhibit provided publicity for his new book—a publication of his state security file together with a short biographical exposé bragging about his involvement in sexual escapades and Vatican political intrigues while working as a "cultural spy" in Italian museums and libraries in the 1970s.[15]

The cultural legacy of socialism was on display again in May 2015 when the prime minister inaugurated a new museum complex, Square 500, in the

FIGURE 40.   The Home Monument of the Party on Buzludzha in summer 2019. The graffiti, damaged ceiling, and missing red star are visible even from a distance. Photo by author.

building of the former Gallery for International Art. This building had first opened in 1985 to showcase the cultural endeavors initiated by Zhivkova. At the time, it represented the first systematic showing of foreign art.[16] The current museum features an eclectic collection of Bulgarian, European, and world art. Notably, it houses numerous works of Russian-Indian artist

Nicholas Roerich (the first "multifaceted personality" celebrated in 1978) donated by his son as well as extensive collections of ancient Indian, classic Japanese, African, and Central and Latin American art assembled under Zhivkova's patronage. Its chief curator was the aforementioned Svetlin Rusev, one of Zhivkova's closest associates, who had been instrumental in the efforts to promote her image as a cultural innovator. He single-handedly oversaw the arrangement of the exposition that featured some 42,000 artifacts and unapologetically defended the choices he made in his conception of it—or the lack of conception, as art experts have charged.[17] Despite the conflicting opinions regarding this cultural investment during times of precarity, a familiar refrain dominated discussions on the "Bulgarian Louvre": culture is a good strategy for a small state to showcase its accomplishments to a global audience.

The tension between political, national, cultural, and international factors continues to define Bulgaria's cultural programs today. Political debates related to the communist legacy result in split opinions. Yet, public space is witnessing the remarkable embrace of an allegedly organic Bulgarianness, including omnipresent historical monuments and national symbols as well as official celebrations of the glorious past and popular fascination with allegedly authentic rites, traditional costumes, and folk traditions. A specter from the socialist past is haunting postsocialist Bulgaria: under the democratic political order, cultural nationalism is successfully building a social consensus on the unique historical destiny of small Bulgaria at the crossroads of civilizations.

Notes

Introduction

1. TNA, FCO 28/3732, U.S. Ambassador Jack Perry, "First Impressions from Bulgaria," 20 November 1979.

2. "Bulgaria: A Modern Nation Salutes Its Past," *UNESCO Courier* 34 (May 1981): 13.

3. While cultural bureaucrats likely inflated the numbers, what matters here is the geographical breakdown of Bulgaria's international cultural outreach. Of the total events counted, 7,894 occurred in socialist countries and 7,420 in developed capitalist countries while 542 occurred in the Balkans. Some 15,413 cultural events were organized in Asia, 3,442 in the Arab countries, 2,973 in Latin America, and 1,170 in Africa. TsDA, f. 1b, op. 55, a.e. 780, 1–32, Information-Sociological Center of the BKP, "Public Opinion for the 1300-Year Jubilee," February 1982.

4. "Bulgaria: A Modern Nation Salutes Its Past," *UNESCO Courier* 34 (May 1981), 5–13.

5. "Bulgaria 1981," *Bulgaria Today* 1 (January 1981): 3.

6. OSA/RFE, 300/20/1/36, "Zhivkov's Daughter Making Her Mark," Reuters, Sofia, 11 May 1976.

7. OSA/RFE, 300, 20/1/149, *Guardian*, 8 January 1976.

8. "Golden Artifacts," *Washington Post*, 15 February 1976.

9. OSA/RFE, 300/20/1/26, "Culture Boss," *Observer*, 29 February 1976.

10. OSA/RFE, 300/20/1/162, "The Un-Polish News," *Economist*, 21 November 1981.

11. TsDA, f. 405, op. 9, a.e. 497, clippings of press materials, including "Thracian Treasures from Bulgaria," *National Herald*, 18 February 1981, and "Bulgarian History of 1300 Years," *National Herald* (New Delhi), 2 February 1981.

12. MVnR, op. 38, a.e. 1171, 45–49, speech by Indira Gandhi, December 1981.

13. TsDA, f. 405, op. 10, a.e. 438, meeting of representatives of national jubilee committees in Western Europe, Vienna, 25–26 February 1981. The speech of Karl Blecha (Austria) is on p. 27.

14. TNA, FCO 28/4092, embassy in Sofia, annual review for 1979.

15. OSA/RFE, 300/20/1/162, RFE situation report, "The Bulgarian Military, Macedonia, and the 'Ludmila Effect,'" 18 April 1983.

16. See Laurien Crump and Susanna Erlandsson, eds., *Margins for Manoeuvre in Cold War Europe: The Influence of Smaller Powers* (New York: Routledge, 2019), 1–2, 244–246. The authors take "the concept of smallness as a starting point" and propose the notion of "margins for manoeuvre" to emphasize the agency of smaller states in the Cold War.

17. Mark Mazower, "Histories of the Big and Small: An Interview with Mark Mazower," Toynbee Prize Foundation, 20 February 2019, https://toynbeeprize.org/posts/mark-mazower/; Maria Todorova, *The Lost World of Socialists at Europe's Margins: Imagining Utopia, 1870–1920* (London: Bloomsbury, 2020), 15.

18. Akira Iriye, "Historicizing the Cold War," in *Oxford Handbook of the Cold War*, ed. Richard H. Immerman and Petra Goedde (Oxford: Oxford University Press, 2013); and Odd Arne Westad, "The New International History of the Cold War: Three (Possible) Paradigms," *Diplomatic History* 24, no. 4 (2000): 551–565.

19. Akira Iriye defines cultural internationalism as the exchange of cultural events across borders to foster the development of shared values in his *Cultural Internationalism and World Order* (Baltimore, MD: Johns Hopkins University Press, 1997). See also Petra Goedde, "Global Cultures," and Akira Iriye, "Making a Transnational World," in *Global Interdependence: The World after 1945*, ed. Akira Iriye (Cambridge, MA: Harvard University Press, 2014), 537–678, 681–847.

20. David Engerman, "Ideology and the Origins of the Cold War, 1917–1962," in *The Cambridge History of the Cold War*, ed. Melvyn P. Leffler and Odd Arne Westad (Cambridge: Cambridge University Press, 2010), 20–43.

21. Naoko Shibusawa, "Ideology, Culture, and the Cold War," in Immerman and Goedde, *The Oxford Handbook of the Cold War*, 32.

22. Christopher Endy, "Power and Culture in the West," in Immerman and Goedde, *The Oxford Handbook of the Cold War*, 324.

23. Charlotte Faucher, "Cultural Diplomacy and International Cultural Relations in Twentieth-Century Europe," *Contemporary European History* 25, no. 2 (2016): 373–385; Nancy Snow and Philip M. Taylor, eds., *Routledge Handbook of Public Diplomacy* (New York: Routledge, 2009).

24. Some examples include Kristen Ghodsee, *Muslim Lives in Eastern Europe: Gender, Ethnicity, and the Transformation of Islam in Postsocialist Bulgaria* (Princeton, NJ: Princeton University Press, 2010); Cristofer Scarboro, *The Late Socialist Good Life in Bulgaria: Meaning and Living in a Permanent Present Tense* (Lanham, MD: Lexington Books, 2011); and Karin Taylor, *Let's Twist Again: Youth and Leisure in Socialist Bulgaria* (Vienna: LIT Verlag, 2006).

25. Poland and Hungary had more open relations with both the West and the world. See Malgorzata Fidelis, "The Other Marxists: Making Sense of International Student Revolts in Poland in the Global Sixties," *Zeitschrift für Ostmitteleuropa-Forschung* 62, no. 3 (2013): 425–449; James Mark and Péter Apor, "Socialism Goes Global: Decolonization and the Making of a New Culture of Internationalism in Socialist Hungary, 1956–1989," *Journal of Modern History* 87, no. 4 (2015): 852–891; and Malgorzata Fidelis, *Imagining the World: Youth and the Global Sixties in Poland* (New York: Oxford University Press, forthcoming).

26. Arjun Appadurai, *Modernity at Large: Cultural Dimensions of Globalization* (Minneapolis: University of Minnesota Press, 1996) highlights the more rapid circulation of people, capital, technology, and ideas as key features of the new global trends in the postcolonial period. For a work that links Cold War cultural exchange and globalization, see Danielle Fosler-Lussier, *Music in America's Cold War Diplomacy* (Oakland: University of California Press, 2015).

27. For the concept of "cultural opening," see Iskra Baeva, ed., *Kulturnoto otvariane na Bâlgariia kâm sveta* (Sofia: Universitetsko izdatelstvo Sv. Kliment Ohridski, 2013).

28. See Johanna Bockman, *Markets in the Name of Socialism: The Left-Wing Origins of Neoliberalism* (Stanford, CA: Stanford University Press, 2011); Besnik Pula, *Globalization under and after Socialism: The Evolution of Transnational Capital in Central and Eastern Europe* (Stanford, CA: Stanford University Press, 2018); and James Mark, Artemy Kalinovsky, and Steffi Marung, eds., *Alternative Globalizations: Eastern Europe and the Postcolonial World* (Bloomington: Indiana University Press, 2020).

29. For an appeal to disentangle the agendas of the Soviet Union and its Eastern European allies, see Theodora Dragostinova and Malgorzata Fidelis, "Introduction," in "Beyond the Iron Curtain: Eastern Europe and the Global Cold War," special issue, *Slavic Review* 77, no. 3 (2018): 577–587.

30. Łukasz Stanek, *Architecture in Global Socialism: Eastern Europe, West Africa, and the Middle East in the Cold War* (Princeton, NJ: Princeton University Press, 2020).

31. Kristen Ghodsee, *Second World, Second Sex: Socialist Women's Activism and Global Solidarity during the Cold War* (Durham, NC: Duke University Press, 2019).

32. Niall Ferguson et al., eds., *The Shock of the Global: The 1970s in Perspective* (Cambridge, MA: The Belknap Press of Harvard University Press, 2010).

33. Thomas Borstelmann, *The 1970s: A New Global History from Civil Rights to Economic Inequality* (Princeton, NJ: Princeton University Press, 2011), 3.

34. Tony Judt, *Postwar: A History of Europe since 1945* (New York: Penguin, 2005), 456, 477, 576.

35. Matthew Connelly, "Future Shock: The End of the World as They Knew It," in Ferguson et al., *The Shock of the Global*, 346.

36. See Paulina Bren, *The Greengrocer and His TV: The Culture of Communism after the 1968 Prague Spring* (Ithaca, NY: Cornell University Press, 2010), 111, 145, 173, 187.

37. Alexei Yurchak, *Everything Was Forever, Until It Was No More: The Last Soviet Generation* (Princeton, NJ: Princeton University Press, 2006), 4, 28.

38. Angela Romano and Federico Romero, Introduction to *European Socialist Regimes' Fateful Engagement with the West: National Strategies in the Long 1970s*, ed. Angela Romano and Federico Romero (New York: Routledge, 2021), 3. This volume is based on the findings of the PanEur1970s project carried out at the European University Institute, Florence. I thank Angela Romano for sharing the draft introduction with me.

39. B. R. Tomlinson, "What Was the Third World?," *Journal of Contemporary History* 38, no. 2 (2003): 307–321.

40. Tony Smith, "New Bottles for New Wine: A Pericentric Framework for the Study of the Cold War," *Diplomatic History* 24, no. 4 (2000): 567–591.

41. Jeremi Suri, *Power and Protest: Global Revolution and the Rise of Détente* (Cambridge, MA: Harvard University Press, 2003).

42. TsDA, f. 405, op. 9, a.e. 670, 162–197, "Future Development of Cultural Cooperation between Bulgaria and the United States," undated.

1. The Contradictions of Developed Socialism

1. Todor Zhivkov, "Address to the Bulgarian People on the Occasion of the 1300th Anniversary of the Bulgarian State," 20 October 1981, abridged English translation in *Bulgaria Today* 4 (1981): 2–3, 6. For the full speech in Bulgarian, see "1981–13

veka Bâlgarska dârzhava," Bulgarian National Radio, 21 April 2015, http://bnr.bg/radiobulgaria/post/100547908/1981-13-veka-balgarska-darjava.

2. TNA, FCO 28/4865, FCO on an embassy in Sofia report, 6 May 1982.

3. TNA, FCO 28/4851, embassy in Sofia, annual review for 1981.

4. TNA, FCO 28/4865, "Bulgaria: A National Identity," 22 April 1982.

5. TNA, FCO 28/2700, embassy in Sofia report, 10 December 1974.

6. TNA, FCO 28/2498, "Bulgaria: First Impressions," 24 August 1973; embassy to FCO, 12 February 1974.

7. TNA, FCO 28/2863, embassy in Sofia, annual review for 1975.

8. OSA/RFE, 300/20/1/126, "Folgsames Bulgarien," *Frankfurter Allgemeine Zeitung*, 30 March 1976; "Bulgariens Kurs als Mustersatellit," *Neue Zürcher Zeitung*, 13 June 1977.

9. TNA, FCO 28/2865, U.S. embassy in Sofia to State Department, 18 and 24 March 1976.

10. TNA, FCO 28/3732, U.S. Ambassador Perry, "First Impressions from Bulgaria," 20 November 1979.

11. TNA, FCO 28/3732, "What Use Is Bulgaria?," 30 July 1979.

12. TNA, FCO 28/3732, embassy in Sofia report, 20 November 1979.

13. OSA/RFE, 300/20/1/162, "The Un-Polish News," *Economist*, 21 November 1981.

14. TNA, FCO 28/2698, RFE situation report, "Criticism in Mass Media Discussed," 4 December 1975.

15. TNA, FCO 28/2863, embassy in Sofia, annual review for 1975.

16. TNA, FCO 28/3024, "Unaesthetic Education," 24 October 1977.

17. TNA, FCO 28/2862, "Bulgaria: Valedictory," 29 June 1976.

18. TNA, FCO 28/4851, embassy in Sofia, annual review for 1978.

19. TNA, FCO 28/3318, embassy in Sofia report, 17 October 1978.

20. I use the term normalization in its literal meaning, and not in reference to the process of normalization in Czechoslovakia after 1968, which has country-specific meaning related to the Warsaw Pact invasion of the country.

21. TNA, FCO 28/4447, embassy in Sofia, annual review for 1980.

22. For succinct but comprehensive overviews, see the contributions in Ivaĭlo Znepolski, ed., *Istoriia na Narodna Republika Bâlgariia: Rezhimât i obshtestvoto* (Sofia: Siela, 2009); and Ivaĭlo Znepolski, ed., *NRB ot nachaloto do kraia* (Sofia: Siela, 2011).

23. Ivaĭlo Znepolsi, "'Konsensusnata diktatura' i sotsialnata i baza: Korumpirane na masite," in Znepolski, *Istoriia*, 395–437.

24. Martin Ivanov, "Ikonomika na komunisticheska Bâlgariia," in Znepolski, *Istoriia*, 314–321. For economic policies under socialism, see also Rumen Avramov, *Pari i de/stabilizatsiia v Bâlgariia 1948–1989* (Sofia: Siela, 2008).

25. Mihail Gruev, "Politicheskoto razvitie na Bâlgariia," in Znepolski, *Istoriia*, 161–164.

26. Iskra Baeva and Evgeniia Kalinova, *Bâlgarskite prehodi, 1939–2002* (Sofia: Paradigma, 2002), 176–179; for the recent role of Russia in the Balkans, see Dimitar Bechev, *Rival Power: Russia's Influence in Southeast Europe* (New Haven, CT: Yale University Press, 2017).

27. Baeva and Kalinova, *Bâlgarskite prehodi*, 178–182; and Znepolski, *NRB ot nachaloto do kraia*, 314–321.

28. Irina Gigova, "The Feeble Charm of National(ist) Communism: Intellectuals and Cultural Politics in Zhivkov's Bulgaria," in *Beyond Mosque, Church, and State: Alternative Narratives of the Nation in the Balkans*, ed. Theodora Dragostinova and Yana Hashamova (Budapest: Central European University Press, 2016), 153–154, 156. See also Tchavdar Marinov, "Ot internatsionalizâm kâm natsionalizâm: Komunisticheskiiat rezhim, Makedonskiiat vâpros i politikata kâm etnicheskite i religioznite obshtnosti," in Znepolski, *Istoriia*, 479–529.

29. Two comprehensive studies are Mihail Gruev and Alexeï Kalionski, *Vâzroditelniiat protses: Miusiulmanskite obshtnosti i komunistichedkiia rezhim* (Sofia: Siela, 2008); and Rumen Avramov, *Ikonomika na "Vâzroditelniia protses"* (Sofia: CAS, 2016). See also Marinov, "Ot internatsionalizâm kâm natsionalizâm," 500–515. For a recent study in English, see Tomasz Kamusella, *Ethnic Cleansing during the Cold War: The Forgotten 1989 Expulsion of Turks from Communist Bulgaria* (London: Routledge, 2018).

30. OSA/RFE, 300/20/1/44, RFE situation report, 30 October 1979.

31. TNA, FCO 28/2700, embassy in Sofia report, 10 December 1974.

32. Ivaïlo Znepolski, *Bâlgarskiiat komunizâm: Sotsiokulturni cherti i vlastova traektoriia* (Sofia: Siela, 2008), 221–250.

33. Ulf Brunnbauer and Karin Taylor, "Creating a 'Socialist Way of Life': Family and Reproduction Policies in Bulgaria, 1944–1989," *Continuity and Change* 19, no. 2 (2004): 284–285. For a similar approach, see Taylor, *Let's Twist Again*.

34. Ulf Brunnbauer, "Making Bulgarians Socialist: The Fatherland Front in Communist Bulgaria, 1944–1989," *East European Politics and Societies* 22, no. 1 (2008): 72.

35. Brunnbauer, "Making Bulgarians Socialist," 73–74. This article is based on a larger work on socialist Bulgaria, used here in its Bulgarian translation. Ulf Brunnbauer, *Sotsialisticheskiiat nachin na zhivot: Ideologiia, obshtestvo, semeistvo i politika v Bâlgariia (1944–1989)*, trans. Rumiana Stankova (Sofia: Elias Kaneti, 2010). Confirming the contradictory social processes during late socialism, Cristofer Scarboro talks about "a move towards embourgeoisement and the creation of middle-class socialists" in the 1970s in his *The Late Socialist Good Life in Bulgaria*.

36. The quotations come from Brunnbauer, "Making Bulgarians Socialist," 50, who dates the speech to 1968. According to Evgeniia Kalinova, *Bâlgarskata kultura i politicheskiiat imperativ, 1944–1989* (Sofia: Paradigma, 2011), 269, Zhivkov gave that speech at a meeting with Bulgarian writers in 1966.

37. Ivan Elenkov, *Trud, radost, otdih i kultura* (Sofia: CAS, 2013), 154–156.

38. For Bulgarian writers, see Irina Gigova, "Writers of the Nation: Intellectual Identity in Bulgaria, 1939–1953" (PhD diss., University of Illinois Urbana-Champaign, 2005).

39. This uneasy "thaw" is described in Atanas Slavov, *The "Thaw" in Bulgarian Literature* (Boulder, CO: East European Monographs, 1981).

40. Nick Rutter, "Look Left, Drive Right: Internationalisms at the 1968 Youth World Festival," in *The Socialist Sixties: Crossing Borders in the Second World*, ed. Anne E. Gorsuch and Diane Koenker (Bloomington: Indiana University Press, 2013), 193–212.

41. Kalinova, *Bâlgarskata kultura*, 245–291.

42. Kalinova, *Bâlgarskata kultura*, 295–298, 301.

43. Ivan Elenkov, "Kulturnata politika," in Znepolski, *Istoriia*, 550–551.

44. Katherine Verdery, *National Ideology under Socialism: Identity and Cultural Politics in Ceaușescu's Romania* (Berkeley: University of California Press, 1991).

45. For the rise of cultural nationalism, see Gigova, "The Feeble Charm of National(ist) Communism"; Marinov, "Ot internatsionalizâm kâm natsionalizâm"; and Zhivka Valiavicharska, "Post-Stalinism's Uncanny Symbioses: Ethno-nationalism and the Global Orientations of Bulgarian Socialism during the 1960s and 1970s," in "Decolonial Theory and Practice in Southeast Europe," special issue, *dVersia* (March 2019), 78–99.

46. Kalinova, *Bâlgarskata kultura*, 300–305. See also OSA/RFE, 300/20/1/36, RFE situation report, 1 June 1977.

47. Kalinova, *Bâlgarskata kultura*, 308–310.

48. Ivan Elenkov, *Kulturniiat front: Bâlgarskata kultura prez epohata na komunizma—politichesko upravlenie, ideologicheski osnovaniia, institutsionalni rezhimi* (Sofia: Siela, 2008), 309.

49. Kalinova, *Bâlgarskata kultura*, 312–313; Elenkov, "Kulturnata politika," 551–553.

50. Elenkov, "Kulturnata politika," 551.

51. Elenkov, "Kulturnata politika," 551; Elenkov, *Kulturniiat front*, 286.

52. Elenkov, *Kulturniiat front*, 317–318.

53. Elenkov, *Kulturniiat front*, 320. This choice is linked to the personal connections between Zhivkova and Svetoslav Roerich, the son of Nicholas Roerich, himself an artist who lived in India and shared her interest in Eastern philosophies and meditation. Roerich donated close to 250 of his father's artworks to the Bulgarian state.

54. Elenkov, *Kulturniiat front*, 344. For a study of the role of UNESCO for other Balkan states in the context of the global Cold War, see Bogdan C. Iacob, "Southeast by Global South: The Balkans, UNESCO, and the Cold War," in *Alternative Globalizations: Eastern Europe and the Postcolonial World*, ed. James Mark, Artemy M. Kalinovski, and Steffi Marung (Bloomington: Indiana University Press, 2020), 251–271.

55. Elenkov, *Kulturniiat front*, 317–356; Kalinova, *Bâlgarskata kultura*, 316–318.

56. Elenkov, *Kulturniiat front*, 357–411; Elenkov, "Kulturnata politika," 553–556; and Kalinova, *Bâlgarskata kultura*, 324–325.

57. Kalinova, *Bâlgarskata kultura*, 324.

58. Elenkov, *Kulturniiat front*, 320–321, 327–336. In the end, the Roerich celebrations focused on India, a decision in line with Zhivkova's personal interest in theosophy and mysticism.

59. One of those "cultural spies" was Bozhidar Dimitrov, a prolific nationalist historian and long-term director of the National History Museum. See Bozhidar Dimitrov, *Za kozhata na edno chenge* (Sofia: Unikart, 2015).

60. Kalinova, *Bâlgarskata kultura*, 321–323.

61. *Telegraph*, London, 18 September 1972. For this and other international events, see Valiavicharska, "Post-Stalinism's Uncanny Symbioses."

62. OSA/RFE, 300/20/1/149, BTA dispatch, 3 February 1973.

63. OSA/RFE, 300/20/1/39, RFE report, Munich, 3 June 1977; RFE special report, 18 July 1977. There were subsequent meetings in 1979, 1980, 1982, 1984, and 1986.

64. OSA/RFE, 300/20/1/44, correspondence regarding meetings of the Congress of Bulgaria Studies in May 1981 and July 1984.

65. Kalinova, *Bâlgarskata kultura*, 318–321.

66. Elenkov, "Kulturnata politika," 555.

67. Elenkov, *Kulturniiat front*, 411; Elenkov, "Kulturnata politika," 556.

68. Gigova, "The Feeble Charm of National(ist) Communism," 164–165.

69. Elenkov, *Kulturniiat front*, 364.

70. Elenkov, *Kulturniiat front*, 362.

71. In official historical interpretation, the Bulgarian nation merged three elements, the Thracians, Proto-Bulgarians, and Slavs.

72. Elenkov, "Kulturnata politika," 554.

73. Elenkov, *Kulturniiat front*, 364.

74. Elenkov, "Kulturnata politika," 553.

75. For a list of the themes, see Elenkov, *Kulturniiat front*, 404.

76. For domestic policies related to 1300, see Elitsa Stanoeva, *Sofia: Ideologiia, gradoustroĭstvo i zhivot prez sotsializma* (Sofia: Prosveta, 2016).

77. TsDA, f. 990, op. 1, a.e. 718, 25, MvNR memo to KK and NKK, 12 April 1978.

78. TsDA, f. 990, op. 1, a.e. 729, 1–12, analysis of millennium events in Krakow, January 1979.

79. TsDA, f. 990, op. 1, a.e. 731, 105–118, "Studies of Foreign Experience: The Polish Millennium," January 1977.

80. TsDA, f. 990, op. 1, a.e. 729, 1–12; TsDA, f. 990, op. 1, a.e. 731, 1–4 and 32–52, information on the participation of Polish émigrés in the millennial celebrations from 1977 and 1978.

81. TsDA, f. 990, op. 1, a.e. 723, 26–53, report on the Iranian 2500th anniversary, 7 January 1977.

82. TsDA, f. 990, op. 1, a.e. 718, 58–65, organizational mechanism of the 1300th anniversary, March 1976.

83. TsDA, f. 990, op. 1, a.e. 742, 8–16, "Studies of Foreign Experience: The USA Bicentennial," December 1976.

84. TsDA, f. 990, op. 1, a.e. 744, 52–56, 62–71, 138, analyses of the U.S. events from 1977.

85. TsDA, f. 990, op. 1, a.e. 719, 1–2, report of Alexander Fol, 10 January 1978.

86. TsDA, f. 990, op. 1, a.e. 444, 3–9, report from November 1979; ibid., a.e. 445, 5, NKK report on foreign propaganda related to the 1300th anniversary, April 1981.

87. TsDA, f. 1b, op. 55, a.e. 780, 1–32, Information-Sociological Center of the BKP, "Public Opinion for the 1300 Jubilee," February 1982.

88. See TsDA, f. 405, op. 9, a.e. 263, 55, NKK, "For the Dignified Celebration of the 1300th Anniversary of the Establishment of the Bulgarian State," June 1979.

89. Elitza Stanoeva, "Bulgaria's 1300 Years and East Berlin's 750 Years: Comparing National and International Objectives of Socialist Anniversaries in the 1980s," *CAS Working Paper Series* 9 (2017): 25.

90. János Kornai, *Economics of Shortage* (Amsterdam: North-Holland, 1980).

91. TNA, FCO 28/3319, embassy in Sofia, annual review for 1977.

92. OSA/RFE, 300/20/1/25, RFE situation report, 8 September 1972.

93. TNA, FCO 28/4091, "Leading Personalities in Bulgaria in 1980."

94. Kalinova, *Bâlgarskata kultura*, 298–300, 330–336.

95. TNA, FCO 28/4091, "Leading Personalities in Bulgaria in 1980."

96. Aleksandâr Vezenkov, *Vlastovite strukturi na Bâlgarskata komunisticheska partiia, 1944–1989* (Sofia: Siela, 2008), 144–145.

97. Elena Savova et al., eds., *Liudmila Zhivkov: Zhivot i delo (1942–1981); Letopis* (Sofia: Izdatelstvo na Bâlgarskata akademiia na naukite, 1987).

98. There have been many studies of Zhivkova in Bulgarian, including that of the journalist Krum Blagov, *Zagadkata Luidmila Zhivkova* (Sofia: Reporter, 2012). Two works by close associates of Zhivkova are Elit Nikolov, *Dâshteriata na nadezhdite* (Sofia: Propeler, 2008); and Bogomil Raĭnov, *Liudmila: Mechti i dela* (Sofia: Iztok-Zapad, 2011). For a study of her interest in Eastern philosophies, see Mihail Gruev, "Liudmila Zhivkova—pâtiat kâm agni ioga," in *Prelomni vremena: Iubileen sbornik v chest na 65-godishninata na profesor Liubomir Ognianov*, ed. Evgeniia Kalinova, Mihail Gruev, and Liudmila Zidarova (Sofia: Universitetsko izdatelstvo Sv. Kliment Ohridski, 2006), 796–816. For a brief study in English, see Ivanka Nedeva Atanasova, "Lyudmila Zhivkova and the Paradox of Ideology and Identity in Communist Bulgaria," *East European Politics & Societies* 18, no. 2 (2004): 278–315. For "enlightened absolutism," see Iliana Marcheva and Mariia Radeva, eds., *Bâlgariski darzhavnitsi, 1944–1989* (Sofia: Skorpio, 2005), 170–183.

99. TNA, FCO 28/4091, "Leading Personalities in Bulgaria in 1980."

100. OSA/RFE, 300/20/1/26, "Culture Boss," *Observer*, 29 February 1976.

101. OSA/RFE, 300/20/1/26, "Communist Rule: All in the Family," *International Herald Tribune*, 24 August 1979.

102. OSA/RFE, 300/20/1/26, RFE special report, "Lyudmila a New Potent Force in Bulgarian Politics," 24 June 1980.

103. OSA/RFE, 300/20/1/26, "Zhivkova Making an Impact," Reuters, 7 November 1980.

104. TNA, FCO 28/4093, "The Two Faces of Bulgaria," 24 June 1980.

105. TNA, FCO 28/4091, "Leading Personalities in Bulgaria in 1980." All quotations in the next three paragraphs, unless noted otherwise, are from this document. I am triangulating that document, which contains some mistakes, with Marcheva and Radeva, *Bâlgariski darzhavnitsi* as well as Vezenkov, *Vlastovite strukturi*, 144–145.

106. For the hunting crew, Kalinova, *Bâlgarskata kultura*, 332–333.

107. Kalinova, *Bâlgarskata kultura*, 332–333.

108. Mihail Gruev, "Komunisticheskiiat elit v Bâlgariia: Genezis i evoliutsiia," *Razum* 1 (2005): 215–224.

109. Kristen Ghodsee, "Pressuring the Politburo: The Committee of the Bulgarian Women's Movement and State Socialist Feminism," *Slavic Review* 73, no. 3 (2014): 538–562.

110. Suri, *Power and Protest*, 213–214.

111. The five writers were Blagoi Dimitrov, who voted against, and Marko Ganchev, Valeri Petrov, Hristo Ganev, and Gocho Gochev who abstained. See Kalinova, *Bâlgarskata kultura*, 348–349; and Gigova, "The Feeble Charm of National(ist) Communism," 164.

112. Kalinova, *Bâlgarskata kultura*, 337–340.

113. Nataliia Hristova, *Spetsifika na bâlgarskoto "disidenstvo": Vlast i inteligentsiia, 1956–1989 g.* (Plovdiv: Letera, 2005) is the most comprehensive study to date. It traces various moments of tension between intellectuals and those in power from 1956 until the late 1980s, but declines to call those episodes "dissidence." For moment of crises in the literary scene, in particular, see Plamen Doĭnov, *Bâlgarskiiat sotsrealizâm 1956 1968 1989: Norma i kriza v literaturata na NRB* (Sofia: Siela, 2011).

114. Kalinova, *Bâlgarskata kultura*, 352–353; Gigova, "The Feeble Charm of National(ist) Communism," 164.

115. Kalinova, *Bâlgarskata kultura*, 361–362.

116. Elenkov, *Trud, radost, otdih i kultura*, 154–156.

117. TNA, FCO 28/3318, embassy in Sofia report, 8 May 1978.

118. OSA/RFE, 300/20/1/182, RFE reports from Vienna, 23 February 1977.

119. For a study of Czechoslovakia, see Jonathan Bolton, *Worlds of Dissent: Charter 77, the Plastic People of the Universe, and Czech Culture under Communism* (Cambridge, MA: Harvard University Press, 2012).

120. OSA/RFE, 300/20/1/182, RFE report, Munich, 21 February 1977; BTA, 22 and 23 February 1977.

121. OSA/RFE, 300/20/1/182, RFE reports, Paris, 8 March 1977.

122. See Kalinova, *Bâlgarskata kultura*, 362; OSA/RFE, 300/20/1/182, RFE situation report "Is There Dissidence in Bulgaria?," 8 December 1977.

123. OSA/RFE, 300/20/1/182, Declaration 78, typed texts in Bulgarian and English, 2 March 1978; *Svoboden narod* 27–28 (1978); *Die Presse*, 3 April 1978; RFE situation report "Declaration 78," 17 April 1978; RFE report, "Dissidence in Bulgaria," 10 July 1978; TNA, FCO 28/3318, embassy in Sofia report, 27 April 1978.

124. Kalinova, *Bâlgarskata kultura*, 353–358; for breakdown of the agents according to cultural institutions, see 357.

125. Kalinova, *Bâlgarskata kultura*, 359–363.

126. OSA/RFE, 300/20/1/182, Radio Sofia Abroad dispatch, 28 July 1977.

127. OSA/RFE, 300/20/1/182, RFE "Zhivkov to Address Bulgaria's Young Writers," 24 February 1978; TNA, FCO 28/3321, embassy in Sofia report, 3 February 1978; see also Kalinova, *Bâlgarskata kultura*, 363, and Gigova, "The Feeble Charm of National(ist) Communism," 164–165.

128. OSA/RFE, 300/20/1/182, BTA dispatch, 4 April 1978.

129. Many of these dispatches are assembled in Georgi Markov, *Zadochni reportazhi za Bâlgariia* (Sofia: Siela, 2008).

130. MVnR, op. 34, a.e. 581, 132–134, 137–139, memos of Maria Zaharieva, January and April 1978.

131. Kalinova, *Bâlgarskata kultura*, 358.

132. For a nuanced study of Markov's choices, see Dimiter Kenarov, "A Captivating Mind," *Nation*, 7 April 2014, https://www.thenation.com/article/archive/captivating-mind/.

133. MVnR, op. 34, a.e. 812, 109–110, MVnR memo, 10 October 1978; a.e. 833, 30–36, "The Anti-Bulgarian Campaign in the FRG Mass Media regarding the Death of Georgi Markov and Vladimir Simeonov," September 1978"; MVnR, op. 34, a.e. 2905, 32–57, "Characteristics of the Anticommunist Propaganda in France," 5 December 1978. For Markov, see ibid., a.e. 2905, 23–25, "Hostile Campaign against Bulgaria in the French Press," 1 October 1978.

134. TNA, FCO 28/3733, annual review for 1978.

135. MVnR, op. 35, a.e. 658, 66–84, report of Filip Bokov, January 1979. A work that supports this thesis is Hristo Hristov, *Ubiîte "Skitnik": Bâlgarskata i Britanskata dârzhâvna politika po sluchaia Georgi Markov* (Sofia: Siela, 2006). See also Kalinova, *Bâlgarskata kultura*, 359n238.

136. MVnR, op. 34, a.e. 2905, 32–57, "Characteristics of the Anticommunist Propaganda in France," 5 December 1978.

137. MVnR, op. 36, a.e. 159, 19–21, Bulgarian translation of *Internationale Politik* article, June 1980.

138. MVnR, op. 36, a.e. 159, 39, Bulgarian translation of *Die Presse* article, 20 November 1980.

139. TNA, FCO 28/4099, embassy in Sofia report, 8 September 1980.

140. For the acrostic, see OSA/RFE, 300/20/1/183, RFE situation report, 1 August 1985.

141. Gigova, "The Feeble Charm of National(ist) Communism," 153.

142. Hristova, *Spetsifika na bâlgarskoto "disidenstvo,"* 360.

143. Kalinova, *Bâlgarskata kultura,* 363–364.

144. Gigova, "The Feeble Charm of National(ist) Communism," 164–165.

145. Bren, *The Greengrocer and His TV,* 91.

146. Verdery, *National Ideology under Socialism.*

147. Maryjane Osa, *Solidarity and Contention: Networks of Polish Opposition* (Minneapolis: University of Minnesota Press, 2003), 59–80.

148. Verdery, *National Ideology under Socialism;* Dennis Deletant, "Romania's Return to Europe: Between Politics and Culture," in *Europe and the Historical Legacies in the Balkans,* ed. Raymond Detrez and Barbara Segaert (Frankfurt: Peter Lang, 2008), 83–98.

149. Stanoeva, "Bulgaria's 1300 Years," 7.

150. Dimitrov examines this trend in the context of 1929 when Bulgaria celebrated a threefold jubilee—the millennium of Simeon the Great, the fiftieth anniversary of the liberation of Bulgaria, and the tenth anniversary of the enthronement of Tsar Boris III—to unite the nation after the wars of the 1910s. See Emil Dimitrov, "Iubileiat kato proekt: Târzhestvata prez 1929 i 'bâlgarskata ideiia,'" *Sledva* 7 (2003): 74, 77–78. I thank Ivan Elenkov for this reference.

151. Elenkov, "Kulturnata politika," 555.

2. Goodwill between Neighbors

1. TsDA, f. 405, op. 9, a.e. 607, 5–6, KK note, 10 December 1975.

2. TsDA, f. 405, op. 9, a.e. 607, 41–42, KK information on cultural cooperation with Yugoslavia in 1975.

3. TsDA, f. 405, op. 9, a.e. 665, 44–45, Bulgarian translation of an article in *Nova Makedoniia* from 4 October 1977, reprinting the *Oko* article. According to the Bulgarian explanation, the map was created by U.S. experts at the Greco-Roman Division of the Metropolitan Museum and contained many other inaccuracies. See TsDA, f. 405, op. 9, a.e. 665, 51, report of the KK, 22 September 1977.

4. MVnR, op. 36, a.e. 595, 1–15, embassy in London report, 10 October 1980.

5. TsDA, f. 405, op. 10, a.e. 487, 108–109, KK information, November 1981.

6. For the role of the Balkans in the early Cold War, see Theodora Dragostinova, "On 'Strategic Frontiers': Debating the Borders of the Post–Second World War Balkans," *Contemporary European History* 27, no. 3 (2018): 387–411. Here, I rely on Svetozar Rajak et al., eds., *The Balkans in the Cold War* (London: Palgrave Macmillan, 2017).

7. On Balkan diplomacy during the 1970s, see Tonka Kostadinova, "Bâlgaro-grâtski otnosheniia prez 70-te godini na XX vek—aspekti na dvustrannoto sâtrudnichestvo i regionalnata integratsiia," in *Evropeiski integratsionni protsesi prez 70-te godini na XX vek,* ed. Iskra Baeva (Sofia: Universitetsko izdatelstvo Sv. Kliment Ohridski, 2014),

183–200; Eirini Karamouzi, "Managing the 'Helsinki Spirit' in the Balkans: The Greek Initiative for Balkan Co-operation, 1975–1976," *Diplomacy & Statecraft* 24 (2013): 597–618; and Lykourgos Kourkouvelas, "Détente as a Strategy: Greece and the Communist World, 1974–9," *The International History Review* 35, no. 5 (2013): 1052–1067.

8. See Aurel Braun, *Small-State Security in the Balkans* (London: Macmillan, 1983).

9. Robert Niebuhr, *The Search for a Cold War Legitimacy: Foreign Policy and Tito's Yugoslavia* (Leiden: Brill, 2018).

10. Dennis Deletant and Mihail Ionescu, "Romania and the Warsaw Pact, 1955–1989," *Cold War International History Project*, Working Paper 43 (April 2004), 1–103.

11. For Albania, see Elidor Mëhilli, *From Stalin to Mao: Albania and the Socialist World* (Ithaca, NY: Cornell University Press, 2017). Bulgarian officials tried to reach out to Albania, but abandoned all efforts to sponsor cultural events in the country due to its open hostility toward the Bulgarian agenda. Thus, I do not engage Albania in my analysis.

12. Here, I take the term "socialist internationalism" to mean the existence of a "transnational socialist community," as described in the fraught "friendship project" between the Soviet Union and Czechoslovakia by Rachel Applebaum, *Empire of Friends: Soviet Power and Socialist Internationalism in Cold War Czechoslovakia* (Ithaca, NY: Cornell University Press, 2019), 3.

13. Kostadin Grozev and Jordan Baev, "Bulgaria, Balkan Diplomacy, and the Road to Helsinki," in *Helsinki 1975 and the Transformation of Europe*, ed. Oliver Bange and Gottfried Niedhart (New York: Berghahn Books, 2008), 160–174; and Baeva and Kalinova, *Bâlgarskite prehodi*, 199–216.

14. Grozev and Baev, "Bulgaria," 171.

15. Eirini Karamouzi, *Greece, the EEC and the Cold War, 1974–1979: The Second Enlargement* (Basingstoke: Palgrave Macmillan, 2014).

16. Mehmet Döşemeci, "Cutting through the Cold War: The EEC and Turkey's Great Westernization Debate," in Rajak, *The Balkans in the Cold War*, 331–350; and William Hale, *Turkish Foreign Policy since 1774* (New York: Routledge, 2012).

17. Grozev and Baev, "Bulgaria," 161.

18. Grozev and Baev, "Bulgaria," 167, 171.

19. Karamouzi, "Managing the 'Helsinki Spirit,'" 600; Kostadinova, "Bâlgaro-grâtski otnosheniia"; Effie Pedaliu, "The US, the Balkans, and Détente," in Rajak, *The Balkans in the Cold War*, 206–208; and Braun, *Small-State Security*.

20. The Conference on Security and Cooperation in Europe (CSCE), first held in Helsinki in 1973, had its second meeting in Belgrade in 1977. I thank Dimitar Bechev for this reminder.

21. TNA, FCO 28/2866, embassy in Sofia report, 2 February 1976.

22. Kostadinova, "Bâlgaro-grâtski otnosheniia," 187–188.

23. Karamouzi, "Managing the 'Helsinki Spirit'"; Kourkouvelas, "Détente as a Strategy"; and Kostadinova, "Bâlgaro-grâtski otnosheniia," 199. For the Ankara conference, see TNA, FCO 28/3747, correspondence on Balkan cooperation, 1979. See also Evgeniia Kalinova, "Iztâniavashtata zheliazna zavesa Bâlgariia-Gârtsiia," in *Bâlgariia i Evropa prez sâvremennata epoha: Sbornik v chest na prof. D. Sirkov*, ed. Dragomir Draganov, Dimitâr Dimmitrov, and Petko Boev (Veliko Tarnovo: Faber, 2010), 194–215.

24. TNA, FCO 28/2866, embassy in Sofia report, 2 February 1976.

25. For recent comparative studies, see Rumen Daskalov and Tchavdar Marinov, eds., *National Ideologies and Language Policies*, vol. 1 of *Entangled Histories of the Balkans* (Leiden: Brill, 2013), and the three subsequent volumes of this series. See also Detrez and Segaert, *Europe and the Historical Legacies*.

26. For the interrelationship between communism and nationalism, see Martin Mevius, ed., "The Communist Quest for National Legitimacy in Europe, 1918–1989," special issue, *Nationalities Papers* 37, no. 4 (2009) and especially Martin Mevius, "Reappraising Communism and Nationalism," *Nationalities Papers* 37, no. 4 (2009): 377–400. See also Verdery, *National Ideology under Socialism*; Bradley F. Abrams, *The Struggle for the Soul of the Nation: Czech Culture and the Rise of Communism* (Lanham, MD: Rowman & Littlefield, 2004); Martin Mevius, *Agents of Moscow: The Hungarian Communist Party and the Origins of Socialist Patriotism, 1941–1953* (Oxford: Clarendon Press, 2005).

27. For an overview of Bulgarian national policies under communism, see Marinov, "Ot internatsionalizâm kâm natsionalizâm."

28. Yannis Sygkelos, *Nationalism from the Left: The Bulgarian Communist Party during the Second World War and the Early Post-War Years* (Leiden: Brill, 2011), 55, 73.

29. For a study of cultural nationalism in socialist Bulgaria, see Gigova, "The Feeble Charm of National(ist) Communism."

30. For an excellent study of historical scholarship in Romania, Greece, and Bulgaria on the topic of ancient ancestors, see Tchavdar Marinov, "Ancient Thrace in the Modern Imagination: Ideological Aspects of the Construction of Thracian Studies in Southeast Europe (Romania, Greece, Bulgaria)," in *Shared Pasts, Disputed Legacies*, vol. 3 of *Entangled Histories of the Balkans*, ed. Rumen Daskalov and Alexander Vezenkov (Leiden: Brill, 2015), 10–117.

31. Stefan Troebst, *Die bulgarisch-jugoslawische Kontroverse um Mazedonien, 1967–1982* (Munich: R. Oldenbourg, 1983); and Tchavdar Marinov, *La question macédonienne de 1944 a` nos jours: Communisme et nationalisme dans les Balkans* (Paris: L'Harmattan, 2010). For a study of the Macedonian question in a Cold War context, see Spyridon Sfetas, "The Fusion of Regional and Cold War Problems: The Macedonian Triangle between Greece, Bulgaria, and Yugoslavia, 1963–1989," in Rajak, *The Balkans in the Cold War*, 307–329.

32. Each national historiography has produced prolific literature on the subject. For two recent works in English, see Keith Brown, *Loyal unto Death: Trust and Terror in Revolutionary Macedonia* (Bloomington: Indiana University Press, 2013); and İpek Yosmaoğlu, *Blood Ties: Religion, Violence, and the Politics of Nationhood in Ottoman Macedonia, 1878–1908* (Ithaca, NY: Cornell University Press, 2014). See also Dimitar Bechev, *Historical Dictionary of North Macedonia*, 2nd ed. (Lanham, MD: Rowman & Littlefield, 2019).

33. This narrative is based on Marinov, "Ot internatsionalizâm kâm natsionalizâm." See also his *La question macédonienne*; and Troebst, *Die bulgarisch-jugoslawische Kontroverse*.

34. MVnR, op. 35, a.e. 3693, 10–15, 135–144, memo on Bulgarian-Yugoslav relations, March 1979; information on the anti-Bulgarian campaign in Yugoslavia in 1978.

35. For the role of history and linguistics in the legitimization of the Bulgarian position on Macedonia, see Marinov, "Ot internatsionalizâm kâm natsionalizâm," 496–499.

36. Theodora Dragostinova, *Between Two Motherlands: Nationality and Emigration among the Greeks of Bulgaria, 1900–1949* (Ithaca, NY: Cornell University Press, 2011); and Dragostinova, "On 'Strategic Frontiers.'"

37. Georgi Daskalov, *Bâlgariia i Gârtsia: Ot razriv kâm pomirenie, 1944–1964* (Sofia: Universitetsko izdatelstvo Sv. Kliment Ohridski, 2004); and Evanthis Hatzivassiliou, "Negotiating with the Enemy: The Normalisation of Greek-Bulgarian Relations," *Journal of Southeast European and Black Sea Studies* 4, no. 1 (2004): 140–161. See also Karamouzi, "Managing the 'Helsinki Spirit'"; and Kostadinova, "Bâlgaro-grâtski otnosheniia," 187–188.

38. Marinov, "Ancient Thrace," 60–63, 75–77, 89–93. These theories were from the interwar period when Bulgarian nationalists wished to eliminate Greek cultural influences and pursued the discovery of "indigenous" populations predating the ancient Greek colonists.

39. Constantin Iordachi, "Diplomacy and the Making of a Geopolitical Question: The Bulgarian-Romanian Conflict over Dobrudja, 1878–1947," in *Concepts, Approaches, and Self-Representations*, vol. 4 of *Entangled Histories of the Balkans*, ed. Rumen Daskalov et al. (Leiden: Brill, 2017), 291–393.

40. As Marinov explains, the Dacians and Getae were the ancient inhabitants of the contemporary Romanian lands, but they were also a part of the larger group of the Thracians. See "Ancient Thrace," 21. For the brief Romanian scholarly attempts to study the Slavs in their territory, see ibid., 32.

41. Deletant, "Romania's Return to Europe," 83–98.

42. Lucian Boia, *History and Myth in Romanian Consciousness* (Budapest: Central European University Press, 2001), 78.

43. Boia, *History and Myth*, 78–79.

44. Deletant, "Romania's Return to Europe," 94.

45. Two comprehensive studies are Gruev and Kalionski, *Vâzroditelniiat protses*; and Avramov, *Ikonomika na "Vâzroditelniia protses."* See also Marinov, "Ot internatsionalizâm kâm natsionalizâm," 500–515. For a recent study in English, see Kamusella, *Ethnic Cleansing.*

46. TsDA, f. 990, op. 1, a.e. 596, 256–260, memo on relations with Romania, May 1980.

47. Grozev and Baev, "Bulgaria," 165.

48. TsDA, f. 990, op. 1, a.e. 596, 244–248, memo on relations with Romania, June 1980.

49. TsDA, f. 990, op. 1, a.e. 596, 256–260, memo on political relations, May 1980.

50. TsDA, f. 405, op. 9, a.e. 547, 12, speech prepared by KK for the meeting of the two associations, undated.

51. TsDA, f. 990, op. 1, a.e. 596, 249–252, memo on cultural cooperation, May 1980; ibid., a.e. 597, 67–102, general report of the embassy in Bucharest, 20 March 1982.

52. TsDA, f. 990, op. 1, a.e. 596, 2–4, plan for 1300 events of the embassy in Bucharest, 8 December 1977; ibid., 5–12, translation of Romanian newspapers on

the 2050th anniversary. See also MVnR, op. 38, a.e. 2199, 2–13, embassy in Bucharest report, 12 November 1980.

53. TsDA, f. 990, op. 1, a.e. 596, 97–103, memo on Romanian interpretations of Bulgarian history, 10 November 1979.

54. TsDA, f. 990, op. 1, a.e. 596, l. 169–179, "New Directions in the National History of Romania," 23 September 1980.

55. TsDA, f. 990, op. 1, a.e. 596, 24–38, translation of Romanian articles published in 1978.

56. TsDA, f. 990, op. 1, a.e. 596, 52–65, plan of the embassy in Bucharest for the 1300th anniversary, 5 October 1978.

57. TsDA, f. 990, op. 1, a.e. 597, 67–102, general report of the embassy in Bucharest, 20 March 1982.

58. TsDA, f. 990, op. 1, a.e. 596, 52–65, embassy in Bucharest plan for cultural events, 5 October 1978.

59. TsDA, f. 990, op. 1, a.e. 596, 52–65, embassy in Bucharest plan for cultural events, 5 October 1978.

60. TsDA, f. 990, op. 1, a.e. 596, 107–116, embassy in Bucharest report, 22 November 1979.

61. TsDA, f. 990, op. 1, a.e. 596, 249–252, memo on cultural cooperation, May 1980.

62. TsDA, f. 990, op. 1, a.e. 596, 200–204, embassy in Bucharest report, 15 September 1980.

63. TsDA, f. 990, op. 1, a.e. 596, 241–242, embassy in Bucharest report, 11 May 1981.

64. TsDA, f. 990, op. 1, a.e. 597, 21–28, report on 1300 events, 2 October 1981.

65. TsDA, f. 990, op. 1, a.e. 597, 67–102, general report of the embassy in Bucharest, 20 March 1982.

66. TsDA, f. 405, op. 9, a.e. 607, 38–40, information on cultural cooperation, 13 October 1975.

67. MVnR, op. 35, a.e. 3693, 135–144, information on the "anti-Bulgarian campaign in Yugoslavia" in 1978–1979. See also MVnR, op. 35, a.e. 3661, 36–44, "Information on the Yugoslav propaganda against Bulgaria in 1978 and early 1979," 28 May 1979.

68. TsDA, f. 990, op. 1, a.e. 667, 37, embassy in Belgrade report, 11 October 1979.

69. TsDA, f. 990, op. 1, a.e. 668, 137–144, memo on Bulgarian-Yugoslav relations, 10 April 1981.

70. MVnR, op. 38, a.e. 3301, 1–5, Petar Mladenov to the Central Committee of the BKP, 3 February 1981.

71. TsDA, f. 990, op. 1, a.e. 667, 40–54 and 57–59, correspondence from summer 1980.

72. TsDA, f. 405, op. 10, a.e. 495, 58–64, report on cultural cooperation, December 1982.

73. TsDA, f. 990, op. 1, a.e. 667, 1–4, plan of the embassy in Belgrade for the 1300th anniversary, 21 February 1979.

74. TsDA, f. 990, op. 1, a.e. 667, 37, embassy in Belgrade report, 11 October 1979.

75. TsDA, f. 990, op. 1, a.e. 667, 40–54 and 57–59, embassy in Belgrade and NKK reports and memos, June–August 1980.

76. TsDA, f. 990, op. 1, a.e. 667, 112–136, NKK plans for the Belgrade and Zagreb fairs, April and May 1981.

77. TsDA, f. 990, op. 1, a.e. 667, 154–155 and 156–158, NKK memos, 6 January and 14 April 1981.

78. TsDA, f. 990, op. 1, a.e. 667, 2–5, embassy in Belgrade plans for 1300 events in 1978.

79. TsDA, f. 990, op. 1, a.e. 667, 19–36, embassy in Belgrade report, 13 June 1979.

80. TsDA, f. 990, op. 1, a.e. 667, 62–64a and 65, embassy in Belgrade report, 15 September 1980; and NKK to Petar Mladenov, 15 September 1980.

81. TsDA, f. 990, op. 1, a.e. 667, 69a–69b and 72–73, notes from 22 September 1980. See also MVnR, op. 38, a.e. 3301, 1–5, Petar Mladenov to the CC of the BKP, 3 February 1981.

82. TsDA, f. 990, op. 1, a.e. 668, 88–90, note from 27 January 1981.

83. TsDA, f. 990, op. 1, a.e. 668, 100–107, note from 24 February 1981.

84. TsDA, f. 990, op. 1, a.e. 668, 108–115, note from 25 February 1981.

85. TsDA, f. 990, op. 1, a.e. 668, 108–115, note from 25 February 1981.

86. TNA, FCO 28/4445, embassy in Sofia report, 13 April 1981.

87. TsDA, f. 990, op. 1, a.e. 668, 137–144, 166–174, memo on Bulgarian-Yugoslav relations; report on the 1300th anniversary in Yugoslavia, 9 June 1982.

88. TsDA, f. 990, op. 1, a.e. 668, 18, note from 17 October 1981.

89. Döşemeci, "Cutting through the Cold War."

90. TsDA, f. 405, op. 10, a.e. 489, 53–69, report on Turkey, May 1981.

91. Baeva and Kalinova, *Bâlgarskite prehodi*, 208–216. See also MVnR, op. 38, a.e. 2–42, report on Turkish-Greek relations, May 1981.

92. MVnR, op. 36, a.e. 2767, 10–23, embassy in Ankara report, January 1980.

93. TsDA, f. 405, op. 9, a.e. 587, 142–143, memo on cultural talks in Turkey, 6 July 1979.

94. TsDA, f. 990, op. 1, a.e. 626, 175, telegram from embassy in Ankara to NKK, 30 January 1981.

95. TsDA, f. 405, op. 9, a.e. 586, 47–79, memo on cultural relations with Turkey in 1975.

96. TsDA, f. 405, op. 9, a.e. 586, 151–153, report of Alexander Fol, 5 May 1976; ibid., a.e. 587, 84–90, information on cultural relations, February 1978.

97. TsDA, f. 405, op. 9, a.e. 587, 55–57, cultural relations with Turkey, undated draft.

98. TsDA, f. 405, op. 9, a.e. 587, 37–45, 46–54, 151–165, drafts of "Plan for Scientific and Cultural Cooperation between Bulgaria and Turkey" in 1976–1977 and 1978–1979.

99. TsDA, f. 405, op. 9, a.e. 587, 11–18, embassy in Ankara report on cultural events in first half of 1978.

100. TsDA, f. 405, op. 9, a.e. 587, 121–129, 130–139, embassy in Ankara report on cultural events in 1979. See also MVnR, op. 36, a.e. 2764, 10–23; ibid., a.e. 2829A, 2–9, reports of the embassy in Ankara and general consulate in Istanbul on cultural work for 1979.

101. MVnR, op. 36, a.e. 2764, 48–50, embassy in Ankara report, 9 October 1980. See also MVnR, op. 36, a.e. 2829A, 34–41, 43–48, reports of the consulates in Istanbul and Odrin.

102. TsDA, f. 405, op. 10, a.e. 487, 95–97, 120–127, 129–132, embassy in Ankara report, October 1980.

103. TsDA, f. 405, op. 9, a.e. 587, 1–3 and 19–23, memos on cultural talks, February 1978.

104. TsDA, f. 990, op. 1, a.e. 627, 64–80, general report of the embassy in Ankara, 30 March 1982.

105. TsDA, f. 405, op. 10, a.e. 487, 8–19, KK report, June 1981.

106. TsDA, f. 405, op. 9, a.e. 587, 96–98 and 111–113, memos from 10 May 1979 and 20 February 1980. In the spirit of reciprocity, the Turkish embassy suggested placing a plaque of the Bulgarian poet Petko Slaveikov in Istanbul.

107. TsDA, f. 405, op. 9, a.e. 587, 151–165, plan for scientific and cultural cooperation between Bulgaria and Turkey, 1980–1981. See also TsDA, f. 990, op. 1, a.e. 626, 166–167, embassy in Ankara report, 3 December 1980.

108. TsDA, f. 990, op. 1, a.e. 627, 64–80, 82–113, general reports of the embassy in Ankara and consulate in Istanbul, 30 March 1982 and 29 April 1981.

109. TsDA, f. 405, op. 10, a.e. 487, 2–7, embassy in Ankara report, 12 March 1980.

110. TsDA, f. 405, op. 10, a.e. 486, 89–90, embassy in Ankara report, 23 December 1981. See also TsDA, f. 990, op. 1, a.e. 627, 64–80, 82–113, general reports on the 1300 events in Turkey, 30 March 1982 and 29 April 1981.

111. TsDA, f. 990, op. 1, a.e. 627, 9, 24–25, NKK memos, 11 September and 1 October 1981. See also TsDA, f. 990, op. 1, a.e. 627, 64–80, 82–113, general reports on the 1300 events in Turkey, 30 March 1982 and 29 April 1981.

112. TsDA, f. 405, op. 10, a.e. 489, 60–63, information on cultural exchange, January 1982.

113. TsDA, f. 990, op. 1, a.e. 499, 2–39, general report of the embassy in Athens, 16 April 1982.

114. MVnR, op. 38, a.e. 906, 2–39, report on Greece after the elections in November 1981.

115. Baeva and Kalinova, *Bâlgarskite prehodi*, 204–208; Kostadinova, "Bâlgaro-grâtski otnosheniia"; Karamouzi, "Managing the 'Helsinki Spirit.'" See also MVnR, op. 38, a.e. 906, 2–39, report on Greece after the elections in November 1981.

116. Baeva and Kalinova, *Bâlgarskite prehodi*, 207. For Greek Ostpolitik, see Kourkouvelas, "Détente as a Strategy."

117. TsDA, f. 405, op. 9, a.e. 566, 3–8, 58, KK memos and reports from December 1975 and January 1976.

118. TsDA, f. 405, op. 9, a.e. 567, 1–12 and 13–21, embassy in Athens memo on cultural and scientific cooperation in 1976.

119. TsDA, f. 405, op. 9, a.e. 566, 77, Alexander Fol to Liudmila Zhivkova, 16 April 1976.

120. TsDA, f. 405, op. 9, a.e. 567, 13–21, report of Zhivkova, 26 July 1976.

121. TsDA, f. 405, op. 9, a.e. 568, 9–13, cultural cooperation with Greece in 1978.

122. TsDA, f. 990, op. 1, a.e 499, 2–39, general report of the embassy in Athens, 16 April 1982.

123. Nikolai Todorov eloquently describes his conversation with Zhivkov in *The Ambassador as Historian: An Eyewitness Account of Bulgarian-Greek Relations in the 1980s* (New Rochelle, NY: A. D. Caratzas, 1999).

124. TsDA, f. 990, op. 1, a.e. 497, 43, Nikolai Todorov to NKK, 31 August 1979.

125. TsDA, f. 990, op. 1, a.e. 497, 89–95, embassy in Athens report, 6 May 1980.

126. TsDA, f. 990, op. 1, a.e. 497, 89–95, embassy in Athens report, 6 May 1980.

127. TsDA, f. 990, op. 1, a.e. 497, 60–63, report to Liudmila Zhivkova, 29 May 1980.

128. TsDA, f. 990, op. 1, a.e. 497, 186, embassy in Athens report, 24 February 1981.

129. TsDA, f. 990, op. 1, a.e. 497, 223–228, Bulgarian translation of the article.

130. TsDA, f. 990, op. 1, a.e. 498, 58–69, embassy in Athens report, 22 June 1981.

131. TsDA, f. 990, op. 1, a.e. 497, 3–6, General Consulate to NKK, 13 December 1977.

132. TsDA, f. 990, op. 1, a.e. 497, l. 220–222, embassy in Athens report, 26 February 1981.

133. TsDA, f. 990, op. 1, a.e. 497, l. 189–190, NKK report, 2 March 1981.

134. TsDA, f. 990, op. 1, a.e. 497, l. 177–178, embassy in Athens report, 2 February 1981.

135. TsDA, f. 405, op. 9, a.e. 568, 151–152, memo on a meeting between the NKK and MVnR regarding 1300 events in the Balkans, 20 January 1980.

136. TsDA, f. 990, op. 1, a.e. 498, 136, NKK memo, undated.

137. TsDA, f. 990, op. 1, a.e. 498, 91, Roumen Spasov to NKK, 12 June 1981.

138. TsDA, f. 990, op. 1, a.e. 498, 58–69, embassy in Athens report, 22 June 1981.

139. TsDA, f. 990, op. 1, a.e. 498, 91, Roumen Spasov to NKK, 12 June 1981.

140. TsDA, f. 990, op. 1, a.e. 498, 251–252, NKK report, 10 February 1982.

141. TsDA, f. 990, op. 1, a.e. 498, 111 and 129, embassy in Athens telegrams from September and October 1981.

142. TsDA, f. 990, op. 1, a.e. 500, 1–2, undated Bulgarian translations of the two statements.

143. TNA, FCO 28/4445, "12th Congress of the BKP: Balkan Policy," 13 April 1981.

144. TNA, FCO 28/4449, *Sofia News*, 21 October 1981. For earlier Romanian initiatives in this sphere, see Corina Mavrodin, "Denuclearisation and Regional Cooperation: Romania's Tactical Approaches to Escaping Bloc Rigidities," in Crump and Erlandsson, *Margins for Manoeuvre*, 187–204.

145. TNA, FCO 28/4449, embassy in Sofia report, 16 October 1981. It should be noted that the Soviet Union supported this position, because unlike the United States in Turkey, the Soviets had no nuclear arms deployed in the region. I thank Dimitar Bechev for this information.

146. TNA, FCO 28/4449, embassy in Athens report, 8 December 1981.

147. TNA, FCO 28/4449, embassy in Athens report, 8 December 1981.

3. Culture as a Way of Life

1. OSA/RFE, 300/20/1/149, BTA and Radio Sofia dispatches, 1973.

2. MVnR, op. 34, a.e. 890, 11–39, report on FRG mass media in 1977.

3. OSA/RFE, 300/20/1/174, BTA dispatch, 11 February 1977.

4. OSA/RFE, 300/20/1/174, RFE report, Munich, 1 November 1977.

5. OS/RFE, 300/20/1/39, RFE report, Munich, 3 June 1977; RFE special report, 18 July 1977.

6. TsDA, f. 1b, op. 55, a.e. 780, 1–32, Information-Sociological Center of the BKP, "Public Opinion for the 1300-Year Jubilee," February 1982.

7. MVnR, op. 36, a.e. 877, 3, memo, 19 June 1980; ibid., a.e. 895a, correspondence between MVnR and the embassy of the FRG in Sofia, March 1980.

8. MVnR, op. 36, a.e. 866, 9–13, report, 24 December 1979.

9. For a study of the "friendship project" between the Soviet Union and Czechoslovakia, see Applebaum, *Empire of Friends*.

10. OSA/RFE, 300/20/1/174, RFE special report "Ideological Struggle in Full Swing," 21 July 1972; RFE report, Munich, 28 November 1975; RFE report, Munich, 8 February 1977.

11. MVnR, op. 35, a.e. 658, 26–30, embassy in London report, February 1979.

12. For two sophisticated analyses of the topic of international cultural contact in the Cold War, see Goedde, "Global Cultures," and Iriye, "Making a Transnational World."

13. Oliver Bange and Gottfried Niedhart, eds., *Helsinki 1975 and the Transformation of Europe* (New York: Berghahn Books, 2008), 2.

14. James Mark, Bogdan C. Iacob, Tobias Rupprecht, and Ljubica Spaskovska, *1989: A Global History of Eastern Europe* (Cambridge: Cambridge University Press, 2019), 133.

15. Carole Fink and Bernd Schäfer, eds., *Ostpolitik, 1969–1974: European and Global Responses* (New York: Cambridge University Press, 2008), 1, 269.

16. Judt, *Postwar*, 496–500.

17. Fink and Schäfer, *Ostpolitik*, 1, 269. See also Annika Frieberg, *Peace at All Costs: Catholic Intellectuals, Journalists, and Media in Postwar Polish-German Reconciliation* (New York: Berghahn Books, 2019).

18. Sarah Snyder, *Human Rights Activism and the End of the Cold War: A Transnational History of the Helsinki Network* (New York: Cambridge University Press, 2011), 27, 7. For global human rights discourse in the 1970s, see Samuel Moyn, *The Last Utopia: Human Right in History* (Cambridge, MA: The Belknap Press of Harvard University Press, 2010).

19. Suri, *Power and Protest*, 213–214.

20. See Mark et al., *1989*, 132–136 for the beginning of the convergence between the East and the West in the 1970s. For Bulgaria, see Elitza Stanoeva, "The Imperative of Opening to the West and the Impact of the 1968 Crisis: Bulgaria's Cooperation with Denmark and West Germany in the 1960s," in Crump and Erlandsson, *Margins for Manoeuvre*, 110–129.

21. TsDA, f. 405, op. 10, a.e. 549, 1–85, general report of the embassy in Vienna, March 1982.

22. TsDA, f. 405, op. 9, a.e. 558, 52–63, memo on Austria, March 1980.

23. OSA/RFE, 300/20/1/80, RFE situation report, 1 June 1981.

24. OSA/RFE, 300/20/1/80, RFE report, Munich, 12 May 1981; RFE situation report, 1 June 1981.

25. OSA/RFE, 300/20/1/80, RFE report, 9 May 1975. For Zhivkov's subsequent state visit to Vienna, see RFE situation report, 2 October 1978.

26. OSA/RFE, 300/20/1/80, RFE report, Munich, 12 May 1981; RFE situation report, 1 June 1981.

27. MVnR, op. 38, a.e. 2917j, 3–11, report, "Meaning of the Differential Approach of France vis-à-vis the Brotherly Socialist States," December 1981.

28. OSA/RFE, 300/20/1/93, RFE special report, Paris, 7 April 1976.

29. MVnR, op. 38, a.e. 2917j, 38–39, relations between Bulgaria and France in 1980.

30. TNA, FCO 28/3742, embassy in Sofia dispatches, April and October 1979.

31. Jordan Baev, "The Establishment of Bulgarian-West German Diplomatic Relations with the Coordinating Framework of the Warsaw Pact," *Journal of Cold War Studies* 18, no. 3 (2016): 158–180; and Stanoeva, "The Imperative of Opening."

32. OSA/RFE, 300/20/1/94, RFE special report, 3 January 1974.

33. OSA/RFE, 300/20/1/95, RFE report "Bonn Regrets Lag in Cultural Ties with East Europe," Bonn, 21 September 1977.

34. OSA/RFE, 300/20/1/95, RFE report, Bonn, 30 April 1979.

35. MVnR, op. 34, a.e. 812, reports and memos on political relations, 1978; OSA/RFE, 300/20/1/95, RFE report, Bonn, 28 June 1978.

36. OSA/RFE, 300/20/1/95, RFE report, Bonn, 30 April 1979; BTA, 2 and 4 May 1979.

37. TNA, FCO 28/4099, embassy in Sofia report, 2 July 1980.

38. MVnR, op. 36, a.e. 546, 2–18, information on British policies in the Balkans, June 1980.

39. TNA, FCO 28/4092, embassy in Sofia, annual review for Bulgaria, 1979.

40. MVnR, op. 35, a.e. 658, 139–156, embassy in London report, June 1979.

41. Vitka Toshkova, *Bâlgariia i SASht, 1919–1989* (Sofia: Sineva, 2007).

42. For a chronology of Zhivkova's public engagements, see Savova et al., *Liudmila Zhivkova*; for her U.S. visit in 1977, ibid., 185–187.

43. MVnR, op. 36, a.e. 360, relations between Bulgaria and the United States; and Savova, *Liudmila Zhivkova*, 292.

44. "Bulgaria Closely Follows the Soviet Model," *Los Angeles Times*, 29 June 1980.

45. MVnR, op. 36, a.e. 360, relations between Bulgaria and the United States, 1980. See also MVnR, op. 38, a.e. 793v, 29–38, relations between the United States and Western Europe, October 1981.

46. OSA/RFE, 300/20/1/122, RFE report, Washington, 14 September 1979.

47. MVnR, op. 36, a.e. 546, 20–21, memo on a meeting with Deputy Foreign Office Secretary Douglas Herd.

48. OSA/RFE, 300/20/1/80, RFE report, Munich, 12 May 1981; RFE situation report, 1 June 1981.

49. MVnR, op. 38, a.e. 2886, 27–29, embassy in Paris report, 7 August 1981.

50. TsDA, f. 990, op. 1, a.e. 638, 210–239, memo on a meeting for 1300 in Bonn, July 1980.

51. OSA/RFE, 300/20/1/95, RFE report, Bonn, 7 July 1981.

52. OSA/RFE, 300/20/1/95, BTA dispatch, 9 July 1981.

53. For an analysis of Polish, Hungarian, and Yugoslav cultural initiatives, which functioned in similar ways, see Mark et al., *1989*, 132–136.

54. Recent works on cultural diplomacy include Michael David-Fox, *Showcasing the Great Experiment: Cultural Diplomacy and Western Visitors to Soviet Union, 1921–1941* (New York: Oxford University Press, 2011); Kiril Tomoff, *Virtuosi Abroad: Soviet Music and Imperial Competition during the Early Cold War, 1945–1958* (Ithaca, NY: Cornell University Press, 2015); and Fosler-Lussier, *Music.* Other works are David Caute, *The Dancer Defects: The Struggle for Cultural Supremacy during the Cold War* (New York: Oxford University Press, 2003); Yale Richmond, *Cultural Exchange and the Cold War: Raising the Iron Curtain* (University Park: Pennsylvania State University Press,

2003); and Laura A. Belmonte, *Selling the American Way: U.S. Propaganda and the Cold War* (Philadelphia: University of Pennsylvania Press, 2008).

55. Nigel Gould-Davies, "The Logic of Soviet Cultural Diplomacy," *Diplomatic History* 27, no. 2 (2003): 195, 212, 213.

56. Danielle Fosler-Lussier, "Music Pushed, Music Pulled: Cultural Diplomacy, Globalization, and Imperialism," *Diplomatic History* 36, no. 1 (2012): 53.

57. Gould-Davies, "The Logic of Soviet Cultural Diplomacy," 203.

58. Eleonory Gilburd, "The Revival of Soviet Internationalism in the Mid to Late 1950s," in *The Thaw: Soviet Society and Culture during the 1950s and 1960s*, ed. Eleonory Gilburd and Denis Kozlov (Toronto: University of Toronto Press, 2012), 362–401; and Eleonory Gilburd, *To See Paris and To Die: The Soviet Lives of Western Culture* (Cambridge, MA: The Belknap Press of Harvard University Press, 2018).

59. Fosler-Lussier, *Music*.

60. Anne E. Gorsuch and Diane Koenker, eds., *Turizm: The Russian and East European Tourist under Capitalism and Socialism* (Ithaca, NY: Cornell University Press, 2006); György Péteri, ed., *Imagining the West in Eastern Europe and the Soviet Union* (Pittsburgh: University of Pittsburgh, 2010); Paulina Bren and Mary Neuberger, eds., *Communism Unwrapped: Consumption in Cold War Eastern Europe* (New York: Oxford University Press, 2012); Gorsuch and Koenker, *The Socialist Sixties*; Patryk Babiracki and Kenyon Zimmer, eds., *Cold War Crossings: International Travel and Exchange across the Soviet Bloc, 1940s–1960s* (College Station: Texas A&M Press, 2014); Cathleen M. Guistino, Catherine J. Plum, and Alexander Vari, eds., *Socialist Escapes: Breaking Away from Ideology and Everyday Routine in Eastern Europe, 1945–1989* (New York: Berghahn, 2015); and Sune Bechmann Pedersen and Christian Noack, eds., *Tourism and Travel during the Cold War: Negotiating Tourist Experiences across the Iron Curtain* (New York: Routledge, 2019). See also Mark Keck-Szajbel and Dariusz Stola, eds., Introduction to "Crossing the Borders of Friendship: Mobility across Communist Borders," special section, *East European Politics and Societies* 29, no. 1 (2015): 92–95; and Malgorzata Fidelis, "Pleasures and Perils of Socialist Modernity: New Scholarship on Post-War Eastern Europe," *Contemporary European History* 26, no. 3 (2017): 533–544.

61. Frieberg, *Peace at All Costs*.

62. OSA/RFE, 300/20/1/179, BTA dispatch, 23 February 1977.

63. TsDA, f. 405, op. 10, a.e. 545, 1–12, "Objectives of Bulgarian Cultural Policies in Developed Capitalist States," undated.

64. The Bulgarian scholar Evgeniia Kalinova characterizes the 1960s as a period of modest "cracking of the door" (*otkrehvane*). See Evgeniia Kalinova, "Politikata na Liudmila Zhivkova za kulturnoto otvariane na Bâlgariia kâm sveta—predpostavki i spetsifika," in Baeva, *Kulturnoto otvariane*, 41.

65. MVnR, op. 36, a.e. 360, relations between Bulgaria and the United States.

66. TsDA, f. 405, op. 10. a.e. 546, 1–12, "International Cultural Work in the First Half of 1983: Capitalist States."

67. TsDA, f. 990, op. 1, a.e. 477, 113–120, report on British cultural institutions in 1979.

68. TsDA, f. 405, op. 10, a.e. 545, 1–12, "Objectives of Bulgarian Cultural Policies in Developed Capitalist States," undated.

69. MVnR, op. 38, a.e. 3215, 16–22, memo of Maria Zaharieva, February 1981.

70. MVnR, op. 38, a.e. 2897, 40–41, embassy in Paris report, 11 July 1980.

71. TsDA, f. 405, op. 10. a.e. 546, 1–12, "International Cultural Work in the first Half of 1983: Capitalist States, undated.

72. TsDA, f. 405, op. 9, a.e. 670, 162–197, "Future Development of Cultural Cooperation between Bulgaria and the United States," undated.

73. TsDA, f. 405, op. 10. a.e. 545, 1–12, "Objectives of Bulgarian Cultural Policies in Developed Capitalist States," undated.

74. TsDA, f. 405, op. 9, a.e. 670, 162–197, "Future Development of Cultural Cooperation between Bulgaria and the United States," undated.

75. TsDA, f. 990, op. 1. a.e. 642, 25–78, general report of the embassy in Bonn, 10 May 1982.

76. TsDA, f. 405, op. 10, a.e. 545, 1–12, "Objectives of Bulgarian Cultural Policies in Developed Capitalist States," undated.

77. TsDA, f. 405, op. 9, a.e. 263, 55, NKK, "For the Dignified Celebration of the 1300th Anniversary of the Establishment of the Bulgarian State," June 1979, 10, 195. Zhivkova's speech from 1978 on pp. 9–15.

78. TsDA, f. 405, op. 10, a.e. 546, 1–12, "International Cultural Work in the first Half of 1983: Capitalist States," undated.

79. TsDA, f. 990, op. 1, a.e. 637, 1–11, plan for 1300 celebrations in the FRG, April 1978.

80. "Bulgaria: A Modern Nation Salutes Its Past," *UNESCO Courier* 34 (May 1981): 13.

81. TsDA, f. 405, op. 9, a.e. 597, "Information regarding the Thracian Culture and Art Exhibition in Paris in 1974."

82. OSA/RFE, 300/20/1/149, BTA dispatch, 21 January 1976. It was so successful that Bulgarian experts put together a second exhibition of icons to satisfy the demand of museums worldwide.

83. OSA/RFE, 300/20/1/149, RFE report, Vienna, 3 March 1975.

84. OSA/RFE, 300/20/1/36, "Zhivkov's Daughter Making Her Mark," Reuters, Sofia, 11 May 1976.

85. OSA/RFE, 300/20/1/149, RFE special report, London, 4 January 1976.

86. OSA/RFE, 300/20/1/93, BTA dispatch, 27 January 1978.

87. Stanoeva, "Bulgaria's 1300 Years", 23.

88. TsDA, f. 990, op. 1, a.e. 639, 102–123, report on 1300 events in 1981.

89. Excerpts from the French press in 1980 found in TsDA, f. 990, op. 1, a.e. 647, 106–118.

90. TsDA, f. 405, op. 10, a.e. 405, 100–111, memo on Bulgarian-French cultural cooperation, 1982.

91. MVnR, op. 34, a.e. 2905, 32–57, "Characteristics of the Anticommunist Propaganda in France," 5 December 1978.

92. TsDA, f. 405, op. 9, a.e. 597, "Information regarding the Thracian Culture and Art Exhibition in Paris in 1974." The exhibition drew 70,000 visitors, a huge success for the Bulgarian organizers.

93. OSA/RFE, 300/20/1/93, RFE report, Paris, 7 April 1976.

94. TsDA, f. 405, op. 10, a.e. 553, 100–111, KK memo on Bulgarian-French cultural cooperation, 1982–1983, which lists key events over the years.

95. TsDA, f. 990, op. 1, a.e. 647, 1–14, plan for cultural events in France, November 1978.

96. MVnR, op. 36, a.e. 3030, 2–8, embassy in Paris report, 8 July 1980.

97. TsDA, f. 405, op. 10, a.e. 549, 1–85, general report of the embassy in Vienna, March 1982.

98. For the Thracian exhibit, which was put together in 1972, see TsDA, f. 405, op. 9, a.e. 552, 186–189, 283–287, KK information about the exhibition in Vienna, 1974–1975.

99. TsDA, f. 405, op. 9, a.e. 555, 96–103, embassy in Vienna information, 26 April 1978.

100. TsDA, f. 405, op. 9, a.e. 557, 20–28, embassy in Vienna report, 20 November 1979.

101. TsDA, f. 405, op. 10, a.e. 549, 1–85, general report of the embassy in Vienna, March 1982.

102. OSA/RFE, 300/20/1/149, BTA dispatch, 5 Jan 1972.

103. OSA/RFE, 300/20/1/94, RFE special report "Diplomatic Relations with West Germany Established," 3 January 1974.

104. MVnR, op. 34, a.e. 866; MVnR, op. 35, a.e. 1009; a.e. 1010; a.e. 915, 1–4; MVnR, op. 36, a.e. 877, 28; TsDA, f. 405, op. 9, a.e. 593, 1–32, records on cultural work in 1980.

105. The book was also published in English in the UK. See Ludmila Zhivkova, *Anglo-Turkish Relations, 1933–1939* (London: Secker and Warburg, 1976).

106. TsDA, f. 405, op. 9, a.e. 126, 107–129, report of Alexander Fol, April 1976. See also ibid., a.e. 559 for documents related to the organization of the exhibitions and a.e. 561 for press coverage.

107. MVnR, op. 34, a.e. 612, 15–22, 38–49, 60–67; TsDA, f. 405, op. 9, a.e. 560, 5–6, 33, 73, 96–97, 101–102, 158–165, 220–224, 237–244, correspondence between MvNR and KK, September–October 1978.

108. TsDA, f. 405, op. 9, a.e. 668, 270–278, cultural relations with the United States, undated.

109. MVnR, op. 36, a.e. 360, relations between Bulgaria and the United States, 1980; and Savova, *Liudmila Zhivkova*, 292.

110. TsDA, f. 405, op. 9, a.e. 666, 188–198, correspondence between KK and embassy in Washington, September–October 1976.

111. TsDA, f. 405, op. 9, a.e. 666, 17–19, 23–25, 26–34, correspondence between embassy in Washington and KK, October–November 1976.

112. TsDA, f. 405, op. 9, a.e. 668, 253–258, KK report, 20 April 1979.

113. TsDA, f. 405, op. 9, a.e. 126, 107–129, report of Alexander Fol, April 1976.

114. TsDA, f. 405, op. 9, a.e. 667, 1–7, plan for *Thracian Treasures from Bulgaria* from 1977.

115. MVnR, op. 34, a.e. 862; a.e. 865; a.e. 866, 34–42; op. 35, a.e. 988, 41–58. TsDA, f. 405, op. 9, a.e. 589, 93–101; ibid., a.e. 590, 91–108, cultural events in the FRG in 1978.

116. TsDA, f. 405, op. 9, a.e. 667, 1–7, plan for *Thracian Treasures from Bulgaria* from 1977.

117. "Thracian Art: A Treasury of Gold and Silver," *Philadelphia Inquirer*, 10 July 1977.

118. TsDA, f. 405, op. 9, a.e. 670, 1–11, KK information, 10–21 November 1980.

119. "Bulgarian Poetry Moves Audience," *Centre Daily Times*, 14 November 1980.

120. TsDA, f. 990, op. 1, a.e. 647, 100–105 and 122–129, embassy in Paris report on 1300 events in France, 21 July 1980, and report on cultural events in first half of 1980; ibid., a.e. 648, 1–6, 13, 31–34, 35–38, correspondence between MVnR, embassy in Paris, KK, and NKK, June 1980.

121. TsDA, f. 405, op. 10, a.e. 549, 1–85, general report of the embassy in Vienna, March 1982.

122. MVnR, op. 34, a.e. 866; MVnR, op. 35, a.e. 1009; a.e. 1010; a.e. 915, 1–4; MVnR, op. 36, a.e. 877, 28. TsDA, f. 405, op. 9, a.e. 593, 1–32, cultural work in 1980.

123. TsDA, f. 990, op. 1, a.e. 477, 86–97 and 98–109, plans for 1300 events, 1979.

124. TsDA, f. 1B, op. 66, a.e. 2726, 63–80, activities for the 1300 anniversary, 25 December 1980, Index 1.

125. TsDA, f. 990, op. 1, a.e. 647, 90, NKK note, 19 March 1980.

126. TsDA, f. 990, op. 1, a.e. 638, 116–147, cultural activities in 1980; ibid., a.e. 639, 102–123, report from April 1981.

127. TsDA, f. 990, op. 1, a.e. 480, 23–25, 33–35, and 138–142, correspondence between NKK, KK, MVnR, and embassy in London, 1981.

128. MVnR, op. 38, a.e. 350, 14–15, memo on most important events in the United States in 1981.

129. The countries included were Austria, Belgium, Cyprus, Denmark, Finland, France, FRG, Greece, Holland, Iceland, Italy, Luxemburg, Malta, Norway, Portugal, Spain, Sweden, Switzerland, and the UK.

130. TsDA, f. 405, op. 10, a.e. 549, 1–85, general report of the embassy in Vienna, March 1982.

131. OSA/RFE, 300/20/1/95, "Days of Bulgarian Culture in FRG," BTA, 18 April 1981.

132. TsDA, f. 405, op. 10, a.e. 555, 72–73; TsDA, f. 990, op. 1, a.e. 641, 62–89, report on 1300th anniversary events in 1981.

133. TsDA, f. 990, op. 1, a.e. 648, 43 and 68–73, embassy in Paris telegram, 6 March 1981, and report, 4 April 1981.

134. MVnR, op. 38, a.e. 2897, 60–63; MVnR, op. 38, a.e. 2896, CC to MVnR, 26 February 1981, on cultural exchange with France. TsDA, f. 405, op. 10, a.e. 405, 100–111, memo on Bulgarian-French cultural cooperation, 1982. See also TsDA, f. 990, op. 1, a.e. 648, 101–11, 165–178, reports on the 1300 events in France in 1981.

135. MVnR, op. 38, a.e. 350, 14–15, information on the most important events in the United States in 1981. I thank Predrag Matejic, Charles Gribble, and Victor Friedman for sharing their extensive insights on this topic.

136. TsDA, f. 990, op. 1, a.e. 603, facsimiles of the two telegrams, June and November 1981.

137. MVnR, op. 38, a.e. 598, 23–25; MVnR to the CC of the BKP, 24 February 1981.

138. TsDA, f. 405, op. 9, a.e. 563, 228–233, embassy in London reports, May 1981. See also MVnR, op. 38, a.e. 597, 55–87; TsDA, f. 990, op. 1, a.e. 479, 232–239 and a.e. 480, 98–99, correspondence between MVnR, KK, and NKK, May–September 1981.

139. TsDA, f. 405, op. 9, a.e. 265, 1–20, "Development and Problems of the 1300th Anniversary Preparations Abroad," February 1980.

140. TsDA, f. 405, op. 10, a.e. 549, 1–85, general report of the embassy in Vienna, March 1982.

141. TsDA, f. 405, op. 10. a.e. 66, 55–87, Georgi Iordanov, "The Program 1300 Years Bulgaria—Results and Future Perspectives," 28 December 1983.

142. TsDA, f. 405, op. 10, a.e. 546, 1–12, "International Cultural Work in the first Half of 1983: Capitalist States"; ibid, 21–23, KK memo on capitalist states in 1983.

143. TsDA, f. 405, op. 10, a.e. 545, 1–12, "Objectives of Bulgarian Cultural Policies in Developed Capitalist States," undated.

144. TNA, FCO 28/3732, Cloake to FCO, 30 July 1979; Bullard to Blaker, 10 September 1979.

145. OSA/RFE, 300/20/1/95, RFE report, Bonn, 28 June 1978.

146. OSA/RFE, 300/20/1/95, RFE report, "Bonn Regrets Lag in Cultural Ties with East Europe," Bonn, 21 September 1977.

147. OSA/RFE, 300/20/1/26, RFE report, "Lyudmila a New Potent Force in Bulgarian Politics," Sofia, 24 June 1980.

148. OSA/RFE, 300/20/1/174, "In the West: The Omnivorousness of Culture," *Vecherni novini*, 20 January 1978.

149. OSA/RFE, 300/20/1/26, "Culture Boss," *Observer*, 29 February 1976.

150. TNA, FCO 28/3331, embassy in Sofia report, 19 September 1978.

151. TsDA, f. 405, op. 10, a.e. 555, 39–44, cultural relations Bulgaria-FRG, May 1982.

152. MVnR, op. 36, a.e. 866, 9–13, report, 24 December 1979.

153. TsDA, f. 405, op. 9, a.e. 563, 28–29, KK memo, 27 February 1979.

154. TNA, FCO 28/3024, embassy in Sofia report, 11 February 1977.

155. TsDA, f. 405, op. 9, a.e. 668, 229–230, report of Liberte Popov, 15 March 1978.

156. MVnR, op. 38, a.e. 836, 81a, 82–84, memos from 10 and 13 November 1981.

157. MVnR, op. 36, a.e. 385, 2–3, memo to the CC of the BKP, June 1980.

158. MVnR, op. 38, a.e. 408, 13–80, correspondence from March–June 1981.

159. TsDA, f. 405, op. 9, a.e. 668, 70–71, embassy in Washington report, 2 July 1978; MVnR, op. 36, a.e. 385, 2–3, memo to the CC of the BKP, June 1980.

160. OSA/RFE, 300/20/1/149, BTA dispatch, 23 January 1976.

161. TsDA, f. 405, op. 9, a.e. 556, 65–68, KK report, 18 October 1978; TsDA, f. 405, op. 10, a.e. 405, 100–111, memo on Bulgarian-French cultural cooperation, 1982.

162. TsDA, f. 405, op. 9, a.e. 563, 28–29, KK information, 27 February 1979.

163. Elenkov, *Kulturniiat front*, 344.

164. TsDA, f. 405, op. 9, a.e. 563, 111–113, 114–118, 120, embassy in London reports and KK memos, March and November 1979.

165. MVnR, op. 35, a.e. 1020, correspondence between MVnR and KK, February–October 1979. OSA/RFE, 300/20/1/95, RFE report, "West German Cultural Week Opens in Sofia," Bonn, 17 November 1980; "FRG Cultural Week," BTA, 17 November 1980.

166. TsDA, f. 405, op. 9, a.e. 593, 33, catalog of exhibition, 17–23 November 1980.

167. MVnR, op. 36, a.e. 886, correspondence between MvNR, embassies in Bonn and Budapest, and KK, December 1979–October 1980; TsDA, f. 405, op. 9, a.e. 593, 136–137, 162–164, 165, KK memos, October–November 1980. See also TsDA, f. 405, op. 9, a.e. 593, 33, catalog of exhibition, 17–23 November 1980.

168. OSA/RFE, 300/20/1/95, RFE report, Bonn, 7 July 1981.

169. TsDA, f. 405, op. 9, a.e. 593, 33, catalog of exhibition, 17–23 November 1980.

170. OSA/RFE, 300/20/1/149, BTA dispatch, 14 March 1981.

171. TsDA, f. 990, op. 1, a.e. 479, 1–3, 14–15, 22–23, 68–6, 107, 154, correspondence between NKK, KK, and MVnR, 1981. See also MVnR, op. 38, a.e. 597, 55–56, KK to MVnR, 7 May 1981.

172. MVnR, op. 38, a.e. 597, 28, 55–56, correspondence between MVnR, KK, and embassy in London, February and May 1981. See also TsDA, f. 405, op. 9, a.e. 563, 220–223, NKK correspondence, 1981.

173. MVnR, op. 38, a.e. 408, 78–83, correspondence between MVnR, KK, and U.S. embassy in Sofia, June and October 1981.

174. OSA/RFE, 300/20/1/122, RFE special report, 12 September 1983; BTA dispatch, 24 September 1983.

175. TsDA, f. 405, op. 10, a.e. 555, 39–44, perspective on cultural relations Bulgaria-FRG, May 1982.

176. OSA/RFE, 300/20/1/93, BTA dispatch, 9 February 1982.

177. OSA/RFE, 300/20/1/174, BTA dispatch, 21 February 1977.

178. See Benjamin Nathans, "Soviet Rights-Talk in the Post-Stalin Era," in *Human Rights in the Twentieth Century*, ed. Stefan-Ludwig Hoffmann (Cambridge: Cambridge University Press, 2011), 166–190.

179. OSA/RFE, 300/20/1/174, BTA dispatch, 14 July 1977.

180. OSA/RFE, 300/20/1/174, RFE report, June 1972; *Rabotnichesko delo*, 20 March 1972.

181. OSA/RFE, 300/20/1/174, BTA dispatch, 13 April 1977.

182. OSA/RFE, 300/20/1/174, RFE report "Minister of Interior Warns of Western Ideological Assaults," 24 September 1980.

183. MVnR, op. 35, a.e. 23, embassy in Vienna on cultural-propaganda work in 1978.

184. TsDA, f. 990, op. 1, a.e. 600, 116–125, MM memo on the meeting of the commission for cultural cooperation in Washington, DC, 22 December 1980.

185. TNA, FCO 28/3024, Lord Gorowny-Roberts to Cloake, 12 December 1977.

186. TNA, FCO 28/3024, Cloake to FCO on "unaesthetic education," 24 October 1977.

187. TNA, FCO 28/3319, embassy in Sofia, annual review for Bulgaria, 1977.

188. TNA, FCO 28/4093, "The Two Faces of Bulgaria: A Valedictory," 24 June 1980.

4. Forging a Diaspora

1. TsDA, f. 141, op. 11, a.e. 387, information, program, and lists of participants in the gathering of Bulgarian emigrants in 1981.

2. TsDA, f. 141, op. 11, a.e. 32, "Program for Work with the Bulgarian Colony in Non-Socialist States, 1982."

3. "Open Letter to the Slavic Committee in Bulgaria," *Luch* (May–July 1983): 60.

4. This observation is not unique to Bulgaria: Ulf Brunnbauer discovers a similar dynamic between friendly and hostile émigrés in Yugoslavia in *Globalizing Southeastern Europe: Emigrants, America, and the State since the Late Nineteenth Century* (Lanham, MD: Lexington Books, 2016).

5. Melissa Feinberg, *Curtain of Lies: The Battle over Truth in Stalinist Eastern Europe* (New York: Oxford University Press, 2017), 88–116.

6. Tara Zahra, *The Great Departure: Mass Migration from Eastern Europe and the Making of the Free World* (New York: Norton, 2016), 217–253.

7. Brunnbauer, *Globalizing Southeastern Europe*, 5, 12, 259. For the polices of socialist Yugoslavia specifically, see 257–310.

8. I rely on James Clifford's classic definition in "Diasporas," *Cultural Anthropology* 9, no. 3 (1994): 302–338, which outlines the essential features of diasporas: "a history of dispersal, myths/memories of the homeland, alienation in the host (bad host?) country, desire for eventual return, ongoing support of the homeland, and a collective identity importantly defined by this relationship."

9. Bolton, *Worlds of Dissent*, examines oppositional intellectuals' writing, public engagements, and mundane experiences to complicate the image of a one-dimensional, heroic dissident by outlining their complex "worlds of dissent." For "spokesvoices," see ibid., 193.

10. This observation is supported by my examination of *Slaviani* published during 1978–1983.

11. TsDA, f. 141, historical overview of the Slavic Committee and its archival holdings, 15 March 1985.

12. TsDA, f. 141, op. 9, a.e. 3, 1–14, MVnR instructions for work with the Bulgarian colony in non-socialist states, most likely from 1977.

13. Boĭko Kiriakov, "Dârzhavata sreshtu emigratsiiata," in Gruev and Mishkova, *Bâlgarskiiat komunizâm*, 195–214.

14. For more information on these organizations and others, see Boĭka Vasileva, *Bâlgarskata politicheska emigratsiia sled Vtorata Svetovna Voĭna* (Sofia: Universitetsko izdatelstvo Sv. Kliment Ohridski, 1999); Elena Statelova, ed., *Drugata Bâlgariia, 1944–1989* (Sofia: Anubis, 2000); Elena Statelova and Vasilka Tankova, *Prokudenite* (Plovdiv: Zhanet, 2002). See also OSA/RFE, 300/20/1/66, RFE report, Paris, 30 June and 16 December 1977; Sofia, 1 March 1978.

15. For an overview of the organization, see Veselin Traĭkov, *Istoriia na bâlgarskata emigratiia v Severna Amerika* (Sofia: Universitetsko izdatelstvo Sv. Kliment Ohridski, 1993), 169–180. The website of the MPO makes clear the evolution of the organization: http://www.macedonian.org/joomla/, accessed 2 May 2018. For Yugoslav policies in relation to the Macedonian émigrés, see Brunnbauer, *Globalizing Southeast Europe*, 277–283.

16. The evolution of the identities of the Macedonian émigrés in North America is a complicated question. See Chris Kostov, *Contested Ethnic Identity: The Case of Macedonian Immigrants in Toronto, 1900–1996* (Bern: Peter Lang, 2010); and Keith Brown, *Macedonia's Child-Grandfathers: The Transnational Politics of Memory, Exile, and Return, 1948–1998*, Donald W. Treadgold Papers 38 (Seattle, WA: Henry M. Jackson School of International Studies, University of Washington, 2003).

17. For an overview, see Znepolski, *NRB ot nachaloto do kraiia*, 364–366; Traĭkov, *Istoriia na bâlgarskata emigratiia*, 197–199; and the websites of the Bulgarian Diocese of the Orthodox Church of America (https://www.oca.org/dioceses/bulgarian-diocese) and the Bulgarian Eastern Orthodox Diocese of the United States, Canada, and Australia (https://www.bulgariandiocese.org/). The Bulgarian Diocese for Western and Central Europe was established in 1986. See the website of the Bulgarian patriarchate at http://www.bg-patriarshia.bg/index.php?file=east_bul_diocese.xml. All links accessed 3 May 2018.

18. Hristov, *Ubiîte "Skitnik,"* 228–229; Kiriakov, "Dârzhavata sreshtu emigratsiiata"; and Vasileva, *Bâlgarskata politicheska emigratsiia.*

19. TsDA, f. 1b, op. 66, a.e. 2433, 39, 28–33, quoted in Kiriakov, "Dârzhavata sreshtu emigratsiiata," 210.

20. TsDA, f. 41, op. 11, a.e. 32, "Program for Work with the Bulgarian Colony in Non-Socialist States, 1982."

21. Hristov, *Ubiîte "Skitnik,"* 228–229.

22. Hristov, *Ubiîte "Skitnik,"* 233, referring to a Politburo decision from 5 September 1974 to grant amnesty to all who had fled the country after 1944.

23. TsDA, f. 141, op. 10, a.e. 44, 82, 86, Slavic Committee documents from 1974–1975, quoted in Kiriakov, "Dârzhavata sreshtu emigratsiiata," 207–208.

24. For the United States, see MVnR, op. 36, a.e. 360, 5–30, "On Relations between Bulgaria and the United States and the Work of the Embassy in Washington in Light of the Decisions of the National Party Conference," undated (hereafter report, undated); and MVnR, op. 36, a.e. 361, 31–37, plan for work with the Bulgarian colony in the United States from 1980. While these files were supposed to be kept in the embassies, during my work in the archives of the Ministry of Foreign Affairs I was unable to locate such records. For the FRG, see TsDA, f. 990, op. 1, a.e. 642, 25–78, general report on 1300 activities in the FRG, April 1982; and TsDA, f. 990, op. 1, a.e. 641, 51–61, plans for work with the Bulgarian colony in the FRG, June 1981. Some 2,500 Bulgarians in the FRG had registered with the embassy by 1982 while diplomats had identified and created files for another 4,000.

25. TsDA, f. 41, op. 11, a.e. 32, "Program for Work with the Bulgarian Colony in Non-Socialist States, 1982."

26. See TsDA, f. 1b, op. 64, a.e. 504, decision of Politburo, 27 June 1977, quoted in Kiriakov, "Dârzhavata sreshtu emigratsiiata," 206.

27. TsDA, f. 990, op. 1, a.e. 599, 21–52, plan of the embassy in Washington for the 1300th anniversary, 15 December 1978.

28. MVnR, op. 36, a.e. 360, 5–30, report, undated.

29. MVnR, op. 36, a.e. 360, 5–30, report, undated; MVnR, op. 36, a.e. 361, 31–37, plan for work with the Bulgarian colony in the United States from 1980; TsDA, f. 990, op. 1, a.e. 599, 21–52, plan of the embassy in Washington for the 1300th anniversary.

30. MVnR, op. 36, a.e. 360, 5–30, report, undated. See also MVnR, op. 36, a.e. 361, 31–37, plan for work with the Bulgarian colony in the United States from 1980, p. 36–37, for a list of activities planned; MVnR, op. 36, a.e. 336, 135–139, reports on visits to the United States and Canada, November 1980; TsDA, f. 990, op. 1, a.e. 599, 21–52, plan of the embassy in Washington for the 1300th anniversary, 15 December 1978.

31. MVnR, op. 36, a.e. 336, 135–139, reports on visits to the United States and Canada, November 1980.

32. TsDA, f. 990, op. 1, a.e. 599, 215–216, Slavic committee to NKK, May 1980; MVnR, op. 36, a.e. 336, 135–139, embassy in Washington report, May 1980.

33. See, for example, TsDA, f. 990, op. 1, a.e. 599, 137, list of the active members of the Bulgarian colony in Detroit, New York, Pittsburgh, Los Angeles, Seattle, Toledo, Santa Barbara, San Francisco, and Washington, 22 June 1979.

34. TsDA, f. 990, op. 1, a.e. 599, 128, 129–135, embassy in Washington report and attached letter, 3 August 1979.

35. TsDA, f. 990, op. 1, a.e. 602, 230, embassy in Washington telegram, 21 October 1981.

36. TsDA, f. 405, op. 9, a.e. 670, 71–78, 80–84, correspondence between Slavic Committee, embassy in Washington, and KK, February–June 1980.

37. TsDA, f. 990, op. 1, a.e. 602, 130, 131–150, 170–172, embassy in Washington memos about the writings of Louise Dern and her visit to Bulgaria in September 1981.

38. TsDA, f. 990, op. 1, a.e. 641, 237–243, report from July 1982 refers to 13,000–14,000 while TsDA, f. 990, op. 1, a.e. 642, 25–78, from April 1982 talks about 10,000.

39. TsDA, f. 990, op. 1, a.e. 642, 25–78, general report on the 1300 activities in the FRG, 10 May 1982; TsDA, f. 141, op. 9, a.e. 41, 1–6, 14–29, information about work with the Bulgarian colony in FRG from 1975 and 1978.

40. TsDA, f. 990, op. 1, a.e. 641, 51–61, plans for work with the Bulgarian colony, June 1981. Émigrés were presented with information about how to acquire the status of Bulgarian citizens legally residing abroad (according to a new citizenship law) and how to return to Bulgaria based on amnesty laws. They were informed about changes in the compulsory military service law that provided exceptions for males living abroad, assured of the speedy resolution of family reunifications, and afforded the possibility of purchasing homes in Bulgaria with hard currency.

41. TsDA, f. 990, op. 1, a.e. 642, 25–78, general report on the 1300 activities in FRG, 10 May 1982.

42. TsDA, f. 990, op. 1, a.e. 642, 25–78, general report on the 1300 activities in FRG, 10 May 1982.

43. MVnR, op. 34, a.e. 812, 89–90, memo from 6 September 1978 related to publications attacking the pending visit of Todor Zhivkov to Austria.

44. MVnR, op. 34, a.e. 833, 1, telegram from Bonn referring to publications in *Die Welt* from 20 and 29 February 1978.

45. MVnR, op. 34, a.e. 812, 11–13, meeting with the FRG ambassador at MVnR, 28 March 1978.

46. MVnR, op. 34, a.e. 833, 30–36, "The Anti-Bulgarian Campaign in FRG Mass Media regarding the Death of Georgi Markov and Vladimir Simeonov," September 1978; MVnR, op. 36, a.e. 851, 2–29, report on the cultural-propaganda activities of the embassy in Bonn in 1979.

47. TsDA, f. 990, op. 1, a.e. 638, 103–111, report of the embassy in Bonn on 1300 activities among the Bulgarian colony, June 1980.

48. TsDA, f. 990, op. 1, a.e. 642, 25–78, general report on the 1300 activities in the FRG, 10 May 1982; TsDA, f. 141, op. 9, a.e. 41, 1–6, 14–29, information about work with the Bulgarian colony in the FRG from 1975 and 1978.

49. TsDA, f. 990, op. 1, a.e. 642, 25–78, general report on the 1300 activities in the FRG, 10 May 1982.

50. TsDA, f. 990, op. 1, a.e. 642, 25–78, general report on the 1300 activities in the FRG, 10 May 1982.

51. TsDA, f. 141, op. 9, a.e. 41, 22–29, information for events organized for 24 May 1977.

52. TsDA, f. 990, op. 1, a.e. 641, 51–61, plans for work with the Bulgarian colony, June 1981.

53. TsDA, f. 990, op. 1, a.e. 642, 25–78, general report on the 1300 activities in the FRG, 10 May 1982; ibid., a.e. 638, 639, and 641, interim reports from 1980 and 1981.

54. TsDA, f. 141, op. 9, a.e. 41, 1–6, information about work with the Bulgarian colony in the FRG from 1975. See the memoirs of Stefan Popov, *Bezsânitsi* (Sofia: Letopisi, 1992).

55. TsDA, f. 141, op. 11, a.e. 32, long-term program for work with Bulgarians in non-socialist states, 1981–1990.

56. TsDA, f. 141, op. 11, a.e. 51, 1–43, report on Slavic Committee visit to United States and Canada in September and October 1982.

57. Anna Lowenhaupt Tsing, *Friction: An Ethnography of Global Connection* (Princeton, NJ: Princeton University Press, 2005), 3.

58. See Januarius A. MacGahan, *The Turkish Atrocities in Bulgaria: Letters of the Special Commissioner of the "Daily News"* (London: Bradbury, Agnew & Co., 1876).

59. Perry Country Public Library has an extensive collection on the life of Januarius MacGahan. I am grateful to Carma Jean Rausch and Barbara Mooney, longtime organizers of the MacGahan American-Bulgarian Festival, for information they provided during my visits to New Lexington in June 2012 and June 2013. Carma Jean Rausch passed away in April 2019, and her obituary states, "She was very active in the local community and was the organizer of the annual MacGahan Festival, which she was most proud of." See the *Columbus Dispatch*, April 22, 2019, https://www.legacy.com/obituaries/dispatch/obituary.aspx?n=carma-jean-rausch&pid=192633788&fhid=8691.

60. Teodor Dimitrov, *Ianuari Makgahan, 1844–187: Biografiia, dokumenti i materiali* (Sofia: Nauka i izkustvo, 1977). Sculptor Todor Pârvanov created the monument.

61. MVnR, op. 38, a.e. 411, information on émigré activities in New Lexington, the birthplace of MacGahan, 1978–1980.

62. Resolution, Ohio House of Representatives, H.R. No. 676, June 1978, found in TsDA, f. 405, op. 9, a.e. 668, 181.

63. TsDA, f. 405, op. 9, a.e. 668, 175–176, KK information about MacGahan, 1978; and MVnR, op. 36, a.e. 386, 1, embassy in Washington to MVnR, 22 November 1978.

64. Liubomir Dalchev is the sculptor of the Monument of the Soviet Army in Plovdiv, still standing today. For Dalchev's defection, see OSA/RFE, 300/20/1/44, RFE report, 30 October 1979. For Dalchev in the United States, see "Na sto godini v Amerika," *Bulgaria sega*, 29 September 2010, http://www.bulgariasega.com/usa_canada_bulgari/usa-west-coast/8512.html.

65. For a description from a Bulgarian émigré, see TsDA, f. 405, op. 9, a.e. 668, 177–180, Zhenia Pimpirova, "The MacGahan Bulgarian Centennial Commemoration," *Horizons* 1 (August 1978).

66. Franc Grivec, "Der hl. Methodius in Ellwangen," in *Ellwangen 764–1964: Beiträge und Untersuchungen zur Zwölfhundert-Jahnfeier*, ed. Viktor Burr (Ellwangen: Schwabenverlag, 1964), 153–159; and Immo Eberl, "Der hl. Methodius und Ellwangen," in *Die Vita des Heiligen Methodius*, ed. Spatrak Paskalevski (Munich: Biblion Verlag, 2006), 9–13. I am grateful to Pasha Johnson for her help researching this topic.

67. "V Germaniia chestvat Sv. Metodi," *Akademika*, 7 July 2011, http://aka demika.bg/2011/07/в-германия-честват-св-методий/; "NDF 13 Veka Bâlgariia— Fotoizlozhba v Elvagen," *Natsionalen daritelski fond 13 veka Bâlgariia*, 9 June 2008, http://2006.fond.13veka.org/page.php?id=351&category=73; "Pametnitsite na Sv. sv. Kiril i Metodi," 25 May 2007, https://www.pravoslavie.bg/Символика/дума-паметниците-на-св-св-кирил-и-мето/; and "45 godini Metodievi târzhestva v Elvangen, Germaniia," *Rodina*, 9 June 2005, http://rodinabg.net/?action=news&id=3376.

68. TsDA, f. 141, op. 9, a.e. 41, 22–29, information on events organized for 24 May 1977.

69. TsDA, f. 141, op. 9, a.e. 41, 18–21, information on New Year's Eve events in the FRG in January 1977. In 1978, some five hundred Bulgarians visited the reception at the embassy in Bonn. There were also "members of the hostile emigration" but they "did not undertake any action to dampen the celebration." TsDA, f. 141, op. 9, a.e. 41, 14–17, report of the embassy in Bonn, 1 June 1978.

70. TsDA, f. 141, op. 11, a.e. 48, 75–76, conversations between Slavic Committee and compatriots abroad, 1981. I am grateful to Pat French for our email communication. She passed away in January 2019, and her obituary states, "Pat was a first generation American, her parents immigrated from Bulgaria, and while they never forgot their homeland, she took her dedication to that tiny but mighty country to heart," and lists her contributions to cultivating relations between the United States and Bulgaria. See Legacy.com, accessed 24 May 2019, https://www.legacy.com/obituaries/postga zette/obituary.aspx?n=patricia-paina-french&pid=191282515&fhid=9848.

71. TsDA, f. 990, op. 1, a.e. 599, 97–100, embassy in Washington report, 18 June 1979.

72. TsDA, f. 990, op. 1, a.e. 602, 69, embassy in Washington report, 5 May 1981. For other members of the committee, see chapter 3.

73. TsDA, f. 990, op. 1, a.e. 602, 218–224, embassy in Washington report, 24 July 1981.

74. TsDA, f. 141, op. 9, a.e. 82, 56–59; op. 9, a.e. 83, 130–131; op. 11, a.e. 48, 75–76, memos of Slavic Committee meetings with Bulgarians abroad, 1978–1981.

75. These paragraphs are based on my examination of the Dora Gabensky Papers, Hoover Institution Archives. The records are assembled in sixty-four boxes and had no finding aid during the time of my research. Two bios were located in boxes 7 and 13.

76. Dora Gabensky Papers, box 23, Hoover Institution Archives.

77. *Luch*, May–July 1983, 60.

78. These paragraphs are based on my examination of the Atanas Slavov Papers, Hoover Institution Archives (two boxes with materials dated 1978–1981).

79. Slavov, *The "Thaw."*

80. All *Meridian* correspondence is in an orange envelope in Box 2, Atanas Slavov Papers, Hoover Institution Archives.

81. Publications in Bulgaria on the occasion of his passing in 2010 include: "Sbogu-vane s Atanas Slavov," *Kultura*, 10 December 2010, http://newspaper.kultura.bg/bg/ article/view/17750; Hristo Karastoianov, "Za Atanas Slavov nekanonichno," *Trud*, 25 January 2012, https://web.archive.org/web/20140115010502/http://m.trud. bg/Article.aspx?id=1198995; Dimitar Bochev, "Atanas Slavov—buntariat," *Tema*, 16

December 2013, http://archive.is/SQXsZ; and Veselina Sedlarska, "Sled nishtoto," *Tema*, 11 May 2013, http://www.temanews.com/img/tema/762/17228/39.p1.pdf.

82. Clifford, "Diasporas," 304–305.

5. Like a Grand World Civilization

1. TsDA, f. 405, op. 9, a.e. 622, 95–98, draft report of the embassy in New Delhi, 13 May 1980.

2. MVnR, op. 38, a.e. 1208, 44–52, information on the Indo-Bulgarian Friendship Associations, 1981. CPI members staffed the friendship societies in large numbers, but after Indira Gandhi returned to power in 1980, Congress activists took over the societies.

3. TsDA, f. 405, op. 9, a.e. 619, 54–60, "Brisking Up the Activity of the Foreign-Bulgarian Friendship Societies," undated.

4. MVnR, op. 35, a.e. 1339, report from September 1979. The friendship societies celebrated other holidays, such as the Bulgarian centennial in 1978, Georgi Dimitrov's birth, the October Revolution, or the Day of the Bulgarian Alphabet on 24 May.

5. MvnR, op. 33, a.e. 1258, 15–17, embassy in New Delhi report, September 1977.

6. MVnR, op. 38, a.e. 1171, 45–49, materials related to Ghandi's visit to Bulgaria, November 1981; copy of the speech in English.

7. TsDA, f. 405, op. 9, a.e. 679, 3, clipping from *Literaturen front*, undated.

8. Smith, "New Bottles for New Wine," 568.

9. Johanna Bockman, "Socialist Globalization against Capitalist Neocolonialism: The Economic Ideas behind the New International Economic Order," *Humanity: An International Journal of Human Rights, Humanitarianism and Development* 6, no. 1 (2015): 109–128. See also Mark, Kalinovsky, and Marung, *Alternative Globalizations*.

10. For a recent overview of the literature, see Dragostinova and Fidelis, "Introduction." For the role of Eastern European experts in India, see Małgorzata Mazurek, "Polish Economists in Nehru's India: Making Science for the Third World in an Era of De-Stalinization and Decolonization," *Slavic Review* 77, no. 3 (2018): 588–610. For the cultural flirtations between Albania and China, see Elidor Mëhilli, "Globalized Socialism, Nationalized Time: Soviet Films, Albanian Subjects, and Chinese Audiences across the Sino-Soviet Split," *Slavic Review* 77, no. 3 (2018): 611–637. For culture in Soviet development schemes in Central Asia, see Artemy Kalinovsky, *Laboratory of Socialist Development: Cold War Politics and Decolonization in Soviet Tajikistan* (Ithaca, NY: Cornell University Press, 2018).

11. In their recent volume, *1989*, Mark, Bogdan C. Iacob, Tobias Rupprecht, and Ljubica Spaskovska assert that in the aftermath of the Helsinki Final Act in 1975, Eastern Europe started abandoning the Global South and firmly reoriented itself toward the West. In my sources, it is clear that East-South relations were strong well into the 1980s.

12. TsDA, f. 1b, op. 55, a.e. 780, 1–32, Information-Sociological Center of the BKP, "Public Opinion for the 1300 Jubilee," February 1982. There were also 7,894 cultural events in socialist countries, for a total of 38,854 events globally.

13. For a recent study of the role of UNESCO as an intermediary between the Global South and a number of Balkan states, see Iacob, "Southeast by Global South."

14. See Zhivkova's biography in chapter 1 of this book. Some studies that focus on this aspect of her personality are Blagov, *Zagadkata Liudmila Zhivkova*; and Gruev, "Liudmila Zhivkova." In English, see Atanasova, "Lyudmila Zhivkova"; and Veneta Ivanova, "Occult Communism: Culture, Science, and Spirituality in Late Socialist Bulgaria" (PhD diss., University of Illinois Urbana-Champaign, 2016).

15. The case of Japan provides further nuance. See Evgeniĭ Kandilarov," Liudmila Zhivkova i kulturnata diplomatsiia kâm Iaponiia," in Baeva, *Kulturnoto otvariane*, 63–77; and Evgeniĭ Kandilarov, *Bâlgariia i Iaponiia: Ot Studenata vŭina kâm XXI vek* (Sofia: Damian Iakov, 2009).

16. David Engerman, "The Second World's Third World," *Kritika: Explorations in Russian and Eurasian History* 12, no. 1 (2011): 185.

17. The literature on the Third World and development is rich, but two analyses used here include Nick Cullather, "Development? Its History: Research Note," *Diplomatic History* 24, no. 4 (2000): 641–653; and Tomlinson, "What Was the Third World?"

18. Mark Atwood Lawrence, "The Rise and Fall of Nonalignment," in McMahon, *The Cold War*, 139–155.

19. Tomlinson, "What Was the Third World?"; and Odd Arne Westad, "The Cold War and the Third World," in McMahon, *The Cold War*, 213. From an influential emic perspective, see Vijay Prashad, *The Darker Nations: A People's History of the Third World* (New York: New Press, 2007).

20. Bockman, "Socialist Globalization."

21. Tomlinson, "What Was the Third World?", 314; and Cullather, "Development?"

22. The vast majority of the English-language literature has focused on Western economic involvement in Asia, Africa, and Latin America. These narratives often use modernization theory to imply a relationship in which the periphery borrows superior practices from the core and assume that "to be developed is to be Euro-American." See Cullather, "Development?," 646. For two syntheses of the vast literature on development, see Corinna R. Unger, "Histories of Development and Modernization: Findings, Reflections, Future Research," H-Soz-Kult, 9 December 2010, https://www.hsozkult.de/literaturereview/id/forschungsberichte-1130; and Joseph Morgan Hodge, "Writing the History of Development (Part 2: Longer, Deeper, Wider)," *Humanity: An International Journal of Human Rights, Humanitarianism and Development* 7, no. 1 (2016): 125–174.

23. Westad, "The Cold War," 211.

24. Hodge, "Writing the History of Development," 150–151; and Latham, "The Cold War," 263–265.

25. Vladislav Zubok, "Cold War Strategies / Power and Culture—East," in Immerman and Goedde, *The Oxford Handbook of the Cold War*, 309–312.

26. See Jude Howell, "The End of an Era: The Rise and Fall of GDR Aid," *Journal of Modern African Studies* 32, no. 2 (1994): 305–328; Martin Rudner, "East European Aid to Asian Developing Countries: The Legacy of the Communist Era," *Modern Asian Studies* 30, no. 1 (1996): 1–28; Massimilano Trentin, "'Tough Negotiations': The Two Germanies in Syria and Iraq, 1963–74," *Cold War History* 8, no. 3 (2008): 353–380; Phillip Muehlenbeck, *Czechoslovakia in Africa, 1946–1968* (New York: Palgrave Macmillan, 2016); and Dubravka Sekulić, "Energoprojekt in Nigeria: Yugoslav Construction

Companies in the Developing World." *Southeastern Europe/L'Europe du Sud-Est* 41, no. 2 (2017), 200–229.

27. Young-Sun Hong, *Cold War Germany, the Third World, and the Global Humanitarian Regime* (New York: Cambridge University Press, 2015), 13–48.

28. Bockman, "Socialist Globalization," 109–110, 113, 121.

29. Łukasz Stanek, "Architects from Socialist Countries in Ghana (1957–67): Modern Architecture and Mondialisation," *Journal of the Society of Architectural Historians* 74, no. 4 (2015): 416–442; and Łukasz Stanek, "Miastoprojekt Goes Abroad: The Transfer of Architectural Labour from Socialist Poland to Iraq (1958–1989)," *The Journal of Architecture* 17, no. 3 (2012): 361–386.

30. Mark, Kalinovsky, and Marung, *Alternative Globalizations*, 3, 4. I thank James Mark for sharing a draft of the introduction to this excellent volume.

31. Cullather, "Development?," 642–643.

32. Even though my sources do not use the term Third World, I use it interchangeably with Global South and developing states. Scholarship on Bulgarian involvement in the Third World is developing. See Raia Apostolova, "Duty and Debt under the Ethos of Internationalism: The Case of the Vietnamese Workers in Bulgaria," *Journal of Vietnamese Studies* 12, no. 1 (2017): 101–125; and Mariya Ivancheva, "Paternalistic Internationalism and (De)colonial Practices of Cold War Higher Education Exchange: Bulgaria's Connections with Cuba and Angola," *Journal of Labor and Society* 22, no. 4 (2019): 733–748.

33. TNA, FCO 28/3732, "What Use Is Bulgaria?," 30 July 1979.

34. TNA, FCO 28/2866, embassy in Sofia report, 29 December 1976.

35. TNA, FCO 28/3023, embassy in Sofia, annual review for 1976.

36. TNA, FCO 28/4106, embassy in Sofia report, 6 October 1980.

37. Latham, "The Cold War," 264; Engerman, "The Second World's Third World," 188–189.

38. TNA, FCO 28/2866, embassy in Sofia report, 22 March 1976.

39. MVnR, op. 34, a.e. 3794, 16–26, 27–34, materials related to the visit of Zhivkov in Nigeria, 16–19 October 1978.

40. TNA, FCO 28/3330, "Zhivkov's African Tour," 6 November 1978.

41. Maxim Matusevich, *No Easy Row for a Russian Hoe: Ideology and Pragmatism in Russian-Nigerian Relations, 1960–1991* (Trenton, NJ: Africa World Press, 2003).

42. TNA, FCO 28/4106, embassy in Sofia report, 6 October 1980.

43. TNA, FCO 28/3733, embassy in Sofia, annual review of Bulgaria for 1978; FCO evaluation of report, 20 February 1979. The memoir of the Bulgarian ambassador in Mexico at the time capture this enthusiasm well. See Bogomil Gerasimov, *Diplomatsiia v zonata na kaktusa* (Sofia: Trud, 1998).

44. TNA, FCO 28/3330, FCO to Cloake, 15 December 1978; Anderson to Lambert, 22 November 1978; the annex contains a list of visits by Warsaw Pact heads of state to Africa.

45. For a list of the Bulgarian cultural centers and friendship societies abroad, see TsDA, f. 405, op. 9, a.e. 263, 55, NKK, "For the Dignified Celebration of the 1300th Anniversary of the Establishment of the Bulgarian State," June 1979, index 6.

46. TsDA, f. 1b, op. 55, a.e. 780, 1–32, Information-Sociological Center of the BKP, "Public Opinion for the 1300 Jubilee," February 1982.

47. TsDA, f. 405, op. 9, a.e. 263, 55, NKK, "For the Dignified Celebration of the 1300th Anniversary of the Establishment of the Bulgarian State," June 1979, 10, 195.

48. I borrow this term from Kate Brown, *Plutopia: Nuclear Families, Atomic Cities, and the Great Soviet and American Plutonium Disasters* (New York: Oxford University Press, 2013).

49. In November 1976 and February 1981, Liudmila Zhivkova took two consecutive trips to India and Mexico to sign cultural exchange agreements and open exhibitions for the 1300-year jubilee. See Savova et al., *Liudmila Zhivkova*, 158–159, 394–399.

50. TNA, FCO 28/3330, embassy in Mexico City report, 27 April 1978.

51. Mark et al., *1989*, 56–59, discusses the authoritarian capitalist path that Eastern European elites were willing to follow in the 1970s, as evident in their relations with South Korea, Chile, and Panama.

52. MVnR, op. 38, a.e. 1171, 93–98, 104–109, information on India, November 1981.

53. TsDA, f. 405, op. 9, a.e. 675, 44–52, memo on Mexico, undated.

54. MVnR, op. 35, a.e. 2091, 36–42, materials related to Zhivkov's visit to Mexico, April 1979; memo on Mexico.

55. MVnR, op. 38, a.e. 1171, 110–116, relations between CPI and the Congress Party, November 1981.

56. MVnR, op. 36, a.e. 1243, reports on Indian elections, 1980.

57. MVnR, op. 35, a.e. 2091,14–17, information on Mexico, 24 February 1979.

58. MVnR, op. 35, a.e. 2091, 36–42, materials related to Zhivkov's visit to Mexico, April 1979; memo on Mexico.

59. Diplomats to India and Mexico were carefully chosen to satisfy Zhivkova's preferences and reported personally to her on various matters. These included Toshho Toshhev, ambassador in New Delhi; Bogomil Gerasimov, ambassador in Mexico City; and Morfi Skarlatov, director of the Bulgarian Cultural-Informational Center in New Delhi.

60. MVnR, op. 38, a.e. 1171, 45–49, materials related to Ghandi's visit to Bulgaria, November 1981; copy of the speech in English.

61. Achin Vanaik, *The Painful Transition: Bourgeois Democracy in India* (New York: Verso, 1990), 259.

62. Gerasimov, *Diplomatsiia v zonata na kaktusa*.

63. MVnR, op. 35, a.e. 2091, 43–49, 136–140, materials related to Zhivkov's visit to Mexico, April 1979.

64. OSA/RFE, 300/20/1/26, "Die Herscher im sozialischtische Ostblock bauer Dynastien auf," *Muencher Merkur*, 27 September 1979; and "Communist Rule: All in the Family," *International Herald Tribune*, 24 Aug 1979.

65. "Bulgaria's 'Princess' Leads Drive for Culture," *Chicago Tribune*, 19 July 1980; and "President's Daughter Plays Major Role in Bulgaria," *New York Times*, 9 November 1980.

66. OSA/RFE, 300/20/1/26, "Zhivkov's Daughter Making Her Mark," Reuters, Sofia, 11 May 1976.

67. Zhivkova's biographers confirm the importance of her personal interests in the way official Bulgarian cultural policies evolved. See Blagov, *Zagadkata Liudmila Zhivkova*.

68. OSA/RFE, 300/20/1/26, "Culture Boss," *Observer*, 29 February 1976.

69. A growing literature has shown that to think about Third World choices simply in terms of Western and Eastern models is simplistic. Third World states—such as India and Mexico—merged elements of East and West while they also prioritized local factors in their international choices. See Engerman, "The Second World's Third World," 184; Ragna Boden, "Cold War Economics: Soviet Aid to Indonesia," *Journal of Cold War Studies* 10, no. 3 (2008): 110–128; and Matusevich, *No Easy Row*.

70. See Andrew J. Rotter, "South Asia," in Immerman and Goedde, *Oxford Handbook of the Cold War*, 211–229; and Artemy M. Kalinovsky, "The Cold War in South and Central Asia," in *Routledge Handbook of the Cold War*, ed. Artemy M. Kalinovsky and Craig Daigle (New York: Routledge, 2016), 178–191. See also Dennis Kux, *Estranged Democracies: India and the United States, 1941–1991* (Thousand Oaks, CA: Sage, 1993); and Vojtech Mastny, "The Soviet Union's Partnership with India," *Journal of Cold War Studies* 12, no. 3 (2010): 50–90.

71. For the role of Soviet and Polish experts in India, see David Engerman, "Learning from the East: Soviet Experts and India in the Era of Competitive Coexistence," *Comparative Studies of South Asia, Africa and the Middle East* 33, no. 2 (2013): 227–235; and Mazurek, "Polish Economists." Most recently, David Engerman has examined the competing superpower agendas in India in *The Price of Aid: The Economic Cold War in India* (Cambridge, MA: Harvard University Press, 2018).

72. For general overviews of India after 1947, see Vanaik, *The Painful Transition*; Bipan Chandra, Mridula Mukherjee and Aditya Mukherjee, *India after Independence, 1947–2000* (New York: Oxford University Press, 2000); Ramachandra Guha, *India after Gandhi: The History of the World's Largest Democracy* (London: Macmillan, 2007); and Wendy Singer, *Independent India, 1947–2000* (New York: Pearson Longman, 2012).

73. For a recent overview of the scholarship, see Gilbert M. Joseph, "Border Crossings and the Remaking of Latin American Cold War Studies," *Cold War History* 19, no. 1 (2019): 141–170, on Mexico, see 152–153. See also Gilbert M. Joseph and Daniela Spenser, eds., *In from the Cold: Latin America's New Encounter with the Cold War* (Durham, NC: Duke University Press, 2008); Hal Brands, *Latin America's Cold War* (Cambridge, MA: Harvard University Press, 2010), 142–147; Virginia Garrard-Burnett, Mark Atwood Lawrence, and Julio E. Moreno, eds., *Beyond the Eagle's Shadow: New Histories of Latin America's Cold War* (Albuquerque: University of New Mexico Press, 2013); and Patrick Iber, *Neither Peace nor Freedom: The Cultural Cold War in Latin America* (Cambridge, MA: Harvard University Press, 2015).

74. Tobias Rupprecht, *Soviet Internationalism after Stalin: Interaction and Exchange between USSR and Latin America during the Cold War* (Cambridge: Cambridge University Press, 2015); Renata Keller, *Mexico's Cold War: Cuba, the United States, and the Legacy of the Mexican Revolution* (New York: Cambridge University Press, 2015); and Nicola Miller, *Soviet Relations with Latin America, 1959–1987* (New York: Cambridge University Press, 1989), 180–182.

75. Joseph, "Border Crossings," 153. See also Burton Kirkwood, The History of Mexico (Santa Barbara, CA: Greenwood Press, 2010), 185–192; and Philip Russell, *The History of Mexico: From Pre-Conquest to Present* (New York: Routledge, 2010), 478–482.

76. MVnR, op. 38, a.e. 1171, 93–98, 104–109, 117–125, information on India, November 1981.

77. MVnR, op. 38, a.e. 1173, 9–10, report from December 1980; MVnR, op. 35, a.e. 1339, 1–2, report from February 1979.

78. MVnR, op. 35, a.e. 2091, 85–96, political situation in Latin America, March 1979.

79. MVnR, op. 35, a.e. 2091, 14–17, information on Mexico, 24 February 1979.

80. TsDA, f. 405, op. 9, a.e. 675, 44–52, memo on Mexico, undated.

81. MVnR, op. 38, a.e. 1171, 93–98, 104–109, information on India, November 1981.

82. TNA, FCO 28/2866, British High Commission in New Dehli, 29 November 1976; joint communiqué, 21 November 1976.

83. TsDA, f. 405, op. 9, a.e. 616, 161–175, draft project for cooperation with India, 1976–1980; MVnR, op. 38, a.e. 1171, 93–98, 99–103, materials related to Gandhi's visit to Bulgaria, November 1981.

84. For the cooperation between Bulgaria and India in computing, see Victor Petrov, "The Rose and the Lotus: Bulgarian Electronic Entanglements in India, 1967–89," *Journal of Contemporary History* 54, no. 3 (2019): 666–687.

85. MVnR, op. 36, a.e. 1243, 85–86; a.e. 1244, 50–52, 70–72; and a.e. 1245, 5–8, 12–32, correspondence between the embassy in New Delhi and MVnR, 1980. According to this selection of documents, India exported leather, dyes, and some engineering goods to Bulgaria, while Bulgaria sent fertilizers, soda ash, pharmaceuticals and chemicals, electronics, fibers and yarns, high tension coils, steel products, bulk carriers, and defense items to India.

86. TNA, FCO 28/2866, embassy in Sofia report, 30 November 1976.

87. MVnR, op. 35, a.e. 2091, 36–42, materials related to Zhivkov's visit to Mexico, April 1979; memo on Mexico.

88. MVnR, op. 36, a.e. 2019, clippings from *Uno mas uno*, 12 August 1980; Gerasimov, *Diplomatsiia v zonata na kaktusa*.

89. TNA, FCO 28/3330, embassy in Mexico City report, 27 April 1978.

90. MVnR, op. 35, a.e. 2091, 43–46, 60–67, 101–106, materials related to Zhivkov's visit to Mexico, April 1979; memos on Bulgarian-Mexican relations and COMECON and Mexico.

91. MVnR, op. 38, a.e. 1173, 66–69, Radio India coverage of Zhivkova's visit to India, February 1981.

92. TsDA, f. 405, op. 9, a.e. 675, 131–135, memo on cultural relation, 1978.

93. *Pogled*, 3 March 1981, found in TsDA, f. 405, op. 9, a.e. 679.

94. TsDA, f. 405, op. 9, a.e. 675, 44–52, memo on Mexico, undated.

95. Russell, *The History of Mexico*, 480–481, 516, 526–527. For the role of culture in post-1940 Mexico, see Gilbert M. Joseph, Anne Rubenstein, and Eric Zolov, eds., *Fragments of a Golden Age: The Politics of Culture in Mexico since 1940* (Durham, NC: Duke University Press, 2001). See also Anne Rubenstein, "Mass Media and Popular Culture in the Post-revolutionary Era," in *The Oxford History of Mexico*, ed. Michael C. Meyer and William H. Beezley (New York: Oxford University Press, 2010), 598–634.

96. Singer, *Independent India*, 53.

97. MVnR, op. 32, a.e. 1402, 24–39, cultural relations with India, 1976.

98. MVnR, op. 38, a.e. 1173, 66–69, Radio India coverage of Zhivkova's visit to India, February 1981.

99. Gerasimov, *Diplomatsiia v zonata na kaktusa*, 298.

100. *Excelsior*, 4 March 1981, found in MVnR, op. 38, a.e. 1894.

101. TsDA, f. 405, op. 9, a.e. 616, 114–135, cultural relations with India, April 1976.

102. TsDA, f. 405, op. 9, a.e. 616, 114–135, 180–196, cultural relations with India, April and December 1976.

103. MVnR, op. 32, a.e. 1402, 24–39, cultural relations with India, 1976.

104. TsDA, f. 405, op. 9, a.e. 616, 180–196, cultural relations with India, December 1976.

105. MVnR, op. 33, a.e. 1260, 71–77; ibid., a.e. 1261, 57–58, correspondence on cultural matters, 1977.

106. MVnR, op. 34, a.e. 1218, 10–24, embassy in New Delhi report, May 1978; TsDA, f. 405, op. 9, a.e. 617, 103–118, report, December 1977.

107. TsDA, f. 405, op. 9, a.e. 617, 31, 42, *News from Bulgaria*, February and March 1977.

108. TsDA, f. 405, op. 9, a.e. 618, 98–99, KK correspondence on cultural cooperation with India in 1979. In 1979, there were sixty-six Indian-Bulgarian Friendship Societies in India, but their number grew to eighty-three in 1980. See ibid., a.e. 622, 95–98, draft report of the embassy in New Delhi, 13 May 1980.

109. MVnR, op. 34, a.e. 1224, correspondence on the Bulgarian Studies program, Delhi University, 1978.

110. MVnR, op. 38, a.e. 1218, 35, 36–39, MVnR and KK correspondence, December 1980–January 1981.

111. MVnR, op. 38, a.e. 1207, 12–17, memo on cultural relation with India, 1980.

112. TsDA, f. 405, op. 9, a.e. 616, 114–135, cultural relations with India, April 1976.

113. MVnR, op. 35, a.e. 1372; MVnR, op. 36, a.e. 1295 and 1299, correspondence on cultural relations, 1980.

114. For Bulgarian cultural relations with India, which also includes a detailed explanation of the study of Indology in Bulgaria, see Violina Atanasova, "Liudmila Zhivkova i ambitsioznite bâlgarski proekti v Indiia," in Baeva, *Kulturnoto otvariane*, 78–84.

115. TsDA, f. 405, op. 10, a.e. 539, 1–7, memo on cultural relations, February 1981.

116. TsDA, f. 405, op. 10, a.e. 539, 1–7, memo on cultural relations, February 1981.

117. TsDA, f. 405, op. 9, a.e. 675, 44–52, memo on Mexico, undated.

118. After London, the exhibition first went to Cuba and, after Mexico, it visited the Metropolitan Museum of Art in New York City.

119. TsDA, f. 405, op. 9, a.e. 675, 131–135, memo on cultural relations, 1978.

120. TsDA, f. 405, op. 10, a.e. 539, 1–7, memo on cultural relations, February 1981.

121. TNA, FCO 28/2866, embassy in Sofia report, 30 November 1976.

122. TsDA, f. 405, op. 10, a.e. 539, 1–7, memo on cultural relations, February 1981.

123. TsDA, f. 990, op. 1, a.e. 515, 259–314, general report on 1300 activities in India, 31 March 1982.

124. TsDA, f. 405, op. 10, a.e. 539, 23–28, memo on 1300 preparations, February 1981; TsDA, f. 990, op. 1, a.e. 570, 149–178, memo on jubilee activities in Mexico, December 1981.

125. TsDA, f. 990, op. 1, a.e. 570, 149–178, memo on jubilee activities in Mexico, December 1981.

126. The exhibition was arranged in a museum in Plovdiv Old Town. Today most works are in the permanent collection of the Municipal Art Museum of Plovdiv.

127. Zhivkova was in India 17–27 February. See Savova et al., *Liudmila Zhivkova*, 394–399; MVnR, op. 36, a.e. 1298, 23–25, 33–36; MVnR, op. 38, a.e. 1173, 1193, correspondence on the *Thracian Treasures* exhibition and Zhivkova's visit to India, December 1980–February 1981. By this point, the exhibition had already toured Paris, Moscow, Leningrad, Vienna, Warsaw, Budapest, London, Havana, Mexico City, New York City, Boston, Munich, Cologne, and Tokyo.

128. TsDA, f. 405, op. 9, a.e. 497, clipping from the speech reprinted in the *Statesman* (New Delhi), 2 March 1981, and *Sunday Standard* (New Delhi), 22 February 1981.

129. TsDA, f. 990, op. 1, a.e. 515, 259–314, 246–254, general report on 1300 activities in India, 31 March 1982; report on Zhivkova's visit to India in February 1981.

130. Zhivkova was in Mexico 28 February–6 March, with a twelve-hour stay in Sofia after India. Savova et al., *Liudmila Zhivkova*, 394–399.

131. Savova et al., *Liudmila Zhivkova*, 394–399; TsDA, f. 405, op. 9, a.e. 679, 1–5, 63–65, clippings and report about the *Bulgarian Medieval Civilization* exhibition and other activities in Mexico, March 1981.

132. TsDA, f. 405, op. 9, a.e. 679, 1–5, 63–65, an overview of cultural events until early 1981; TsDA, f. 405, op. 10, a.e. 539, 1–7, memo on cultural relations, February 1981.

133. TsDA, f. 405, op. 9, a.e. 679, 1–5, 63–65, KK report, 21 May 1981, and press clippings, March 1981 and undated.

134. Blagov, *Zagadkata Liudmila Zhivkova*.

135. See TsDA, op. 38, a.e. 88, 1–13, information on foreign press coverage of Zhivkova's death, July 1981; indicatively, in the "developing countries" section of this report, the most extensive discussions are on Mexico and India. See also OSA/RFE, 300/20/1/26, which contains a collection of foreign press obituaries and reports in the aftermath of Zhivkova's death in July 1981.

136. TsDA, f. 990, op. 1, a.e. 570, 149–178, memo on jubilee activities in Mexico, December 1981.

137. MVnR, op. 38, a.e. 1162 and 1171, materials on India related to Gandhi's visit to Bulgaria, November 1981.

138. MVnR, op. 38, a.e. 1171, 45–49, materials related to Gandhi's visit to Bulgaria, November 1981; copy of the speech in English.

139. See Kandilarov, "Liudmila Zhivkova."

140. Scholars are only now starting to analyze the historical record for such encounters. See Petrov, "The Rose and the Lotus," who carries his analysis of Bulgarian-Indian economic cooperation into the 1980s.

141. TNA, FCO 28/4447, embassy in Sofia, annual review for 1980.

142. TNA, FCO 28/3732, "What Use Is Bulgaria?," 30 July 1979.

6. Culture under Special Conditions

1. MVnR, op. 36, a.e. 4623, 48–49, embassy in Lagos information, 29 September 1980.

2. MVnR, op. 36, a.e. 4623, 16–17, embassy in Lagos information, 13 July 1980.

3. MVnR, op. 38, a.e. 3803, 52–55, embassy in Lagos report, 1981.

4. MVnR, op. 38, a.e. 3805, 110–112, embassy in Lagos report, November 1981.

5. Artemy Kalinovsky notes a similar interplay of economic and cultural messages in Soviet development projects in Tajikistan in his *Laboratory of Socialist Development*.

6. For civilizational rhetoric in the imperial context, see Alice Conklin, *A Mission to Civilize: The Republican Idea of Empire in France and West Africa, 1895–1930* (Stanford, CA: Stanford University Press, 1997). For a critical exploration of the concept in the Soviet context, see Adeeb Khalid, "Backwardness and the Quest for Civilization: Early Soviet Central Asia in Comparative Perspective," *Slavic Review* 65, no. 2 (Summer 2006): 231–251. Kalinovsky, *Laboratory of Socialist Development*, 10, claims in his study of Soviet Tajikistan that "promoting kul'turnost' [culturedness] . . . implied a transfer of European models of behavior and thought to supposedly uncultured subjects."

7. For the "civilizational bordering" of Eastern Europe during late socialism, see Mark et al., *1989*, 127–128, 140–141. For the attitude to Black students in the Soviet Union, see Julie Hessler, "Death of an African Student in Moscow—Race, Politics, and the Cold War," *Cahiers du monde Russe* 47, no. 1–2 (2006): 33–63; and Maxim Matusevich, "An Exotic Subversive: Africa, Africans, and the Soviet Everyday," Race and Class 49, no. 4 (2008): 57–81; "Black in the U.S.S.R.: Africans, African Americans, and the Soviet Society," *Transition: An International Review* 100, no. 1 (2009): 56–75; and "Expanding the Boundaries of the Black Atlantic: African Students as Soviet Moderns," *Ab Imperio*, no. 2 (2012): 325–350. For East Germany, see Quinn Slobodian, ed., *Comrades of Color: East Germany in the Cold War World* (New York: Berghahn Books, 2015).

8. Grigor Doytchinov, "Pragmatism, Not Ideology: Bulgarian Architectural Exports to the 'Third World,'" *The Journal of Architecture* 17, no. 3 (2012): 453–473. Other scholarship on the Bulgarian presence in the Third World includes Apostolova, "Duty and Debt"; and Ivancheva, "Paternalistic Internationalism."

9. Matusevich, *No Easy Row*; and Alessandro Iandolo, "The Rise and Fall of the 'Soviet Model of Development' in West Africa, 1957–64," *Cold War History* 12, no. 4 (2012): 683–704. For two other works on Eastern Europe in Africa, see Gareth Winrow, *The Foreign Policy of the GDR in Africa* (Cambridge: Cambridge University Press, 1990); and Muehlenbeck, *Czechoslovakia in Africa*.

10. Andrew Apter, *The Pan-African Nation: Oil and the Spectacle of Culture in Nigeria* (Chicago: University of Chicago Press, 2005).

11. Stanek, "Architects from Socialist Countries," 435. See also Łukasz Stanek, "Introduction: The 'Second World's' Architecture and Planning in the 'Third World,'" in "Cold War Transfer: Architecture and Planning of Socialist Countries in the Third World," special issue, *Journal of Architecture* 17, no. 3 (2012), 302, and especially "Miastoprojekt Goes Abroad," 361–386; and Sekulić, "Energoprojekt in Nigeria." See also James Mark and Quinn Slobodian, "Eastern Europe in the Global History of Decolonization." In *The Oxford Handbook of the Ends of Empire*, ed. Martin Thomas and Andrew Thompson (Oxford: Oxford University Press, 2018). DOI: 10.1093/oxfordhb/9780198713197.013.20.

12. Mark, Kalinovsky, and Marung, *Alternative Globalizations*.

13. Stanek, "Architects from Socialist Countries"; Stanek, "Miastoprojekt Goes Abroad."

14. Ghodsee, *Second World, Second Sex*, 25.

15. Iu. Cherkasov, ed., *Ekonomicheskie problemy Afriki: Stat'i bolgarskikh uchenykh* (Moscow: Nauka, 1974), 28.

16. Doytchinov, "Pragmatism, Not Ideology."

17. TNA, FCO 28/3330, embassy in Sofia, "Zhivkov's African Tour," 6 November 1978; TNA, FCO 28/3023, annual review of Bulgaria for 1976.

18. Cherkasov, *Ekonomicheskie problemy Afriki*, 3–4, 6.

19. Evgeni Kamenov, ed., *Afrika, politiko-ikonomicheski spravochnik* (Sofia: Partizdat, 1973), 87.

20. Kamenov, *Afrika*, 32–38.

21. Kamenov, *Afrika*, 87.

22. Kamenov, *Afrika*, 20.

23. For this definition of "cooperation," see Kamenov, *Afrika*, 105. More information is available in E. Kamenov, T. Vulchev, and E. Malhasian, "Ekonomicheskie sviazi Bolgarii s razvivaiushtimisia stranami," in Cherkasov, *Ekonomicheskie problemy Afriki*, 42–58.

24. Kamenov, *Afrika*, 111–112.

25. For a critique of Western "aid," see Kamenov, *Afrika*, 91–92.

26. "In the Interest of Friendship: In the Interest of Peace," *Bulgaria Today*, February 1979, 10–11.

27. TNA, FCO 28/3330, "Zhivkov's African Tour," 6 November 1978.

28. TNA, FCO 28/3733, embassy in Sofia, annual review of Bulgaria for 1978; FCO evaluation of report, 20 February 1979.

29. TNA, FCO 28/3330, FCO to Cloake, 15 December 1978; Anderson to Lambert, 22 November 1978.

30. For "jungle offensive," see TNA, FCO 28/4106, embassy in Sofia report, 6 October 1980.

31. Toyin Falola and Matthew M. Heaton, *A History of Nigeria* (Cambridge: Cambridge University Press, 2008), chapter 7.

32. MVnR, op. 34, a.e. 3794, 35–44, memos of mutual relations Bulgaria-Nigeria, October 1978.

33. Ehimika A. Ifidon and Charles O. Osarumwense, "Politics without Commerce? Explaining the Discontinuity in Soviet-Nigerian Relations, 1971–1979," *African & Asian Studies* 14, no. 4 (2015): 301. According to this account, Soviet bloc military aid to Nigeria continued after the civil war, and in 1974 and 1975 Bulgarian arms imports accounted for 25 percent and 22.5 percent of all arms sales.

34. Falola and Heaton, *A History of Nigeria*, 182; Frederick Cooper, *Africa since 1940: The Past of the Present* (Cambridge: Cambridge University Press, 2002), 172.

35. Falola and Heaton, *A History of Nigeria*, 184.

36. MVnR, op. 34, a.e. 3778, 11–18, memo on relations between Bulgaria and Nigeria, August 1978.

37. Matusevich, *No Easy Row*, 145.

38. MVnR, op. 34, a.e. 3794, 35–44, memos on relations between Bulgaria and Nigeria, October 1978.

39. Doytchinov, "Pragmatism, Not Ideology," 463–466. See also Falola and Heaton, *A History of Nigeria*, 194–195. For a detailed analysis of the architectural elements of the building, completed with numerous plans and photographs, see *Arhitektura* 4 (1977).

40. Falola and Heaton, *A History of Nigeria*, 188–195.

41. MVnR, op. 34, a.e. 3794, 27–34, information on Nigeria, October 1978.

42. MVnR, op. 34, a.e. 3794, 27–34, information on Nigeria, October 1978. See also ibid., 35–44, relations between Bulgaria and Nigeria, October 1978.

43. MVnR, op. 34, a.e. 3775 and 3778, correspondence between MVnR and the embassy in Lagos on Nigerian political relations in 1978.

44. MVnR, op. 34, a.e. 3793, 20–24, report to CC of the BKP about Zhivkov's visit, October 1978.

45. MVnR, op. 34, a.e. 3794, 27–34, materials related to Zhivkov's visit to Nigeria, 16–19 October 1978.

46. MVnR, op. 34, a.e. 3794, 16–26, 27–34, materials related to Zhivkov's visit to Nigeria, 16–19 October 1978.

47. Matusevich, *No Easy Row*, 157.

48. MVnR, op. 34, a.e. 3778, 11–18, relations between Bulgaria and Nigeria, August 1978. See also MVnR, op. 34, a.e. 3794, 16–26, materials related to Zhivkov's visit to Nigeria, 16–19 October 1978.

49. TNA, FCO 28/3330, report of the British High Commission, Lagos, 31 October 1978.

50. MVnR, op. 34, a.e. 3778, 11–18, relations between Bulgaria and Nigeria, August 1978. See also MVnR, op. 34, a.e. 3794, 16–26, materials related to Zhivkov's visit to Nigeria, 16–19 October 1978.

51. MVnR, op. 38, a.e. 3802, 37–40, 62–66, information related to the position of Nigeria on key international issues, 1981. See also Winrow, *The Foreign Policy of the GDR*; and Muehlenbeck, *Czechoslovakia in Africa*.

52. MVnR, op. 34, a.e. 3794, 16–26, materials related to Zhivkov's visit to Nigeria, 16–19 October 1978.

53. Matusevich, *No Easy Row*, 191. See also Kenneth E. Noble, "Nigeria's Monumental Steel Plant: Nationalist Mission or Colossal Mistake?" *New York Times*, 11 July 1992.

54. MVnR, op. 38, a.e. 3803, 26–28, 45, memos on UK-Nigerian relations, March 1981.

55. TNA, FCO 28/3330, report of the British High Commission, Lagos, 31 October 1978.

56. MVnR, op. 38, a.e. 3803, 11–17, Nigerian relations with socialist states, January 1981.

57. Matusevich, *No Easy Row*, 171.

58. MVnR, op. 35, a.e. 4201, 25–27, embassy in Lagos information, 27 July 1979.

59. Falola and Heaton, *A History of Nigeria*, 198–202.

60. MVnR, op. 38, a.e. 3805, 41–46, information on Shagari's social policies, 18 October 1981.

61. Falola and Heaton, *A History of Nigeria*, 202.

62. MVnR, op. 38, a.e. 3803, 11–17, Nigerian relations with socialist states, January 1981.

63. Falola and Heaton, *A History of Nigeria*, 203–208.

64. For Technoexportstroy's projects, including public buildings in Lagos, Abuja, Benin, and Kano, see http://www.technoexportstroy.bg/indexdetails.php?menu_id=90&country=2, accessed 30 January 2018.

65. For Bulgarian economic plans, see MVnR, op. 35, a.e. 4201, 18–22, embassy in Lagos memo, 14 June 1979.

66. MVnR, op. 34, a.e. 3794, 27–34, information on Nigeria, October 1978.

67. MVnR, op. 34, a.e. 3794, 27–34, information on Nigeria, October 1978. See also ibid., 35–44, relations between Bulgaria and Nigeria, October 1978.

68. MVnR, op. 34, a.e. 3792, 20–33, proposal, 16 November 1978.

69. *Arhitektura* (1977): 4, 13–22, quoted in Doytchinov, "Pragmatism, Not Ideology," 465.

70. MVnR, op. 34, a.e. 3794, 35–40, materials related Zhivkov's visit to Nigeria, 16–19 October 1978.

71. Apter, *The Pan-African Nation*, 45, 213.

72. Apter, *The Pan-African Nation*, 91–93.

73. Murtala Mohammed, "Foreword," in *Two Thousand Years of Nigerian Art*, by Ekpo Eyo (Lagos: Federal Department of Antiquities, 1977), 6.

74. Eyo, *Two Thousand Years of Nigerian Art*, 7.

75. Sarah Van Beurden, *Authentically African: Arts and the Transnational Politics of Congolese Culture* (Athens: Ohio University Press, 2015), 1, 3.

76. Apter, *The Pan-African Nation*, 42, 75.

77. Flora Edouwaye S. Kaplan, "Nigerian Museums: Envisaging Culture as National Identity," in *Museums and the Making of Ourselves: The Role of Objects in National Identity*, ed. Flora E. S. Kaplan and Flora S. Kaplan (Leicester, UK: Leicester University Press, 1996), 47.

78. Apter, *The Pan-African Nation*, 97–98.

79. Falola and Heaton, *A History of Nigeria*, 196.

80. MVnR, op. 35, a.e. 4165, work of the embassy in Lagos in 1978.

81. MVnR, op. 35, a.e. 4200, plan for 1300 events in Nigeria, 1979.

82. MVnR, op. 35, a.e. 4165, work of the embassy in Lagos in 1978.

83. MVnR, op. 35, a.e. 4200, plan for 1300 events in Nigeria, 1979.

84. MVnR, op. 38, a.e. 3838, 69, embassy in Lagos telegram, 20 February 1980.

85. MVnR, op. 35, a.e. 4186, 8–17, report on cultural-propaganda work in Nigeria in the first half of 1980.

86. MVnR, op. 36, a.e. 4609, embassy in Lagos correspondence, 1980.

87. MVnR, op. 36, a.e. 4648, 29–31, correspondence between embassy in Lagos, KK, and MVnR, March 1980.

88. MVnR, op. 38, a.e. 3802, 37–40, 62–66, memos on the position of Nigeria on key international issues, 1981.

89. MVnR, op. 35, a.e. 4171, 7–8, embassy in Lagos information, 5 October 1979.

90. MVnR, op. 36, a.e. 4645, 39–41, embassy in Lagos information, 27 February 1980.

91. MVnR, op. 36, a.e. 4623, 38–46, embassy in Lagos information on the exhibition *Children in Bulgaria*, 29 August 1980. Held during an event at the Red Cross headquarters in Lagos in August 1980, the exhibition marked the first anniversary of the Banner of Peace Assembly held in Sofia in 1979; the event also featured panels advertising the 1300th jubilee and the successes of contemporary Bulgaria. See also Ghodsee, *Second World, Second Sex*, for contacts between Bulgarian and Zambian women's activists.

92. MVnR, op. 36, a.e. 4620, 6, 7a, embassy in Lagos report, 1 February 1980.

93. MVnR, op. 36, a.e. 4571, 6–7, embassy in Lagos report, February 1980.

94. MVnR, op. 38, a.e. 3804, 2–4, information on the first official celebration of 1 May in Nigeria in 1981.

95. MVnR, op. 36, a.e. 4648, 36–39, embassy in Lagos information, April 1980.

96. MVnR, op. 36, a.e. 4648, 53–55, 56–58, embassy in Lagos information, 3 June 1980; "Agreement for Cooperation Between the Union of Bulgarian Artists and the Society of Nigerian Artists for the Period 1980–1981."

97. MVnR, op. 36, a.e. 4623, 20–29, informational-propaganda and cultural work in 1980.

98. MVnR, op. 36, a.e. 4648, 45–46, embassy in Lagos information, May 1980.

99. MVnR, op. 36, a.e. 4648, 69–70; ibid., a.e. 4623, 33–34, embassy in Lagos reports, July 1980.

100. MVnR, op. 36, a.e. 4648, 98, embassy in Lagos information, 16 November 1980.

101. MVnR, op. 36, a.e. 4623, 2–5, 16–17, and 18, embassy in Lagos reports, February and July 1980. Such combinations of historical and contemporary topics were evident during the visits in Kaduna, Bauchi, and Jos in February, and Port Harcourt in the state of Rivers in July.

102. MVnR, op. 38, a.e. 3804, 40–41, embassy in Lagos to MVnR, June 1981.

103. MVnR, op. 38, a.e. 3817, 4–6, embassy in Lagos report, 18 January 1981.

104. MVnR, op. 38, a.e. 3817, correspondence between MVnR and embassy in Lagos, 1981.

105. MVnR, op. 36, a.e. 4657, 1, embassy in Lagos to president Shagari, 7 February 1980.

106. MVnR, op. 38, a.e. 3838, 53–54, embassy in Lagos report, 15 May 1981; ibid., a.e. 3816, 11–14, information on cultural events in the first quarter of 1981.

107. MVnR, op. 38, a.e. 3816, 7–9, embassy in Lagos information, 3 March 1981.

108. MVnR, op. 38, a.e. 3816, 11–14 and 16–17, information on cultural events in the first quarter of 1981; and embassy in Lagos information, March 1981.

109. MVnR, op. 36, a.e. 4648, 53–55, embassy in Lagos information, 6 June 1980.

110. MVnR, op. 36, a.e. 4620, correspondence on cultural cooperation, 1980; and MVnR, op. 38, a.e. 3816, 2, embassy in Lagos information, 15 February 1981.

111. MVnR, op. 38, a.e. 3848, embassy in Lagos correspondence, 1981.

112. MVnR, op. 38, a.e. 3845, 21, embassy in Lagos telegram, 21 February 1981.

113. MVnR, op. 38, a.e. 3845, 31–32, embassy in Lagos information on the visit to the state of Benue in June 1981. To recognize the accomplishments of the Bulgarian lecturers at the Federal Polytechnic School in Ida, the embassy donated the photo exhibit *Electronics in Bulgaria* to the school.

114. MVnR, op. 38, a.e. 3805, 32–33, speech from September 1981; ibid., a.e. 3845, 49–50, embassy in Lagos information, September 1981.

115. MVnR, op. 38, a.e. 3805, 41–46.

116. MVnR, op. 38, a.e. 3824, 17–21; ibid., a.e. 3817, 4–6, embassy in Lagos reports, January 1981.

117. MVnR, op. 38, a.e. 3816, 2–2a, embassy in Lagos information, 15 February 1981.

118. MVnR, op. 38, a.e. 3805, 118–119, 121–123, embassy in Lagos reports, February 1981 and 7 March 1981.

119. Kalinovsky, *Laboratory of Socialist Development*, 7, also discusses the notion of *kul'turnost'* (culturedness) in Soviet development ideas.

120. Frederick Cooper, "Modernizing Bureaucrats, Backward Africans, and the Development Concept," in *International Development and the Social Sciences: Essays on the History and Politics of Knowledge*, ed. Frederick Cooper and Randall M. Packard (Berkeley: University of California Press, 1997), 64–92; and David Engerman, "Development Politics and the Cold War," *Diplomatic History* 41, no. 1 (2017): 5–7. See also, Frederick Cooper, "Writing the History of Development," *Journal of Modern European History* 8, no. 1 (2010): 5–23.

121. Cullather, "Development?," 642–643.

Epilogue

1. See Nikolai Vukov, "The 'Unmemorable' and the 'Unforgettable': 'Museumizing' the Socialist Past in Post-1989 Bulgaria," in *Past for the Eyes: East European Representations of Communism in Cinema and Museums after 1989*, ed. Oksana Sarkisova and Peter Apor (Budapest: Central European University Press, 2008), 307–334; and Zhivka Valiavicharska, "History's Restless Ruins: On Socialist Public Monuments in Postsocialist Bulgaria," *boundary 2* 41, no. 1 (2014): 171–201.

2. For a summary of the main trends in Bulgarian scholarship, see Gruev and Mishkova, *Bâlgarskiiat komunizâm*. For studies that put Bulgaria in a comparative context, see Maria Todorova, ed., *Remembering Communism: Genres of Representation* (New York: Social Science Research Council, 2010); and Maria Todorova, Augusta Dimou, and Stefan Troebst, eds., *Remembering Communism: Private and Public Recollections of Lived Experience in Southeast Europe* (Budapest: Central European University Press, 2014).

3. Two works of close associates are Nikolov, *Dâshteriata na nadezhdite*; and Raǐnov, *Liudmila*.

4. See writer Liubomir Levchev's commentary on occasion of the seventieth anniversary of Zhivkova's birth, "Smârtta niama rozhden den: Za bezsmârtieto vseki mig e novo nachalo," 22 November 2012, https://www.lentata.com/page_5160.html.

5. "Zhenata, koiato izprevari svoeto vreme," Facebook, 8 March 2014, https://www.facebook.com/Peoples.Republic.memories/photos/a.439625529435279.106942.371517049579461/681668758564287/?type=1.

6. http://www.foreignartmuseum.bg/bg/archive/temporary_exhibition.html, accessed 11 October 2012. Website discontinued.

7. The proceedings of the conference were published in Baeva, *Kulturnoto otvariane*. For the controversies surrounding the event, see Yavor Siderov, "Liudmila Zhivkova triabva da se istorizira," *Liberalen pregled*, 24 October 2012, http://www.librev.com/discussion-bulgaria-publisher/1816-2012-10-24-10-14-28. Two critical views include "Kniaginiata Liudmila Zhivkova," *Webcafe*, 31 October 2012, http://www.webcafe.bg/id_1550239094; and "Kakva ni e Liudmila Zhivkova," *Dnevnik*, 4 October 2012, http://www.dnevnik.bg/analizi/2012/10/04/1919600_kakva_ni_e_ljudmila_jivkova/.

8. Valentin Starchev, "Demokratsiiata otprishti energiiata na lumpena," *Sega*, 10 December 2005, http://www.segabg.com/article.php?issueid=2052&sectionid=5&id=0001001.

9. "Okonchatelno: Pametnikât pred NDK otiva vistoriiata," *Vesti*, 14 December 2014, https://www.vesti.bg/bulgaria/obshtestvo/okonchatelno-pametnikyt-pred-ndk-otiva-v-istoriiata-6029182; and "Pametnikât pred NDK—za i protiv," *Kultura*, 4 December 2012.

10. For the interwar monument, see "Lâvât ot Voinishkiia memorial na miastoto na pametnika pred NDK," *Ploshtad Slaveikov*, 4 July 2017, http://www.ploshtadslaveikov.com/lavat-ot-vojnishkiya-memorial-na-myastoto-na-pametnika-pred-ndk/; and "Gotov proekt za-voinishkiia pametnik ima ot godini, no memorial—ne," BTV, 18 July 2017, https://btvnovinite.bg/bulgaria/gotov-proekt-za-vojnishkija-pametnik-ima-ot-godini-no-memorial-ne.html.

11. See "Eyewitness: Buzludzha, Bulgaria," *Guardian*, 14 September 2014, https://www.theguardian.com/world/picture/2014/sep/14/eyewitness-bulgaria-derelict-monument; and "Visit an Eerie, Spaceship-Like Monument in the Balkan Mountains," *National Geographic*, 18 January 2018, https://www.nationalgeographic.com/travel/destinations/europe/bulgaria/things-to-do-buzludzha-monument/.

12. For the Getty Foundation announcement, see https://www.getty.edu/foundation/initiatives/current/keeping_it_modern/grants_awarded_2019.html. The website of the Buzludzha Project Foundation contains detailed information about the monument in English and Bulgarian: http://www.buzludzha-monument.com/.

13. For a positive evaluation of the exhibition, see an interview with Academician Vasil Gyuzelev, "Zlatoto na trakite nad 50 godini shestva iz Evropa," *Epicenter*, 18 April 2015, http://epicenter.bg/article/Zlatoto-na-trakite-nad-50-godini-shestva-iz-Evropa/71305/11/34. For criticism of Borisov's self-promotion, see "Predozirane: Izlozhbata v Luvâra ni izvadi ot izolatsiiata v Evropa," *Dnevnik*, 15 April 2015, http://www.dnevnik.bg/bulgaria/2015/04/15/2512931_predozirane_izlojbata_v_luvura_ni_izvadi_ot/.

14. Excerpts from the minutes of the State Council's meeting, "Sbâdna se mechtata na Liudmila Zhivkova," *Dnevnik*, 15 April 2015, http://www.dnevnik.bg/bulgaria/2015/04/15/2513232_iz_stenogramata_na_ministerskiia_suvet_sbudna_se/.

15. Dimitrov, *Za kozhata*.

16. For a report that makes connections to the socialist past, see "Otkrivaneto na 'Kvadrat 500'—'Dozhiviahme da se sâizmervame s velichieto na evropeiskoto izkustvo,'" *Dnevnik*, 28 May 2015, http://www.dnevnik.bg/bulgaria/2015/05/28/2542514_otkrivaneto_na_kvadrat_500_-_dojiviahme_da_se/.

17. For Rusev's opinions, see his interview in *Dnevnik*, "Rabotata mi po 'Kvadrat 500' e avtorska, ne me interesuva kakvo pishe vâv feisbuk," 25 May 2015, http://www.dnevnik.bg/intervju/2015/05/25/2539919_svetlin_rusev_rabotata_mi_po_kvadrat_500_e_avtorska_ne/. For a critical view, see "Kvadrat 500: Magnum opus na Svetlin Rusev," *Ploshtad Slaveikov*, 29 May 2015, http://www.ploshtadslaveikov.com/kvadrat-500-magnum-opus-na-svetlin-rusev/.

Bibliography

Archives

Bulgaria

Archives of the Ministry of Foreign Affairs (MVnR), Sofia

op. 32–36 (1976–1980) and op. 38 (1981), records relating to Bulgarian foreign relations with a number of countries (countries are arranged alphabetically in Bulgarian, as listed below):

Austria (1), the United States (5), Argentina (6), Great Britain (13), Germany (17), Greece (18), India (26), Iraq (29), Mexico (45), Poland (56), Romania (58), Russia (64), Turkey (66), Hungary (67), France (71), Czechoslovakia (78), Yugoslavia (80), Japan (82), and Nigeria (100)

Central State Archive (TsDA), Sofia

f. 1B, Central Committee of BKP (various)

f. 1B, op. 55, Information-Sociological Center of BKP (1971–1990)

f. 1B, op. 65, Plenums of the Central Committee of BKP (1976–1989)

f. 1B, op. 66 and op. 67, Politburo of the Central Committee of BKP (1976–1984)

f. 1B, op. 78, Cultural Department of the Central Committee of BKP (1974–1989)

f. 141, Slavic Committee (Organization for the Bulgarians Abroad)

f. 405, Committee for Culture

f. 720, Bulgarian Photography

f. 990, National Coordinating Committee "Thirteen Centuries Bulgaria" (microfilm)

Hungary

Open Society Archives (OSA), Budapest

Radio Free Europe / Radio Liberty Research Institute

United Kingdom

The National Archives (TNA), Kew

BW 18, British Council
FCO 28, Foreign Office and Foreign and Commonwealth Office
FCO 34, Foreign Office and Foreign and Commonwealth Office: East-West Contacts Department

United States

Hoover Institution Archives, Stanford, California

Kyril Drenikoff papers
Dora Gabensky papers
Radio Free Europe / Radio Liberty Broadcast and Corporate Records
Spas Raikin papers
Ivan Slavov papers

Library of Congress, Washington, DC

Bulgarian Newspaper Collection

National Archives (NARA), College Park, Maryland

RG 59: General Records of the Department of State Central Foreign Policy File, 1973–1979, Electronic Telegrams
RG 306: US Information Agency

Perry Country Public Library, New Lexington, Ohio

Januarius MacGahan Collection

Periodicals

Official Bulgarian Periodicals

Bulgaria (later *Bulgaria Today*)
Bulgarian Horizons
Kulturen front (Cultural front)
Literaturen front (Literary front)
Obzor (Overview)
Otechestven front (Fatherland front)

Rabotnichesko delo (Workers' deed)
Slaviani (Slavs)
Vecherni novini (Nightly news)

Émigré Press

Bâdeshte (Future), Paris
Bâlgarski voĭn (Bulgarian soldier), Frankfurt
Borba (Struggle), Chicago
Luch (Ray), Los Angeles
Spektâr (Spectrum), Munich
Svoboden narod (Free People), Vienna

Secondary Sources

Abrams, Bradley F. *The Struggle for the Soul of the Nation: Czech Culture and the Rise of Communism*. Lanham, MD: Rowman & Littlefield, 2004.

Apostolova, Raia. "Duty and Debt under the Ethos of Internationalism: The Case of the Vietnamese Workers in Bulgaria." *Journal of Vietnamese Studies* 12, no. 1 (2017): 101–125.

Appadurai, Arjun. *Modernity at Large: Cultural Dimensions of Globalization*. Minneapolis: University of Minnesota Press, 1996.

Applebaum, Rachel. *Empire of Friends: Soviet Power and Socialist Internationalism in Cold War Czechoslovakia*. Ithaca, NY: Cornell University Press, 2019.

Apter, Andrew. *The Pan-African Nation: Oil and the Spectacle of Culture in Nigeria*. Chicago: University of Chicago Press, 2005.

Atanasova, Ivanka Nedeva. "Lyudmila Zhivkova and the Paradox of Ideology and Identity in Communist Bulgaria." *East European Politics & Societies* 18, no. 2 (2004): 278–315.

Atanasova, Violina. "Liudmila Zhivkova i ambitsioznite bâlgarski proekti v Indiia." In Baeva, *Kulturnoto otvariane*, 78–84.

Avramov, Rumen. *Ikonomika na "Vâzroditelniia protses."* Sofia: CAS, 2016.

Avramov, Rumen. *Pari i de/stabilizatsiia v Bâlgariia 1948–1989*. Sofia: Siela, 2008.

Babiracki, Patryk, and Kenyon Zimmer, eds. *Cold War Crossings: International Travel and Exchange across the Soviet Bloc, 1940s–1960s*. College Station: Texas A&M University Press, 2014.

Baev, Jordan. "The Establishment of Bulgarian-West German Diplomatic Relations with the Coordinating Framework of the Warsaw Pact." *Journal of Cold War Studies* 18, no. 3 (2016): 158–180.

Baeva, Iskra, ed. *Kulturnoto otvariane na Bâlgariia kâm sveta*. Sofia: Universitetsko izdatelstvo Sv. Kliment Ohridski, 2013.

Baeva, Iskra, and Evgeniia Kalinova. *Bâlgarskite prehodi, 1939–2002*. Sofia: Paradigma, 2002.

Bange, Oliver, and Gottfried Niedhart, eds. *Helsinki 1975 and the Transformation of Europe*. New York: Berghahn Books, 2008.

Bechev, Dimitar. *Historical Dictionary of North Macedonia*. 2nd ed. Lanham, MD: Rowman & Littlefield, 2019.

Bechev, Dimitar. *Rival Power: Russia's Influence in Southeast Europe*. New Haven, CT: Yale University Press, 2017.

Bechmann Pedersen, Sune, and Christian Noack, eds. *Tourism and Travel during the Cold War: Negotiating Tourist Experiences across the Iron Curtain*. New York: Routledge, 2019.

Belmonte, Laura A. *Selling the American Way: U.S. Propaganda and the Cold War*. Philadelphia: University of Pennsylvania Press, 2008.

Blagov, Krum. *Zagadkata Liudmila Zhivkova*. Sofia: Reporter, 2012.

Bockman, Johanna. *Markets in the Name of Socialism: The Left-Wing Origins of Neoliberalism*. Stanford, CA: Stanford University Press, 2011.

Bockman, Johanna. "Socialist Globalization against Capitalist Neocolonialism: The Economic Ideas behind the New International Economic Order." *Humanity: An International Journal of Human Rights, Humanitarianism and Development* 6, no. 1 (2015): 109–128.

Boden, Ragna. "Cold War Economics: Soviet Aid to Indonesia." *Journal of Cold War Studies* 10, no. 3 (2008): 110–128.

Boia, Lucian. *History and Myth in Romanian Consciousness*. Budapest: Central European University Press, 2001.

Bolton, Jonathan. *Worlds of Dissent: Charter 77, the Plastic People of the Universe, and Czech Culture under Communism*. Cambridge, MA: Harvard University Press, 2012.

Borstelmann, Thomas. *The 1970s: A New Global History from Civil Rights to Economic Inequality*. Princeton, NJ: Princeton University Press, 2011.

Brands, Hal. *Latin America's Cold War*. Cambridge, MA: Harvard University Press, 2010.

Braun, Aurel. *Small-State Security in the Balkans*. London: Macmillan, 1983.

Bren, Paulina. *The Greengrocer and His TV: The Culture of Communism after the 1968 Prague Spring*. Ithaca, NY: Cornell University Press, 2010.

Bren, Paulina, and Mary Neuburger, eds. *Communism Unwrapped: Consumption in Cold War Eastern Europe*. New York: Oxford University Press, 2012.

Brown, Kate. *Plutopia: Nuclear Families, Atomic Cities, and the Great Soviet and American Plutonium Disasters*. New York: Oxford University Press, 2013.

Brown, Keith. *Loyal unto Death: Trust and Terror in Revolutionary Macedonia*. Bloomington: Indiana University Press, 2013.

Brown, Keith. *Macedonia's Child-Grandfathers: The Transnational Politics of Memory, Exile, and Return, 1948–1998*. Donald W. Treadgold Papers 38. Seattle, WA: Henry M. Jackson School of International Studies, University of Washington, 2003.

Brunnbauer, Ulf. *Globalizing Southeastern Europe: Emigrants, America, and the State since the Late Nineteenth Century*. Lanham, MD: Lexington Books, 2016.

Brunnbauer, Ulf. "Making Bulgarians Socialist: The Fatherland Front in Communist Bulgaria, 1944–1989." *East European Politics and Societies* 22, no. 1 (2008): 44–79.

Brunnbauer, Ulf. *Sotsialisticheskiiat nachin na zhivot: Ideologiia, obshtestvo, semeistvo i politika v Bŭlgariia (1944–1989)*. Translated by Rumiana Stankova. Sofia: Elias Kaneti, 2010.

Brunnbauer, Ulf, and Karin Taylor. "Creating a 'Socialist Way of Life': Family and Reproduction Policies in Bulgaria, 1944–1989." *Continuity and Change* 19, no. 2 (2004): 283–312.

Caute, David. *The Dancer Defects: The Struggle for Cultural Supremacy during the Cold War.* New York: Oxford University Press, 2003.

Chandra, Bipan, Mridula Mukherjee, and Aditya Mukherjee. *India after Independence, 1947–2000.* New York: Oxford University Press, 2000.

Cherkasov, Iu., ed. *Ekonomicheskie problemy Afriki: Stat'i bolgarskikh uchenykh.* Moscow: Nauka, 1974.

Clifford, James. "Diasporas." *Cultural Anthropology* 9, no. 3 (1994): 302–338.

Conklin, Alice. *A Mission to Civilize: The Republican Idea of Empire in France and West Africa, 1895–1930.* Stanford, CA: Stanford University Press, 1997.

Connelly, Matthew. "Future Shock: The End of the World as They Knew It." In Ferguson et al., *The Shock of the Global*, 337–350.

Cooper, Frederick. *Africa since 1940: The Past of the Present.* Cambridge: Cambridge University Press, 2002.

Cooper, Frederick. "Modernizing Bureaucrats, Backward Africans, and the Development Concept." In *International Development and the Social Sciences: Essays on the History and Politics of Knowledge*, edited by Frederick Cooper and Randall M. Packard, 64–92. Berkeley: University of California Press, 1997.

Cooper, Frederick. "Writing the History of Development." *Journal of Modern European History* 8, no. 1 (2010): 5–23.

Crump, Laurien, and Susanna Erlandsson, eds. *Margins for Manoeuvre in Cold War Europe: The Influence of Smaller Powers.* New York: Routledge, 2019.

Cullather, Nick. "Development? Its History: Research Note." *Diplomatic History* 24, no. 4 (2000): 641–653.

Daskalov, Georgi. *Bâlgariia i Gârtsiia: Ot razriv kâm pomirenie, 1944–1964.* Sofia: Universitetsko izdatelstvo Sv. Kliment Ohridski, 2004.

Daskalov, Rumen, and Tchavdar Marinov, eds. *National Ideologies and Language Policies.* Vol. 1 of *Entangled Histories of the Balkans.* Leiden: Brill, 2013.

Daskalov, Rumen, and Alexander Vezenkov, eds. *Shared Pasts, Disputed Legacies.* Vol. 3 of *Entangled Histories of the Balkans.* Leiden: Brill, 2015.

Daskalov, Rumen, Diana Mishkova, Tchavdar Marinov, and Alexander Vezenkov, eds. *Concepts, Approaches, and Self-Representations.* Vol. 4 of *Entangled Histories of the Balkans.* Leiden: Brill, 2017.

David-Fox, Michael. *Showcasing the Great Experiment: Cultural Diplomacy and Western Visitors to the Soviet Union, 1921–1941.* New York: Oxford University Press, 2011.

Deletant, Dennis. "Romania's Return to Europe: Between Politics and Culture." In Detrez and Segaert, *Europe and the Historical Legacies*, 83–98.

Deletant, Dennis, and Mihail Ionescu. "Romania and the Warsaw Pact, 1955–1989." *Cold War International History Project*, Working Paper 43 (April 2004), 1–103.

Detrez, Raymond, and Barbara Segaert, eds. *Europe and the Historical Legacies in the Balkans.* New York: Peter Lang, 2008.

Dimitrov, Bozhidar. *Za kozhata na edno chenge.* Sofia: Unikart, 2015.

Dimitrov, Emil. "Iubileiat kato proekt: Târzhestvata prez 1929 i 'bâlgarskata ideiia.'" *Sledva* 7 (2003): 72–83.

Dimitrov, Teodor. *Ianuari Makgahan, 1844–1878: Biografiia, dokumenti i materiali.* Sofia: Nauka i izkustvo, 1977.

Doĭnov, Plamen. *Bâlgarskiiat sotsrealizâm 1956 1968 1989: Norma i kriza v literaturata na NRB.* Sofia: Siela, 2011.

Döşemeci, Mehmet. "Cutting through the Cold War: The EEC and Turkey's Great Westernization Debate." In Rajak, *The Balkans in the Cold War,* 331–350.

Dosev, Georgi, and Stefan Zhelev, eds. *Bâlgariia, 40 godini po pâtia na sotsializma.* Sofia: Sofiia Press, 1984.

Doytchinov, Grigor. "Pragmatism, Not Ideology: Bulgarian Architectural Exports to the 'Third World.'" *The Journal of Architecture* 17, no. 3 (2012): 453–473.

Dragostinova, Theodora. *Between Two Motherlands: Nationality and Emigration among the Greeks of Bulgaria, 1900–1949.* Ithaca, NY: Cornell University Press, 2011.

Dragostinova, Theodora. "The East in the West: Bulgarian Culture in the United States of America during the Global 1970s." *Journal of Contemporary History* 53, no. 1 (2018): 212–239.

Dragostinova, Theodora. "Empty Fountains: Communist-Era Monuments Revisited." *Origins* 4 (2014). Accessed 13 July 2018, http://origins.osu.edu/connecting-history/1142014-empty-fountains-communist-era-monuments-revisited.

Dragostinova, Theodora. "The 'Natural Ally' of the 'Developing World': Bulgarian Culture in India and Mexico." *Slavic Review* 77, no. 3 (2018): 661–684.

Dragostinova, Theodora. "On 'Strategic Frontiers': Debating the Borders of the Post–Second World War Balkans." *Contemporary European History* 27, no. 3 (2018): 387–411.

Dragostinova, Theodora, and Malgorzata Fidelis. "Introduction." In "Beyond the Iron Curtain: Eastern Europe and the Global Cold War." Special issue, *Slavic Review* 77, no. 3 (2018): 577–587.

Eberl, Immo. "Der hl. Methodius und Ellwangen." In *Die Vita des Heiligen Methodius,* edited by Spatrak Paskalevski, 9–13. Munich: Biblion Verlag, 2006.

Elenkov, Ivan. "Kulturnata politika." In Znepolski, *Istoriia na Narodna Republika Bâlgariia,* 550–551.

Elenkov, Ivan. *Kulturniiat front: Bâlgarskata kultura prez epohata na komunizma—politichesko upravlenie, ideologicheski osnovaniia, institutsionalni rezhimi.* Sofia: Siela, 2008.

Elenkov, Ivan. *Trud, radost, otdih i kultura.* Sofia: CAS, 2013.

Endy, Christopher. "Power and Culture in the West." In Immerman and Goedde, *The Oxford Handbook of the Cold War,* 323–340.

Engerman, David. "Development Politics and the Cold War." *Diplomatic History* 41, no. 1 (2017): 1–19.

Engerman, David. "Ideology and the Origins of the Cold War, 1917–1962." In Leffler and Westad, *Cambridge History of the Cold War,* 20–43.

Engerman, David. "Learning from the East: Soviet Experts and India in the Era of Competitive Coexistence." *Comparative Studies of South Asia, Africa and the Middle East* 33, no. 2 (2013): 227–238.

Engerman, David. *The Price of Aid: The Economic Cold War in India.* Cambridge, MA: Harvard University Press, 2018.

Engerman, David. "The Second World's Third World." *Kritika: Explorations in Russian and Eurasian History* 12, no. 1 (2011): 183–211.

Eyo, Ekpo. *Two Thousand Years of Nigerian Art*. Lagos: Federal Department of Antiquities, 1977.

Falola, Toyin, and Matthew M. Heaton. *A History of Nigeria*. Cambridge: Cambridge University Press, 2008.

Faucher, Charlotte. "Cultural Diplomacy and International Cultural Relations in Twentieth-Century Europe." *Contemporary European History* 25, no. 2 (2016): 373–385.

Feinberg, Melissa. *Curtain of Lies: The Battle over Truth in Stalinist Eastern Europe*. New York: Oxford University Press, 2017.

Ferguson, Niall, Charles Maier, Erez Manela, and Daniel J. Sargent, eds. *The Shock of the Global: The 1970s in Perspective*. Cambridge, MA: The Belknap Press of Harvard University Press, 2010.

Fidelis, Malgorzata. *Imagining the World: Youth and the Global Sixties in Poland*. New York: Oxford University Press, forthcoming.

Fidelis, Malgorzata. "The Other Marxists: Making Sense of International Student Revolts in Poland in the Global Sixties." *Zeitschrift für Ostmitteleuropa-Forschung* 62, no. 3 (2013): 425–449.

Fidelis, Malgorzata. "Pleasures and Perils of Socialist Modernity: New Scholarship on Post-War Eastern Europe." *Contemporary European History* 26, no. 3 (2017): 533–544.

Fink, Carole, and Bernd Schäfer, eds. *Ostpolitik, 1969–1974: European and Global Responses*. New York: Cambridge University Press, 2008.

Fol, Aleksandâr et al., eds. *Bâlgariia prez vekovete: Ochertsi*. Sofia: Nauka i izkustvo, 1982.

Fosler-Lussier, Danielle. *Music in America's Cold War Diplomacy*. Oakland: University of California Press, 2015.

Fosler-Lussier, Danielle. "Music Pushed, Music Pulled: Cultural Diplomacy, Globalization, and Imperialism." *Diplomatic History* 36, no. 1 (2012): 53–64.

Frieberg, Annika. *Peace at All Costs: Catholic Intellectuals, Journalists, and Media in Postwar Polish-German Reconciliation*. New York: Berghahn Books, 2019.

Garrard-Burnett, Virginia, Mark Atwood Lawrence, and Julio E. Moreno, eds. *Beyond the Eagle's Shadow: New Histories of Latin America's Cold War*. Albuquerque: University of New Mexico Press, 2013.

Gerasimov, Bogomil. *Diplomatsiia v zonata na kaktusa*. Sofia: Trud, 1998.

Ghodsee, Kristen. *Muslim Lives in Eastern Europe: Gender, Ethnicity, and the Transformation of Islam in Postsocialist Bulgaria*. Princeton, NJ: Princeton University Press, 2010.

Ghodsee, Kristen. "Pressuring the Politburo: The Committee of the Bulgarian Women's Movement and State Socialist Feminism." *Slavic Review* 73, no. 3 (2014): 538–562.

Ghodsee, Kristen. *Second World, Second Sex: Socialist Women's Activism and Global Solidarity during the Cold War*. Durham, NC: Duke University Press, 2019.

Gigova, Irina. "The Feeble Charm of National(ist) Communism: Intellectuals and Cultural Politics in Zhivkov's Bulgaria." In *Beyond Mosque, Church, and State: Alternative Narratives of the Nation in the Balkans*, edited by Theodora Dragostinova and Yana Hashamova, 151–180. Budapest: Central European University Press, 2016.

Gigova, Irina. "Writers of the Nation: Intellectual Identity in Bulgaria, 1939–1953." PhD diss., University of Illinois Urbana-Champaign, 2005.

Gilburd, Eleonory. "The Revival of Soviet Internationalism in the Mid to Late 1950s." In *The Thaw: Soviet Society and Culture during the 1950s and 1960s*, edited by Eleonory Gilburd and Denis Kozlov, 362–401. Toronto: University of Toronto Press, 2012.

Gilburd, Eleonory. *To See Paris and Die: The Soviet Lives of Western Culture*. Cambridge, MA: The Belknap Press of Harvard University Press, 2018.

Goedde, Petra. "Global Cultures." In *Global Interdependence: The World after 1945*, edited by Akira Iriye, 537–678. Cambridge, MA: Harvard University Press, 2014.

Gorsuch, Anne E., and Diane Koenker, eds. *The Socialist Sixties: Crossing Borders in the Second World*. Bloomington: Indiana University Press, 2013.

Gorsuch, Anne E., and Diane Koenker, eds. *Turizm: The Russian and East European Tourist under Capitalism and Socialism*. Ithaca, NY: Cornell University Press, 2006.

Gould-Davies, Nigel. "The Logic of Soviet Cultural Diplomacy." *Diplomatic History* 27, no. 2 (2003): 193–214.

Grivec, Franc. "Der hl. Methodius in Ellwangen." In *Ellwangen 764–1964: Beiträge und Untersuchungen zur Zwölfhundert-Jahnfeier*, edited by Viktor Burr, 153–159. Ellwangen: Schwabenverlag, 1964.

Grozev, Kostadin, and Jordan Baev. "Bulgaria, Balkan Diplomacy, and the Road to Helsinki." In Bange and Niedhart, *Helsinki 1975*, 160–174.

Gruev, Mihail. "Komunisticheskiiat elit v Bâlgariia: Genezis i evoliutsiia." *Razum* 1 (2005): 215–224.

Gruev, Mihail. "Liudmila Zhivkova—pâtiat kâm agni ioga." In *Prelomni vremena: Iubileen sbornik v chest na 65-godishninata na profesor Liubomir Ognianov*, edited by Evgeniia Kalinova, Mihail Gruev, and Liudmila Zidarova, 796–816. Sofia: Universitetsko izdatelstvo Sv. Kliment Ohridski, 2006.

Gruev, Mihail. "Politicheskoto razvitie na Bâlgariia." In Znepolski, *Istoriia*, 161–164.

Gruev, Mihail, and Alexeï Kalionski. *Vâzroditelniiat protses: Miusiulmanskite obshtnosti i komunistichedkiia rezhim*. Sofia: Siela, 2008.

Gruev, Mihail, and Diana Mishkova. *Bâlgarskiiat komunizâm: Debati i interpretatsii*. Sofia: CAS, 2013.

Guha, Ramachandra. *India after Gandhi: The History of the World's Largest Democracy*. London: Macmillan, 2007.

Guistino, Cathleen M., Catherine J. Plum, and Alexander Vari, eds. *Socialist Escapes: Breaking Away from Ideology and Everyday Routine in Eastern Europe, 1945–1989*. New York: Berghahn Books, 2015.

Hale, William. *Turkish Foreign Policy since 1774*. New York: Routledge, 2012.

Hatzivassiliou, Evanthis. "Negotiating with the Enemy: The Normalization of Greek-Bulgarian Relations." *Journal of Southeast European and Black Sea Studies* 4, no. 1 (2004): 140–61.

Hessler, Julie. "Death of an African Student in Moscow—Race, Politics, and the Cold War." *Cahiers du monde Russe* 47, nos. 1–2 (2006): 33–63.

Hodge, Joseph Morgan. "Writing the History of Development (Part 2: Longer, Deeper, Wider)." *Humanity: An International Journal of Human Rights, Humanitarianism and Development* 7, no. 1 (2016): 125–174.

Hong, Young-Sun. *Cold War Germany, the Third World, and the Global Humanitarian Regime*. New York: Cambridge University Press, 2015.

Howell, Jude. "The End of an Era: The Rise and Fall of GDR Aid." *Journal of Modern African Studies* 32, no. 2 (1994): 305–328.

Hristov, Hristo. *Ubiîte "Skitnik": Bâlgarskata i Britanskata dârzhâvna politika po sluchaia Georgi Markov*. Sofia: Siela, 2006.

Hristova, Nataliia. *Spetsifika na bâlgarskoto "disidenstvo": Vlast i inteligentsiia, 1956–1989 g*. Plovdiv: Letera, 2005.

Iacob, Bogdan C. "Southeast by Global South: The Balkans, UNESCO, and the Cold War." In *Alternative Globalizations: Eastern Europe and the Postcolonial World*, edited by James Mark, Artemy M. Kalinovski, and Steffi Marung, 251–227. Bloomington: Indiana University Press, 2020.

Iandolo, Alessandro. "The Rise and Fall of the 'Soviet Model of Development' in West Africa, 1957–64." *Cold War History* 12, no. 4 (2012): 683–704.

Iber, Patrick. *Neither Peace nor Freedom: The Cultural Cold War in Latin America*. Cambridge, MA: Harvard University Press, 2015.

Ifidon, Ehimika A., and Charles O. Osarumwense. "Politics without Commerce? Explaining the Discontinuity in Soviet-Nigerian Relations, 1971–1979." *African and Asian Studies* 14, no. 4 (2015): 289–314.

Immerman, Richard H., and Petra Goedde, eds. *The Oxford Handbook of the Cold War*. Oxford: Oxford University Press, 2013.

Iordachi, Constantin. "Diplomacy and the Making of a Geopolitical Question: The Bulgarian-Romanian Conflict over Dobrudja, 1878–1947." In Daskalov et al., *Concepts, Approaches, and Self-Representations*, 291–393.

Iriye, Akira. *Cultural Internationalism and World Order*. Baltimore, MD: Johns Hopkins University Press, 1997.

Iriye, Akira, ed. *Global Interdependence: The World after 1945*. Cambridge, MA: Harvard University Press, 2014.

Iriye, Akira. "Historicizing the Cold War." In Immerman and Goedde, *The Oxford Handbook of the Cold War*, 15–31.

Iriye, Akira. "Making a Transnational World." In Iriye, *Global Interdependence*, 681–847.

Ivancheva, Mariya. "Paternalistic Internationalism and (De)colonial Practices of Cold War Higher Education Exchange: Bulgaria's Connections with Cuba and Angola." *Journal of Labor and Society* 22, no. 4 (2019): 733–748.

Ivanov, Martin. "Ikonomika na komunisticheska Bâlgariia." In Znepolski, *Istoriia*, 314–321.

Ivanova, Veneta. "Occult Communism: Culture, Science and Spirituality in Late Socialist Bulgaria." PhD diss., University of Illinois Urbana-Champaign, 2016.

Joseph, Gilbert M. "Border Crossings and the Remaking of Latin American Cold War Studies." *Cold War History* 19, no. 1 (2019): 141–170.

Joseph, Gilbert M., Anne Rubenstein, and Eric Zolov, eds. *Fragments of a Golden Age: The Politics of Culture in Mexico since 1940*. Durham, NC: Duke University Press, 2001.

Joseph, Gilbert M., and Daniela Spenser, eds. *In from the Cold: Latin America's New Encounter with the Cold War*. Durham, NC: Duke University Press, 2008.

Judt, Tony. *Postwar: A History of Europe since 1945*. New York: Penguin, 2005.

Kalinova, Evgeniia. *Bâlgarskata kultura i politicheskiiat imperativ, 1944–1989*. Sofia: Paradigma, 2011.

Kalinova, Evgeniia. "Iztâniavashtata zheliazna zavesa Bâlgariia-Gârtsiia." In *Bâlgariia i Evropa prez sâvremennata epoha: Sbornik v chest na prof. D. Sirkov*, edited by Dragomir Draganov, Dimitâr Dimitrov, and Petko Boev, 194–215. Veliko Tarnovo: Faber, 2010.

Kalinova, Evgeniia. "Politikata na Liudmila Zhivkova za kulturnoto otvariane na Bâlgariia kâm sveta—predpostavki i spetsifika," in Baeva, *Kulturnoto otvariane*, 39–55.

Kalinovsky, Artemy M. "The Cold War in South and Central Asia." In Kalinovsky and Daigle, *The Routledge Handbook of the Cold War*, 178–191.

Kalinovsky, Artemy M. *Laboratory of Socialist Development: Cold War Politics and Decolonization in Soviet Tajikistan*. Ithaca, NY: Cornell University Press, 2018.

Kalinovsky, Artemy M., and Craig Daigle, eds. *The Routledge Handbook of the Cold War*. New York: Routledge, 2016.

Kamenov, Evgeni, ed. *Afrika: Politiko-ikonomicheski spravochnik*. Sofia: Partizdat, 1973.

Kamenov, E., T. Vulchev, and E. Malhasian. "Ekonomicheskie sviazi Bolgarii s razvivaiushtimisia stranami." In Cherkasov, *Ekonomicheskie problemy Afriki*, 42–58.

Kamusella, Tomasz. *Ethnic Cleansing during the Cold War: The Forgotten 1989 Expulsion of Turks from Communist Bulgaria*. London: Routledge, 2018.

Kandilarov, Evgeniĭ. *Bâlgariia i Iaponiia: Ot Studenata voĭna kâm XXI vek*. Sofia: Damian Iakov, 2009.

Kandilarov, Evgeniĭ. "Liudmila Zhivkova i kulturnata diplomatsiia kâm Iaponiia." In Baeva, *Kulturnoto otvariane*, 63–77.

Kaplan, Flora Edouwaye S. "Nigerian Museums: Envisaging Culture as National Identity." In *Museums and the Making of "Ourselves": The Role of Objects in National Identity*, edited by Flora E. S. Kaplan and Flora S. Kaplan, 45–78. New York: Leicester University Press, 1996.

Karamouzi, Eirini. *Greece, the EEC and the Cold War, 1974–1979: The Second Enlargement*. Basingstoke: Palgrave Macmillan, 2014.

Karamouzi, Eirini. "Managing the 'Helsinki Spirit' in the Balkans: The Greek Initiative for Balkan Co-operation, 1975–1976." *Diplomacy & Statecraft* 24, no. 4 (2013): 597–618.

Keck-Szajbel, Mark, and Dariusz Stola, eds. Introduction to "Crossing the Borders of Friendship: Mobility across Communist Borders." Special section, *East European Politics and Societies* 29, no. 1 (2015): 92–95.

Keller, Renata. *Mexico's Cold War: Cuba, the United States, and the Legacy of the Mexican Revolution*. New York: Cambridge University Press, 2015.

Kenarov, Dimiter. "A Captivating Mind." *The Nation*, 7 April 2014. https://www.thenation.com/article/archive/captivating-mind/.

Khalid, Adeeb. "Backwardness and the Quest for Civilization: Early Soviet Central Asia in Comparative Perspective." *Slavic Review* 65, no. 2 (Summer 2006): 231–251.

Kiriakov, Boĭko. "Dârzhavata sreshtu emigratsiiata." In Gruev and Mishkova, *Bâlgarskiiat komunizâm*, 195–214.

Kirkwood, Burton. *The History of Mexico*. Santa Barbara, CA: Greenwood Press, 2010.

Kornai, János. *Economics of Shortage*. Amsterdam: North-Holland, 1980.

Kostadinova, Tonka. "Bâlgaro-grâtski otnosheniia prez 70-te godini na XX vek—aspekti na dvustrannoto sâtrudnichestvo i regionalnata integratsiia." In *Evropeiski integratsionni protsesi prez 70-te godini na XX vek*, edited by Iskra Baeva, 183–200. Sofia: Universitetsko izdatelstvo Sv. Kliment Ohridski, 2014.

Kostov, Chris. *Contested Ethnic Identity: The Case of Macedonian Immigrants in Toronto, 1900–1996*. Bern: Peter Lang, 2010.

Kourkouvelas, Lykourgos. "Détente as a Strategy: Greece and the Communist World, 1974–9." *The International History Review* 35, no. 5 (2013): 1052–1067.

Kux, Dennis. *Estranged Democracies: India and the United States, 1941–1991*. Thousand Oaks, CA: Sage, 1993.

Latham, Michael E. "The Cold War in the Third World, 1963–1975." In Leffler and Westad, *Cambridge History of the Cold War*, 258–280.

Lawrence, Mark Atwood. "The Rise and Fall of Nonalignment." In McMahon, *The Cold War in the Third World*, 139–155.

Leffler, Melvyn P., and Odd Arne Westad, eds. *The Cambridge History of the Cold War*. New York: Cambridge University Press, 2016.

MacGahan, Januarius. *The Turkish Atrocities in Bulgaria: Letters of the Special Commissioner of the "Daily News."* London: Bradbury, Agnew & Co., 1876.

Marcheva, Iliana, and Mariia Radeva, eds. *Bâlgariski darzhavnitsi, 1944–1989*. Sofia: Skorpio, 2005.

Mark, James, and Péter Apor. "Socialism Goes Global: Decolonization and the Making of a New Culture of Internationalism in Socialist Hungary, 1956–1989." *Journal of Modern History* 87, no. 4 (2015): 852–891.

Mark, James, Bogdan C. Iacob, Tobias Rupprecht, and Ljubica Spaskovska. *1989: A Global History of Eastern Europe*. Cambridge: Cambridge University Press, 2019.

Mark, James, Artemy Kalinovsky, and Steffi Marung, eds. *Alternative Globalizations: Eastern Europe and the Postcolonial World*. Bloomington: Indiana University Press, 2020.

Mark, James, and Quinn Slobodian. "Eastern Europe in the Global History of Decolonization." In *The Oxford Handbook of the Ends of Empire*, edited by Martin Thomas and Andrew Thompson. Oxford: Oxford University Press, 2018. https://doi.org/10.1093/oxfordhb/9780198713197.013.20.

Marinov, Chavdar. "Ot internatsionalizâm kâm natsionalizâm: Komunisticheskiiat rezhim, Makedonskiiat vâpros i politikata kâm etnicheskite i religioznite obshtnosti." In Znepolski, *Istoriia*, 479–529.

Marinov, Tchavdar. "Ancient Thrace in the Modern Imagination: Ideological Aspects of the Construction of Thracian Studies in Southeast Europe (Romania, Greece, Bulgaria)." In Daskalov and Vezenkov, *Shared Pasts, Disputed Legacies*, 10–117.

Marinov, Tchavdar. *La question macédonienne de 1944 à nos jours: Communisme et nationalisme dans les Balkans*. Paris: L'Harmattan, 2010.

Markov, Georgi. *Zadochni reportazhi za Bâlgariia*. Sofia: Siela, 2008.

Mastny, Vojtech. "The Soviet Union's Partnership with India." *Journal of Cold War Studies* 12, no. 3 (2010): 50–90.

Matusevich, Maxim. "Black in the U.S.S.R.: Africans, African Americans, and the Soviet Society." *Transition: An International Review* 100, no. 1 (2009): 56–75.

Matusevich, Maxim. "An Exotic Subversive: Africa, Africans, and the Soviet Everyday." *Race and Class* 49, no. 4 (2008): 57–81.

Matusevich, Maxim. "Expanding the Boundaries of the Black Atlantic: African Students as Soviet Moderns." *Ab Imperio*, no. 2 (2012): 325–350.

Matusevich, Maxim. *No Easy Row for a Russian Hoe: Ideology and Pragmatism in Russian-Nigerian Relations, 1960–1991*. Trenton, NJ: Africa World Press, 2003.

Mavrodin, Corina. "Denuclearisation and Regional Cooperation: Romania's Tactical Approaches to Escaping Bloc Rigidities." In Crump and Erlandsson, *Margins for Manoeuvre*, 187–204.

Mazower, Mark. "Histories of the Big and Small: An Interview with Mark Mazower." Toynbee Prize Foundation. 20 February 2019, https://toynbeeprize.org/posts/mark-mazower/.

Mazurek, Małgorzata. "Polish Economists in Nehru's India: Making Science for the Third World in an Era of De-Stalinization and Decolonization." *Slavic Review* 77, no. 3 (2018): 588–610.

McMahon, Robert J., ed. *The Cold War in the Third World*. New York: Oxford University Press, 2013.

Mëhilli, Elidor. *From Stalin to Mao: Albania and the Socialist World*. Ithaca, NY: Cornell University Press, 2017.

Mëhilli, Elidor. "Globalized Socialism, Nationalized Time: Soviet Films, Albanian Subjects, and Chinese Audiences across the Sino-Soviet Split." *Slavic Review* 77, no. 3 (2018): 611–637.

Mevius, Martin. *Agents of Moscow: The Hungarian Communist Party and the Origins of Socialist Patriotism, 1941–1953*. Oxford: Clarendon Press, 2005.

Mevius, Martin. "Reappraising Communism and Nationalism." In "The Communist Quest for National Legitimacy in Europe, 1918–1989." Special issue, *Nationalities Papers* 37, no. 4 (2009): 377–400.

Miller, Nicola. *Soviet Relations with Latin America, 1959–1987*. New York: Cambridge University Press, 1989.

Moyn, Samuel. *The Last Utopia: Human Rights in History*. Cambridge, MA: The Belknap Press of Harvard University Press, 2010.

Muehlenbeck, Philip. *Czechoslovakia in Africa, 1946–1968*. New York: Palgrave Macmillan, 2016.

Nathans, Benjamin. "Soviet Rights-Talk in the Post-Stalin Era." In *Human Rights in the Twentieth Century*, edited by Stefan-Ludwig Hoffmann, 166–190. Cambridge: Cambridge University Press, 2011.

Niebuhr, Robert. *The Search for a Cold War Legitimacy: Foreign Policy and Tito's Yugoslavia*. Leiden: Brill, 2018.

Nikolov, Elit. *Dâshteriata na nadezhdite*. Sofia: Propeler, 2008.

Osa, Maryjane. *Solidarity and Contention: Networks of Polish Opposition*. Minneapolis: University of Minnesota Press, 2003.

Pedaliu, Effie. "The US, the Balkans, and Détente." In Rajak, *The Balkans in the Cold War*, 197–218.

Péteri, György, ed. *Imagining the West in Eastern Europe and the Soviet Union*. Pittsburgh: University of Pittsburgh, 2010.

Petrov, Victor. "A Cyber-Socialism at Home and Abroad: Bulgarian Modernization, Computers, and the World, 1967–1989." PhD diss., Columbia University, 2017.

Petrov, Victor. "The Rose and the Lotus: Bulgarian Electronic Entanglements in India, 1967–89." *Journal of Contemporary History* 54, no. 3 (2019): 666–687.

Popov, Stefan. *Bezsânitsi*. Sofia: Letopisi, 1992.

Prashad, Vijay. *The Darker Nations: A People's History of the Third World*. New York: New Press, 2007.

Pula, Besnik. *Globalization under and after Socialism: The Evolution of Transnational Capital in Central and Eastern Europe*. Stanford, CA: Stanford University Press, 2018.

Raĭnov, Bogomil. *Liudmila: Mechti i dela*. Sofia: Iztok-Zapad, 2011.

Rajak, Svetozar, Konstantina E. Botsiou, Eirini Karamouzi, and Evanthis Hatzivassiliou, eds. *The Balkans in the Cold War*. London: Palgrave Macmillan, 2017.

Richmond, Yale. *Cultural Exchange and the Cold War: Raising the Iron Curtain*. University Park: Penn State University Press, 2003.

Romano, Angela, and Federico Romero, eds. *European Socialist Regimes' Fateful Engagement with the West: National Strategies in the Long 1970s*. New York: Routledge, 2021.

Rotter, Andrew J. "South Asia." In Immerman and Goedde, *The Oxford Handbook of the Cold War*, 211–229.

Rubenstein, Anne. "Mass Media and Popular Culture in the Post-revolutionary Era." In *The Oxford History of Mexico*, edited by Michael C. Meyer and William H. Beezley, 598–634. New York: Oxford University Press, 2010.

Rudner, Martin. "East European Aid to Asian Developing Countries: The Legacy of the Communist Era." *Modern Asian Studies* 30, no. 1 (1996): 1–28.

Rupprecht, Tobias. *Soviet Internationalism after Stalin: Interaction and Exchange between USSR and Latin America during the Cold War*. Cambridge: Cambridge University Press, 2015.

Russell, Philip. *The History of Mexico: From Pre-Conquest to Present*. New York: Routledge, 2010.

Rutter, Nick. "Look Left, Drive Right: Internationalisms at the 1968 Youth World Festival." In Gorsuch and Koenker, *The Socialist Sixties*, 193–212.

Savova, Elena, Zdravka Micheva, and Kiril Avramov, eds. *Liudmila Zhivkova: Zhivot i delo (1942–1981); Letopis*. Sofia: Izdatelstvo na Bâlgarskata akademiia na naukite, 1987.

Scarboro, Cristofer. *The Late Socialist Good Life in Bulgaria: Meaning and Living in a Permanent Present Tense*. Lanham, MD: Lexington Books, 2011.

Sekulić, Dubravka. "Energoprojekt in Nigeria: Yugoslav Construction Companies in the Developing World." *Southeastern Europe/L'Europe du Sud-Est* 41, no. 2 (2017): 200–229. https://brill.com/view/journals/seeu/41/2/article-p200_200.xml.

Sfetas, Spyridon. "The Fusion of Regional and Cold War Problems: The Macedonian Triangle between Greece, Bulgaria, and Yugoslavia, 1963–1989." In Rajak, *The Balkans in the Cold War*, 307–329.

Shibusawa, Naoko. "Ideology, Culture, and the Cold War." In Immerman and Goedde, *The Oxford Handbook of the Cold War*, 32–49.

Singer, Wendy. *Independent India, 1947–2000*. New York: Pearson Longman, 2012.

Slavov, Atanas. *The "Thaw" in Bulgarian Literature*. Boulder, CO: East European Monographs, 1981.

Slobodian, Quinn, ed. *Comrades of Color: East Germany in the Cold War World*. New York: Berghahn Books, 2015.

Smith, Tony. "New Bottles for New Wine: A Pericentric Framework for the Study of the Cold War." *Diplomatic History* 24, no. 4 (2000): 567–591.

Snow, Nancy, and Philip M. Taylor, eds. *Routledge Handbook of Public Diplomacy*. New York: Routledge, 2009.

Snyder, Sarah. *Human Rights Activism and the End of the Cold War: A Transnational History of the Helsinki Network*. New York: Cambridge University Press, 2011.

Stanek, Łukasz. "Architects from Socialist Countries in Ghana (1957–67): Modern Architecture and Mondialisation." *Journal of the Society of Architectural Historians* 74, no. 4 (2015): 416–442.

Stanek, Łukasz. *Architecture in Global Socialism: Eastern Europe, West Africa, and the Middle East in the Cold War*. Princeton, NJ: Princeton University Press, 2020.

Stanek, Łukasz. "Introduction: The 'Second World's' Architecture and Planning in the 'Third World.'" In "Cold War Transfer: Architecture and Planning of Socialist Countries in the Third World." Special issue, *Journal of Architecture* 17, no. 3 (2012): 299–307.

Stanek, Łukasz. "Miastoprojekt Goes Abroad: The Transfer of Architectural Labour from Socialist Poland to Iraq (1958–1989)." *Journal of Architecture* 17, no. 3 (2012): 361–386.

Stanoeva, Elitsa. *Sofiia: Ideologiia, gradoustroĭstvo i zhivot prez sotsializma*. Sofia: Prosveta, 2016.

Stanoeva, Elitza. "Bulgaria's 1300 Years and East Berlin's 750 Years: Comparing National and International Objectives of Socialist Anniversaries in the 1980s." *CAS Working Paper Series* 9 (2017): 1–40.

Stanoeva, Elitza. "The Imperative of Opening to the West and the Impact of the 1968 Crisis: Bulgaria's Cooperation with Denmark and West Germany in the 1960s." In Crump and Erlandsson, *Margins for Manoeuvre*, 110–129.

Statelova, Elena, ed. *Drugata Bâlgariia, 1944–1989*. Sofia: Anubis, 2000.

Statelova, Elena, and Vasilka Tankova. *Prokudenite*. Plovdiv: Zhanet, 2002.

Suri, Jeremi. *Power and Protest: Global Revolution and the Rise of Détente*. Cambridge, MA: Harvard University Press, 2003.

Sygkelos, Yannis. *Nationalism from the Left: The Bulgarian Communist Party during the Second World War and the Early Post-War Years*. Leiden: Brill, 2011.

Taylor, Karin. *Let's Twist Again: Youth and Leisure in Socialist Bulgaria*. Vienna: LIT Verlag, 2006.

Todorov, Nikolai. *The Ambassador as Historian: An Eyewitness Account of Bulgarian-Greek Relations in the 1980s*. New Rochelle, NY: A. D. Caratzas, 1999.

Todorova, Maria. *The Lost World of Socialists at Europe's Margins: Imagining Utopia, 1870–1920*. London: Bloomsbury, 2020.

Todorova, Maria, ed. *Remembering Communism: Genres of Representation*. New York: Social Science Research Council, 2010.

Todorova, Maria, Augusta Dimou, and Stefan Troebst, eds. *Remembering Communism: Private and Public Recollections of Lived Experience in Southeast Europe*. Budapest: Central European University Press, 2014.

Tomlinson, B. R. "What Was the Third World?" *Journal of Contemporary History* 38, no. 2 (2003): 307–321.

Tomoff, Kiril. *Virtuosi Abroad: Soviet Music and Imperial Competition during the Early Cold War, 1945–1958.* Ithaca, NY: Cornell University Press, 2015.

Toshkova, Vitka. *Bâlgariia i SASht, 1919–1989.* Sofia: Sineva, 2007.

Traĭkov, Veselin. *Istoriia na bâlgarskata emigratsiia v Severna Amerika.* Sofia: Universitetsko izdatelstvo Sv. Kliment Ohridski, 1993.

Trentin, Massimiliano. "'Tough Negotiations': The Two Germanies in Syria and Iraq, 1963–74." *Cold War History* 8, no. 3 (2008): 353–380.

Troebst, Stefan. *Die bulgarisch-jugoslawische Kontroverse um Makedonien, 1967–1982.* Munich: R. Oldenbourg, 1983.

Tsing, Anna Lowenhaupt. *Friction: An Ethnography of Global Connection.* Princeton, NJ: Princeton University Press, 2005.

Unger, Corinna R. "Histories of Development and Modernization: Findings, Reflections, Future Research." H/Soz/Kult. 12 September 2010, https://www.hsoz kult.de/literaturereview/id/forschungsberichte-1130.

Valiavicharska, Zhivka. "History's Restless Ruins: On Socialist Public Monuments in Postsocialist Bulgaria." *boundary 2* 41, no. 1 (2014): 171–201.

Valiavicharska, Zhivka. "Post-Stalinism's Uncanny Symbioses: Ethno-nationalism and the Global Orientations of Bulgarian Socialism during the 1960s and 1970s." In "Decolonial Theory and Practice in Southeast Europe." Special issue, *dVersiia* (March 2019): 78–99.

Van Beurden, Sarah. *Authentically African: Arts and the Transnational Politics of Congolese Culture.* Athens: Ohio University Press, 2015.

Vasileva, Boĭka. *Bâlgarskata politicheska emigratsiia sled Vtorata Svetovna Voĭna.* Sofia: Universitetsko izdatelstvo Sv. Kliment Ohridski, 1999.

Verdery, Katherine. *National Ideology under Socialism: Identity and Cultural Politics in Ceauşescu's Romania.* Berkeley: University of California Press, 1991.

Vezenkov, Aleksandâr. *Vlastovite strukturi na Bâlgarskata komunisticheska partiia, 1944–1989.* Sofia: Siela, 2008.

Vukov, Nikolai. "The 'Unmemorable' and the 'Unforgettable': 'Museumizing' the Socialist Past in Post-1989 Bulgaria." In *Past for the Eyes: East European Representations of Communism in Cinema and Museums after 1989,* edited by Oksana Sarkisova and Peter Apor, 307–334. Budapest: Central European University Press, 2008.

Westad, Odd Arne. "The Cold War and the Third World." In McMahon, *The Cold War in the Third World,* 208–220.

Westad, Odd Arne. *The Global Cold War: Third World Interventions and the Making of Our Times.* New York: Cambridge University Press, 2005.

Westad, Odd Arne. "The New International History of the Cold War: Three (Possible) Paradigms." *Diplomatic History* 24, no. 4 (2000): 551–565.

Winrow, Gareth. *The Foreign Policy of the GDR in Africa.* Cambridge: Cambridge University Press, 1990.

Yosmaoğlu, İpek. *Blood Ties: Religion, Violence, and the Politics of Nationhood in Ottoman Macedonia, 1878–1908.* Ithaca, NY: Cornell University Press, 2014.

Yurchak, Alexei. *Everything Was Forever, Until It Was No More: The Last Soviet Generation.* Princeton, NJ: Princeton University Press, 2006.

Zahra, Tara. *The Great Departure: Mass Migration from Eastern Europe and the Making of the Free World*. New York: Norton, 2016.

Zhivkov, Todor. "Address to the Bulgarian People on the Occasion of the 1300th Anniversary of the Bulgarian State." *Bulgaria Today* 4 (1981): 2–6.

Zhivkova, Ludmila. *Anglo-Turkish Relations, 1933–1939*. London: Secker and Warburg, 1976.

Znepolski, Ivaïlo. *Bâlgarskiiat komunizâm: Sotsiokulturni cherti i vlastova traektoriia*. Sofia: Siela, 2008.

Znepolski, Ivaïlo, ed. *Istoriia na Narodna Republika Bâlgariia: Rezhimât i obshtestvoto*. Sofia: Siela, 2009.

Znepolski, Ivaïlo. "'Konsensusnata diktatura' i sotsialnata i baza: Korumpirane na masite," in Znepolski, *Istoriia*, 395–437.

Znepolski, Ivaïlo, ed. *NRB ot nachaloto do kraia*. Sofia: Siela, 2011.

Zubok, Vladislav. "Cold War Strategies/Power and Culture—East." In Immerman and Goedde, *The Oxford Handbook of the Cold War*, 309–312.

INDEX

Page numbers followed by letter *f* refer to figures.

Lightning Source UK Ltd.
Milton Keynes UK
UKHW011117090721
386819UK00013B/547